Politics and Policy Making
in Developing Countries

THE INTERNATIONAL CENTER FOR ECONOMIC GROWTH is a non-profit research institute founded in 1985 to stimulate international discussions on economic policy, economic growth, and human development. The Center sponsors research, publications, and conferences in cooperation with an international network of correspondent institutes, which distribute publications of both the Center and other network members to policy audiences around the world. The Center's research and publications program is organized around five series: Sector Studies; Country Studies; Studies in Human Development and Social Welfare; Occasional Papers; and Reprints.

The Center is affiliated with the Institute for Contemporary Studies, and has headquarters in Panama and a home office in San Francisco, California.

For further information, please contact the International Center for Economic Growth, 243 Kearny Street, San Francisco, California, 94108, USA. Phone (415) 981-5353; Fax (415) 986-4878.

ICEG Board of Overseers

Politics and Policy Making in Developing Countries

Perspectives on the New Political Economy

Edited by Gerald M. Meier

An International Center for Economic Growth Publication

ICS PRESS
San Francisco, California

Inquiries, book orders, and catalog requests should be addressed to ICS Press, 243 Kearny Street, San Francisco, California 94108. Telephone: (415) 981-5353; FAX: (415) 986-4878. For book orders and catalog requests, call toll free in the contiguous United States: **(800) 326-0263**. Distributed to the trade by National Book Network, Lanham, Maryland.

Cover design by Lisa Tranter.

Index by Shirley Kessel.

Library of Congress Cataloging-in-Publication Data

Politics and policy making in developing countries : perspectives on
the new political economy / edited by Gerald M. Meier.
      p.   cm.
"An International Center for Economic Growth Publication."
Includes bibliographical references and index.
ISBN 1-55815-095-1 (cloth). — ISBN 1-55815-079-X (pbk.)
    1. Developing countries—Economic policy. I. Meier, Gerald M.
HC59.7.P5774 1991
338.9′009172′4—dc20   90-20395
                                           CIP

Contents

Preface

In recent decades economists have learned a great deal about how to stimulate growth and alleviate poverty in developing countries. Yet much of their advice to developing-country policy makers is deemed politically infeasible and goes unheeded. If the worldwide development effort is to succeed, one of the most crucial tasks is to learn how political factors affect economic policy making. This knowledge will permit successful implementation of effective economic policy in the political arena.

In July 1989 the International Center for Economic Growth and the Banco de la República de Colombia sponsored a conference, directed by Gerald M. Meier, on politics and development policy making. Economists, political scientists, and policy makers from many countries gathered in Paipa, Colombia, to consider whether the new political economy, a framework created largely to analyze conditions in the democratic, industrialized countries, can offer insights into economic policy making in developing countries. The participants looked at how elements of the framework such as interest groups, rent-seeking behavior, and the "predatory state" manifest themselves in developing countries and how they influence policy related to trade, land reform, poverty alleviation, privatization, and inflation and stabilization. *Politics and Policy Making in Developing Countries: Perspectives on the New Political Economy* presents the arguments and discussions from that conference.

A fuller understanding of the interaction between politics and economics is essential if politics is to be a tool for sound development policy making rather than a hindrance. And without constructive use of political processes, there is little chance for successful economic reform. By advancing what economists know about policy making in developing countries, this volume increases the potential for positive policy change.

Many individuals and organizations helped make this project possible. In particular, we would like to thank the Banco de la República de Colombia, the World Bank, and the International Development Research Centre (IDRC) of Canada for their financial support. Our gratitude also goes to Francisco Ortega, general manager of the Banco de la República, and his staff, without whose support the conference could not have taken place.

Nicolás Ardito-Barletta
General Director
International Center for Economic Growth

Panama City, Panama
May 1991

Editor's Preface

This book is an outgrowth of a conference that explored how various public policies have advanced or impeded economic development over the past four decades. The conference had two unique features. It was unusual in bringing together not only development economists but also political scientists and policy makers from developing countries and international organizations. And it focused intensively on the strengths and limitations of the "new political economy" in contributing to an understanding of the political determinants of economic policy making in less-developed countries. From the perspective of the new political economy, the participants looked at past experience to see how future policy reform can be undertaken.

The conference was held in Paipa, Colombia, July 12–15, 1989. It was sponsored by the International Center for Economic Growth and the Banco de la República de Colombia. Grateful acknowledgment is made for the support of these organizations and for the funding from other contributors acknowledged in the Preface.

Appreciation is also extended to the participants who accepted the invitation to yet another conference, and especially to the participants who undertook the difficult task of writing the papers and offering the comments now included in this volume.

Thanks are also due to Frieda Martin, Julie Hirshen, and Heidi Fritschel of the International Center for Economic Growth and to Pat Sharp of Stanford University for their logistical or editorial help.

Gerald M. Meier

PART I

INTRODUCING THE NEW POLITICAL ECONOMY

Policy Lessons and Policy Formation

Despite all the attention given to problems of economic development, we still have much to learn about why some countries develop faster than others. The development record since 1950 is varied. Some countries—such as the East Asian newly industrializing countries (NICs)—have been success stories, achieving rapid growth in per capita income and alleviation of poverty. In contrast, others have developed slowly or are in decline. An economic policy that has been successful in one country has failed in another. One type of policy has been effective in a country while another type of policy in the same country has not. How are we now to account for these differences in policy performance? How can policy choices and outcomes be explained?

These contrasting policy performances have led economists to draw a number of policy lessons from the post-1950 development experience. Arnold Harberger, for instance, has compiled thirteen such lessons that are the shared conclusions of most professional practitioners and students of economic policy (1984: 428–35). These lessons focus on controlling budget deficits and monetary emission; taking advantage of international trade; valuing neutrality in tax and tariff policy; avoiding excessive income tax rates and excessive tax incentives; steering clear of quotas, licenses, and wage and price controls; and stressing efficiency and financial profitability in public enterprises.

Similarly, Helen Hughes concludes that "many aspects of policy effectiveness remain unsolved, but enough is known to accelerate growth in slowly growing countries. There is now no excuse for the governments of developing countries that do not approach the high, long-run GNP growth of the East Asian countries" (Ranis and Schultz 1988: 142).

Against the background of development policy experience, development economists, political scientists, and policy makers are seeking insights that might help narrow the gap between good economic analysis and good policy making. To do this, they are giving increasing attention to the new political economy as a mode of identifying and interpreting the political determinants of development policy. This book explores the uses and limitations of the new political economy in the belief that attention to formal political economy issues in policy formulation in developing countries is likely to heighten our understanding of development issues and contribute to necessary policy reform.

At the end of World War II, development problems were thrust upon economists. Political independence could be legislated, but economic development could not be established by fiat. How then was development to be achieved? Awakening with the emergence of the new nations, the subject matter of development economics became at once both analytical and policy oriented. Governments needed to make policy choices, and the instrumental character of the state became important. The state was active, and policy advice was sought and given. Much of this advice was based on the welfare economics of the mid-1950s and emphasized the correction of market failure. Government interventions, however, often resulted in policy-induced distortions. Nonmarket or government failure became prevalent. As the shortcomings of the initial policies became apparent, there was the plea to "get prices right" (Timmer 1973). And with the neoclassical resurgence came the more general exhortation to get policies right (Little 1982).

If there is one thing developing countries have not lacked, it is economic advice. Frequently, however, this advice has been ignored. Economists have urged export promotion, but countries continue to follow import-substitution policies. Economists have urged rural development and the removal of urban bias, but governments still emphasize industrialization and neglect agriculture. Economists argue for stabilization, but inflation still prevails.

Why are the development economists not listened to? Why are Harberger's policy lessons not heeded? Part of the answer may be the ineffectiveness of the economist as communicator to the policy maker. Even assuming that economists know what policies are best and that they are united in one voice, they may be ineffective as advisers. The problem is not lack of understanding by the policy maker. Rather the burden lies on the economist to be understandable and persuasive in giving advice. Often advice is too subtle or too complicated to be persuasive. Furthermore, policy prescriptions presented to the policy maker frequently defy any feasible application. Where is there any government that can compute and administer the lump-sum and nondistortionary taxes and subsidies of welfare economics? For most developing countries, even the machinery for direct income taxes is rudimentary. Whereas the economist too often deals with the "first-best" optimal policy, the government must live with the "second-best" or "third-best" in any hierarchy of policy choices.

Moreover, the political calendar has a short time horizon whereas the economist considers longer-term tendencies. But as Lord Keynes observed, "The long run is a misleading guide to current affairs. In the long run we are all dead. Economists set themselves too easy, too useless a task if in tempestuous seasons they can only tell us that when the storm is long past the ocean is flat again" (Keynes 1923).

To explain nonmarket failure by the ineffectiveness of the economist as adviser is, however, too ad hoc and simplistic. A deeper explanation lies in the interaction of economics and politics. Such an explanation may be sought in the new political economy. This is to return to the grandest theme in economics—the role of the state and markets. But we now do so in a more rigorous and systematic fashion than that of the old political economy as represented by Adam Smith, Karl Marx, and John Stuart Mill or by contemporary political scientists who do not use the techniques of economic analysis.

Features of the New Political Economy

By the new political economy (NPE) is meant a neoclassical economic theory of politics. The analytical concepts and principles—as applied to political markets and political phenomena—are analogous to those of neoclassical economic analysis. The unit of analysis is the individual, group, or enterprise. In chapter 5, T. N. Srinivasan defines NPE by "the axiom that agents behave rationally; that is, they have a consistent set of preferences over the outcomes of their actions, and they choose an action whose outcome is preferable to the outcome of other actions they find also feasible, given the constraints within which they act. . . . Agents are assumed to behave rationally, whether they are consumers using available information to form expectations about the future, bureaucrats fighting for turf or distributing publicly created rents, or lobbyists and voters."

The concept of self-interest or self-goal choice is relevant for the NPE, and hence the techniques of maximization, minimization, and optimization apply. Marginal analysis and equilibrium outcomes can be applied to political markets and political objective functions.

Unlike much normative economic analysis, however, the NPE does not assume that the government is composed of Platonic guardians and that the state acts benevolently in seeking the public interest. Economists may refer to a state devoted to the public interest, a social welfare function, Pareto efficiency, and first-best policies. In contrast, the rational choice political economists now focus on other types of states—the Leviathan state, bureaucratic state, or factional state. The Leviathan or bureaucratic state is often a predatory state,[1] preying on its citizens for the economic benefit of an autocracy, policy elite, or bureaucracy. The factional state responds to the interests of pressure groups. It is often a transfer state, redistributing income or wealth from one faction to another. In both the Leviathan state and the factional state, an underdeveloped economy has commonly given rise to an overextended state. For those who apply the new political economy, this overextended state is, as Merilee Grindle observes in chapter 3, a negative state.

The NPE was first related to political processes in the more developed countries, especially those with liberal democratic political institutions.[2] In such countries, the techniques of neoclassical economics have been applied to an economic theory of legislation, reciprocal (pork-barrel) patronage, log rolling, lobbying, and voting by the electorate. Especially prominent has been the use of rent seeking as the basis of modeling political behavior to explain foreign trade intervention and domestic economic regulation. Early contributions were by Downs (1957), Riker (1962), Buchanan and Tullock (1962), Niskanen (1971), and Stigler (1971).

Thus in one type of model—that of endogenous tariff theory—trade restrictions balance the power of narrow interests (lobbies) against that of broad interests (voters). The trade policies are equilibrating variables that clear political (redistributive) markets; they are analogous to prices in product markets that balance the quantity demanded against the quantity supplied. The policy maker is like an auctioneer in a product market, and the demand for protection gives rise to the supply of protection (Magee 1984).

In the mid-1970s, the new political economy began to be applied to political phenomena in the less-developed countries (LDCs). Initial applications were based on rent seeking; Krueger (1974), for example, showed the cost of rent seeking caused by quantitative trade restrictions. Bhagwati (1982) offered a more general analysis of tariff seeking, revenue seeking, and other restriction-seeking activities. The early rent-seeking studies, however, were without political content: the quantitative restriction or tariff was simply imposed exogenously.

The special feature of this volume is that it applies the new political economy more extensively to policy making in the developing countries: contributors endogenize policy variables and analyze the political determinants of a range of economic policies, extending beyond simple foreign trade restrictions.

The neoclassical resurgence was ahistorical and apolitical: it did not focus on the central role played by government (Sandbrook 1986). The new political economy now removes this deficiency by enunciating a positive theory of political behavior that does not assume government is an exogenous force, external to the economist's model, but is instead at least partially endogenous, to be explained by relationships within the economist's model. Such an analysis disaggregates and operationalizes the "state." It emphasizes political rationality on the part of policy makers instead of economic rationality: it observes how rational self- interested choice with respect to goals and instruments shapes the decisions of politicians, bureaucrats, and administrators. It analyzes the effects of political behavior and motivations on economic policy as analogous to that of economic behavior and market institutions. In so doing, it opens windows in the black box of the state by using various strands of thought: public choice, collective choice, transaction costs, property rights, rent seeking, and directly unproductive profit-seeking activities.

The Economic Role of the State

When applying the new political economy to developing countries, the analyst may focus on the economic role of the state. The "state" is, however, one of the most problematic concepts in politics (Evans et al. 1985; Vincent 1987; Jasay 1985). The crucial formal feature of the state is that it incorporates certain power rights associated with legislative, executive, and judicial authority. The state generally has maximal control over resources as well as force. Law also originates with the state. The state, as continual public power, embodies the central administrative and legal apparatus with the authority to make binding decisions for people and organizations juridically located in a particular territory and to implement these decisions (Evans et al. 1985: 46–47).

The various theories of public power are explained by one author as follows (Vincent 1987: 222–23):

> 1. In absolutist theory the public power *is* the absolute sovereign person (whether fictional or real) embodying divine right and owning the realm. The sovereign's interests are the state's interests.
> 2. In constitutional theory the public power *is* the complex institutional structure which, through historical, legal, moral and philosophical claims,

embodies self-limitation and diversification of authority and power and a complex hierarchy of rules and norms, which act to institutionalize power and regulate the relations between citizens, laws and political institutions.

3. In ethical theory the public power *is* the *modus operandi* of the citizens, groups and institutions of a constitutional monarchy, directed to the maximal ethical self-development and freedom of the citizen body.

4. In class theory the public power *is* the institutional form of the condensation of dominant class interests, which is ultimately directed at the accumulation of capital and the defense of private property.

5. In pluralist theory the public power *is*, in general terms, the synthesis of living semi-independent groups (understood as real legal persons). Groups are integrated not absorbed. Narrowly focused public power implies a government acting for the common good of groups.

The state, is, however, more than an abstract entity. It is simultaneously the people who do whatever it is that the state does (Alt and Chrystal 1983: 28). There are therefore agents of the state—individual policy makers, bureaucrats, and administrators who are placed in authority over others.

An issue that runs throughout the new political economy is whether the state is autonomous—that is, has its own objectives—or is merely passive, responding to the demands of various interests or classes in society. In liberal pluralist theory, policies are formulated in accordance with the demands of interest groups, and the state simply reacts to various interest groups contending "horizontally." Stigler (1971) argues that politician-regulators supply economic regulations over industry because there is a demand for them. The demand for such regulations is made with votes and other resources, such as monetary support for campaign contributions by effective political coalitions. In vulgar Marxism, the state is simply the "executive committee of the ruling class." Ronald Findlay sets forth in chapter 2 a theory of the autonomous state that can be applied to conditions prevailing in LDCs of different types. From other chapters in this volume, however, it will be evident that the new political economy embodies both society-centered and state-centered theories of policy making.

The economic role of the state can be described in (at least) three ways, as simply sketched in Figure 1.1 (Alt and Chrystal 1983: 28–29). These roles can be described as protective or neutral, productive or positive, and exploitative or negative.

The protective state is the minimal state of classical liberal theory, with functions limited to the provision of public goods of defense and law and order. The protective state is neutral and essentially policyless. The productive state is the public interest state of welfare economics, in

FIGURE 1.1   The Economic Role of the State

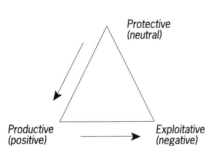

SOURCE: Adapted from J. E. Alt and K. A. Chrystal, *Political Economics* (Brighton: Wheatsheaf, 1983), 28–29.

which the state is positive and public policies correct market failure and lead to the maximum net benefit for the population at large. The exploitative state is also active, but it is negative since its interventions maximize the benefit to those in the state apparatus and to those groups who act as principals for whom the policy makers are agents.

The exploitative or negative state creates nonmarket failure as the political market conflicts with the economic market. The movement (both in political thought and in reality) has been away from the protective state toward the productive state—and for many LDCs along the bottom axis from the positive state to the negative state.

How can the movement now be reversed? How can government failures be diminished and a closer approach to the productive state achieved? How can policy reform be instituted? For these changes to occur, professional economic advice must have some influence in the developing world. But the dilemma is that in showing why governments do what they do, the new political economy at the same time shows why economists are not listened to. If the economists' advice is now to be more persuasive, economists must give more consideration to the political economy aspects of policy formation.

The Process of Policy Formation

A schematic description of the policy formation process is offered in Figure 1.2. The usual approach is to consider a linear process that goes from the predictions and prescriptions given by economists to the policy maker, to policy choice by the policy maker, to implementation, and finally to the policy outcome. A richer view of the policy formation process, however, requires a consideration of other forces that act on the

FIGURE 1.2   The Policy Formation Process

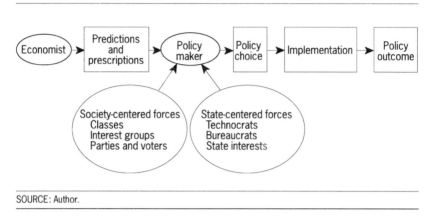

SOURCE: Author.

policy maker. These forces can be grouped in two categories: society-centered forces and state-centered forces.

According to the society-centered approach the government is passive. There are societal inputs to government, and the policy choice is a dependent variable. The demand from society creates the supply of policy. The society-centered forces include the inputs from classes whether in Marxist, neo-Marxist, or dependency theory; the interest groups of pluralist theory and public choice theory; and political parties and voters.

The state-centered approach views the state as having its own objectives. The state is autonomous, and policy elites are active. State-centered forces include the technocrat's approach of a benevolent government that is devoted to increasing the national welfare, bureaucratic politics, and forces on the policymaker on behalf of state interests.

The new political economy rejects explanations based on classes and technocrats. Instead the NPE focuses on interest groups, parties and voters, bureaucrats, and state interests.

The NPE, however, should offer not only positive analysis, but also normative analysis. The political economist Bernard Schaffer observed, "Public policy is, after all, what it does. The point is to explain what that is, and then see if that explanation can itself be an instrument for change and improvement, through its own revelations and expositions" (Schaffer 1984: 189). That is our task in the remainder of this volume.

When reading the following chapters, some overriding questions may be kept in mind:

- Does the new political economy adequately explain why governments undertake the policies they do? Can it identify—ex ante and not simply ex post—the determinants of state intervention in different types of political regimes? And can the NPE explain the variance in policies over time and across countries?

- How does the explanatory value of the models of the NPE compare with the older concepts in political economy? What roles, for example, are played by class, legitimacy, ideology, culture, values, and power?

- Does the NPE indicate how policy reform might now be instituted? Can it identify the political impediments to reform? How can they be overcome?

These questions are initially addressed in the major conceptual chapters by Ronald Findlay, Merilee Grindle, and Gustav Ranis. Findlay presents an affirmative analysis of the uses of the new political economy for developing countries. In contrast, Grindle emphasizes limitations of the NPE and suggests alternative approaches for the analysis of the politics of development policy making. Ranis emphasizes the need for a typology of developing countries and presents a conceptual framework for investigating the political economy of policy change, explicitly differentiating between policy linearity and policy oscillation in different countries.

These conceptual chapters are followed by a set of applied sectoral studies. T. N. Srinivasan analyzes the political economy of foreign trade policies. He considers situations in which policy instruments are set exogenously and then examines the consequences of making the choice of the instruments endogenous, as in the NPE. He relates the broad issue of the political economy of choice of a development strategy to the choice of particular trade policy instruments.

Yujiro Hayami considers the effects of government interventions in land and labor markets through the mechanism of land reform. He illuminates problems of land reform, drawing on the Philippine experience, through the positive theory of the NPE rather than through the ideological discussions of traditional political economy.

Guy Pfeffermann inquires whether the NPE can help achieve poverty alleviation. He is especially concerned with the institution of policy measures that will help the poor in the weakest countries.

Leroy Jones, Ingo Vogelsang, and Pankaj Tandon seek to identify the winners and losers from a policy of public enterprise divestiture. They examine current efforts at privatization and link the normative and positive by assigning economic costs and benefits to particular interest groups with varying political influence.

Stephan Haggard relates inflation to its political roots and examines the political dilemmas posed by stabilization policies. In so doing, he draws on the NPE to suggest some hypotheses on the variation in macro-economic policy in the middle-income developing countries.

Chapters 10 and 11 present the views of two special groups who respond to the analyses and proposals of the economists. First, political scientists Robert Bates, Stephan Haggard, and Joan Nelson confront the NPE with some insights from the traditional or older political economy. Next, Nicolás Ardito-Barletta summarizes the experiences of policy makers, mostly from Latin America, who have had to balance economic concerns with political realities. He also presents his own views on the role of the economist as policy maker.

The concluding chapter acts as a summary for the volume by considering the uses and limitations of the NPE from the standpoint of explaining government behavior and the possibilities for policy reform.

The New Political Economy:
Its Explanatory Power for LDCs

The term new political economy refers to the extensive analysis done during the 1970s and 1980s under a variety of names, such as public choice, rent seeking, directly unproductive profit-seeking activities, and, most recently, new institutional economics. The pioneers have been Anthony Downs, Mancur Olson, James Buchanan, Gordon Tullock, and Douglass North, whose work has attracted increasing attention from economists specializing in more traditional areas such as international trade and industrial organization.[1]

For the most part this literature has postulated a framework of political institutions and behavior that corresponds to that of the advanced industrial countries and, even more specifically, to that prevailing in the

For helpful comments and encouragement I would like to thank Pranab Bardhan, Jagdish Bhagwati, Gerald Meier, Gustav Ranis, T. N. Srinivasan, Augustine Tan, John Toye, and Stan Wellisz. The paper was mostly written while I was visiting the Faculdade de Economia, Universidade Nova de Lisboa, in the summer of 1989. I am grateful to the director, Professor Jaime Reis, Luis Cunha, and other colleagues for their kind hospitality and generous support during my visit.

contemporary United States. This framework portrays the state as passive and emphasizes the efforts of interest groups to obtain legislation favorable to themselves through the intermediation of political parties whose only concern is with electoral success. Other work has considered voting schemes and problems of constitutional design, areas that also presume pluralist democracies of the Anglo-Saxon or Swiss type.

It is, of course, an unfortunate fact that most less-developed countries (LDCs) today are ruled by military juntas or one-party dictatorships, in none of which does it appear that economic policy is decided by the kind of equilibrium between contending interest groups that is such a prominent feature of the new political economy. In LDCs the state tends to dominate civil society, which is weak and fragmented, whereas in advanced industrial democracies the rich texture of organized private interests in civil society emasculates the state as an autonomous entity. One might ask, therefore, whether or not the new political economy is relevant for the LDCs. My answer is a resounding "yes," even though most of the existing literature on the new political economy generally presumes political conditions vastly different from those prevailing in the typical LDC.

The basic reason for my positive position on this question is that one can use the methods and the spirit of the new political economy to develop a theory of the autonomous state, which can then be applied to conditions prevailing in LDCs of different types. This approach makes possible a parsimonious and, one hopes, credible explanation of several major features of third world experience. These are the extensive growth of government relative to the private sector, the pervasiveness of corruption in varied forms, the intensity of trade restrictions and the associated phenomenon of the import-substitution syndrome, the urban bias of economic policy and resource allocation, and the degree of dependence on foreign capital.

Because the notion of the state is central to my argument, the first section of this chapter is a brief survey and analysis of the emergence of the state in the experience of Western Europe and its nature in the contemporary third world. The next section presents an economic model of the state that attempts to integrate the productive and predatory aspects of this institution. The third section applies the insights of this approach to the state to some simple general equilibrium models of trade theory that consider the activities of a public sector in an open economy in which trade taxes provide the main source of revenue. The final section offers comments on the relations between the present analysis and recent work on the political economy of some selected countries that might be of general interest.

To avoid misunderstanding I should stress that the objective of this chapter is strictly positive in nature; that is, it aims to present hypotheses and models based on the insights of the new political economy to see how far they can go toward being consistent with at least some of the major features, or "stylized facts," of third world experience. It is not intended as yet another diatribe against state intervention and in praise of the "magic of the market." The question of what the appropriate role of the state in economic development is—the normative issue—is left entirely aside, though of course the analysis presented may have some relevant implications for any attempt to address it.

The Autonomy of the State

Bringing the State Back In is the title of an interesting book edited by P. B. Evans, D. Rueschmeyer, and Theda Skocpol (1985).[2] The common theme that Skocpol finds in much recent social science literature, further emphasized in the papers of the edited volume, is the rediscovery by a number of authors, Marxists as well as mainstream scholars, of the "autonomy of the state." According to this idea, the state is neither a passive agent of society at large and its various interest groups contending "horizontally," as in liberal pluralist theory, nor an "executive committee of the ruling class," as in vulgar Marxism, but rather, a dynamic independent force. This issue of the autonomy of the state can be addressed through many theoretical avenues, which are not only not mutually exclusive but which can possibly contribute to a wider understanding. Marxists, following Engels in *Origin of the Family* and *Private Property and the State* and Marx in his *Eighteenth Brumaire of Louis Napoleon*, see class interests achieving a deadlock in their natural antagonism, allowing a dynasty, dictator, or ruling clique of some sort to pursue independent policies of aggrandizement that may diverge from the interests of each of the classes themselves, though a prudent ruler would be careful to play off one group against another by partial concessions and favors. Some of these autonomous ends might be the wealth and privileges of the ruling circles, military glory, or, what is most likely in the modern world, an enlargement of the state's bureaucratic apparatus for its own sake. The sociological distinction between latent and manifest motives and objectives is crucial in this regard. "Economic development," "national security," and "socialist construction" are all objectives that have been used with greater or less sincerity but all of which operate at the manifest level. The task of the social scientist is to penetrate these myths, while recognizing their force, and to discover the latent core of individual or group self-interest that underlies them.[3]

Perhaps the most natural approach to this problem for an economist is in terms of the principal-agent framework. Thus whether one views the government as the agent of "the people," as in Locke or Rousseau, or of the "ruling class," as in the cruder Marxian variant, the principal has the difficult problem of monitoring the activities of the agent to see whether or not they are in keeping with the implicit social contract that underlies both cases. The conventional principal-agent problem is of course enormously compounded by the fact that the agent in this case is empowered with the "monopoly of the use of force" that is necessary for the enforcement of the conventional types of contract between principals and agents. Once the people, or the bourgeoisie, or the proletariat appoint or accept a guardian, then who is to guard them from the guardian? Recognition of this problem probably led Hobbes to his conception of the sovereign as necessarily absolute.

The modern state as we know it evolved in the West during the course of a millennium from the feudalism of the Carolingian empire, through the *Ständestaat* and the absolutist state to the constitutional state of the nineteenth century, culminating in the universal suffrage and the welfare state of today.[4] At each stage of this development, the state was intimately involved with the evolution of civil society, both shaping and being shaped by it. Even in its most primitive form, the feudalism of the Middle Ages, it was marked by an acknowledgment of the limitations of the ruler in relation to his subjects. Lord and vassal both shared in the status of knighthood and were therefore in one sense equals, though not in terms of circumstances and power. The Magna Charta is the best known but by no means the only acknowledgment by a sovereign of the limits beyond which he cannot encroach on the rights of his aristocratic vassals. The urban merchants and craftsmen in the rising towns of the Middle Ages were also able to secure rights and privileges for themselves in relation to the crown, in exchange for the financial assistance they could provide the monarchs in their struggles to pacify the unruly barons. The Church, furthermore, had always been a powerful institution whose vast landed wealth augmented its spiritual influence on civil society. Thus the *Ständestaat* or "estate society" was marked by a dualism of power between crown and estates.

Despite their appellation, the absolutist states of early modern Europe were sharply constrained by the historical circumstances within which they emerged, with the inherited structure of rights and privileges enjoyed by the various segments of civil society. Thus, although the fact that the Estates General of France were not summoned between 1618 and 1789 is generally taken as indicating the power of the Bourbons to rule unhindered, the other side of the coin is that there were "no new taxes" they could levy. They had to supplement the rising yield from the traditional taxes by a variety of expedients, such as the sale of offices, the farming of the tax revenues, and of course the issue of public debt. All of these created trouble for the future since they were accompanied by the granting of exemptions and privileges to wider segments of society. The very efficiency of the *intendants*, the royal officials who administered France, most of whom were a meritocracy of "new men," undermined the social basis of the ancien régime, as Alexis de Tocqueville pointed out, because it rendered the aristocracy superfluous as a functional class. The French Revolution continued the trend toward a more centralized administration but with the extension of civil rights to the people as a whole. In England the Whig oligarchy that ruled after 1689 gradually extended the franchise and reformed the electoral system in the nineteenth century.

The modern state can be thought of as a contrivance or invention of administrative technology, capable of being transferred or imported into societies that originally did not possess it. As it moved eastward in Europe to the German principalities and Russia, it became more authoritarian in nature. In his book *The Well-Ordered Police State* historian Mark Raeff (1983) examined the concept of the authoritarian state. Rulers in the German principalities, particularly Prussia, he points out, established bureaucracies that meticulously attempted to regulate and modernize (which at that time of course meant imitating the French) civil society in the spheres of education and the economy. This transplanted version of the modern state worked relatively well in the German case despite its authoritarian character and legacy, since civil society itself was sufficiently developed to respond positively to the detailed regulations and intervention. In the case of Russia, however, the succession of revolutions from above, from Peter the Great to Mikhail Gorbachev, have yet to succeed in transforming civil society according to the Western European model, despite the bloody sacrifices that have been imposed on the people in the attempt.

If the modern state, which attained its ideal form in postrevolutionary France, was modified and distorted in its journey eastward to Germany and Russia, it has certainly spawned an exotic new strain in its recent journey "south" to the former colonies in Asia and Africa that attained their independence in the aftermath of World War II. Particularly in the former British colonies, the modern constitutional state, with its full panoply of checks and balances, privileges and safeguards, was left behind by the departing representatives of the crown as the culmination of decades, if not centuries, of "preparation for self-government." If the Western state took a millennium to develop from feudal anarchy to constitutionalism, the third world states have sadly given the impression, in many cases, of running the film backward at an accelerated rate that covers the same distance in less than half a century. Although there are many notable exceptions to this gloomy spectacle, it is fair to say that the record has on the whole been a dismal one, especially in the light of the hope and enthusiasm initially aroused by the national independence movements.

Some conservative critics have said that the colonial powers left too soon, before their "civilizing mission" was fully accomplished. This argument is unconvincing, particularly when one notes that the longer and harder the colonial power resisted the demand for independence, the more violent and radical has been the regime that eventually took over. Another, more pernicious argument has been that third world people do not share the values of individual freedom and civil liberty with the West and are thus reverting to meek acceptance of despotic rule with which they are familiar from their precolonial past. It is hard to maintain this view in the light of the dramatic popular protests in the Philippines, South Korea, Burma, Algeria, and China that have all taken place recently.

What then is the problem? Why has not the modern constitutional state "taken" in its transplantation into the less-developed world? The basic answer is that there is a disproportion in the third world between the state and the development of civil society, such that the state is turned into an instrument to repress the mass of the people in the interests of a small minority. This minority is not defined, as in Marxism, by its ownership or control of the means of production but by its control over the "means of administration," which ultimately consists, of course, in the effective monopoly of the use of force. The closest approximation to a Marxian ruling-class view of the state is in parts of Central and South America, where landowning elites exercise domination through political parties that closely represent their interests, backed by armies whose officers come from the same social stratum.

In their effort to characterize the third world state, social scientists have turned to Max Weber's typology of authority under the rubrics *patrimonial, charismatic,* and *rational-legal.* The first generation of nationalist leaders tended to be striking figures, such as Kemal, Nasser, Nehru, and Nkrumah. These were natural candidates for the charismatic category, and indeed some of their achievements could perhaps only be accounted for in terms of the force of their personalities. Social scientists also sought to explain subsequent developments by Weber's notion of the "routinization of charisma." The explanatory power of this approach seems however to have faded along with the transient glories of the modernizing dictator. A more illuminating application of Weber's categories is Christopher Clapham's (1985) view of neopatrimonialism as the general underlying characteristic of third world states. By this he means the use of modern rational-legal forms—that is, impersonal, universalistic systems and rules—for private, particularistic purposes. A pure patrimonial ruler would bestow gifts on his followers and kinsmen to cement their loyalty to him in his struggles with his opponents; these gifts would come out of his own personal resources, since such a system would lack any distinction between the private and public purse. A modern third world leader, however, who wanted to perform essentially the same activity of rewarding followers and kinsmen would typically do so by assigning them jobs or import licenses or contracts that ostensibly ought to go only to those satisfying certain impersonal objective criteria of functional qualification.

Many widely noted aspects of third world experience fall into place in the light of this fruitful characterization. The pervasiveness of the state in the economy and society at large, and the extent and persistence of economic controls and regulations, can be seen as maximizing the resources with which the neopatrimonial ruler can reward himself and his followers. Admonitions by the International Monetary Fund (IMF) and the World Bank, universal guardians of the rational-legal order in the economic sphere, to "get the prices right" will obviously be resisted directly or by a barrage of subterfuges. Third world leaders will tend to respond to negative external shocks by borrowing rather than adjustment, since the latter would lead not only to a cut in present consumption of the ruling group but also to an erosion of its essential political support.

The more successful the neopatrimonial state is in its predatory exactions on society, however, the less legitimate the regime is in the eyes of the people, since the more blatant is the violation of the publicly proclaimed rational-legal norms. The regime's response to challenges to its legitimacy is typically political repression of varying degrees of severity, depending upon the magnitude of the perceived threat. Also, the more valuable the "prize" of the control of the state, the more intense will be the pressure of rival claimants, and so the regime will face the problem of how wide or narrow to make the coalition that enjoys the benefits of rule. Much of the politics of the third world is concerned with the ebb and flow of these concessions and retractions to various segments of the society.

A Typology of Third World States

Despite its appeal as a characterization of third world states, the neopatrimonial concept needs to be supplemented by some typology or classification of the scores of actual states that at present exist in Asia, Africa, and Latin America, among which there is enormous variation in size, ideology, and political organization, even if they all share the feature of neopatrimonialism to some degree. Democracy versus dictatorship is one axis along which they might be situated, and market orientation versus central planning is another, giving us four categories if each of these distinctions is applied dichotomously. I had hoped that the literature on comparative politics would have produced some usable classification but have not yet come across one. What follows is therefore a very rough and ready one of my own devising, which I will gladly discard if a superior alternative can be found.

Traditional monarchies. A number of significant and interesting cases can be placed in this category; one thinks readily of Saudi Arabia and the Gulf oil sheikdoms, Morocco, and Jordan, as well as of Ethiopia under Haile Selassie. In each of these cases, the ruler could claim legitimacy on the basis of the traditional authority of the institution of the monarchy and of the dynasty in particular. These examples correspond more to Weber's patrimonial category then to the modern mixture of patrimonialism with rational-legal norms that Clapham stresses. Operationally, the difference is that the extraction and redistribution of rents from the economy and society can be made more openly, with the sanction of royal authority, than under regimes in which this is done behind a facade of impersonal and objective rules. In other words the distinction between the public treasury and the private purse of the monarch is blurred.

Traditional dictatorships. In this category are such states as Paraguay under Stroessner, the Dominican Republic under Trujillo, Cuba under Batista, Haiti under the Duvaliers, Nicaragua under Somoza, and the Philippines under Marcos. Like the monarchies, these regimes are based on absolute personal rule, but they lack the legitimacy of the former. Their exploitation of their countries is more blatant and on a greater scale, not being tempered by the awareness of past and future obligation that constrains a royal dynasty. They do not seriously espouse any ideology of national development and can perhaps best be described as "kleptocracies."

Authoritarian states. The next two categories I shall distinguish are right- and left-wing authoritarian states. These are either strictly one-party states, with no opposition parties allowed, or states in which opposition parties have never been able to take power. In many of them, the military plays a dominant role, either directly or behind the scenes.

Right-wing authoritarian states. This category includes Turkey and Egypt in the Islamic world; Argentina, Brazil, and Chile for most of their recent history, as well as Mexico, in Latin America; Kenya, Nigeria, Ghana, the Ivory Coast, and Malawi in Africa; and a number of states in East and Southeast Asia including Korea, Taiwan, Singapore, Malaysia, Thailand, and Indonesia. In some of these states, such as Turkey and Thailand, there has been a fair amount of democratic politics with parties competing quite actively, but the army defines "the narrow limits of the possible" for the political arena. Economic policy is generally market oriented, but this is consistent either with protectionism and import substitution, as in Latin America, or with outward orientation, as in much of East and Southeast Asia. On the whole there is much less corruption than in the traditional dictatorships identified above, and the army or ruling party genuinely attempts to promote national development, with varying degrees of success in different countries.

Left-wing authoritarian states. Here I would include the explicitly communist states of China, North Korea, Vietnam, and Cuba, with Nicaragua under the Sandinistas and Ethiopia under Mengistu as close cousins, and Algeria, Libya, Syria, Iraq, Tanzania, Angola, and Mozambique in the Middle East and Africa. Burma, with its military socialism and one-party state, is the only noncommunist example in Asia of left-wing authoritarianism. State intervention and controls are much more pervasive in these states than in their right-wing counterparts, though many, most notably China, are experimenting with greater reliance on markets.

Democratic states. In this final category are India, Sri Lanka, Venezuela, Costa Rica, Jamaica, and the other former British West Indies islands, as well as Malta and Mauritius. In all of these states, there have been peaceful transfers of state power determined by elections and considerable freedom of civil society to modify the authority of the state by the threat of defeat at the polls. This does not mean, however, that the state itself is weak or insignificant. On the contrary, the role of the state is quite extensive, in production as well as in the scope for the disbursement of patronage.

An Economic Model of the State

Economists have traditionally not had much to say about the theory of the state. The view of the state that most commonly prevails in economics is that of a functional or instrumental agency that performs the traditional tasks of providing public goods and offsetting externalities and other market failures by corrective taxes and subsidies. Insofar as the state undertakes income redistribution through its tax and expenditure policy, it is in relation to some ethically specified social welfare function. In the tradition of A. C. Pigou and James Meade, the state is seen as a benevolent guardian of the public interest. Baumol's *Welfare Economics and the Theory of the State* (1952) is perhaps still the most explicit and thorough statement of this approach.

The public choice theorists, however, have taken a more cynical view of the state; they see it as a grasping monster, a Leviathan that

extracts revenue from its subjects for the private interests and enjoyment of the individuals or groups who rule. Machiavelli and Hobbes,
rather than Bentham and his modern disciples, inspire these writers.
The literature does not include, however, an approach flexible enough
to handle the tension between these two aspects of the state, the productive and the predatory. In the rest of this section, I will present a model
of the state that will attempt to address this tension in the simplest
possible way. I will then relate this model to the general discussion of
the role of the state in LDCs that was given in the previous section.[5]

The productive role of the state is expressed in this model by the
hypothesis that public expenditure on public goods—administration,
law and order, roads, justice, and so on—acts as an externality to private
economic activities, enhancing the private output from private inputs. I
thus treat public goods as intermediate inputs in the provision of final
private goods, rather than as final goods in their own right.

This idea is embodied in the following simple formal structure. Let
Y be national income, a composite commodity for which the production
function is

$$Y = A(L_g)F[L_p, \bar{K}] \tag{2.1}$$

with

$$L_g + L_p = \bar{L} \tag{2.2}$$

and

$$A'(L_g) > 0, A''(L_g) < 0, A(0) = 1 \tag{2.3}$$

where L_g and L_p are labor in government and private employment, respectively. The function F is the familiar neoclassical type and, for simplicity, is homogeneous of the first degree.

When $L_g = 0$ and therefore $A(0) = 1$, we get the level of output under
anarchy or the Hobbesian "state of nature" in which $Y_o = F[\bar{L}, \bar{K}]$. As L_g
is increased, the marginal productivity of a worker will be higher in the
public than in the private sector and so output will rise initially, but then
it will decline after reaching a maximum when the condition

$$FA'(L_g) = A(L_g)F_L(L_p) \tag{2.4}$$

is met, in which the left-hand side is the marginal product of labor in the
public sector and the right-hand side the marginal product of labor in
the private sector. This condition determines the optimal allocation of
labor L_g^* and L_p^* between the two sectors, making final output a maximum at Y^*. The wages in the two sectors would obviously have to be
equalized to achieve (2.4), and so the shadow price of labor in the public
sector will be the marginal productivity of labor in the private sector.

The optimal level of public expenditure wL_g^*, where w denotes the common wage, is then determined, and so a proportional tax rate $\tilde{t}$ can be calculated to satisfy

$$\tilde{t}Y^* = \tilde{w}L_g^* \tag{2.5}$$

where

$$\tilde{w} = (1 - \tilde{t})A(L_g^*)F_L(L_p^*) \tag{2.6}$$

Once state authority is vested in an autonomous ruler, however, there is no guarantee that he will bring society to this optimal allocation. If the ruler is conceived as literally absolute, with no constraints at all on his ability to secure his will at the expense of society, he will indeed find it in his own interest to maximize Y by meeting condition (2.4), but he will then proceed to appropriate the entire surplus, $Y^* - Y_o$, above that obtainable by his subjects in the state of nature. Hobbes explicitly recognizes that there is nothing to prevent his absolute sovereign from proceeding in this fashion should he be so inclined. This makes it difficult for those like C. B. Macpherson (1962) who sought to regard Hobbes as the apostle of "possessive individualism" and a "bourgeois revolution."

As mentioned in the previous section, however, even the absolutist monarchs of early modern Europe were not unconstrained to this extent, since they were limited by historical precedents in the degree to which they could tax their subjects and otherwise violate private property rights. Let us suppose therefore that the monarch cannot raise the tax rate on output above some specified level, which we can take to be the $\tilde{t}$ of the optimal solution just obtained. In addition we assume that he cannot conscript labor; that is, he has to pay public employees the after-tax wage they could earn in the private sector.

Under these circumstances a self-interested ruler would choose L_g so as to maximize

$$S \equiv \tilde{t}A(L_g)F[L_p\overline{K}] - (1 - \tilde{t})AF_L L_g \tag{2.7}$$

subject to (2.2). The condition necessary to achieve this is

$$\tilde{t}[FA'(L_g) - A(L_g)F_L] = (1 - \tilde{t})[A(L_g)F_L + L_g\{A'(L_g)F_L - A(L_g)F_{LL}\}] \tag{2.8}$$

The left-hand side is the marginal gain in the surplus obtained by transferring a worker from the private to the public sector. The right-hand side is the marginal cost of doing this, that is, the rise in the cost of public employment. The surplus is maximized when these two magnitudes are equated. Because $F_{LL} < 0$, the right-hand side is positive, and therefore

FIGURE 2.1   Surplus Maximization and Budget Maximization

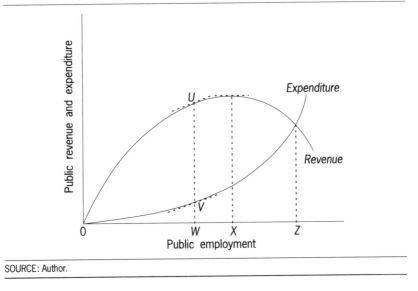

SOURCE: Author.

$$FA'(L_g) > A(L_g) F_L, \tag{2.9}$$

which means that the surplus is maximized when L_g is less than the optimal level. The surplus-maximizing ruler will provide less than the optimal level of public services, since to increase L_g further would raise Y but reduce S. The situation is conveniently depicted in Figure 2.1.

The concave and convex functions in Figure 2.1 represent public revenue and public expenditure, respectively. The expenditure function is convex because the wage rate is an increasing function of public expenditure, for marginal labor productivity in the private sector increases with rising public employment. The surplus is the vertical distance between these functions at each level of public employment, and is maximized where the slopes of the two functions are equal, with public employment equal to OW, public expenditure equal to VW, and the surplus equal to UV. This surplus is available for the consumption of the ruler or for disposition in any other way that he sees fit. Public employment is thus less than the socially optimal level OX, at which the final output Y is maximized.

Alternatively, an autonomous state may maximize the level of public expenditure, subject only to the revenue constraint. This hypothesis is the one advanced by students of bureaucracy from Parkinson (1958) to Niskanen (1971). In this case public employment would expand to OZ, and the surplus would be zero. Thus instead of being too few, as under the hypothesis of surplus maximization, public services could be too great.

Notice that the state becomes analogous to an economy-wide firm in our model. The surplus-maximizing absolutist state becomes like a "natural monopoly," while the bureaucratic case corresponds to the "sales maximization" hypothesis of the "divorce of ownership and control" in the modern corporation.

These two hypotheses, of course, are extremes. Any particular instance is likely to involve some level of public employment between OW and OZ and surplus between UV and zero. The surplus could be allocated to any purpose whatsoever, from worthy causes like transfers to widows and orphans to "rents" to social parasites of various types. A state committed to development could allocate it to public investment.

Thus far we have assumed that the tax rate and the labor supply are both exogenously given. It would clearly be desirable to extend the model in such a way that each of these is determined endogenously by the maximization process, along with all the other variables of the system.

In order to do this we first observe that for any tax rate and labor supply the model already defines a maximized level of surplus. Furthermore, it is readily seen that the surplus is increased by a rise in either of these parameters. This enables us to define a family of isosurplus contours

$$S = S(t,L) \tag{2.10}$$

$$S_t > 0, \, S_L > 0$$

as indicated by the curves SS^0, SS^*, and SS' convex to the origin in Figure 2.2, along each of which the maximized level of surplus is constant.

Assume now that labor supply is not fixed but an increasing function of the after-tax wage rate. This gives rise to the concave frontier TT' depicted in Figure 2.2, which shows the trade-off to the state between the tax rate and the labor supply, upon which the revenue base depends, a higher tax rate having a negative repercussion on the supply of labor and hence on the revenue base. Although intuitively plausible, the frontier TT' has to be derived from the model itself, and this can be conveniently done by use of Figure 2.3.

The positively sloped curve AA' is simply the supply curve of labor as a function of the after-tax wage. The negatively sloped curve BB' shows the equilibrium after-tax wage corresponding to each level of labor supply, for a given tax rate. Thus for any level of labor supply and the tax rate (which is constant at all points on BB') the model determines the surplus-maximizing allocation of labor between the public and private sectors and hence the equilibrium after-tax wage. An increase in the tax rate reduces the after-tax wage for each level of labor input and so shifts the BB' curve to the left, thus reducing the equilibrium labor supply. We have therefore shown why the frontier TT' in Figure 2.2 displays a negative relationship between the tax rate and the labor supply. The

FIGURE 2.2   Optimal Tax Rate and Labor Supply

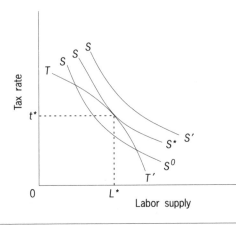

SOURCE: Author.

FIGURE 2.3   Effect of Higher Tax Rate on Labor Supply

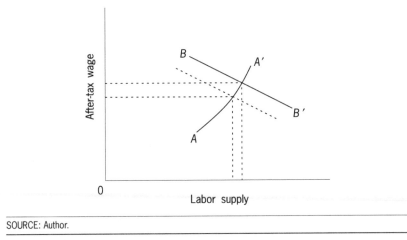

SOURCE: Author.

tangency of SS^* with TT' in Figure 2.2 determines the equilibrium tax rate t^* and labor supply L^* for the surplus-maximizing case.

The budget-maximizing bureaucratic version of the model can be solved in analogous fashion. Given the tax rate and labor supply, the model already determines the maximized budget level, so that we can define the isobudget contours

$$B = B(t,L) \qquad\qquad\qquad\qquad (2.11)$$

$$\frac{\delta B}{\delta t} > 0, \frac{\delta B}{\delta L} > 0$$

since the level of the budget is obviously an increasing function of the tax rate and labor supplies as well. The frontier showing the labor supply as negatively related to the tax rate can also readily be obtained in this case. The supply curve of labor as a positive function of the after-tax wage in Figure 2.3 is invariant to the nature of the maximizing hypothesis for the state. It is easy to see, however, that the negatively sloped "demand curve" for labor will lie to the right of the corresponding case for the surplus-maximizing hypothesis. This is because for any given tax rate and labor input the demand for labor, and hence the after-tax wage, will be higher under the "bureaucratic" hypothesis, as we have already seen from Figure 2.1. This means that for any tax rate the equilibrium supply of labor will be greater than under surplus maximization so that the frontier lies outside that of the previous case. The optimal point on the frontier is where it is tangential to the highest isobudget contour. Thus the state squeezes more resources out of society under the bureaucratic than under the surplus-maximization hypothesis.

We can now link the two versions of the autonomous state analyzed in this section with the typology of third world states presented in the previous section. The surplus-maximization case would appear to correspond to the traditional monarchies and traditional dictatorships. In the first case the ruler's legitimacy is conferred by right of dynastic succession while in the second his authority over civil society is sufficiently strong for him not to have to bother with an extensive apparatus of control. In both cases, therefore, it would seem that there would be some level of resource-using public services, but with a considerable margin between revenue and the cost of public services, which is available for the enjoyment of the ruler and those on whom he chooses to confer special favor or buy off with bribes.

The authoritarian states, however, are dominated by armies or parties that need to justify their rule over society by the apparent execution of grandiose tasks, for which they seek to maximize the available budgetary resources. Key personnel would no doubt live well, primarily because of officially sanctioned "perks" rather than simple graft, though the line may be hard to draw in many cases.

Democratic states do not really fit into the model since in this case the levels of public revenue and public expenditure (in the resource-using sense), as well as the beneficiaries of transfer payments, are determined by electoral competition. The situation is thus oligopolistic rather than monopolistic, as in the simple model. In this case the more standard approach of the new political economy comes into its own.

Factor Proportions, Trade Taxes, and the State

In this section I will apply the hypotheses regarding the behavior of the state that were discussed in the previous section to models of a "typical" LDC economy to see whether they can generate outcomes that are consistent with the "stylized facts" of LDC experience. Since the vast majority of LDCs are highly open economies, we will naturally stress the relationship between the fiscal behavior of the state and international trade and capital movements.

A Viner-Ricardo model. In this well-known model there is a primary sector producing output as a function of labor and a specific input called "land," but which can of course be thought of as a natural resource of any kind, and a manufacturing sector that produces output with labor and another specific input called "capital," which may be either exogenously fixed or internationally mobile as a function of the rate of return obtainable. Both sectors compete for the same homogenous labor pool. Relative prices of the two goods are fixed on world markets but are of course internally variable as a result of state policy.

Let us suppose that capital is perfectly mobile internationally at an exogenous rate of return $\bar{r}$. Assuming constant returns to scale in the production function for manufacturing, this means that

$$f'(k_m) = \bar{r} \tag{2.12}$$

where k_m is the capital-labor ratio and $f'(k_m)$ is the marginal productivity of capital. From (2.12) it follows that

$$f(k_m) - f'(k_m)\, k_m = w \tag{2.13}$$

The externally fixed $\bar{r}$ thus determines k_m and the real wage w in terms of manufactures for the LDC. The allocation of the fixed labor pool between the two sectors is determined by

$$\bar{p}[g(q_a) - g'(q_a)\, q_a] = w \tag{2.14}$$

where $g(q_a)$ is output per worker in the agricultural or primary sector, q_a is the land-labor ratio in the sector, and $\bar{p}$ is the exogenously given world price ratio of the two goods. Since the total supply of "land," specific to the primary sector, is fixed, q_a depends only on employment L_a in that sector. We also have

$$L_a + L_m = \bar{L} \tag{2.15}$$

and since L_a is uniquely determined by (2.14) we also uniquely determine L_m. Since k_m is determined by (2.12) we therefore also know the endogenous capital input K_m. This is divided between an initially fixed domestic component K_m^d and the foreign capital inflow K_m^f which is

$$K_m^f = K_m - K_m^d \tag{2.16}$$

National income would be

$$Y = w\overline{L} + r\,\overline{K}_m^d + \overline{p}g'(q_a)\,q_a\,L_a \tag{2.17}$$

where the first term is total wages, the second is profits of domestically owned capital, and the third is the natural resource rents of the primary sector. Since the economy is "small" in world markets, Y represents the maximum income that domestic residents can obtain and therefore corresponds to the socially optimal level, if distributive problems are either ignored or taken care of by the usual fiction of nondistortionary lump-sum transfers.

Into this idyllic "first-best" world we now introduce, like a serpent in the garden, the autonomous state. While the previous section stressed the productive role of the state, despite its perversion to predatory ends, here we will simplify either by assuming that there is already a pool of resources set aside for public use, at a level just sufficient to sustain private activity at the optimal level, or more blatantly by just ignoring that aspect of the problem, since it is irrelevant to the present objective.

We will assume, with good reason, that the state finds it most convenient to tax trade rather than wealth or incomes. There is ample evidence that states in the third world do just this. We are ignoring productive public expenditure; therefore, maximizing surplus and maximizing revenue are now equivalent. It is instructive to consider the popular use of a "marketing board" to tax the resource-intensive primary sector, which is the source of the country's exports and foreign exchange earnings.

The impact of a revenue-maximizing marketing board on the economy is illustrated in Figure 2.4. The horizontal axis measures employment in the primary sector and the vertical axis indicates the wage and marginal product of labor in this sector, evaluated at the world price $\overline{p}$ in terms of manufactures. The distance OW indicates the wage, and the line AV is the marginal productivity curve of labor in the primary sector (drawn as linear for convenience of exposition). Employment is equal to OG, the rent from natural resources is the triangle AWV, and the wage-bill in the primary sector is $OWVG$.

The marketing board, acting as a maximizing monopsonist, drives a wedge equal to ST between the world and domestic prices of the primary export, T being the point where the horizontal wage line is

FIGURE 2.4   The Effects of Marketing Board Policy

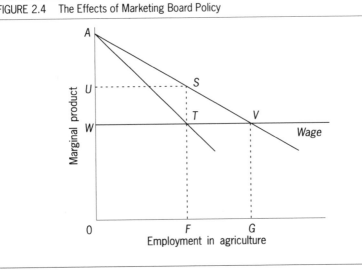

SOURCE: Author.

intersected by the line *AT*, the marginal revenue product curve. The maximum revenue of the marketing board is the area of the rectangle *UWST*. The rents to private citizens in the primary sector fall to the triangle *AUS*, while the triangle *STV* is the deadweight loss to the economy as a whole from the restrictive policies of the marketing board. Employment in the primary sector contracts to *OF*, so that *FG* workers are released to the manufacturing sector. Additional foreign capital will flow in to employ these workers, who will earn the same wage as before. The returns to capital, however, will not be a part of national income because they will accrue to the foreign owners. The economy has become (1) more industrialized, since the primary sector contracts and manufacturing expands, (2) more dependent on foreign capital because of the additional induced inflow, (3) less well off than before because of the net loss of real national income equal to the area of the triangle *STV*, and (4) restricted in its trade since the contraction of primary output is at the expense of exports, so that imports must decline as well because of the decline in net foreign earnings.

What does the state do with its revenue? There are a number of possibilities. If the state is one of the first two types considered in the previous section, a traditional monarch or dictator could simply enjoy the revenue as private income. Swiss bank accounts, luxury imports, and construction of monuments using some of the released labor are all possible uses of the surplus, each of which can be amply illustrated by recent and contemporary third world examples.

Alternatively, if the state is of a more modern left- or right-wing authoritarian type, the regime could establish a public bureaucracy that may enhance the productivity of the economy to some extent but is more likely to be a parasite on the civil society, engaging in phantom tasks defined in terms of those old standbys national unity, security, development, and the like. Wages in the public sector could be above market levels, to reward friends and favorites or simply to create commitments and dependence on the regime.

Another effect of the "squeeze" on agricultural rents is that the price of the product is lowered to domestic consumers, which is particularly important when the primary product is a food staple, such as rice in Southeast Asia or beef and wheat in Argentina. The state could, of course, charge the world price to domestic consumers and thus maximize its returns from exports to the world market. This strategy would present administrative difficulties, however, and in any case there is a substantial political benefit to providing a subsidy to urban dwellers, the likeliest source of visible opposition to the regime. Thus in virtually all known cases the benefit of the squeeze on the primary sector is passed on to the domestic consumers as an implicit or even explicit subsidy.

The model is easily adapted to the case where there is no capital mobility at all or where foreign capital inflow is an increasing function of the rate of return obtainable in the economy. In both cases the rate of return becomes an endogenous variable, along with the foreign capital inflow in the latter case. The tax on the primary sector will result in a diversion of the labor force into manufacturing, raising the rate of return and the inflow of foreign capital to that sector. Domestic as well as foreign capitalists are indirect beneficiaries of the squeeze on the primary sector. Thus the state would get an additional payoff from the goodwill this generates, which can of course be converted into revenue or private connections between functionaries and the relevant firms. Foreign and domestic capital interact in complex ways, some competitive and some complementary. The state can mediate these relationships to serve its own purpose as well as the private interests of those who rule in its name.

Finally, the state could use the revenue to accumulate capital in new state-owned enterprises. Although these may originally be set up as statutory boards to be run on commercial principles, they can soon be turned to political ends as rewards to the members of the ruling elite or as bribes to potentially threatening outsiders (which may include army officers if these are not already in the inner circle). A new bureaucratic bourgeoisie can be built up in this way, some of whom could establish private enterprises out of the rents that they initially obtained from the state.

A Heckscher-Ohlin model. Similar implications can be derived from a Heckscher-Ohlin model, with a state that maximizes its budget in Parkinson-Niskanen fashion. We assume a two-factor, two-good, small open economy, with fixed endowments of capital and labor. The export good is labor-intensive and the import-competing good is capital-intensive. Revenue comes from the proceeds of a tariff, the level of which is determined endogenously, along with the level of public employment.

Since the world price-ratio is fixed, the domestic price-ratio is uniquely determined by the level of the tariff. This domestic price-ratio in turn, by the Stolper-Samuelson theorem, uniquely determines the real wage and return to capital. Since imports are capital-intensive, the higher the tariff the lower the real wage and the higher the return to capital.

The government's problem is to choose the tariff rate, t, and the level of public employment, L_g, in such a way as to maximize $w(t) L_g$ subject to

$$w(t) L_g \leq tp^* M \{(1 + t) p^*, L_g\} \tag{2.18}$$

where p^* is the world price-ratio, M is the level of imports, and $w(t)$ is the wage rate, which is a negative function of t. The level of imports varies negatively with the domestic price-ratio, which is equal to $(1 + t) p^*$. It also depends on L_g, since employment in the public sector withdraws labor from the production of the two tradable goods. With the capital stock fixed, more public employment reduces the labor force in the tradable sector, and hence by the Rybczynski theorem increases the output of the capital-intensive import-competing good and therefore reduces the level of imports and hence tariff revenue as well.

The solution to the problem is indicated in Figure 2.5. The concave frontier FF' shows the maximum feasible $w(t)$ for any given value of L_g. Suppose L_g is at some positive level and the tariff t is at zero. The wage $w(t)$ would then be at its maximum free-trade level but revenue would be zero, so that the government budget constraint would be violated. As the tariff is increased $w(t)$ will decrease, so that expenditure falls, and revenue rises. Thus corresponding to the given value of L_g we can find a tariff t and hence a wage rate $w(t)$ at which the budget constraint is satisfied with equality. A higher value of L_g will involve a lower revenue for a given value of t, since the volume of imports will be lower. Hence we must have a higher tariff, and thus a lower wage rate, at a higher level of public employment. This explains why FF' is negatively sloped.

The objective function $w(t) L_g$ can be represented in Figure 2.5 by a family of rectangular hyperbolas. The optimal point α is where FF' is tangential to the highest of these, yielding the optimal values $w(t^*)$ and L_g^*.

FIGURE 2.5   Public Employment under Revenue Maximization

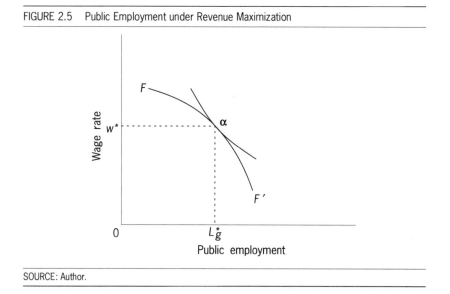

SOURCE: Author.

Our hypothesis of a budget-maximizing bureaucratic regime has thus determined the tariff level endogenously, along with the size of the public sector, in the setting of a small open economy. More standard models of endogenous tariffs, such as Findlay and Wellisz (1982) and Mayer (1984), postulate democratic pluralist regimes, less consistent with third world reality, and are therefore more suited to conditions in the advanced countries. The model presented here is a refinement of an earlier version contained in Section II of Findlay and Wellisz (1983). This model points to the possibilities of a bureaucratic-capitalist alliance, which have often been noted in the Latin American context and which will be elaborated upon in the potentially richer model in the next section.

An "Australian" model. Finally let us consider a model that neatly combines Viner-Ricardo and Heckscher-Ohlin features. This model can be found in a paper by Fred Gruen and Max Corden (1970) and is also used to good effect in Anne Krueger's (1977) Graham Lecture. The Australian connection of all three authors is responsible for the appellation I have given it.

Suppose the economy has two sectors, a primary sector and a manufacturing sector. The primary sector continues to produce a single good, using "land" and labor, but manufacturing is now differentiated between capital-intensive and labor-intensive goods, both using capital and labor. Labor is therefore used for all three goods, capital for two, and land for only one. All endowments are given, and relative prices, as before, are determined exogenously on world markets. In the absence of state intervention, suppose that technology, preferences, and endowments are such that the economy exports the primary good and the labor-intensive industrial good and imports the capital-intensive good.

Since the industrial sector has a Heckscher-Ohlin specification, the relative price of the two industrial goods on the world market would determine the return to capital and the real wage. Let us say that the numeraire is the labor-intensive good. With the price of the primary export also given in terms of the numeraire, it is apparent that employment in the primary sector, and hence rent and output, are all determined by the equality of the marginal product of labor with the real wage. This gives the labor force for the industrial sector and hence the production levels of both goods produced by that sector. National income as well as both relative prices now being given, domestic consumption of each good can be determined and therefore so can the volume of trade in all three goods.

One of the most interesting features of this model, from a political economy standpoint, is that it is possible for a tariff on industrial imports to benefit landowners. Consider a tariff on the import of the capital-intensive good. By the Stolper-Samuelson theorem again the real wage will be lower, while the price of the primary good will be unchanged, both in terms of the numeraire. Thus the effect will be to increase employment, and hence rents, in the primary sector. All agents in the model will be worse off as consumers, because of the distortion in domestic prices caused by the tariff, but it is clearly possible for landowners to gain on a net basis. Thus both capitalists and landowners can gain as a result of a tariff on capital-intensive imports, while workers of course are definitely worse off.

An export tax on agriculture, or the pricing policies of a marketing board, clearly depresses the returns to this sector and reduces the level of employment within it. The influx of labor to the industrial sector would, however, increase the output of labor-intensive goods, while reducing the output of capital-intensive goods. Real wages remain unchanged in terms of the manufactured goods but they *rise* in terms of the primary good, since the internal price of that good has fallen as a result of the policy of taxing agriculture. The decline in output of capital-intensive goods would also be accompanied by an increase in imports. Protectionist interests in industry, together with the ever-present thirst for revenue on the part of the state could lead to imposition of, or a rise in, tariffs on capital-intensive imports. This would offset at least part of the increase in real wages of the workers and produce a rise in the return to capital.

The scenario of the previous paragraph has considerable relevance to the case of Argentina.[6] In its heyday, that country was an agro-export oligarchy where the grain and beef exports produced by the fertile pampas created one of the most prosperous societies in the entire southern hemisphere. Politics was dominated by the rich landowners and the professional urban middle class that arose as an offshoot of this group. Workers, who tended to be recently arrived immigrants from Italy and Spain, did not succeed in entering the political arena significantly, since the anarchist and syndicalist parties that attempted to represent them were crushed by armed forces that reflected the domination of the rural magnates and the urban bourgeoisie. The difficulties caused by the depression of the 1930s resulted in military intervention of a conservative, even reactionary, character. The adverse shift of the terms of trade and isolation during World War II stimulated the development of urban industry and thus expanded the very class that was kept out of the political system.

This situation provided a clear opportunity for someone to mobilize this latent political base. The opportunity was seized by Juan Perón in 1946. Though Perón's personal rule ended in 1956, Peronism has become a permanent feature of Argentine political life, the latest chapter of which opened with the victory at the polls of Carlos Menem in 1989. The Peronist formula was to squeeze the primary sector by taxes and price controls that provided revenue to the state, lowered the workers' cost of living (since grain and beef were such important components of their consumption baskets), and enabled the regime to gain credit by opposing the landed oligarchy in the interest of the common man. Nationalization and an expanding bureaucracy also kept the urban middle class happy by providing career opportunities in the expanded realm of the state. Combined with the charisma of Evita Perón, the formula was extraordinarily effective.

The losers, however, particularly the landowners, associated sections of the army, and financial and industrial interests, were never defeated outright and were able to mount effective resistance, particularly when the excesses of the Peronists, combined with unfavorable external developments, produced crises. These crises would lead to waves of economic liberalization combined with political repression, since the attempts to revive lagging primary exports through higher relative prices were resisted by workers anxious to preserve their real wages. The Peronist defeat of 1956 led to orthodox stabilization and liberalization attempts by Arturo Frondizi, Arturo Illia, Juan Carlos Onganía, and others, which in turn led to collapse and the return of Peronism in the early 1970s. The ensuing chaos again led to a military regime and the orthodox liberalization measures, which again failed. Like his Radical party predecessors Frondizi and Illia, Raúl Alfonsín was not able to defeat Peronism at the polls by providing a workable economic framework, and the stage is apparently set for yet another turn of the wheel.

Some Particular Experiences

In this section I attempt to complement the rather abstract character of the analysis with some observations on experiences in different countries and regions. There is no particular principle underlying the choices made, which have been dictated partly by the availability of relevant literature.

Turkey. The case of Turkey is particularly interesting in the political economy of development. Among other reasons, this is because of the country's early experience with a "developmental dictatorship" under Kemal Atatürk during the interwar years, providing a preview of many recent third world scenarios of development. My discussion is heavily indebted to the excellent historical study by Keyder (1987).

The original system of the Ottoman Empire fits into our model of a surplus-maximizing traditional monarchy, with the surplus shared between the monarch and the class of state functionaries that administered the system. Unlike Europe of the ancien régime or Latin America, Turkey had no class of large landowners, the soil being mainly worked by peasants who were heavily taxed. Turkey was drawn into the great expansion of world trade from 1870 to 1914 as an exporter of primary products, with Greek and Armenian merchants acting as intermediaries between the world market and the Turkish peasant producers. Needless to say, the state was not slow to take the opportunity to substantially increase its revenue, thus enhancing the traditional power of the bureaucracy in Turkish society. The foreign merchant community was certainly not able to challenge this hegemony. The ravages of World War I and the associated conflicts with the Greeks and Armenians led to the almost total disappearance of the merchant community as a result of persecution and flight. The 1920s saw a continuation of agricultural exports under the new regime of Kemal.

The situation was drastically altered by the effects of the Great Depression. Relative prices turned sharply against agriculture, and the consequent stimulus to industry was enhanced by import restrictions. A new class of Turkish industrialists, closely associated with the bureaucracy, emerged. The two forces joined in support of the policy of etatism, inspired by Mussolini's "corporate" state, that characterized Turkey from this period on. The country followed the familiar import-substitution pattern of industrialization, with the boards of the large banks and productive enterprises containing large proportions of bureaucrats, many of whom were also more directly involved in industry. Civil liberties were suppressed, and a firm alliance of state and capital was forged, squeezing the agricultural sector and the working class. The situation thus corresponded to the models of the previous section of this paper, with relative prices turned against land and labor in favor of profits and state revenue.

In 1946 the one-party state was abolished and a democratic system established, which led to the victory of Adnan Menderes and his Democratic party in 1950. This liberalization of the polity was also accompanied by economic changes favoring market-oriented policies. Combined with the boom in primary product prices, this shift brought prosperity to the small cultivator class, which was an important constituency for the competing parties. U.S. foreign aid and political influence was also significant, perhaps even crucial, in bringing about the new configuration. The bureaucracy lost some of its primacy over the economy and society. The external environment, however, eventually turned unfavorable, and the attempt by Menderes to sustain growth through inflation led to disruption that triggered a military coup in 1960. Civilian rule was eventually restored, with a new program of import-substituting industrialization, and the bureaucracy was back in full force with a plethora of planning agencies that allocated scarce inputs, particularly foreign exchange, with the predictable rent-seeking consequences. In fact Anne Krueger's (1974) original article on rent seeking appears to have been based on her experience working in Turkey. Buoyed by foreign aid and the large inflow of remittances from the flood of Turkish workers to Western Europe, the system expanded until it was brought to a crisis by the oil shocks of the 1970s and the associated world recession. Violence erupted in civil society between the extreme right and left, leading to military intervention in 1980. Since then there has been success with outward-looking policies, leading to rapid growth of manufactured exports. It remains to be seen, however, whether bureaucratic authoritarianism in Turkey will follow the East Asian or the Latin American pattern.

India. India, like Turkey and Iran, is a successor state to the three great "gunpowder empires" of the Ottomans, Safavids, and Moguls. The long British colonial interlude modernized the traditional bureaucratic system and left a democratic parliamentary regime as its legacy. The question therefore arises as to whether the modern Indian polity functions as an autonomous centralized state insulated from the pressures of civil society or as a pluralistic democracy of the Western type, distinguished only by a lower standard of living from its Western European and North American counterparts.

Bardhan (1984), in a brief but stimulating study of the political economy of Indian development, begins with the hypothesis of the relative autonomy of the postcolonial state, building on the heritage of the Moguls and the scarcely less imperial British viceroys. He points out that the authority of the Nehru generation, derived from its leadership of the independence struggle, enabled the Indian state initially to impose a pattern of development that stressed the role of the public sector in bringing about a "socialistic pattern of society" while raising per capita incomes. He argues, however, that the subsequent generations of the Nehru dynasty have increasingly yielded to pressures from three main groups—big industrialists and the bureaucracy in the cities and large farmers in the rural areas. The result, although Bardhan does not draw this conclusion, seems to me to be hardly distinguishable from the kind of "churning" redistributive state that we are familiar with in the more developed countries.

The combination of an extremely extensive role for the state, with sweeping control over finance, industry, transport and trade, together with an open polity that is subject to lobbying pressures from almost any organized interest group has resulted in disappointing growth performance in India over the last two decades, despite some successes in agriculture. The surplus has tended to be frittered away in subsidies to farmers and inefficient state enterprises, while an expanding bureaucracy continues its lucrative hegemony over a labyrinthine maze of regulations and controls. No substantial free enterprise coalition has been able to form to push the state back from its control over key sectors, and the bureaucracy is always able to undermine tentative attempts by the leadership to liberalize the system. The dependence of the ruling party on contributions from rent-seeking lobbies also imparts stability to the existing structure. Gunnar Myrdal's well-known complaint about the "soft state" in India is related to the government's inability to insulate itself from these intrusions and to pursue its "higher" developmental objectives.[7]

Yet even though India has not fulfilled the outstanding potential for development provided by her entrepreneurs and diverse base of human capital, it remains a remarkable achievement to have maintained such a vibrant and stable democratic regime for so long when so many of her neighbors have fallen into dictatorial rule.

Africa. The model of a marketing board in a Viner-Ricardo economy presented earlier fits the African experience remarkably well.[8] The institution of the marketing board, particularly in West Africa, owes its origin to the colonial regimes, which built up large surpluses during World War II and the period preceding independence. In the case of cash crops such as cocoa, coffee, sugar, sisal, groundnuts, and so on, producers, particularly if they are peasant smallholders, are natural victims of the predatory state we have analyzed. Our general equilibrium model also accounts for the induced bias in favor of urban industry and capital, as well as for the diversion of the rents to the ruling elite, popularly known as the WaBenzi, the Mercedes-Benz tribe, in much of Africa.

The exceptions that prove the rule, the Ivory Coast and Kenya, are also interesting. In both of these states an indigenous planter class was an important part of the independence movement that took over power. Félix Houphouët-Boigny, in fact, was cofounder and president of the Syndicat Agricole Africain, an organization devoted to the interests of indigenous planters, many of whom were from his tribe, the Baoulé.[9] It is therefore not surprising that in these cases the independent African state has done well by permitting export agriculture to flourish and allowing foreign participation. The benefits of development are still channeled toward the ruling elite, but it is done in a more efficient or rational manner for the functioning of the system as a whole.

The work of Robert Bates (1972, 1983) has provided excellent analysis and documentation of the political economy logic of agricultural pricing policies in Africa in a spirit that is entirely consistent, so far as I can see, with that of the approach taken here.

Latin America. Latin America presents the greatest variation in economic and political experience in the third world, not only because of its diversity in resource base and social structure, but also because of its longer history of independence. Discussions of this experience have tended to identify three broad phases or stages in the development of most of the countries of the region. These are (1) an oligarchic phase of domination by a landowning elite, with an economic orientation geared to the export of land-intensive primary products to the world market; (2) populism, a regime in which a charismatic leader such as Perón in Argentina or Vargas in Brazil adopts more nationalistic economic policies, stressing industrialization and import substitution, restrictive measures against the former oligarchs, redistribution in favor of the "popular classes," and their incorporation into the political arena; and (3) bureaucratic-authoritarianism, a term coined by the Argentine political scientist Guillermo O'Donnell, in which there is an alliance among the upper echelons of the military and civilian bureaucracy, foreign capital in the form of multinational corporations, and "advanced," or capital-intensive sectors of domestic industry. This type of regime attempts to follow "liberal" economic policies in the macroeconomic sphere, though it is concerned with continuing and furthering import-substituting industrialization. Politically it is repressive and excludes mass participation, since this is regarded as disruptive of orderly progress.[10]

It seems that our models are well adapted to embody the features of each of these different politico-economic regimes. The technocratic bias and orientation of the bureaucratic-authoritarian regime is consistent with our budget-maximizing version of the autonomous state. The alliance between the bureaucracy and foreign and domestic capital emerges clearly in our Heckscher-Ohlin and Australian models. This last model is also able to capture the relationships between different interest groups—the landowners, workers, advanced industry, and of course the state itself. The model could also be adapted to handle differentiation within the primary sector between large-scale, land-intensive production of livestock and subsistence production in a labor-intensive peasant sector. "Dualistic" societies such as Peru and Bolivia, with extensive peasant hinterlands, could be analyzed in corresponding terms.

The East Asian NICs. The four East Asian newly industrializing countries (NICs)—Korea, Taiwan, Singapore and Hong Kong—have clearly been the star performers in the development field over the past two decades or more. It is therefore of particular importance to ask what, if anything, the new political economy can contribute toward an understanding of the reasons for their success. It is not enough simply to point out that they have been just about the only group of LDCs to have made a systematic and sustained commitment to outward orientation in their economic policies. In fact the crucial political economy question is precisely why this is so.

Certainly the major theme of this chapter, the relative autonomy of the state, continues to hold in these cases. By comparison with, say, India, or even Brazil, the state and its economic policy apparatus has been insulated from the pressures of lobbies and special interests in all four cases—military dictatorships in two, a dominant-party state in another, and British guardians in the case of Hong Kong. Thus the subsidies, transfers, regulations, and bureaucratic proliferation that have shackled the Indian entrepreneurs have been either absent or channeled toward export performance in the NICs. Except in the case of Hong Kong, this has not meant laissez-faire but rather allowed the state to pursue a sustained strategy of export-led growth.[11]

But if generals in Korea and Taiwan have succeeded because of the autonomy of the states that they set up, why not the Latin American juntas or the legion of African soldiers ranging in rank from field marshal to master sergeant that have taken over control of their societies? In the case of the African countries, one could perhaps say that the levels of physical and social infrastructure are as yet inadequate for a policy of growth based on labor-intensive manufactured exports, and that the temptation to squeeze the natural resource–based export sectors is too strong. In Latin America the infrastructure is available in many cases, but the military is itself too caught up in the complex antagonisms of civil society, which has a richer texture than in the East Asian cases, to follow a sustained path of export orientation. Chile is close to becoming an exception in this regard since the long rule of the Pinochet regime has enabled it to embark on a successful economic course. It is very much to be hoped that the restoration of democracy will not cause a setback in the development of the economy.

The New Political Economy:
Positive Economics and Negative Politics

As they enter the 1990s, many development economists are deeply concerned about the future of developing countries. In Latin America, they are perplexed about how to alter development strategies that generate systemic inflation and recurring balance of payments crises. Crippling foreign debt, linked to increased energy prices and recession in the international economy, can also be traced to the policies of governments that dreamed too grandly, grew too large, spent too much, and taxed hardly at all (Sachs 1985; Balassa, Bueno, Kuczynski, and Simonsen 1986; Kuczynski 1988; Fishlow 1985). In much of Africa, only the most bright-spirited would not find cause for disillusion. Corrupt and personalistic governments have almost ceased to exert authority in many societies, and populations have come to rely on the family, ethnic, or

An earlier version of this chapter was thoughtfully reviewed and commented upon by Robert Paarlberg, Dwight Perkins, Stephen Reifenberg, Michael Roemer, and Judith Tendler. I am extremely grateful for their insightful advice. In addition, T. N. Srinivasan and David Abernethy provided valuable comments on the conference paper.

village security systems and parallel, or black, markets as substitutes for the formal legal and economic systems that no longer function (Sandbrook 1986; Hyden 1983; World Bank 1984; Jones and Roemer 1989). In such conditions, poverty, strife, inefficiency, and administrative collapse confound plans for short- or medium-term recovery. Despite a number of success stories in Asia, some countries there have also experienced stymied growth, inefficient agricultural and industrial sectors, and policy-making systems that serve only a narrow range of interests (Haggard 1989; Bardhan 1984; Johnson 1983; Rudolph and Rudolph 1987).

The 1980s were a decade in which these conditions cut deeply into the consciousness of development economists. Not surprisingly, the issue of policy reform came to dominate discussions among specialists. Increasingly, governments were urged to establish a macroeconomic policy context more conducive to growth, to adjust sectoral policies to increase efficiency and responsiveness to the market, and to lessen the regulatory and interventionist presence of the state in economic interactions (see Roemer 1988; Perkins 1988). Neoclassical economists stressed structural adjustment, liberalization, privatization, and decentralization as important elements of a successful development strategy. Nevertheless, this concern about the importance of policy reform fueled increasing disillusion when many governments proved reluctant to introduce reoriented policies, even when under considerable pressure from international financial institutions. Despite the impetus of the worst economic crisis in the modern era, policies damned as inimical to growth often proved difficult to alter. Authoritarian and democratic governments alike frequently appeared unable to adopt strategies that policy advisers recommended as being more efficient and more effective than existing policies in generating growth. Many economists echoed the concerns expressed by Gerald Meier:

> Governments continue to undertake policies contrary to the normative principles of development economics and in contradiction to the policy lessons from development experience. Inward-looking policies, inflationary budgets, policies of deliberate industrialization, urban bias, and factor market distortions continue despite the policy recommendations of development economists (1989: 1).

After at least three decades of research, analysis, and advice giving, it is understandable that some development economists are tempted by pessimism.

The sense of disillusion is perhaps all the greater because neoclassical economics had traditionally held high expectations about the motives behind state policy.[1] Policy analysis, focused on achieving optimal solutions to given problems, had assumed a benign and welfare-maximizing state, a state that was disembodied from the identity of its leadership, the diverse claims of its citizens, or the orientations of its historical evolution. Planning models of the 1960s assumed that policy makers, planners, and the institutions of the state held notions of the public interest that corresponded to economic notions of welfare maximization.[2] In short, behind policy analysis, advice, and planning was an implicit notion of states whose purpose was to do good (see Colander 1984a; Bardhan 1988). Presented with technical evidence of how to achieve increased welfare, states would adopt appropriate policy. Within such a perspective, failure to achieve goals was the result of incomplete information, faulty analysis, or institutional weaknesses in carrying out policy (see especially Killick 1976: 164–65).

The harsh realities of the 1980s made it increasingly difficult to sustain assumptions about welfare-maximizing states. In fact, research, experience, and frustration combined to encourage considerable interest in the study of political economy among development economists. Among diverse political economy models that are being explored in this context, recent neoclassical models have helped resolve the clash between theory and empirical observation by replacing the image of the benign state with its mirror opposite, the negative state. Whereas the benign state was assumed to be motivated to do good, the negative state of neoclassical approaches was characterized as a creature of self-seeking interest groups and/or self-serving leaders and could be expected to do harm to societal welfare unless it was carefully restricted in its activities. Scholars in the 1970s and 1980s utilized concepts such as the rent-seeking society and the predatory state to explain why states adopted and then persisted in pursuing policies that increased distortions in the economy, exacerbating inefficiency, stagnation, and inequality (see especially Lal 1984; Conybeare 1982; Krueger 1974; Bhagwati 1982; Srinivasan 1985). Politicians and bureaucrats ceased to be seen as value-neutral public servants and became, in narrative and in model construction, motivated only to stay in power or to maximize their individual gains through rent seeking and the encouragement of directly unproductive profit seeking (DUP). Moreover, while the benign state was always empirically elusive, the image of the negative state has strong empirical referents for many economists who have worked in developing countries. Intuitively and conceptually, then, neoclassical political economy provided answers to a number of questions about the role of the state and public policy in economic development.[3]

This new political economy, a theoretical orientation developed primarily by economists and encompassing the perspectives of public choice, collective choice, and social choice theory, has proved extraordinarily useful as a construct for explaining economically irrational policy to neoclassical economists and political scientists alike. It offers parsimonious formal theory to respond to Robert Bates's challenging question, "Why should reasonable men adopt public policies that have harmful consequences for the societies they govern?" (Bates 1981: 3).

Although there are distinct strains of thought within this neoclassical approach, they are based in a set of basic assumptions about human behavior. In neoclassical political economy, traditional microeconomic assumptions about the primacy of individual self-interest are applied with equal consistency to the political claims of citizens, to the actions of politicians and policy makers, to the behavior of bureaucrats, and even to the actions of states more generally (see Conybeare 1982; Hirshleifer 1985). Through the lens of self-interest, politics becomes endogenous to policy choice and can be modeled along with more traditional economic variables. Moreover, neoclassical political economy offers an explanatory framework to help development specialists understand why governments of developing countries do not adopt their advice with greater regularity.

The new political economy also offers a profoundly cynical view of the political process. Clearly there is much empirical evidence to support a deeply skeptical attitude about the existence of a benign state. The neoclassical approach, however, adopts the notion that individually rational behavior in politics leads to economically irrational outcomes. That is, individual self-interest pursued in a political arena results in policies that are collectively wasteful and, ultimately, individually irrational as well. Moreover, neoclassical political economy suggests that politically rational behavior for an individual is capable of fairly consistently overwhelming the demonstrable logic of good economic policy advice. It thus makes the task of explaining the potential for economic reform extremely difficult and limits the applicability of policy-relevant advice. Carried to its logical conclusions, it may well be a trap for those who wish to bring about change in existing policies and institutional arrangements. The new political economy has many strengths, but it is weakened as an approach to understanding policy making in developing countries and as a tool for policy analysis by the assumption that politics is a negative factor in attempting to get the policies right. This chapter presents a critique of an explanation of policy making that predicts negative outcomes for society and that emphasizes the inability to introduce significant change in development policy.

In the following pages, I assess the relevance of neoclassical political economy for explaining policy making in developing countries and consider its utility in policy analysis. I am less concerned here with a critique of the basic assumptions of the models that have been developed than with the utility of the models in capturing the nature and process of policy dynamics. Granting the assumptions, I ask how accurate and useful the tools of neoclassical political economy are in the analysis of public policy in developing countries. This is, then, primarily a critique not of formal theory, but of the utility of formal theory.

Briefly, I argue that society-centric political economy models adopted from the U.S. experience are not particularly relevant for most developing countries. State-centric adaptations come somewhat closer to reflecting how public policy is formulated and implemented in these contexts. Even with more appropriate applications, however, the new political economy is most useful for explaining stasis rather than change and "bad" policy choices rather than "good" ones.[4] That is, I argue that the perspective is reductionist in a way that impedes efforts to conceptualize or explain what is most sought after by many of its adherents— change and improvement in the nature of development policy in a society. A model of policy making relevant for this era of economic crisis and political upheaval would be one in which politics is assumed to be neither inherently negative nor inherently positive for the selection and pursuit of public policy. It would accept politics, not as a spanner in the economic works, but as the central means through which societies seek to resolve conflict over issues of distribution and values. In such a perspective, politically rational behavior would not be viewed as a constraint on the achievement of collectively beneficial public policy.

The New Political Economy: The Logic of Argument

Neoclassical political economy asserts that the basic unit of social analysis is the individual (see, for example, Buchanan and Tullock 1962; Colander 1984b; Riker and Ordeshook 1973; Barry and Hardin 1982). Individuals are rational, and as such they seek to maximize individual utilities or values; in other words, they pursue their self-interest. Self-interest is theoretically contentless until individual preferences are revealed through behavior, although it is generally assumed that self-seeking individuals will pursue enhanced economic welfare or economic security. Individuals will try to maximize their gains from economic interaction; simultaneously, they will try to use government to increase and protect these gains. The new political economy attempts to understand the noneconomic market of political activity, using the language and analytic tools of the economist (see Hirshleifer 1985: 53).

Central to understanding politics through this perspective is the assertion that individuals cannot always achieve their self-interest individually. At times it will be rational for them to join together with other individuals whose self-interest corresponds with their own, to press for the achievement of individual goals. In this way individuals

can transform their pursuit of self-interest into group action (see especially Riker and Ordeshook 1973). The payoff to members of the group
for joint action is the enhanced possibility that individual goals will be
realized. Rational individuals, therefore, cooperate with likeminded
others if and when such cooperation clearly results in a more optimal
individual payoff than solitary action. When the achievement of such
goals involves making claims on government, the basis for political
action is laid. Generally, politics is considered to be activities in pursuit
of self-interest through voting by individuals and lobbying for favorable policy outcomes by groups (see Alt and Chrystal 1983; Buchanan
and Tullock 1962).[5] Lobbying involves seeking access to benefits that
cannot be acquired through a competitive market; lobbying activities
will increase the more government intervenes in the economy (see
Buchanan 1980). Economic benefits sought through noneconomic markets are considered by most neoclassical political economists to be
wasteful in that they result in a loss of social welfare (Srinivasan 1985:
43; see Bhagwati 1982 for a discussion). The use of the state to maximize economic gains for specific interests has been dubbed "rent seeking" (see Samuels and Mercuro 1984: 55–56; Krueger 1974).[6]

Mancur Olson, in considering the problem of collective action,
notes the difficulty of sustaining joint activities if individuals perceive
they will achieve the sought-after benefits even without contributing
their time, effort, or money to group action (see Olson 1965). This problem of the free rider means that groups tend to remain small and narrowly focused on achieving specific goals that will accrue only to group
members if action is successful. In politics, therefore, narrowly focused
special interest groups tend to emerge in order to press government for
specific benefits for their members—a special tax exclusion or allotment
of funds for a neighborhood school, for example.[7] For neoclassical political economists, then, politics is characterized by a plethora of special
interest groups competing for access to the benefits that can be allocated
by government and by individual voting behavior that is motivated by
self-interest, electing those who promise to deliver these benefits and
punishing those who fail to make such promises or who fail to make
good on them if they are elected (Downs 1957). According to Olson
(1965, 1982), public policy reflects the existence of distributional coalitions in society that seek to shape and control the allocation of public
resources to the benefit of their members.

This perspective on politics is similar in many regards to a long
tradition of democratic political theory in the United States. In the pluralist model often adopted by political scientists, society is also composed of self-interested individuals. Motivated by the majoritarian
requisites of democratic government, they join together in groups and
then coalitions of likeminded individuals to press for favorable govern-

ment action.[8] Interests are usually economic, but groups also form around shared concerns for neighborhood, ethnicity, religion, values, region, or other goals. They lobby, they contribute to campaigns, and they vote in order to influence public officials to act on their behalf. In the pluralist tradition, democratic politics is based on large numbers of such groups competing and coalescing around the promotion or protection of common policy goals.[9] Political conflict in democratic society is moderated by the fact that individual group members have multiple interests and affiliations that tend to be crosscutting, limiting the intensity of their commitment to any one goal, and by the need of the group to join in coalitions with other groups in order to have enough power (that is, votes) to influence government. Party competition is also moderated by the need of parties to attract voters, most of whom reside in the middle of the spectrum of political opinion (see Downs 1957).

In the pluralist tradition, as in much neoclassical political economy, public policy is the result of the pushing and hauling among interest groups and their efforts to influence government through lobbying—this is a society-centric view of the determinants of policy, as we will see later. Interest groups raise issues to public attention and place them on the agenda for government action, and it is their lobbying activities that determine decisional outcomes. The actions of public officials reflect the distribution of power among interests in society. Pluralist and neoclassical political economy theories clearly agree that the key to understanding politics and public policy is to understand the composition and interaction of interest groups in the society and the claims they make on government.[10]

Pluralists and neoclassical political economists tend to part company, however, over the issue of how the public interest is achieved in policy. In the pluralist tradition, the public interest is ultimately served through the conflict and competition of interest groups. The tendency for interests to be fragmented is counteracted by the need in democratic government to achieve majoritarian consent—in the population at large or within representative bodies of lawmakers—that requires groups to compromise on positions and form coalitions around more broadly defined interests. Minorities are protected because of the difficulty of putting together majority coalitions and the need, in doing so, to moderate extreme positions. Those affected adversely by proposed or actual legislation have an opportunity to organize to oppose it. The impediments to acquiring the consent of the majority under democratic rules are—at least theoretically—supposed to act as a control on the growth of government, ensuring the widest possible scope for pursuit of self-interest in the economic marketplace. This pluralist view that the public interest emerges from competition in the political marketplace is a clear analogy to the notion of efficiency achieved in the economic marketplace through the competition among numerous firms. In the democracy they formed, the Founding Fathers of the United States institutionalized this pluralist political economy. James Madison defended the notion of a federal republic, for instance, by arguing that " . . . the society itself will be broken into so many parts and classes of citizens, that the rights of individuals or of the minority will be in little danger from interested combinations of the majority" (Federalist Paper no. 51).

In contrast, neoclassical political economy perceives in the conflict and competition among interest groups a clear threat to the ability of government to respond to the public interest with policies that are economically rational for society in general. The logic of collective action tends to enforce smallness in groups and to keep their interests narrowly focused on specific benefits for group members. The result of their activities to influence government is a parceling out of benefits to the narrowly defined interests and a growth in the size and incoherence of government as elected public officials scurry to respond to a multitude of interest groups. Government policy distorts economic interactions and encourages inefficiency through excessive regulation designed to protect or promote the plethora of interests (Buchanan 1980; Olson 1982). While an "invisible hand" regulates economic markets, an "invisible foot" results in their distortion through politics (see Magee 1984).

Limited government is the neoclassical solution to this problem (see Colander 1984a: 5). Restricting the activities of government means that it will have less with which to reward specific interests (Buchanan 1980). If there is less to acquire through efforts to influence government, there will be less political activity focused on extracting benefits from government and a more unfettered economic system, able to respond with greater speed to market forces. According to Bennett and DiLorenzo (1984: 217), "The problem of reforming the rent-seeking society is widely perceived to be the adoption of an appropriate set of rules to limit the burdens of government." In this formulation, less politics generally means better economics. For neoclassical political economists, interest-group competition in the absence of specific rules to control its scope breeds big government and distorts the normal functioning of the market:

> . . . so long as governmental action is restricted largely, if not entirely, to protecting individual rights, persons and property, and enforcing voluntarily negotiated private contracts, the market process dominates economic behavior. . . . If, however, government action moves significantly beyond the limits defined by the minimal or protective state . . . the tendency toward the erosion or dissipation of rents is countered and may be shortly blocked (Buchanan 1980: 9).

Thus, in the neoclassical view, politics and markets are often in conflict because the efficient operation of competitive markets is easily threatened by policy interventions resulting from interest-group pressures on government. Public policy tends in this way to reflect politically rational choices that lead to economically irrational outcomes.

When the new political economy has probed inside the state and inquired into the decision making of political and bureaucratic elites, it has also presented rational political choice as an impediment to achieving the collective economic good. Although the focus of most work has been society-centric, in which government action is presumed to reflect vested interests found in society, some analysts have sought to explain the behavior of actors within the state or of the state itself. In more state-centered explanations of the politics of economic policy making, politicians are as rational and self-seeking as are voters. Their self-interest, however, is expressed as the desire to maximize their hold on power. They will therefore be motivated to use government resources to reward those who support their hold on power and, at times, to punish those who seek to unseat them (see, for example, Ames 1987; Bates 1981). In this way, policy elites become less reactive to interest group pressures and more active in attempting to maximize their chances of staying in power by putting together supportive coalitions and using public resources to "buy" support. The actions of political elites are contentless in terms of normative preferences in policy; they will take any policy position if it promises to maximize their short-term goal of staying in power. The policy that tends to emerge from this situation is largely incoherent and even inimical to economic stability and growth because of the short-term time horizons of the politicians and their lack of commitment to the content of public policy.[11]

Neoclassical political economy, when it takes a more state-centric approach, also makes a series of statements about the behavior of non-elected public officials. Bureaucrats are also individualistic self-seekers. Generally, their pursuit of self-interest involves maximizing their own economic welfare, but can also entail enhancing their power or benefiting their home village or ethnic group. When provided with policy resources to distribute—import licenses, for example, or the location of school sites—they will seek to maximize their self-interest either by selling the resource to whomever offers the highest price or by allocating it to preferred clients. Corruption and clientelism can therefore be understood to result from noneconomic markets that function through bureaucratic resource allocations. The new political economy thus provides a third explanation for the economically irrational allocation of public resources.

A fourth application of the new political economy is the idea of the predatory state (see Lal 1984). Here the state is the unit of analysis, not the citizen, the politician, or the bureaucrat. The state as a rational actor seeks to maximize short-term revenues and pursues a variety of forms of taxation that allow it to increase its wealth and to grow in size, even at the cost of overall economic development. Predatory states are particularly likely to tax trade, maintain an overvalued exchange rate, and support a large inefficient bureaucracy (see Killick 1988: 7; Conybeare 1982). These states, acting in rational ways to enhance their power, thus introduce and perpetuate economically irrational development strategies.

Neoclassical political economy provides a compelling explanation of economically irrational policy outcomes in developing countries. It asserts that individuals, politicians, bureaucrats, and states purposely use the authority of the state to distort economic interactions to their own benefit. Empirically, developing countries provide numerous cases of such economically irrational outcomes. There are many examples, for instance, of predominantly agrarian societies whose governments have followed policies that have systematically overtaxed agriculture in the interests of urban and industrial development (Bates 1981; Anderson and Hayami 1986). It is not difficult to find cases of countries locked into unproductive development strategies by the combined economic and political power of vested interests; the continued pursuit of import substitution is often credited to this situation. There are also numerous examples of policies with short-term benefits but long-term costs—an overvalued exchange rate or extensive protectionist measures, for instance. Similarly, many governments adopt cumbersome and inefficient policy mechanisms such as import licensing when more administratively efficient mechanisms, such as tariffs, are readily available. Moreover, governments often invest widely in projects rather than formulating and implementing more general policies; in neoclassical analysis, this is because specific interests lobby for specific benefits, not general ones, or because politicians are concerned with buying the support of specific groups in their single-minded pursuit of power (Olson 1982; Bates 1981). It is also true that development resources are often systematically misallocated during implementation (see Grindle 1980). Neoclassical political economy explains these outcomes without assuming ignorance, stupidity, or willful misbehavior on the part of citizens, policy makers, or bureaucrats.

How Applicable Is the New Political Economy to Conditions in Developing Countries?

While a large number of economically irrational outcomes in public policy can be explained with neoclassical political economy, it is worth considering whether this approach correctly captures the *dynamics* that lead to such outcomes in developing countries. That is, current work in political economy identifies—often correctly—certain policy outcomes, from which it infers political processes that led to such outcomes. The question here is whether the inferences are warranted, given what is known about processes of decision making and policy implementation in developing countries. In particular, can the process of government decision making in developing countries be explained through recourse to the activities of rent-seeking lobbies? Power-seeking politicians? Rent-seeking bureaucrats? Predatory states?

The first of these alternatives, that policy choice reflects the interests of pressure groups, is a society-centric explanation of policy making (see Grindle and Thomas 1989). In this perspective, the activities of states and policy elites are dependent variables. Whenever the new political economy has tried to explain the policy preferences of politicians, bureaucrats, or states in general, it has adopted a state-centric approach in which these actors have greater autonomous capacity to shape policy outcomes. In the society-centric explanation of public policy, economic agents use political markets for economic ends; in the state-centric applications, political agents make use of economic resources for political ends.[12]

In this chapter, I suggest that neoclassical political economy is least applicable to the dynamics of policy making in developing countries when it takes a society-centered approach, that is, when it is based on assumptions about interest mobilization and more or less acquiescent government response to lobbying activities. It is more applicable when it replaces this society-centric view with a more state-centric perspective based on political elites who are actively engaged in maximizing their political power or on rent-seeking bureaucrats. Even here, however, the approach tends to misrepresent the political meaning of the actions of political elites and bureaucrats. Finally, while the notion of predatory states has been adopted for predictive purposes in some cases, there is little theoretical support in either economics or politics for treating states as unitary actors or assuming purposive behavior by the state as a collectivity. In what follows, the notion of predatory states is not dealt with because of the difficulty of assuming that unitary states act out of individual self-interest in the sense developed by neoclassical economists.

Lobbying by interest groups. Some economists and political scientists have found the new political economy to be useful as a way of understanding public policy in the United States (see especially Alt and Chrystal 1983 and Keech, Bates, and Lange 1989 for reviews). In particular, they find its explanation of the activities of lobby groups and elected officials to be consistent with aspects of contemporary American politics such as "hyperpluralist" fragmentation of interest groups, the power of small, focused lobbies over the substance of policy in specific areas, the extreme difficulty of aggregating interests, the sensitivity of lawmakers to the demands of narrow constituencies and the reelection imperative, and the reactive and incoherent nature of much public policy (see Alt and Chrystal

1983; Riker 1982).[13] There is much evidence in contemporary politics in the United States that public policy has been parceled out to organized interests and that the government has moved far from its original role of protecting rights and enforcing contracts to one that is highly interventionist and regulatory. In fact, much policy making in the United States tends to be an extremely open and highly visible public pulling and hauling among narrowly focused interest groups, legislatures, and executive offices, and the accumulation of legislation is vast and often contradictory. Many have referred to the "iron triangle" of lobby groups, legislators, and executive agencies that results in extensive allocation of benefits to special interests.

This pattern of policy driven by societal interests, of the state as a more or less neutral arena in which competitive lobbies fight for control of policy resources, is much less in evidence in the vast majority of developing countries. In these countries policy making tends to be more closed, less visible, and more centered in the political executive (see Grindle and Thomas 1989). Citizens often have their first information about policy when it is formally announced or decreed by the political leadership. In general, high-level administrators and political leaders dominate the policy-making process. It is they, not legislators, who tend to be the targets of those who would influence the decision-making process. They may or may not retain office through elections, and their tenure in office is often highly ambiguous. Perhaps most important, extensive organized interest-group activity tends to be less clearly defined in developing countries than in the industrialized democracies of the West. Large portions of the population—peasants and urban shantytown residents, for instance—are generally not organized for sustained political activity, although they may, from time to time, make their demands known through actions such as protest marches, riots, or strikes. Ethnic or family identities may play critical roles in politics even though they are not publicly organized. Additionally, many authoritarian regimes in the third world actively discourage representation of societal interests through formally constituted interest groups. "Interests" clearly exist in developing countries, of course, but the extent to which they are or can be formally constituted to represent goals of a membership, and their capacity to gain access to the state, must always be identified empirically. In many cases, "barriers to entry" are high and any assumptions about democratic responsiveness need to be scrutinized carefully.

Lobbying activity is consequently difficult to identify in many developing countries. In some cases elite organizations—the ubiquitous national chamber of manufacturers or the national agricultural society, for instance—may be well organized and vociferous but wield their real political influence behind the scenes in informal interactions with political leaders, not through votes or more visible lobbying activities. In other cases the most important economic interests in a society may not even be formally organized. The power of some interests over particular policy choices may be more implicit than explicit—few decision makers are unaware of the concerns of the military or foreign investors, for instance, although these "interests" may not articulate their needs explicitly or publicly. In still other cases organizations lack access to policy makers or even the capacity to control their followings. Some organized groups may actually be dependent clientele organizations of bureaucratic agencies or of particular political leaders, with little capacity to press a policy agenda on their patrons in government. Similarly, political parties in one-party or dominant-party states have very little power independent of government leadership. In clientelistic states, interest-group activities tend to be highly disaggregated and personalized and to focus more on influencing implementation than on affecting policy choice. Thus, the assumption that policy outcomes represent societal interests and that policy is made in response to the activities of lobby groups seriously misrepresents the dynamics of policy making in large numbers of developing countries.[14] In addition, the political economy analyses that have emerged in the United States concern political interactions that occur within the context of agreed-upon rules for political competition or how those rules come to be agreed upon (see Riker 1982; Barry and Hardin 1982; Buchanan 1980). In developing countries, however, it cannot always be assumed that the rules of the game are established or agreed upon. Where this is the case, the use of society-centric political economy models is misleading.

The actions of policy makers. In its more state-centric applications, the new political economy has sought to provide insight into the behavior of policy elites. It asserts that elected political leaders want to stay in power; they will maximize their chances of achieving this end by using policy resources to reward supporters or potential supporters (see Lindbeck 1976; Ames 1987; Bates 1981; Anderson and Hayami 1986; Bennett and DiLorenzo 1984). According to this view, policy outcomes can be systematically traced to the efforts of policy elites to buy political support and to establish and maintain supportive coalitions.[15] This perspective corresponds to much that can be observed in developing countries, where, as we have argued, policy elites are central to policy making. Political stability and the maintenance of power tend to be major preoccupations of these political actors because, in many cases, they are vulnerable to the loss of political power (see Grindle and Thomas 1989). Moreover, the regimes they lead are also often vulnerable. Coups and leadership changes are regularly noted phenomena that can result in imprisonment, exile, or even death for those who held prominent roles in the overthrown government. For this reason, it is reasonable to expect that such elites are extremely sensitive to the need to satisfy certain societal and government (military, public servants) interests in repeated bids to establish or maintain support. According to Ames's (1987) analysis of budgetary politics in Latin America, for instance, normal politics is the politics of survival. "Given the frequency of military coups, the dismal reelection record of incumbents, and the volatility of open economies, executives can rarely take political survival for granted. To the maximum degree possible, every program must be subjected to the executive's drive for security" (p. 211).

Nevertheless, the new political economy overemphasizes the direct link between policy and political support building. In fact, policy elites may have little direct information on the interests of particular groups in society or on the limits of tolerance for policy actions that do not directly benefit, or that even harm, these interests. As noted, policy making tends to occur in relatively closed circles and the decision-making process may be highly centralized in a few critical leadership positions. Similarly, interest-articulation structures (lobby groups) are often much less visible, dense, or apparent than is the case with long-established Western democracies. This is not to argue that policy elites are unconstrained by societal interests, but only that it is not always easy to determine how societal policy preferences are made known to decision makers. Policy elites are vulnerable to the claims of many interests, but they may survive politically on the basis of astute intuition about politically relevant groups rather than through the more direct knowledge that results from organized interest-group lobbying. They know that some of their decisions can have personally harmful consequences, but they often have little direct information about the limits of societal tolerance for policy change. Support coalition formation, or mobilizing non-elite groups for political support, may be especially difficult under conditions of very imperfect information.

Given the problems of interest representation in policy making in developing countries, there is considerable scope for the preferences of policy elites to influence the choice of policy and to define acceptable policy (see Grindle and Thomas 1989). There is also considerable potential for mistaken judgments. In addition, there is extensive evidence that policy elites are not idea-free and that politicians are not contentless in terms of their preferences. They generally have very explicit notions of what constitutes good policy and, although clearly concerned about staying in power, they are not undiscriminating in terms of maximizing their capacity to do so. They have historically and ideologically determined coalition partners and support groups, as well as clearly defined opponents whose support they will not seek, even in the interest of staying in power. Once this is acknowledged, the idea of power maximization should become a less central assumption about what drives policy elites. Power is less an end than a means to an end.[16] Moreover, where states have played significant roles in defining and directing the course of economic development, it is reasonable to assume that policy elites have definite ideas about the national interest or the public good that go beyond individual self-interest. Similarly, where the role of the state is large, it is reasonable to expect that policy elites will have some scope to act on these ideas (see Bardhan 1988).

In addition, of course, many decisions made by policy elites are not directly relevant to staying in power. Decentralizing the ministry of health, selling certain parastatals, raising interest rates marginally, or refocusing rural school curriculum are decisions of a different magnitude than a devaluation or an end of subsidies on urban transportation or basic foodstuffs. Although these latter decisions can bring down a regime or a political leader, the former are unlikely to have such consequences and cannot be easily explained through a strategic "calculus of survival" (see Ames 1987; Grindle and Thomas 1989). Thus, if policy elites play critical roles in decision making, it makes sense to try to understand how their preferences are formed and how they are influenced in ways that go beyond the banality of asserting that they wish to stay in office. Specifying preferences more fully than is done in current political economy applications would result in a better capacity to predict the content of policy.

The activities of bureaucrats. A second state-centered application of current political economy analysis focuses on the rent-seeking behavior of bureaucratic officials. This approach has proved a fertile ground for neoclassical political economists, particularly in discussions of trade policy (see Krueger 1974). Public officials in developing countries are thought to exchange access to disaggregated public resources—an import license, for example—for some personal benefit, usually economic in nature. In trade theory, this transaction explains the preference for highly disaggregable protectionist measures, the corrupt behavior of public officials, and the difficulty of altering inefficient policy tools. Importers gain preferential access to scarce goods, and bureaucrats not only enjoy enhanced power, but can also feather their nests. This is an important application of the new political economy because it allows analysts to focus on the resource distribution that occurs during the implementation of policy in developing countries. It also highlights the extent to which societal interests interact with state officials in the normal functioning of government through day-to-day decisions about resource allocation.

Although policy analysts in the United States have long pointed to the important role that implementation plays in developed countries,

this process is even more central in developing countries. There, because policy making tends to be a closed and executive-centered activity, large portions of the population are excluded from influencing the
formulation of laws, decrees, and policies that often have direct impact
on their lives. In contrast, during policy implementation they may have
much greater capacity to reach the bureaucrats charged with pursuing
the policy and to bring pressure to bear on these officials (see Grindle
1980). Bending the rules, seeking exceptions to generalized prescriptions, proffering bribes for special consideration, having a friend in city
hall—these are immensely important aspects of political participation
in developing countries, and they often become more important the
more closed the policy-making process. For political economists, the
venality of public officials mirrors the interest of societal groups or individuals in acquiring access to the resources of the state.

Nevertheless, the interaction of individualistic rent-seeking bureaucrats and individualistic rent-seeking citizens does not explain the most
critical aspects of the politics of policy implementation in developing
countries. Implementation activities, for example, tend to be closely tied
to regime maintenance goals. Political elites and policy makers often
recognize, at least implicitly, the importance of the policy implementation process because of the vulnerability of the regimes or administrations they serve. Policies may have implicit goals—to provide payoffs to
those who can strengthen regime stability—as well as explicit goals—to
achieve the stated goals of the policy—that become apparent only
through the accommodation, rule bending, and resource allocation that
occurs after policy decisions have been made (see Grindle 1980). Similarly, clientelism often serves to hold a tenuous political regime together,
a regime that must continue to provide specific benefits through piece-
meal resource allocations where it is not accorded widespread legitimacy (see Bratton 1980; Sandbrook 1986). Thus, the slippage that occurs
between what is stated as policy and what is actually implemented,
resulting from the myriad times that rules are bent and particular un-
derstandings are reached, may be more than simply venal. It may be a
direct result of the need to provide tangible benefits or immunity from
policy to individuals or groups throughout a social hierarchy. "Accommodation of interests," rather than corruption or rent seeking, may
more fully capture the dynamics of policy implementation because it
draws attention to complex and intentional use of the process, not only
by bureaucratic officials, but also by political leaders. Again, although
neoclassical political economy correctly describes a series of economically irrational policy outcomes, it is often making incorrect inferences
about how those outcomes were generated. The approach can easily
lose sight of the political consequences of such interactions that are
more significant than nest-feathering.

If current political economy analyses correctly describe a series of policy outcomes, is there any reason to be concerned that the approach makes a series of inappropriate inferences about the power of organized interest groups and the motivations of policy elites and bureaucratic officials? I believe there is, because understanding how policy is made and implemented makes it possible to assess how and when policy changes come about and, thus, how policy reforms can be introduced and sustained. A better understanding of process, for example, can provide insights into how problems become policy issues; what circumstances surround efforts to change policy; what role policy elites, technocrats, advisers, and others play in defining alternatives; how choices are determined; and what factors influence the implementation and sustainability of new policy initiatives. Without such insights, the effort to change bad policy into better policy is a directionless enterprise. In the next section, I consider the problem of getting from here to there in terms of reforming policy in developing countries.

Getting from Here to There

The new political economy has provided a number of policy prescriptions for restraining rent-seeking behavior and for limiting the extent to which such politically rational behavior can lead to collectively irrational outcomes. Analysis of rent seeking, for example, has led economists to compare policy mechanisms that differ in terms of their susceptibility to such behavior. Thus, Krueger (1974) is able to recommend tariffs over licensing as a policy tool because the welfare loss associated with tariffs is demonstrated to be less than what is lost through licensing. Tariffs are more general policy instruments and consequently less susceptible to rent seeking by individuals. Similarly, using the analytic tools provided by the neoclassical political economy, political economists have examined the extensive evidence of behavior that is individually rational but socially destructive, such as "the tragedy of the commons," and made recommendations for its amelioration (Hardin 1968; Russell and Nicholson 1981).[17] They have suggested alternative policy and institutional mechanisms to limit or control the destruction of common property, such as binding rules for its use, institutions of private property, or conditions under which collective management can be effective (see Runge 1986; Popkin 1988).

More generally, Kenneth Koford and David Colander (1984) have suggested several mechanisms to limit rent seeking, such as increasing the availability of information about who benefits from it, using moral sanctions to limit its extent, establishing laws to restrict policies that encourage rent seeking, and taxing rent-seeking activities. At the broadest level the central policy prescriptions of the new political economy support much current development policy advice—liberalize the economy, privatize some public activities, and restrict the scope of state intervention in the economy. As suggested in previous pages, according to this perspective, limiting the extent to which politics can intrude in the workings of the economy limits the extent to which state intervention and regulation can overwhelm the efficiency of economic interactions (see Bennett and DiLorenzo 1984).[18]

These policy prescriptions would be fairly easy to apply in developing countries if one were to begin with a political, institutional, and policy tabula rasa. The problem, of course, is that such prescriptions are addressed to governments that have long histories of state intervention in the economy, that have helped create powerful groups in the society that benefit from existing policy, and that have become well acquainted with the use of disaggregated policy tools that can be parceled out for political ends. According to neoclassical political economy such situations result from rational behavior on the part of individuals. Although the new political economy provides tools for understanding bad situations and for recommending policies that will engender better situations, it provides no logically apparent means of moving from bad to better. For example, as we have seen, some argue that tariffs are more economically efficient than import-licensing mechanisms in rent-seeking societies. If import licenses are widely used in a particular country, however, and they are contributing to a variety of individual self-interests, then there is nothing to explain how or why these politically useful mechanisms would be traded in for mechanisms that offer politicians, bureaucrats, and importers less individual utility. If one is locked into an ahistorical explanation of why things are the way they are and the notion that existing situations demonstrate an inevitable rationality, it is hard to envision how changes in such situations occur except through catastrophic events or the exogenous introduction of wise statesmen or technocrats who are above petty political rationality. Both of these alternatives have been used to explain policy change, and both are inadequate.

Mancur Olson, in *The Rise and Decline of Nations* (1982), presents a tightly argued explanation for the inevitability of economic decline in countries where rent seeking has become widespread. Such activities are likely to be most pervasive in stable societies, where the number and diversity of lobbies grow over time and increasingly make claims for rents. Lobbies cause the government to intervene on behalf of specific interests and eventually constrict the normal functioning of an economy so much that it is difficult for new technology to be introduced and for the economy to adapt effectively to new conditions. As a result, growth slows and may even stop, especially in situations where there are few incentives for rent seekers to join in large organizations such as unions or broad-based associations. Rent seekers, Olson argues, will not voluntarily relinquish their hold on policy in the interest of improving general economic performance. They can only be dislodged when a society experiences some catastrophic event, such as a revolution, an invasion, or a war. In the absence of such a shock, little improvement in economic policy can be expected.

Robert Bates (1981), in applying public choice theory to the African context, presents an equally disheartening scenario for the possibilities of change. At independence, he argues, African leaders, motivated by the desire to modernize their societies through industrialization, impose policies to extract resources from their overwhelmingly agricultural societies for use in urbanizing and industrializing. Relatively autonomous in their choice of policy at the outset, they soon become captive to the beneficiaries of the policies they have introduced and lose their capacity to alter policy. Urban middle-class bureaucrats, the new industrial class, the urban working class—sectors created by state policy—increase in wealth and political power to the extent that they can demand the perpetuation and increase of policies to benefit them. Aware of the potential for unrest in the rural population, which pays the costs of urban and industrial development, governments buy the loyalty of rural elites, and their assistance in keeping the rural peace, through projects and subsidies even while more general policies continue to discriminate heavily against the sector. The mass of disadvantaged farmers, as rational actors with low potential to acquire political power, respond in economically rational ways to burdensome public policies—they stop producing for the market and withdraw into self-sufficiency, barter, or black-market activities. The effect of this behavior then rebounds in national terms: declining agricultural productivity and foreign exchange from agricultural exports cause governments to squeeze the sector, borrow extensively abroad, and undertake massive deficit spending to respond to the demands of increasingly insistent urban interests. Politicians, wanting to remain in power, become locked into a cycle of increasingly irrational policy—subsidizing a few rural interests while destroying agricultural productivity; rewarding inefficient industrialists, workers, and bureaucrats while destroying the economy. Ultimately, military coups and other forms of political upheaval are the only way out of this spiral of increasing demands and decreasing resources. In all likelihood, however, newly installed governments will quickly degenerate into equally destructive cycles, to be replaced by other governments, and so on.

To explain policy changes that reflect increases in economic wisdom in rent-seeking societies, other scholars have introduced enlightened technocrats or statespeople who are somehow liberated from the pursuit of self-interest and thus able to see beyond short-term goals to long-term public interests. In the general context of negative politics predicted by neoclassical political economists, change is explained exogenously by benign leadership or disinterested advice. For example, at the conclusion of a lucid article on the new political economy and development policy, T. N. Srinivasan introduces benign leadership as a way out of the political trap created by extensive rent seeking. "Let me conclude," he writes, "with an encouraging note. It would appear that leaders in developing countries are becoming increasingly aware of the negative economic and political consequences of rent-seeking interventions in the economy" (Srinivasan 1985: 58). He goes on to cite examples of leadership in India, China, and some African countries where significant public policy reforms have occurred. He offers no explanation, however, for the appearance of these leaders or their ability to escape the logic that binds ordinary mortals, unless, of course, the concept of self-interest is expanded to include the capacity to view the long-term public interest as individual utility maximization. In this case the concept of self-interest becomes effectively meaningless.

If cataclysms or benign leaders are necessary for policy reform to occur, the introduction of changed policy could be expected to happen only sporadically. Several examples of significant policy changes in the 1980s suggest, however, that despite the universally agreed upon difficulty of initiating reform in public policy, change has not, in fact, been as elusive as neoclassical political economy would suggest. Consider, for instance, the case of The Gambia. During an eighteen-month period beginning in 1985, policy makers in that country introduced a series of significant policy and institutional changes that affected virtually all aspects of the economy (see Radelet 1988; McPherson 1988). Macroeconomic reforms included a float of the national currency, an increase in interest rates by the central bank, and a moratorium on contracting important debt obligations. At the sectoral level, rates for public transportation, water, and electricity were raised in 1985 and again in 1986. In agriculture, markets for domestic and international trade in rice were liberalized, the producer price of groundnuts was greatly increased in both years, and fertilizer marketing was deregulated. In addition, taxes on fish exports were abolished, and prices for petroleum products were raised. Institutionally, the government froze the wages of the civil service and, through several measures, reduced the number of government jobs by almost 18 percent. It also initiated a cleanup of the customs agency. Greater changes were introduced in 1987 and 1988. These reforms, even in conjunction with a series of supportive external conditions, imposed significant and immediate costs on broad sectors of the population and on virtually all politically important interests. Taken together, it is hard to imagine how such changes could be explained through the microeconomic reasoning of neoclassical political economy.

While the case of The Gambia may be unusual for the number and extent of the changes introduced, many countries in the developing world adopted important, if more limited, sets of reforms in the 1980s. Consider the case of Ghana. In the context of declining economic growth and considerable political instability, the government devalued the currency significantly in 1983, imposed an austerity budget, reduced price supports and controls on many consumer products, privatized some state-owned enterprises, and improved public sector efficiency (see World Bank 1988: 116; Younger 1989). The introduction of these politically difficult measures was supported by external financing, increased investment in key economic sectors, and an increase in public sector salaries. From the perspective of neoclassical economics, all of these changes could be viewed as improvements in existing economic conditions. Nevertheless, despite "sweeteners" to some groups, the policy changes had negative short-term effects on important groups and imposed heavy social costs on broad sectors of the population, changes that politicians motivated primarily by the desire to maximize their power might wish to avoid at all costs. Given the initial context, neoclassical political economists would not have predicted such reforms nor would they be able to explain the reforms, once enacted, using the political logic of the approach. The rent-seeking behavior that explains economically irrational policy choices cannot readily explain the adoption of choices that conform to neoclassical notions of enlightened policy.

Significant structural reforms would certainly not have been predicted in Mexico, an almost classic case of rent-seeking lobbies associated with a strategy of import substitution holding policy captive to their economic interests. A currency float that meant massive ongoing devaluations, drastic cutbacks in imports, removal of nontariff barriers to trade, restructuring of public enterprise, tax reforms, decreases in important consumer subsidies, as well as many other economic reforms were introduced over a seven-year period and generally sustained despite a major drop in real income, massive unemployment, high rates of inflation, and a significant threat to the hegemony of the ruling political party (see Carr and Anzaldúa Montoya 1986; Maxfield and Anzaldúa Montoya 1987). The economic and political crises were real, but they engendered neither further rent-seeking accommodations nor coups, revolutions, or other cataclysms. Instead, the crises resulted in ongoing negotiations, a sustained commitment to implement a changed development strategy, and a search for a new basis of consensus in society. All of this occurred with virtually no payoffs available to the large number of politically important groups that were affected by the changes.

The list of countries that have made major changes in basic development policies is extensive.[19] Stabilization and structural adjustment programs have been sustained in Costa Rica, Bolivia, Thailand, Korea, Ghana, and Turkey, among other countries (see Lindenberg 1989; World Bank 1988; Younger 1989). Indonesia has introduced significant trade and financial market changes (Flatters 1988; Usman and Robinson 1988). Bolivia has introduced extensive new tax policies, as have Colombia, India, Jamaica, and Malawi (see World Bank 1988). Bangladesh has introduced and sustained trade and industrial policy changes (see Mallon and Stern 1988). The case of China after Mao is well known. Some countries, such as Bolivia, Sri Lanka, and Ghana, have undertaken major initiatives to target low-income groups most affected by stabilization and structural adjustment measures, even in the absence of significant political power among such groups (see Thomas and Chibber 1989). Social expenditures have been redirected to low-income groups in Mexico, Morocco, Brazil, and Ivory Coast (see Thomas and Chibber 1989). In Mauritius a policy aimed at reducing environmental degradation was instituted in the face of opposition from industrial interests that were causing pollution.

These countries vary significantly in regime type, history of political stability, and nature of vested interests. Clearly, each of them faced severe economic conditions and many confronted political crises of various sorts and degrees of magnitude, but neoclassical political economy offers no insight into the processes through which change occurred or into the ability of governments to select policies they believed would bring longer-term benefits to their societies. Explaining change is a far more challenging task than explaining stasis.

The new political economy recommends itself for its analytic rigor and parsimony. Overall, it allows analysts to understand the pursuit of policies that distort economic interactions, the systematic leakage of policy resources for political ends, and the resistance of policy makers and publics to altering existing practice. It indicates that existing practice represents a politically optimal solution to the problem of staying in power or extracting rents. These characteristics, however, make the theory inadequate for explaining what ought to be of great interest to development specialists, especially those who proffer advice about development policy—an understanding of how change occurs. This gap translates into an inability to explain how to get from here to there by way of alternative policies. This is a critical weakness of the theoretical approach and one that presents a challenge to policy analysts: can alternative models of politics be conceptualized that address issues of change, predict the content of change, and maintain a role for those who seek both politically and economically viable solutions to the major problems facing developing countries in the decades ahead?

Bases for an Alternative Political Economy

The limitations of the new political economy derive not from the fact that it is reductionist, as all theory must be, but that it is reductionist in a way that makes it difficult to explain change and the content of change or to envision a constructive role for politics, even though it accepts politics as an inevitable part of economic systems. In developing countries, where historical and contextual factors are extremely complex, a model of political economy should provide a means of understanding these factors. One possibility is to consider an alternative model, directed less at parsimony and more at capturing critical moments when change occurs, for such moments reveal essential political dynamics at work in a society. Some elements of such a model are sketched out below.

First, given the centrality of policy elites and the state to the policy outcomes, an approach that examines what occurs within the state and at the intersection of state and society would be an appropriate way to begin the task of explaining policy in developing countries. For instance, how do policy elites and policy managers perceive the issues, stakes, options, and constraints surrounding a particular policy problem? In response to such questions, concepts such as self-interest and power maximization explain little that is substantively interesting. Instead, a model of political economy should provide a means of understanding what the preferences of policy elites are, how they are formed, and how interaction among policy elites and between them and other groups influences the choices made about the content of public policy. A recent study of twelve reformist initiatives, for example, found that policy elites come into a decision-making situation with general policy references formed by ideological predispositions, professional expertise and training, memories of similar policy situations, position and power resources, political and institutional commitments, and personal attributes and goals (Grindle and Thomas 1989). Explaining particular instances of policy change is difficult without taking these factors into consideration.

In order to understand the preferences of policy elites in policy reform situations and to sketch out the range of options available to them, an appropriate model of political economy should also address the contextual issues that surround any particular decision-making situation. Policy choices are not made in a void but are part of ongoing patterns of conflict and conflict resolution in a society as well as means through which "optimal" solutions are molded by what appears to be possible. Considering these patterns introduces the very real possibility that states, for historical and ideological reasons, have interests and preferences that cannot be reduced to individual self-interest (see, for example, Bennett and Sharpe 1985; Grindle 1986; Haggard and Moon

1983). The organization of societal interests, historical and international contexts, the administrative capacity of government, and the influence of prior and coterminous policies all shape the preferences of decision makers and play an important role in explaining similarities and differences among countries. Thus, for example, the fact that some states tend to select statist solutions to public problems while others consistently favor market solutions or that unmobilized low-income groups are favored in one and ignored in another can only be convincingly explained by broad contextual factors.

The values of policy elites and the context within which they make decisions form a basis for considering policy making in general. Additionally, a model of political economy that can explain change should explain the specific outcomes of particular decision-making situations. For example, the circumstances surrounding the emergence of a particular issue have been shown to be of critical importance in explaining how that issue will be treated by decision makers (see Grindle and Thomas 1989). A particularly important distinction in explaining variable outcomes is whether policy elites perceive that an issue is tied to a crisis, be it economic, political, or social, or whether they consider it an issue to be dealt with on a politics-as-usual basis (see Hampson 1986). In other words, do decision makers believe they have no choice but to act to avoid a more threatening situation, or, conversely, do they believe that dealing with a problem, although important, is not particularly urgent and that failure to act will not lead to disaster? This distinction is critical because, depending on how the issue is perceived, different policy makers will be involved, the scope of change considered appropriate will differ, and the appraisal of the political and economic stakes will differ. Thus, in a context of perceived crisis, policy elites tend to be most concerned about macropolitical issues such as legitimacy, social stability, the costs and benefits of alternatives to major political coalitions in society, and the longevity of the regime. They will perceive not only that the stakes are very high, but also that such difficult conditions require significant and timely response, often a reversal of prior policy. Major innovative change could be anticipated in such a situation of perceived crisis.

In contrast, if a particular issue emerges under conditions that can be considered politics-as-usual, the dynamics of decision making will be very different, and change will take the form of an incremental or marginal adjustment or series of such adjustments. Little sense of urgency will surround the reform, and policy elites will have more autonomy either to take up the issue of change or to place it on a back burner. Under these politics-as-usual circumstances, decision makers are likely to be most concerned about bureaucratic compliance with change and about micropolitical issues such as clientelism and narrow coalition building. Moreover, high-level decision makers are likely to be only peripherally involved in such issues. Therefore, the politics, preferences, and options of policy elites regarding a devaluation are likely to be very different than those regarding the decentralization of the ministry of public works or a reforestation initiative. A model that allows for the analysis of agenda-setting circumstances and the specific concerns of decision makers can therefore have much more predictive value than a simpler analysis based solely on notions of individual self-interest.

After decisions to change policy have been made, a useful model of political economy should also be able to assess the extent to which those decisions will be successfully pursued by considering the nature of conflict surrounding efforts to implement changes (see Thomas and Grindle 1990). All actions to alter existing policies will encounter opposition or resistance, and the nature of that conflict is important in determining the course of policy implementation and the resources needed to sustain such initiatives. Research by Grindle and Thomas (1989) indicates that the type of conflict surrounding efforts to carry out policy change is strongly conditioned by the characteristics of the policies being implemented. Some policies, for example, have a short-term impact on broad sectors of the population or on particularly important sectors—the ending of a consumer subsidy program, for example, that results in higher prices for basic staples. Benefits, however, are often highly concentrated—removal of pressure on the public budget, for instance. This kind of policy change also tends to have an immediate cost because it is not administratively or technically difficult to implement—it may be almost self-implementing. Policy characteristics such as these add up to visible and immediate change and are likely to engender reactions and conflicts that are public and explicitly political in nature. Riots, protests, public debate, and extensive criticism of public leaders, for instance, tend to be strongly related to policies with such characteristics. These public and political responses mean that the stakes tend to be quite high, not only for the durability of the reform but also for the reputation and tenure of political leaders and even for the life of the regime itself. Policy elites undertaking such initiatives will require considerable political resources, such as high levels of legitimacy, popularity, and regime stability, or an external threat, if policy changes with visible and immediate costs are to be sustained.

In contrast, many policy changes have costs that are concentrated on individuals or narrow groups and benefits that may not be immediately apparent and that are imposed in highly disaggregated fashion, often over a considerable period of time—an import tax levied on certain luxury goods is an example of this kind of policy change. Generally, such changes entail a period of administrative and technical refinement. The benefits to public policy and economic welfare will therefore be visible only in the medium or long term. Policy changes with these

characteristics tend to engender conflict that is played out within bureaucratic arenas, either through the resistance of public officials or the
personalistic claims of client groups or some combination of these. Re-
formers need to be concerned about issues of bureaucratic compliance
and responsiveness in these situations. The stakes for policy elites tend
to be much lower for these kinds of reforms than for those that are
carried out in more public arenas. The responses of bureaucrats and
client groups may call into question the sustainability of the change but
not, usually, the viability of the regime or its leadership. Those promoting reform will require resources that have meaning within bureaucratic
contexts—hierarchical authority, incentive systems, financial resources,
technical criteria to control resource allocations, and the like.

This alternative model of policy making in developing countries
employs a complex set of elements. It emphasizes developing the capacity to explain the timing, nature, and scope of policy change and to
consider its viability once introduced. It stresses the preferences and
perceptions of policy elites and the possibility that they may miscalcu-
late the potential risks in introducing changed policy. It makes a distinction between crisis and noncrisis decision making and between the
macropolitical and micropolitical concerns of decision makers. In doing
so, it enables analysts to begin to explain and even to predict the content
of reform initiatives. Above all, it presents the possibility that policy
elites are strategic managers within complex policy contexts who have
a set of complex preferences and who are seeking politically, bureau-
cratically, and economically viable outcomes. It also lays the basis for
predictions about success or failure in the introduction of reform.

What is important to an alternative political economy model, then,
is not examining the pursuit of individual self-interest as if it existed in
a void, but conceptualizing the ongoing bargains, pacts, and compromises that are made in an effort to craft policy that is acceptable to those
with the greatest stakes in the outcome and to those with the greatest
capacity to stymie or to support the effort. Rather than the sum total of
individuals seeking their self-interest, the view of politics that this alternative presents is one of efforts at problem solving through negotiation
and the use of political resources in the context of great uncertainty.

The results of such processes of problem solving can be good, bad, or
indifferent for the economic system, for society, or for individual sectors
of society. This is an important point, for it suggests the possibility that
there often exists a "space" in which policy elites can maneuver to
achieve policy choices that are both politically and economically wise
and that the institutional and historical context within which policy decisions are reached help define a space for negotiation, problem solving,
and conflict resolution. If this space exists in a large number of situations,
then there would be an important role for the policy advice that develop-

ment economists can provide. It may well be worthwhile to attempt to model this space and to use such models to help craft policy advice.

Ultimately, both economists and political scientists need to abandon notions and models of politics that cast it necessarily as an obstacle to achieving optimal economic outcomes. Helpfully, neoclassical political economy has credited politics with a basis in rational behavior; less helpfully, it has done so in a way that puts economics at odds with politics. Development economists might feel less beleaguered by what they see as the inevitable hegemony of politically rational behavior over the collective economic good if they believed more fully in the possibility that some political values—the compromise of conflicting interests, the achievement of social and political stability based on a reasonable set of rules about how collective problems are best resolved, the creation of public trust based on a shared sense of legitimate authority, the search for basic consensus on the nature of the public interest, the definition of an agreed-upon role for government—have value equal to the achievement of economic efficiency. An effective model of political economy would be one that is fully interactive, not one that demonstrates how politics systematically eats away at economic goals.

The Political Economy of
Development Policy Change

For contemporary less-developed countries (LDCs), the post-1950 era has been a unique period of attempted transition from colonial agrarianism to modern economic growth. During the transition effort, these countries, given a wide variety of initial conditions, used a broad range of macroeconomic policy instruments to promote growth.

The record of the postwar period also reveals that the success of this almost universal development effort, in achieving some combination of growth and distribution, has varied enormously among countries. The statistical evidence clearly indicates that of all the LDCs, the newly industrializing countries of East Asia (the so-called Gang of Four—Taiwan, South Korea, Singapore, and Hong Kong) have registered by far the best development performance in such bottom-line indicators as GDP growth rates and income distribution over the past thirty-five years, whereas performance has been more modest in other parts of the developing world, such as Latin America and the rest of Asia.

The author wishes to acknowledge the substantial contributions of John C. H. Fei and Syed A. Mahmood.

The relative success of the East Asian countries has been attributed by many, including academicians and economists from the World Bank, the International Monetary Fund, and bilateral donor agencies, to these systems' more pronounced external orientation and their greater overall willingness to subject themselves to the competitive discipline of the market. Although these countries, like most LDCs, started with a primary import-substituting subphase, with its associated controls and interventions, they have also shown a pronounced linear trend toward greater external orientation and liberalization in various markets.

In other parts of the developing world, however, once primary import substitution came to an end, the statistical record of economic performance was accompanied by a more oscillatory pattern of policy choice, with market-oriented episodes temporarily followed by a return to import-substitution (IS) policies in a more or less continuous fashion. This pattern is particularly evident for the Latin American countries but is also observable in other LDCs.

The associated trends toward greater external orientation and greater market liberalization have helped to fundamentally transform the economies of the small group of East Asian countries and have made them more successful than other LDCs. These strategies have instilled in them flexibility, sensitivity to technological change, and the ability to adjust to inevitable exogenous shocks—three qualities that are hallmarks of the industrially advanced market economies. Successful LDCs, in other words, show a particular pattern of organizational and institutional choice and display Kuznets's well-known structural characteristics of the mixed, mature developed economy. But they remain the exception among LDCs, and that is the basic puzzle to which this chapter is addressed.

Six developing countries have been chosen for analysis because they represent three subfamilies as indicated by their initial conditions (see Table 4.1). The differences in performance over time of these six countries are illustrated in Table 4.2. Colombia and Mexico represent the archetypal Latin American case: they are relatively rich in natural resources and intermediate in the extent of population pressure on the land and in the quality of human capital. Latin Americans share a long history of industrialization dating back to the pre–World War II period. During the 1950s they followed a common strategy of primary import substitution (PIS, based on nondurable consumer goods), followed during the 1960s by a strategy of secondary import substitution (SIS, based on durable consumer goods and producer goods), tinged with an element of export promotion (the subsidization of nontraditional exports).

At the other end of the spectrum are the East Asian countries, Taiwan and South Korea—examples of systems that are relatively poor in natural resources and rich in labor and human capital. Both countries

TABLE 4.1	Initial Conditions for Six LDCs (approximately 1950)		
	Population (thousands)	Labor surplus[a]	Natural resources
Colombia	11,334	3.0 (1951)	Rich (some oil, gold, silver, iron ore, copper, and emeralds; abundant cash crops)
Mexico	25,826	1.0 (1950)	Rich (zinc, lead, copper, silver, iron ore, mercury, sulfur, oil)
South Korea	20,513	8.3 (1949)	Poor (poor-quality coal, some gold, tungsten)
Taiwan	7,981	4.0 (1950)	Poor (good coal, some natural gas, little oil)
Philippines	19,910	2.2 (1948)	Rich (iron ore, copper, gold, chromite, timber, some cash crops such as sugar and copra)
Thailand	18,488	3.3[b] (1947)	Moderate (tin, rubber, few cash crops, abundant rice)

	Human capital resources				
	Adult literacy rate (%)		Enrollment in primary and secondary schools (%)[c]		
	1950	1960	1950	1955	1960
Colombia	60.0	63.0	30	41	50
Mexico	56.8	65.4	37	43	53
South Korea	76.8 (1955)	82.2	54	60	64
Taiwan	51.1	73.0	47	57	74
Philippines	60.0 (1948)	74.9 (1958)	89	70	70
Thailand	52.0 (1947)	67.7	48	50	58

a. Ratio of rural population to arable land (in persons per hectare).
b. Arable land refers to land devoted to main crops only.
c. These are the ratios of total enrollment at the two levels to the estimated population in the age group corresponding to the actual duration of schooling in each country.
SOURCE: United Nations *Demographic Yearbook*; Food and Agriculture Organization *Production Yearbook*; UNESCO *Statistical Yearbook*; United Nations *Statistical Yearbook*.

pursued a mild PIS form of the strategy during the 1950s but switched at the beginning of the 1960s to a strategy of primary export substitution (PES, based on labor-intensive manufactures), requiring a considerable change in policies.

In between we find Thailand and the Philippines. Although these Southeast Asian countries are neighbors, the Philippines is closer to the

TABLE 4.2   Postwar Performance Indicators for Six LDCs, 1950–1986

	Average real per capita GDP growth rate (% per year)			
	1950–59	1960–69	1970–79	1980–86
Colombia	1.7 (1951–59)	1.9	3.9	0.7
Mexico	3.0 (1952–59)	4.1	1.9	–0.7
Taiwan	4.7 (1952–59)	5.9	8.1	5.6
South Korea	1.3 (1953–59)	4.9	7.5	4.3
Philippines	3.2	2.1	3.3	–1.5
Thailand	2.8	5.0	5.0	3.1

	Income distribution (Gini coefficient)[a]			
	1950	1960	1970	1980
Colombia	n.a.	0.53	0.56	0.52 (1982)
Mexico	n.a.	0.54	0.58	0.50 (1977)
Taiwan	0.56	0.44 (1959)	0.29	0.29 (1978)
South Korea	n.a.	n.a.	0.37	0.38 (1976)
Philippines	0.49 (1956)	0.50 (1961)	0.49 (1971)	0.50 (1977)
Thailand	n.a.	0.41 (1962)	0.44 (1968)	0.45 (1981)

	External-orientation ratio (exports as % of GDP)				
	1950	1960	1970	1980	1986
Colombia	10.9	15.7	14.6	16.3	18.9
Mexico	17.0	10.6	8.2	22.4	17.0
Taiwan	10.1	11.1	29.6	52.2	60.6
South Korea	2.1	3.3	14.3	37.7	40.7
Philippines	10.5	11.0	18.1	17.1	24.5
Thailand	15.0	17.0	18.7	25.8	28.2

NOTE: n.a. = not available.
a. The Gini coefficient can vary between 0 and 1, with 0 representing completely equal income distribution and 1 representing completely unequal distribution.
SOURCE: United Nations, *Statistical Yearbook*, various years, and *National Income Statistics, Analysis of Main Aggregates*, 1983; R. Summers and A. Heston, "Improved International Comparisons of Real Product and Its Composition," *The Review of Income and Wealth* 30 (June 1984): 207–62; S. Jain, *Size Distribution of Income* (Washington, D.C.: World Bank, 1975); J. Fei, G. Ranis, and S. Kuo, *Growth with Equity: The Taiwan Case* (Oxford: Oxford University Press, 1979); International Monetary Fund, *International Financial Statistics*, various years; World Bank, *World Tables* and *World Development Report*, various issues; *Statistical Yearbook of the Republic of China*, various issues; *Philippine Statistical Yearbook*, various issues; *National Income of the Republic of China*, various issues.

Latin American type in its initial conditions and long-term behavior. Both countries are relatively large, favorably endowed with natural resources, and intermediate in both the labor surplus and human capital dimension. Both countries pursued a PIS strategy during the 1950s, although the Philippines adopted a much more severe form than Thailand. Subsequently, at the beginning of the 1960s, the Philippines followed a typical Latin American path of SIS combined with export promotion, while Thailand gradually adopted a strategy closer to the PES pattern of the East Asians.

Countries also differ in the level of their initial organic national-ism—their national cohesion and geographic and cultural homogeneity. The contrast between Latin America and East Asia is clear. Even within subfamilies there exist marked differences. The Philippines, for exam-ple, which suffered two demoralizing colonial experiences, is character-ized by substantial geographic, cultural, religious, and even linguistic diversity, and a lack of secure integrative national moorings. Thailand, in contrast, had no direct colonial experience to break away from and, more important, had a more homogeneous population and a monarchy that has since the mid-nineteenth century been a focus for national re-form and helped pull together disparate national interest groups.

The data in Table 4.2 show that whereas a typical East Asian econ-omy such as Taiwan achieved remarkable rates of growth of real per capita gross domestic product (GDP) virtually throughout the postwar period, and particularly since the 1960s, growth has been far more mod-est in the Latin American prototype cases. Colombia, for example, did not achieve average real per capita GDP growth rates exceeding 4 per-cent in any decade. Mexico and the Philippines achieved high growth rates in the 1950s, but their performance has declined over time. Thai-land has maintained steady, if unspectacular, growth throughout.

The exceptionally high growth rates of East Asia have, moreover, been accompanied by an increasingly equitable distribution of the fruits of that growth. The Gini coefficient of family income in Taiwan, for example, fell from 0.56 in 1950 to 0.29 in 1970 and has remained at more or less that level. In contrast, the Latin American countries have been characterized not only by slower growth but also by a greater concen-tration of income; in both Colombia and Mexico, Gini coefficients ex-ceeded 0.50 in all periods, and there is no consistent trend of improvement in evidence. Once again, Thailand is intermediate in terms of income distribution, whereas the Philippines is typically Latin American.

Countries, of course, differ in initial conditions, including their size, but the striking differences in the trend of external orientation over time from not so disparate beginnings is shown in Table 4.2. In 1950 the degree of external orientation, as represented by the exports/GDP ratio, was no higher in the East Asian countries than in Latin America or Southeast Asia. Since then, however, there has been a marked change in the relative degree of external orientation of these countries. In both Taiwan and South Korea, the exports/GDP ratio has increased in a lin-ear fashion so that by 1980 exports constituted more than one-half of GDP in Taiwan and more than one-third in South Korea. Elsewhere, exports/GDP ratios have either stagnated, as in Colombia after 1960, or actually declined, as in Mexico until 1970. Once again, the Philippines and Thailand are intermediate cases where the exports/GDP ratio has increased over time, although not as much or as linearly as in the East Asian countries.

Given the strong link that seems to exist between policy choice and performance, a study of the marked divergence in policy choices among countries must include not only a description of *what* happened, in terms of economic performance, but also an analysis of *why* certain organizational and policy choices were made along the way. It is fair to assume that all LDCs initiate their transition growth efforts with strong political forces penetrating their mixed economies. To explain the subsequent divergence in organizational and policy choices exclusively on the basis of intrinsic cultural differences or other special characteristics is, in my opinion, inappropriate; such an approach not only challenges the power of positive economics as applied to development but is also undoubtedly factually incorrect. Instead, the explanation for the deviation between monotonicity and oscillation, en route to the convergence of economic and policy structures in the mature economy, is more likely to be found largely in a combination of the initial typological differences among developing countries and of political and economic forces that influence the adoption or rejection of different institutional and policy changes over time. Since policy change is clearly achieved through a political process, our research effort must go beyond the normal confines of economic analysis and include an investigation of the political economy of policy change.

A developing country government can exercise political control over the mixed economy through three basic powers: the power to block trade, the power to transfer income to itself and other favored parties, and the power to decide on the specific allocation of expenditures. I suggest, therefore, that the major development policy instruments deployed over time, such as the interest rate, the foreign exchange rate, the rate of protection, the rate of monetary expansion, and the tax rate, should be interpreted as political instruments to promote growth, in particular by transferring income among social groups, or "manufacturing" profits for one class at the expense of others. In other words, once political force has penetrated the postindependence developing economy, it is necessary not only to trace this behavior over time, but also to differentiate between the conventional on-the-table or overt revenue and expenditure policies of government and the much more pervasive deployment of under-the-table or indirect income transfers among groups. In a political process, such indirect transfers are usually sanctioned by the powerful need of governments (especially the newly independent) to try to solve current problems while putting aside the possibility that a social conflict will arise after a time lag.[1]

When the familiar macroeconomic policy tools are interpreted as growth-promoting instruments to effect income transfers, liberalization then becomes the gradual withdrawal of such political forces from the economic arena over time. Differentiating between the covert and overt types of policy renders the analysis more politically sensitive, as well as more realistic.[2]

This way of looking at the goal of macroeconomic policy instruments and the concepts of the overt and covert transfer of resources provides a basis for explaining the divergent paths of organizational and policy evolutions. In fact, my basic hypothesis is that relatively linear policy change occurs not when the role of government atrophies but when government actions become explicit rather than implicit. Policy oscillation occurs when covert policies adopted for short-term political convenience self-destruct because of the unexpected and delayed adverse effects on some groups whose income is being transferred in the absence of a clear political consensus.

I hope to demonstrate this point more precisely in the theoretical framework of the next section, which provides a detailed exposition of the political economy of policy change over one exogenous shock–induced cycle. This approach offers an appropriate framework for investigating the evolution of policy during the transition effort of the typical mixed LDC economy. Differences between this typical case and developing countries with divergent typological characteristics will be highlighted in the course of the analysis.

Theoretical Framework

During the transition to modern growth the so-called open, dualistic (or small, labor surplus) developing economies, as pointed out earlier, passed through well-recognized evolutionary subphases, namely, an early (or primary) import-substitution subphase and a later external-orientation subphase (EO), either of the export-promotion or export-substitution variety. Superimposed on the long-run trend of growth and structural change en route to modern growth, as emphasized by Simon Kuznets, are disturbances from exogenous shocks originating from fluctuations in the business cycle and in the prices of primary products in world markets. These shocks constitute a primary cause of instability in the LDCs.[3]

In the early PIS subphase, the LDCs, almost without exception, adopted an internal orientation as an essential component of a growth-promotion strategy in which macroeconomic policies were deployed to provide protection from exogenous disturbances. During this period, a cardinal element of the customary strategy was growth promotion through government spending—that is, using macroeconomic policies (especially monetary policies) to accommodate deficit finance and to assist private entrepreneurs by manufacturing profits on their behalf. A corrupted version of the Keynesian monetary approach lurks beneath the surface here; this policy seems to be based on the conviction that (1) interest rates can be repressed to an artificially low level to generate profits, and (2) government can acquire all the goods and services it needs from the market by covert taxation without consent—in other words, inflation. Since the government of a sovereign state has the power to monopolize the printing of money, it can undertake such growth-promotion tasks without difficulty. The government only requires the political will to use this power persistently, giving the LDC a virtually perpetual inflationary bias.[4] The government's political will penetrates the market system to determine not only the overall volume of aggregate demand but even individual investment decisions governing resource allocation.

With the arrival of the EO phase, a liberalization process sets in, and the market mechanism that regulates the exchange behavior among economic actors is gradually depoliticized. There is a gradual atrophying of the growth-focused political will in the sense that Keynesian monetarism is gradually abandoned and replaced by a monetary policy based on the recognition that money (M) should serve primarily as an internal medium of exchange, while the foreign-exchange reserve stock (R) should serve as an external medium of exchange. The manipulation of these quantities as vehicles for exercising the monopoly powers of the government is thus eroded.

The pace of this erosion, will, of course, differ among countries. In the archetypal East Asian case, for example, monetary passivity becomes apparent earlier than in the archetypal Latin American case. This difference is related to the differential choice at the end of PIS between continued import substitution, complemented by export promotion, in Latin America and export substitution in East Asia, as mentioned above. Macroeconomic policies in the LDCs differ from those in the developed countries (DCs) in that, especially during the IS phase, the LDC government's political will penetrates the market system to determine not only the precise direction in which resources are to be transferred but even individual investment decisions and allocations.[5]

The gradual movement toward liberalization also represents a movement toward greater rationalism and an organic nationalism and away from the notion that a newly independent government can and should be all-powerful. Liberalization also means that the government cannot shy away from the onerous task of seeking social compromises in order to replace the inflation tax with taxation by consent, and that private entrepreneurs must learn, as quickly as possible, to earn profits through competitive productive performances in domestic and world markets rather than through rent-seeking activities. This movement toward liberalization, while more pronounced in East Asia, seems to be gaining ascendancy elsewhere. Seen in a long-run historical perspective, it seems to constitute a natural organizational companion to the Kuznetsian characteristics of modern economic growth—especially in the so-called mixed economy.[6]

This liberalization process may not, however, be smooth. Particularly in the archetypal Latin American case, the birth of liberal reform tends to be a slow, painful process. There the very existence and abundance of economic rent (in the production of the exported primary products) invites policies that promote rent-seeking to enter the political stage, and the laissez-faire connotations of liberalization run counter to the lingering political ideology that holds that growth is a public concern to be managed directly, through the exercise of political power. The slow liberalization process is disturbed, moreover, by exogenous shocks, such as fluctuations in the prices of primary products in world markets and in the business cycle, yielding periodic revivals of the earlier PIS phase with all its well-known symptoms.

Basic Framework

As pointed out earlier, the postwar LDC transition process, viewed in historical perspective, has been almost universally characterized by the appearance of a primary import-substitution phase succeeded by an external-orientation (EO) phase. These phases can be measured by the degree of external orientation E/Q (total exports as a fraction of GDP) and by the degree of export diversification E_q/E (nonprimary product exports as a percentage of total exports). As Figures 4.1a and 4.1b show, both of these indices increase markedly during the EO phase.

Superimposed on these long-term trends of E/Q and E_q/E are fluctuations caused by exogenous instability, such as the price fluctuations of primary products in world markets C_i and business cycles in the industrially advanced countries.[7] If the two exogenous cycles coincide, there is an identifiable recovery (+) and a recession (–) subphase within each C_i (see Figure 4.1c). The recovery phase provides the exogenous background favorable for external orientation and export diversification, and hence E/Q and E_q/E temporarily accelerate above their respective trend values. The reverse holds for the recession subphase.

As mentioned above, this exogenous instability may also lead to fluctuations in the long-run trend of policy liberalization. Liberalization packages are adopted and experimented with for a time, only to be abandoned under the impact of external shocks. Policy oscillation between liberalization and a return to import substitution (indicated by

FIGURE 4.1   Trends of Exogenous Instability and Macroeconomic Policies

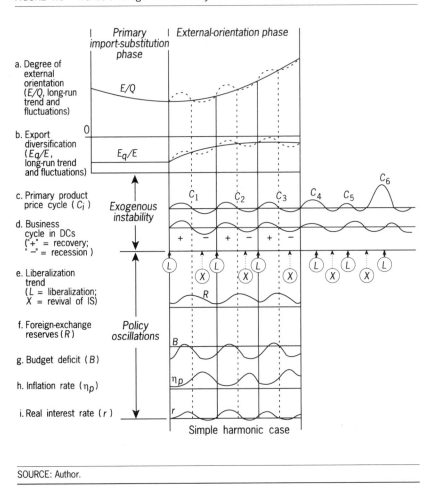

SOURCE: Author.

the Ls and Xs, respectively, in Figure 4.1d) is thus a product of growth and exogenous fluctuations.

It is assumed in this chapter that the phases of the primary product price cycle C_i and of the business cycle coincide as they occur in succession over time (see C_1, C_2, and C_3 in Figure 4.1).[8] Liberalization efforts are assumed to start at the end of PIS or the beginning of C_1. The actual analysis of time series, such as R (the foreign-exchange reserves), B (the government's budget deficit), η_p (the inflation rate), r (the real rate of interest), dM/dt (the rate of monetary expansion), and t (the effective rate of protection), to empirically corroborate the thesis will be based on the historical experience of six LDCs.

Exogenous Instability and the Activation of Government Policies

Real variable indicators. The exogenous fluctuations of an LDC's foreign purchasing power (as proxied by C_i, shown in Figures 4.2a and 4.2b), transmitted by the international market mechanism, produce domestic effects on the GNP growth rate (η_Q) the external-orientation rate ($\eta_{E/Q}$), and the trade balance (D), with an over-the-cycle pattern that naturally coincides with C_i (as shown in the dotted curves of Figures 4.2c, 4.2d, and 4.2e).[9] During the recovery phase η_Q and $\eta_{E/Q}$ are higher than their long-run trend values, as it is a time of relatively rapid growth and a relatively faster rate of external orientation. During the recession η_Q and $\eta_{E/Q}$ are lower than their long-run trends because of relatively slow growth and a relatively slower rate of external orientation.

The "natural" domestic response may not, however, actually occur, because it is affected by political forces that induce policy reactions. The typical LDC interventionist government springs into action during the recovery period of the cycle or falls into inaction during the recession not only because of its sense of mission to promote growth, but also, and just as important, because of the waxing and waning of the feeling that it has the power to spend. What can be statistically observed, ex post, are the magnified fluctuations of η_Q and $\eta_{E/Q}$, which are exacerbated in the recovery period by the expansion of domestic monetary purchasing power and reduced in the recession period by the contraction of such purchasing power. The solid curves in Figures 4.2c and 4.2d thus indicate the ex post, observable pattern and show a sharp contrast between the relatively greater external orientation and rapid growth during the recovery period and the internal orientation and slow growth during the recession period. Similarly, as the result of such political economy effects, the ex post trade balance curve D (Figure 4.2e) shows an export-surplus-raising bias at the beginning of the recovery phase (before time t') and an import-surplus-reducing bias at the end of the recession phase (after time t'''), with a hastening of the arrival of an import surplus in between (at time t'').

Sources of government's power to spend. Exogenous fluctuations cause the government to be active during recovery and passive during recession by way of two channels: its foreign exchange reserves, R (its accumulated external purchasing power), and its tax revenue, T (its internal spending power), both with an over-the-cycle characteristic that can be statistically verified.

Foreign exchange reserves (R) as a source of government power. In a politicized economic system, R represents something considerably more than

FIGURE 4.2   Intracycle Policy Performance in an Open, Dualistic LDC

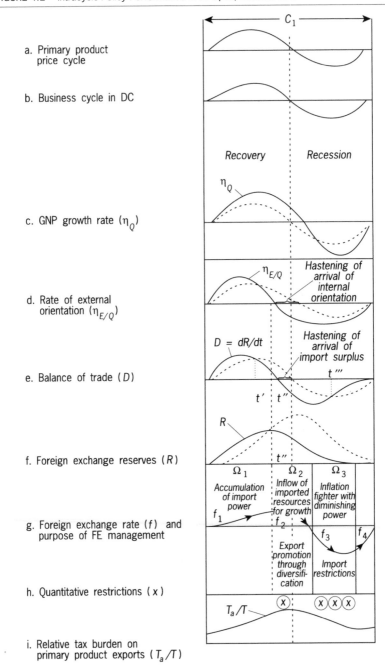

a. Primary product
   price cycle

b. Business cycle in DC

c. GNP growth rate (η_Q)

d. Rate of external
   orientation ($\eta_{E/Q}$)

e. Balance of trade (D)

f. Foreign exchange reserves (R)

g. Foreign exchange rate (f) and
   purpose of FE management

h. Quantitative restrictions (x)

i. Relative tax burden on
   primary product exports (T_a/T)

continued on following page

FIGURE 4.2 (continued)

j. Component 1 of monetary
   expansion ($\Delta m''$)

k. Government revenues (T)
   and expenditures (G)

l. Budget deficit (B) and
   component 2 of monetary
   expansion (Δm)

m. Net commercial bank loans
   and component 3 of monetary
   expansion ($\Delta m'$)

n. Decomposition of monetary expansion

o. Rate of growth of M and Q
   ($\eta_x = \eta_M - \eta_Q$)

p. Inflation with time lag (τ)

q. Real interest rate (r)

r. Savings deposits as share
   of savings (s)

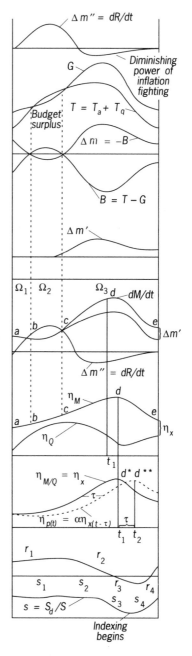

$\Delta m'' = dR/dt$

Diminishing
power of
inflation
fighting

G

$T = T_a + T_q$

Budget
surplus

$\Delta m = -B$

$B = T - G$

$\Delta m'$

Ω_1 Ω_2 Ω_3 d dM/dt

a b c e $\Delta m'$

$\Delta m'' = dR/dt$

d

η_M

c

a b e η_x

η_Q

t_1

$\eta_{M/Q} = \eta_x$ $d^* d^{**}$

τ

$\eta_{p(t)} = \alpha\eta_{x(t-\tau)}$ τ

t_1 t_2

r_1 r_2

s_1 s_2 r_3 r_4

$s = S_d/S$ s_3 s_4

Indexing
begins

SOURCE: Author.

international reserve assets to help defend against short-run fluctuations in the balance of payments. The memory of the experience of previous cycles often leaves the LDC government with little doubt that mercantilist affluence ($dR/dt > 0$) is necessarily good, while the opposite ($dR/dt < 0$) is surely a sign of government weakness that causes national anxiety of crisis proportions.

Thus, an externally sensitive LDC government always tries to stockpile R as much as it can at the beginning of each cycle C_i for later use. Moreover, a sovereign government can always promote exports by buying foreign exchange, thus permitting its own exchange rate to decline in value. In Figure 4.2f, the natural (dotted) R-path is distorted to become the ex post (solid) R-path. Toward the end of each C_i, as the government's political power to rule is threatened by the depletion of the foreign exchange reserves, it becomes increasingly reluctant to release the rapidly diminishing reserves, implying that the import surplus is politically curtailed. Thus the cyclical pattern of foreign exchange management, as depicted in Figure 4.2f, amounts to a distortion of the trade deficit within each C_i by encouraging a country to promote exports or cut imports to allow more imported resources to flow in during the "middle" portions of C_i.

Tax revenue and the power of government spending. Exogenous events also give the government an enhanced sense of the domestic power to spend as total government revenues T increase during the recovery period. The boom and bust nature of the political power to spend is mainly traceable to the appropriation of windfall economic rents from primary producers, which become more abundant in the recovery period. Thus the relative tax burden T_a/T (the tax burden on primary-product exports as a fraction of total tax revenue) rises during the recovery period (see Figure 4.2i). Such an involuntary expansion of the political power to spend then emboldens the government to promote growth through the voluntary act of spending even more with the help of expansionary fiscal policies. Total government expenditures, G, are accordingly likely to zoom up (see Figure 4.2k); a brief, relative budget surplus $B (= T - G)$ will be quickly followed by a deficit as shown in Figure 4.2l. More than the typical DC, the LDC thus tends toward a budget deficit, such that deficit years (more frequent and longer than surplus years) can occur right in the middle of prosperity. Thus fiscal policy has a noncompensatory cast in this period. This internal asymmetry tends to further magnify rather than ameliorate the effects of unavoidable exogenous fluctuations.

Internal purchasing power creation and inflation. Soon after the recovery the activist government begins to manufacture profits for domestic entrepreneurs by printing additional money (dM/dt) through the banking system to accommodate the demand for private investment finance. In LDCs money creation is appropriately interpreted as the creation of market power granted to private entrepreneurs, the government, and state enterprises by the political act of printing money. By way of a footnote to the history of monetary thought, this idea of a demand for finance, that is, a demand for monetary purchasing power to command goods and services in the market, was threatened with obsolescence by the liquidity preference theory of Keynes, according to which an increase in the quantity of money has mainly psychological effects. But Keynes later recanted, even if his followers did not.

Money is printed to solve three types of growth-related problems:

1. As a complement to the centralized foreign exchange system, printing money allows the government to acquire the foreign exchange earnings of exporters forcibly and at no cost. Therefore, component 1 of dM/dt, $\Delta m'' = dR/dt = D$, shown in Figure 4.2j, is referred to in the literature as money of external origin.

2. Printing money gives a government that is running a deficit control over domestic resources without the inconvenience of taxation. The symmetrical curve in Figure 4.2l shows component 2 of dM/dt, $\Delta m = -B$, which is money of internal origin.

3. Printing money allows the government to manufacture profits for private entrepreneurs by accommodating their demand for finance with impunity. Component 3 of dM/dt, $\Delta m'$ in Figure 4.2m, also is of internal origin.

Money creation thus tends to be viewed as a cure-all for the typical LDC government.

The three components of monetary expansion dM/dt ($= \Delta m + \Delta m' + \Delta m''$) are shown by the time path $abcde$ in Figure 4.2n, with three regions ($\Omega_1, \Omega_2, \Omega_3$) marked off. In Ω_1, dM/dt is small because the increase in component 1, $\Delta m''$, is offset by the decrease of component 2, Δm. In Ω_2, dM/dt is moderate because the increase of $\Delta m''$ is partly offset by the government budget surplus (Δm). In Ω_3, dM/dt zooms rapidly to a peak and then declines. Thus, it is in the early part of Ω_3 that the government finds it difficult to resist the temptation to use its sovereign powers of money creation to conveniently solve its growth-related problems. During Ω_3, $\Delta m''$ gradually declines to zero, signifying that the government's capacity to fight inflation by drawing down its reserves rapidly diminishes.

Monetary expansion thus constitutes the most important policy instrument in a typical LDC. Its citizens have no choice but to accept money as the medium of exchange—even when the monetary system functions very badly (such as at times of hyperinflation). In the absence of the tradition of some central bank autonomy, the convenient power of money printing is thus monopolized by the government, with the central bank performing merely as an arm of the executive branch of the "growth-minded" treasury. It is primarily for these reasons that a change in monetary philosophy is essential if the liberalization trend is to become linear.

Analysis of inflation. When the government persistently indulges in money printing, it will, with a time lag, produce inflation. Let $x = M/Q$ be the supply of money as represented by the medium of exchange per unit of real gross national product (GNP). Then the growth rate η_x is indicated as the difference between η_M (derived from dM/dt in Figure 4.2n), and the growth rate of GNP, η_Q (in Figure 4.2c) and is shown in Figure 4.2o. The fact that η_Q is higher in the good years and lower in the bad years implies that a peak value of η_x occurs at t_2. The inflationary pressure is thus much stronger toward the latter part of C_i because, with a decline of η_Q, less money is needed for transactions purposes. A second peak-postponement occurs because the inflation rate (η_p) occurs with a time lag of τ years (say one or two) after the change in x as indicated by the relation $\eta_p(t) = \alpha\eta_x(t - \tau)$ (shown in Figure 4.2p). This equation shows that a stabilized inflation rate (η_p) can be achieved if and only if η_x has been constant for some time in the past. A solution of this differential equation implies a dynamic version of the equation of exchange $p(t) = \alpha[M(t - \tau)]/Q(t - \tau)$, which shows that a constant price level ($\eta_p = 0$) can be achieved only when the condition $\eta_M = \eta_Q$ is fulfilled. This implies that monetary conservatism must have been practiced in the past so that the addition in the supply of money is approximately the same as the additional transactions demand for money.

Therefore the "monetarism" of inflation, especially pronounced in the late phase of C_i, is primarily traceable to the political activism of the recovery phase. At that time the government indulges in money printing (by taking advantage of the necessity of the acceptance of money as a medium of exchange by the nonbank public) while reaping the harvest of inflation only later, after a number of time lags (d, d^*, d^{**} in Figures 4.2o and 4.2p). It is the durability of the circulation of the artificially created purchasing power (η_M) that produces these time lags that "blind" almost everyone into believing in a cost-push theory of inflation. Secondary inflation pressures are, of course, also bound to build, depending on the strength of expectations that raise the value of α (the velocity of circulation in the dynamic exchange equation).

Covert transfers, rational expectations, and indexing. When the government and private entrepreneurs borrow (see B and $\Delta m'$ in Figures 4.2l and 4.2m), the repayment burden that falls due at a later date can be lightened or even rendered negative by inflation.[10] Real interest rates r ($r = i - \eta_p$, the difference between the commercial bank lending rate and the inflation rate) are likely to become negative toward the end of the recession phase, providing an inflationary benefit (see Figure 4.2q). In this way, the creation of purchasing power to meet the investment demands of an earlier date is used as a covert device to transfer income and promote growth. LDC businessmen are well aware that this process helps them substantially by causing negative real interest rates—that is, the delayed inflation lightens the repayment burden. This manufacture of purchasing power plus inflation represents a key growth-promotion mechanism in the LDCs. It has been likened to an "act of burglary" by classical monetary theorists.

In a dualistic financial system (one in which commercial banks-cum-money markets and informal or curb markets coexist), savings deposits in commercial banks, S_d, as a percentage of total savings S, decline when r declines, especially when r becomes negative (Figure 4.2r). Though it is more controversial, the prevailing view is that total savings are also interest elastic. When total savings decline the government is forced to rely even more on money printing, which explains the zooming up of η_M in Figure 4.2o. To prevent the destruction of the "formal" commercial banks as a channel of financial intermediation (in other words, to permit them to attract savings deposits), the real interest rate must then be raised by the competitive pressures of the money market in DCs or of the black or parallel market in LDCs.[11] Although such competitive pressures ultimately force LDCs to eliminate the customary legal ceiling on interest rates as they approach modern growth, they often lead to efforts to index interest rates for inflation during the latter half of the C_i. In a mixed economy, the right to borrow and lend among private parties always imposes an upper bound on the exploitation power of government monetary policies.

When a sequence of cycles (C_1, C_2, C_3, etc.) is viewed in a longer-term perspective, the cyclical pattern of the real interest rate (see Figure 4.2q) illustrates the arguments of the rational expectations school, which make it clear that the "official theft" alluded to earlier can only occur as long as the expectations of savers are not yet fully "rational" (when savers only perceive and defend against the effects of inflation on the real interest rate ex post, rather than anticipate them ex ante). As savers gradually learn from experience, the indexing of bank deposits can become a permanent feature of monetary institutions and thus weaken the government's capacity to act in this fashion. Manufacturing profits by political force is always based on the exploitation of a victimized class—in this case, the savers. With indexing, the market rate of interest is close to its natural level, and the entrepreneurial class must rely on its own entrepreneurial capacity to make a real profit not augmented by political patronage.

"Equity through indexing" is, however, a contradiction in terms, because an agreement on total indexing (at best an unstable pseudo-agreement) is reached only when citizens cannot achieve a consensus on equity under the customary methods of a constitutional democracy. The very fact that governments continue to print money (for deficit finance) in spite of total indexing is concrete proof of this contradiction. For if the body politic has the capacity to agree on something equitable (such as total indexing), the same capacity should have led the citizens to agree on taxation with consent in the first place.

From an evolutionary perspective, however, the practice of indexing the interest rate contributes to the cause of liberalization because it leads to the emergence of the idea that the government, in spite of all its good intentions and power, cannot persistently use an expansionary monetary policy to suppress the interest rate to an artificially low level (that is, one much below the natural rate) according to the loanable-funds theory. Monetary maturity paves the way to political maturity when the citizens demand an explicit accounting of the costs of growth expressed in terms of the dollars-and-cents tax burdens on various groups, instead of accepting the covert transfer of resources to the government by money printing, with inflation used as the mollifier, with or without indexing.

External monetary management. The external monetary management of a country refers to the management of the foreign exchange rate (FE rate) and of its foreign exchange reserves (R). In LDCs, both the internal and external dimensions of monetary management are inseparable from growth-promotion policies and bear little resemblance to the use of R as a first line of defense of the FE rate (under the pressure of a balance of payments imbalance), as in the DCs. In each C_i, there is a three-stage political life of external monetary management complementary to that of the domestic growth-promotion policy.

The cyclical pattern of external monetary management is depicted in Figures 4.2f and 4.2g. With R initially in a state of near depletion, there is first a drive to accumulate R (see Figure 4.2f) by achieving a more realistic FE rate through devaluation (shown by the arrow f_1 in Figure 4.2g). In the absence of a clear-cut Keynesian "precautionary motive," however, there is no assurance that the same reserve stock will not be used up quickly.

In the second stage, denoted by Ω_2 in Figure 4.2f, expansionary domestic monetary and fiscal policies create a tight resources situation and build up pressures for an import surplus. The decline of R, which is calculated and intentional, is accommodated by an overvaluation of the domestic currency (indicated by an arrow f_2 pointing downward in Figure 4.2g). This well-known import-substitution type policy serves to transfer income from the producers of the primary export product to the importing urban entrepreneurial class.[12] This political act of profit manufacture is facilitated by a de facto overvaluation when, with creeping price inflation, the FE rate is pegged (that is, not promptly devalued).

In the final stage—the recession denoted by Ω_3 in Figure 4.2f—the overvaluation of the domestic currency becomes more pronounced (as represented by the sharply dropping arrow f_3 in Figure 4.2g). Some now claim that the FE rate is overvalued because of an accelerated inflation rate that raises the price of exports. Believers in the import cost-push theory of inflation then assert that devaluation at such a time would lead to greater inflation. In the midst of such confusion, one thing is clear: the artificially overvalued domestic currency is expected to act as an inflation fighter, while devaluation is postponed. The rapid, unintentional dissipation of the FE reserves can only mean that their inflation-fighting power is rapidly diminishing. All the symptoms of an IS strategy are revived, as improvised quantitative import restrictions and foreign exchange allocations are installed to protect the quickly depleting R (see Figure 4.2h). And yet, given the customary national anxiety about devaluation, such action is postponed as long as possible, usually until the FE rate has to be devalued abruptly. Finally, when it comes, the devaluation has a "big-bang" effect (shown by arrow f_4 in Figure 4.2g). In the wake of this crisis atmosphere, the economy makes a resolute attempt at liberalization once again, thus starting a new cycle with the expectation that the FE rate will be cleanly floated this time.

An important lesson to be learned here is that although the EO phase is a "natural" phenomenon (see Figure 4.2d), the noncompensatory monetary and fiscal policies of government are likely to shorten that phase and hasten an "unnatural" early return to an internal orientation. Other things being equal, an expansionary policy brings about an import surplus. The application of this principle in an evolutionary perspective implies that the seeds of the revival of the internal orientation phase are planted right in the middle of the recovery phase and blossom fully into a return to the import-substitution policy syndrome in the recession phase.

The organized labor market. Unionism and minimum wage legislation are common phenomena in most LDCs, including those that are labor-abundant. The postwar experience has shown rather conclusively that these policies are primarily political ones stemming from the government's effort to establish a political base and to demonstrate its concern for the working classes. Although the wages, working conditions, and prestige of organized workers, who constitute at most 5 to 10 percent of the total labor force in most LDCs, can be raised, the effects of unionization and minimum wages on the rewards of the laboring class as a whole have been negligible or even negative. Differences between union and nonunion wages represent a form of discrimination against the latter as capitalists can usually protect their profits by increasing the price of the product. The burden of the bilateral oligopoly thus usually falls on labor and consumers.

Artificially created wage differences can also be a serious handicap for an LDC that is "naturally" (from the point of view of comparative advantage) capable of exporting labor-intensive manufactured goods to the rest of the world during the EO phase, since producers of such products stand to lose the intrinsic comparative advantage of the low wage cost generated by the system's relative labor-surplus condition. Consequently, producers either opt for more capital-intensive technologies or do not invest at all, leaving the surplus labor untapped. The coexistence of high wages with substantial open or disguised urban unemployment for the majority makes a mockery of elementary International Labor Organization (ILO) justice. Avoiding it represents a basic development tenet that has been crucial for the success of the labor-surplus economies of East Asia.

In typical developing countries organized labor or union unrest (such as strikes) is also a cyclical phenomenon, an endemic component of the politicized cycle of economic development, C_i, especially at a time of inflation when workers feel they have been unfairly hurt (see Figure 4.2p). At such junctures (that is, between t_2 and t_3 in Figure 4.2p) unions may lead or support protest movements on behalf of all workers against the unfair burdens of covert taxation by inflation. Strikes and unrest can almost be predicted, using η_M and η_p as leading indicators. In that sense labor unrest is an endemic result of the money-printing process over time.

Within the politicized growth cycle, C_i, unions play an odd role. They are both a curse and a blessing for workers. On the one hand, in the recovery phase a union's insistence on a higher wage for the minority hurts the cause of the majority by preventing labor-intensive investment projects and output mixes from being realized. Since union power, along with minimum-wage legislation and civil service emoluments, usually derives from the government, it represents in part a political response to the previously discussed rent-seeking surge associated with the prosperity phase. On the other hand, in the recession phase union leaders are likely to act as spokesmen for all workers and protest against the unfairness of the adjustment process that they are partly responsible for having created. Two monopolistic political powers—the money-printing state and the wage gap–creating union—thus combine to create an odd politico-economic cycle of growth with its own dynamic logic. Unions typically care about all workers at one time in the cycle and only about their own members at another.

Toward a theory of policy oscillation in the EO phase. An examination of all these evolutionary events within a cycle C_i shows that, especially in the downturn—with inflation (Figure 4.2p), currency overvaluation (Figure 4.2g), higher tariffs and quantitative controls (Figure 4.2h), negative real interest rates (Figure 4.2q), etc.—the earlier IS policy syndrome tends to be partially restored. The sequence of such cycles (C_1, C_2, C_3, etc., in Figure 4.1) shows the periodic revival of IS growth. A liberalization package initiates each cycle, only to be abandoned once again to the IS pattern that nobody wanted in the first place. The revival of IS thus occurs almost as a natural result of policy oscillations, traceable through the political economy of a growth-activist LDC, rather than as a consequence of design or conspiracy. Several factors that lie behind this oscillation result that have been hinted at may now be more explicitly identified.

The effects of natural resource abundance. The relative abundance of natural resources in the typical primary export-producing LDC is clearly crucial because it affects the size of the under-the-table rents to be reallocated and the sensitivity to exogenous instability. The tendency for every cycle to start with the accumulation of foreign exchange reserves and to end with a more or less abrupt devaluation can only be explained by the fact that relative resource abundance, in combination with the inevitable exogenous shocks, is a precondition for policy oscillation. The accumulation of FE reserves and the expansion of government revenue (Figures 4.2f and 4.2k) are based on the government's appropriation of the windfall rents of primary product producers that is possible only in a natural resource–rich economy.

Every C_i thus induces a political economy cycle that is relevant for "typical" natural resource–rich LDCs but much less relevant for the natural resource–poor East Asian countries. It is, of course, true that the East Asian countries, like other LDCs, expect their governments to perform growth-related functions with a missionary passion during their primary IS phase. Once they move into the EO phase, however, they are influenced mostly by the business cycle, whose fluctuations are milder than those of the primary product cycle C_i. Moreover, since they liberalize more monotonically—that is, they follow the path of export substitution (ES), rather than that of the secondary import substitution (SIS) with export promotion (EP)—their production and export structures become more diversified and are less affected even by the business cycle.

As a consequence, in the East Asian case at the time of recovery, the rise in total government revenue and FE reserves is not at the expense of producers of export products, which are increasingly manufactured rather than primary products. In other words, in the more typical LDC case the government and the urban elite seek to exploit the usually spatially dispersed primary product producers, but this income transfer–profit manufacture mechanism cannot operate in the natural resource–poor LDC context since, in the relative absence of a "victim class," there is also no pronounced "beneficiary class." Soon after entering the EO phase, the East Asian countries discovered that the diversification into nontraditional exports, the lifeline of their economic future, could be carried out best by the entrepreneurs themselves. There never existed the same political temptation to return to an internal orientation once it had been left behind. Moreover, the government never exercised the same economic power to generate a big push for growth in the middle of C_i in the first place.

Lessons for economic theory. The policies and practices of LDCs during the postwar years (1950–1985) could probably have been rationalized by some theory, such as that of the structuralists. However, the short-run Keynesian message—large government deficits do not matter; inflation is cost pushed; an increase in the supply of money lowers the rate of interest; commercial bank lending does not represent the creation of purchasing power for investment finance; and, above all, governments can and should manage economic affairs—did not help in the early postwar period, especially when accepted out of context.

When all is said and done, what gives unity to the malfunctioning of the economic system, described by the fifteen to twenty policy-related variables summarized in Figure 4.2, is a misconception of the monetary phenomenon—a complex subject that "not one in a million comprehends" (Keynes). Government spending without adequate taxation and the manufacture of profits through the artificial suppression of the interest cost—the cornerstones of macroeconomic policy in the typical LDC—are predicated on a single feature of the monetized economy: namely, the government monopolizes the vast power to acquire goods and services from the market through money printing. The linear trend toward liberalization in LDCs depends, to a large extent, on increased maturity in monetary thinking, which entails using money and the stock of foreign exchange as domestic and international mediums of exchange, respectively, to be separated from the politics of growth promotion.

Second, we must recognize that the LDC government is typically expected to take on more growth-related tasks, such as the accumulation of FE reserves and the use of expansionary purchasing power in ways that few DC governments would attempt. This practice of making covert income transfers, which avoids on-the-table calculations of the benefits and burdens of taxes and expenditures, becomes a root cause of future policy oscillation. Given the political convenience of money creation, growth and income distribution objectives attain a different dimension in the LDC context.

A growth-activist LDC government, moreover, typically has anti-liberalization tendencies built in since, in an evolutionary perspective, liberalization essentially means featuring an increasing role for markets, which are associated with the colonial past. The covert forms of income transfer then generally linger on because the LDC is not yet a pluralistic society in which each of the multiplicity of interest groups can exercise only a relatively small influence on the political stage and the future costs and benefits of government policy are more likely to be carefully calculated in order to reach an ex ante political compromise. Ideological change in the direction of economic liberalization and the emergence of a differentiated, equity-sensitive political pluralism clearly represent more long-run evolutionary organizational accomplishments. That is why policy oscillations (C_1, C_2, C_3, ...) occur in succession during the EO phase. What one can realistically hope for is a diminishing amplitude of such fluctuations in the future.

Assume for a moment, in projecting the long-run economic effects of policy, that the quality of the policy makers of all LDCs is equally high. Under these circumstances, it may well seem that acting responsibly in terms of a long-run societal vision is easier for policy makers in more authoritarian systems, who can presumably afford to take that longer view and do not have to placate public opinion in the short term. In such a situation a tax reform, for example, may seem to be more readily carried out since interest group protests or public demonstrations interfering with the legislative process are less likely. But much depends on the realism of citizens' expectations about government actions in the first place and on the leaders' ability to govern in a way that unifies the country without causing citizens to form unrealistic expectations. These factors, of course, are related to other aforementioned differences in the initial conditions, especially with respect to the strength of a preexisting organic nationalism, itself undoubtedly related to the extent of a population's ethnic and cultural homogeneity. Thus I do not claim that the relative natural resource endowment tells the whole story, but it has a profound effect on the threshold level at which a successful transition can occur.

Summary of Empirical Findings

This section presents brief summaries of empirical studies on the evolution of development policy in six LDCs—Colombia, Mexico, Taiwan, South Korea, the Philippines, and Thailand—grouped into different subfamilies according to their initial conditions and positions on the typological spectrum. Accordingly, Colombia and Mexico are treated as a pair of typical Latin American countries; Taiwan and South Korea represent the "deviant" East Asian family; and the Philippines and Thailand constitute an intermediate case, with the Philippines resembling the Latin American case and Thailand tending toward the East Asian archetype. The empirical findings presented here should help us derive instructive generalizations from the inter- as well as intrafamily differences in the political economy of policy evolution.

A central aspect of the theoretical framework presented in the previous section is the concept of fluctuations in the external environment, as transmitted through the external terms of trade. The main purpose of that section was to trace the policy responses to such changes in various types of LDCs. The first task in the empirical implementation of the framework is to identify the approximate date when the countries in question adopted some form of export orientation; the second is to identify the approximate periods of relatively favorable and unfavorable external shocks. The methodology is thus to estimate the long-run trend in the external terms of trade (defined as the unit value of exports divided by the unit value of imports) from the early 1950s to the mid-1980s for each of the countries and then to examine the deviations from this long-run trend to locate the respective upturns and downturns during their export-oriented phase.

Colombia and Mexico

In the two Latin American cases, the periods of upturn and downturn after the beginning of export orientation were established to be as follows:

	Upturn	Downturn
Colombia	1967–1977	1978–1986
Mexico	1960–1973	1974–1986

It must, however, be pointed out that Mexico's downturn was interrupted by a brief period of bonanza, not well reflected in terms of trade movements, during the oil boom of 1978–1981.

The broad pattern of policy evolution in the two Latin American countries during their phase of external orientation, particularly in the downturn, corresponds quite closely to the scenario described in the theoretical framework. In both countries the government tried to promote growth in good times and to maintain it at high levels during periods of deterioration in the external environment. This strategy, which invariably required increased government expenditures financed by domestic money creation and extensive external borrowing, proved, as the theory predicted, temporarily successful but ultimately self-defeating. It led to serious balance of payments crises—often rendered more serious by further deterioration in the external environment such as a reduced supply or increased cost of foreign capital—and subsequently to lower, often negative, growth for prolonged periods. Both countries also tended to tackle such mounting crises first by reimposing direct controls on the economy, especially on foreign trade, thus reversing previous attempts at liberalization and, ultimately, as predicted in the theoretical framework, by resorting to drastic devaluations, before beginning the next cycle of liberalization.

Although the above summarizes the broad features of the path of development policy change in the two Latin American countries, there are also some instructive differences between the two countries. Colombia achieved fairly respectable growth during the upturn—more than 5.5 percent in all but four years—with a policy package that was initially relatively restrained: modest government deficits (an average of 1 percent of GDP), moderate growth of the money supply (an average of 15 percent), low inflation (an average of 10 percent), no appreciation of the currency, and some trade liberalization measures. Policy behavior, however, later became lax, mainly in the monetary sphere. Expansion of the money supply accelerated to an average of 25 percent from 1972 to 1977, and the rate of inflation jumped from a little over 10 percent in 1972 to more than 30 percent in 1977, resulting in negative real rates of interest throughout the rest of the upturn and, despite some devaluations, in an overall appreciation of the real rate of exchange. Neither the total nor the formal savings ratio (the total savings/GDP ratio and the proportion of total annual savings going into savings deposits) was, however, much affected by interest rate movements. Both stagnated until about 1972–1973, but increased thereafter. Fiscal policy remained more or less restrained, with tax reforms leading to a modest increase in the tax/GDP ratio (from about 8 percent in 1967 to just over 10 percent in 1977). Trade liberalization continued apace.

Once the coffee-led boom was over, the government continued its growth-promotion policies from 1978 until approximately 1982; growth rates averaged 7 percent during 1978–1979, dropping somewhat later. This growth activism was reflected in increased government deficits, which rose to over 2 percent of GDP by 1980 and above 3 percent on average from 1982 to 1984. The larger deficits stemmed from increased expenditures combined with a decreased tax effort (the tax/GDP ratio fell from 11 percent in 1978 to about 9 percent in 1984) and an accelerated growth of the money supply (exceeding 40 percent in 1980). Inflation remained at the high levels reached during the coffee boom. However, flexible interest rates helped to keep real interest rates positive, and flexible exchange rates prevented any significant appreciation of the currency despite high inflation. Nonetheless, the total savings ratio fell until 1982, when it reached 13 percent, increasing slightly afterwards. The formal savings ratio appeared to be relatively more interest rate elastic and remained stable at higher levels during the downturn. There was also further progress on import liberalization.

As would be expected, this relative growth activism ultimately led to a balance of payments and reserves crisis in 1981 and 1982. The government initially reacted by tightening its fiscal policy and imposing import controls, thus postponing a devaluation until late 1984 when it was no longer avoidable and had to be done on a large scale as part of a major adjustment package. A new round of trade liberalization began soon thereafter, starting with the replacement of quotas by tariffs.

Mexico, during much of the 1960–1973 upturn, pursued a basic economic strategy of "development with stability." This strategy implied relative conservatism in economic policy making. Government deficits were low (below 2 percent of GDP until 1971) largely because of restrained expenditures, since the tax effort, which had been low to begin with (about 6 percent of GDP in the early 1960s), increased only modestly. Slow growth of the money supply (mostly around 10 percent) resulted in low rates of inflation (below 5 percent in most years), which helped to keep real interest rates positive. The nominal exchange rate, however, was kept fixed so that even with low inflation there was a steady real appreciation of the currency that was partly responsible for a declining export/GDP ratio during this period. Moreover, unlike Colombia, Mexico showed no persistent trend toward import liberalization; in fact, tariffs were raised while the extensive coverage of quantitative restrictions (QRs) was maintained. The total savings ratio increased only mildly (from 16 percent in 1960 to 18 percent in 1983), and the formal savings ratio remained below 15 percent throughout the upturn.

This era of conservatism in macroeconomic policy came to an end in the early 1970s, just before the downturn started, as growing disenchantment with the development-with-stability strategy led to a shift toward public expenditure–led growth. This approach was temporarily moderated in 1977 following a balance of payments crisis but intensified again following the oil boom. Its core feature was a marked increase in fiscal deficits caused by government expenditure increases far in excess of increases in tax revenues (even during the oil boom years when tax revenues increased significantly). The fiscal deficits, which ranged between 3 and 4 percent of GDP until 1980 before jumping to 6 percent in 1981 and a phenomenal 16 percent in 1982, were financed largely by money creation and external debt. The money supply growth rate increased to over 25 percent in 1974 and exceeded 60 percent in 1982, while the net addition to external debt increased from over 4 percent of GDP in 1973 to about 7.5 percent in 1976 and a record 10 percent in 1981. These rates all exceeded those for Colombia over the same period. They, in turn, led to increases in inflation (which rose from one-digit levels to reach an average of over 20 percent from 1974 to 1981 and over 60 percent from 1982 to 1986) and to negative real rates of interest throughout the downturn period. Savings rates, both total and formal, appeared to be independent of interest rates. The total savings ratio increased steadily until 1980, when it reached about 24 percent, stabilizing thereafter, whereas the formal savings ratio increased from an average of 25 percent from 1974 to 1980 to an average of about 40 percent from 1981 to 1986.

With the end of the oil boom in 1981, the rise in interest rates in international markets, and the drying up of external capital inflows, Mexico's economy collapsed, suffering negative growth, on average, from 1982 to 1986. At least twice during the downturn, the country demonstrated the typical Latin American tendency to delay taking politically unpopular but economically necessary corrective action. First, when faced with a balance of payments crisis during 1974–1976, the government reacted by imposing trade controls and postponing devaluation. In August 1976, when the crisis became serious and capital flight reached critical proportions, it finally floated the peso. Second, during the post-oil-boom crisis of 1981–1982, the government initially imposed trade controls and postponed devaluations. Once these price adjustments were finally carried out, however, renewed attempts at trade liberalization, starting with the replacement of QRs by tariffs, resulted after 1984. By the late 1980s a major liberalization effort was under way, possibly signaling a fundamental shift in Mexico's development pattern.

To summarize, in both countries there is evidence of growth-activist behavior which, although temporarily successful, proved ultimately self-defeating. Both countries tend to prefer politically convenient solutions such as resorting to under-the-table transfers of income through inflationary rather than explicit taxation, negative real rates of interest, and overvalued exchange rates. Finally, both tend to postpone, as long as possible, actions that are economically rational but politically difficult.

There are also differences in behavior within this family. Colombia, at least until very recently, showed relatively greater price flexibility and less policy oscillation. This may be due to differences in the nature of the natural resource endowment; the fact that coffee is grown by a large number of small, dispersed growers may yield smaller scope for rent seeking in Colombia than that provided by oil and minerals in Mexico. The all-too-easy availability of foreign capital in the wake of Mexico's oil bonanza undoubtedly also contributed to its more pathologically Latin American behavior pattern during the 1970s and early 1980s.

South Korea and Taiwan

Although the pattern of policy evolution in most LDCs is likely to mirror, to differing degrees, that described in the theoretical framework, there are a few cases of deviant behavior as exemplified by the East Asian family. Following the methodology described above, the upturn and downturn periods for South Korea and Taiwan were determined to be:

	Upturn	Downturn
South Korea	1962–1972	1973–1986
Taiwan	1960–1970	1971–1986

Our empirical analysis of the history of policy evolution in these two important members of this family reveals that, though there are behavioral differences within the family, the differences that separate them from the Latin American type are indeed pronounced. Specifically, these two countries generally avoided pursuing growth-activist policies and using covert means for transferring incomes to force growth beyond "natural" levels. Their strategy resulted in, among other things, low government deficits, low rates of money growth and inflation, positive real rates of interest, and realistic exchange rates. These countries show a steady trend toward depoliticization of the economic system and linear policy change over the long run.

Both countries achieved overall high real growth rates during both the upturn and downturn phases of their cycle. In Taiwan growth averaged around 9 percent in the upturn and 8.8 percent in the downturn, and in South Korea, it averaged 10 percent and 8 percent, respectively. This performance is not surprising, given the extraordinary success of both countries in their post-1960 export-substitution efforts. In Taiwan the export/GDP ratio rose from 11 percent in 1960 to over 55 percent in 1986 and in South Korea from just over 5 percent in 1962 to about 40 percent in 1986. As production and exports diversified, both economies became less dependent on rents from agriculture and less subject to terms of trade fluctuations. Consequently they found it easier than the

Latin American countries did to maintain a steady policy course. There-fore, early success in liberalization begat more success by moderating policy oscillation in response to exogenous shocks.

There are, however, also differences between the South Korea and Taiwan cases. Taiwan always allowed growth to more or less follow the natural path; for instance, growth was allowed to drop following the two oil shocks before returning to its naturally high levels. South Korea initially made an attempt to maintain growth following the first oil shock, and its annual average growth rate during 1974–1975 was 6.5 percent, compared to 3 percent in Taiwan. From 1976 to 1979 growth was further accelerated to an annual average rate of 11 percent through a huge investment program in heavy and chemical industries and infra-structure, financed to a large extent by foreign borrowing[13] (in contrast, Taiwan achieved the same 11 percent growth rate more naturally). South Korea ultimately had to abandon this strategy, and negative growth resulted in 1980; but, unlike the Latin American cases—espe-cially Mexico—policy adjustment and recovery were much swifter with growth rates averaging 7–8 percent during the difficult years 1981–1986.

The generally more passive attitude toward growth management in East Asia and the temporary deviation from this pattern in South Korea in the mid- to late 1970s are reflected in various areas of our detailed policy analysis. In Taiwan, which provides the best example of consis-tently prudent fiscal policies, budgetary deficits were a rare phenome-non. In fact, after 1964, Taiwan earned surpluses in all years except 1982, when a small deficit appeared. In South Korea, deficits were kept below 1 percent of GDP in all but three years during the upturn and, although higher during the downturn, they were substantially lower than in most LDCs, at below 2 percent in all but four years. There was no significant upward trend during the downturn, but there was a significant jump in the period 1978–1981 when deficits rose from just over 1 percent of GDP to just over 3 percent.

An important factor underlying low fiscal deficits in East Asia is the almost linear trend toward increased tax efforts in both countries. South Korea, whose tax/GDP ratio was lower to begin with—about 6 percent in the early 1960s compared with over 10 percent in Taiwan—increased its ratio in both periods. By 1983, the ratio exceeded 15 percent. Like-wise, Taiwan's tax/GDP ratio increased both during the upturn and during the downturn until 1979, when it reached 17 percent. Underly-ing these trends and levels is a sequence of tax reform measures in the two countries. Taiwan introduced income taxes in 1955, made further reforms in 1970, and implemented the VAT in 1986. South Korea im-posed new taxes and improved tax administration in the late 1960s, introduced a defense tax in 1975 and a VAT and an education tax in 1977, and made further reforms in 1981. The evolution of fiscal policies in both countries, and especially in Taiwan, thus provides a good example of the linearity of policy evolution and shows that these pragmatic governments never had the illusion that a fiscally responsible Treasury could avoid confronting the pain of political compromise.

The restraint and flexibility that characterized fiscal policy in these two countries was also evident in their monetary and exchange rate policies. Once again, the behavior of Taiwan was particularly consistent, and South Korea's slightly less so. In South Korea, the rate of growth of money (M2) ranged between 30 and 40 percent during the latter half of the upturn and the first half of the downturn (1967–1977), but it is interesting to note that although budget deficits rose, money growth fell after 1978. Since 1979 it has, with the exception of 1982, always remained below 20 percent. Inflation hovered around 15 percent for most of the upturn, but increased to a level of 20–25 percent from 1973 to 1980, a trend consistent with the expansionary policies of that period. With the adoption of stabilization policies after 1979, inflation fell dramatically during the 1980s, coming down to below 5 percent in 1983 and remaining there until 1986. Although the interest rate reform of 1965 helped keep nominal rates positive for most of the upturn, a combination of high inflation and low nominal interest rates resulted in negative real rates for most of the downturn. The trend during the downturn, however, was positive, indicating a steady decline in the negative levels and reflecting attempts, albeit not very successful, at restoring positive returns for savers. Both total and formal savings rates appeared to be fairly interest-elastic in South Korea; they increased steadily during the upturn, whereas during the downturn the total savings rate showed some fluctuations and the formal savings ratio stabilized at a lower level. There is evidence that South Korea tried to maintain realistic exchange rates—although somewhat less consistently than Taiwan. South Korea also showed a long-run, gradual trend toward trade liberalization starting from the early reforms of 1964, when it made fundamental exchange rate reforms and replaced QRs with tariffs.

In Taiwan, money growth rates were remarkably stable in both periods, mostly ranging between 20 and 25 percent during the upturn and again during the 1980s, with a slightly higher level in the intervening years. Inflation was also stable and remarkably low, below 6 percent in all but one year during the upturn and in all but five years during the downturn. Low inflation, combined with a flexible nominal interest rate policy, helped keep real interest rates positive and high in most years, with only a few exceptions during the downturn. The total savings ratio increased steadily during the upturn and stabilized at a high level (24–26 percent) during the downturn, while the formal savings ratio remained mostly between 20 and 30 percent, except for the 1980s, when it fell below 10 percent. Taiwan attempted to maintain realistic exchange rates almost throughout the period under observation. It dismantled QRs early, but further trade liberalization, in the sense of tariff reductions, is a more recent phenomenon. The lesson from Taiwan is thus that early monetary restraint and a realistic foreign exchange rate are more important than the elimination of discretionary controls and trade barriers, which can be tackled later in the long-run evolution of policies.

In summary, the policy behavior of the two East Asian countries contrasts sharply with that of the Latin American pair. Although governments in South Korea and Taiwan played an active role in the economy, the general pattern was an almost linear trend toward depoliticization of economic policy making, flexibility in policy formulation, and a reliance on explicit rather than implicit methods of income transfers. Even within this general scenario, however, there are instructive differences between South Korea and Taiwan, especially from 1974 to 1979, when, partly because of political instability at home and partly because of the accelerated inflow of foreign capital, South Korea went off the path. After a brief hiatus, South Korea returned to its previous policies. Such pragmatic flexibility distinguishes South Korea from the typical LDC.

Thailand and the Philippines

Thailand and the Philippines are geographic Southeast Asian neighbors, which have experienced similar external shocks during their external orientation phase. Yet there is a marked contrast in their policy responses to similar shocks: the Philippines exhibits a distinctly Latin American type of behavior, and Thailand behaves more like the deviant East Asian family. This makes for an especially interesting test of the value of the theoretical framework.

For these countries, the periods of upturn and downturn were found to be as follows:

	Upturn	*Downturn*
Thailand	1961–1972	1973–1986
Philippines	1961–1973	1974–1986

As expected, both countries achieved very respectable rates of growth during the upturn: real GDP grew at a rate of 5–6 percent in the Philippines and 7–8 percent in Thailand. However, while Thailand accepted a steady, albeit moderate, decline in growth during the downturn, the Philippines attempted to maintain growth in the face of adverse external circumstances through growth-activist policies financed by domestic and external debt. This strategy initially led to very high growth—about 6–7 percent from 1975 to 1979—but, as predicted by the theoretical framework, it was ultimately self-defeating, for growth rates plummeted in the 1980s, becoming negative in 1984. Both countries experienced an increasing export/GDP ratio during both phases; in the Philippines the export/GDP ratio increased from less than 10 percent in 1961 to about 24 percent in 1984; in Thailand it rose from 19 percent in 1961 to about 26 percent in 1982. The degree of external orientation, however, was higher in Thailand throughout.

The differences in the broad strategy as outlined above were reflected in specific policy areas as well. Encouraged by the relative boom years, both systems expanded government expenditures and ran larger deficits. Once the downturn began, however, Thailand was able to reverse its policies, tighten its belt—partly via higher taxes—and reduce its deficits, while the Philippines attempted to maintain higher growth rates by a combination of larger budget deficits and more foreign borrowing. Government deficits as a percentage of GDP show a significantly positive trend in the Philippines during the downturn, rising from –0.5 percent in 1974 to over 4 percent in 1982. Thailand stabilized its budget deficits after bringing them down to below 3 percent in 1977. The tax effort, as given by the tax/GDP ratio, was lower in the Philippines to begin with—about 7 percent compared with over 11 percent in Thailand in 1961—and, aside from a one-time jump to about 12 percent following the imposition of martial law in 1972, shows no trend in either period. In contrast, Thailand's tax/GDP ratio increased at a steady, though moderate, rate throughout, reaching 14 percent in 1983.

The two countries also exercised sharply contrasting monetary policies. The trends in the rate of growth of the money supply were not as different in the two countries as one might have expected—in both countries the average growth rates were higher during the downturn, about 20 percent on average, compared with about 15 percent on average during the upturn. There were, however, institutional differences: whereas in Thailand the central bank was relatively autonomous, in the Philippines it clearly acted as an extension of an activist government. There were also differences in the public's response in terms of the income velocity of money, as seen in the resulting lagged rate of inflation. In Thailand, the rate of inflation was below 5 percent in all but one year of the upturn and below 10 percent in all but four years of the downturn. In the Philippines it was below 5 percent in only three years during the upturn and below 10 percent in only five years of the downturn. Moreover, Thailand also tended to take prompt remedial policy action, but the Philippines did not. For instance, once inflation reached a peak of 16 percent in 1980 after the second oil shock, Thailand took corrective steps and brought down inflation steadily over the next few years; in the Philippines, by contrast, the drop in inflation following the peak of 15 percent, also in 1980, was only moderate and soon reversed.

The most striking contrast is found in the two countries' interest rate policies. While Thailand succeeded in maintaining reasonably stable positive real rates of interest, the Philippines experienced low or even negative rates most of the time, which led, if not to lower total saving rates, to a more segmented credit market. The Philippines thus appears to epitomize the typical LDC described in the theoretical framework, in which a low interest rate policy is a means of covertly transferring income from certain groups in the society to others.

Finally, the Philippines had initiated liberalization of its exchange rate and trade policies in 1962. It had, for example, replaced QRs with tariffs and devalued the peso. Following the balance of payments crisis in 1967, however, the government, reluctant to devalue the by then substantially overvalued peso, reimposed a series of foreign exchange controls. These actions were not sufficient to prevent another serious payments crisis in 1970, and in February of that year the Philippines, under pressure from the IMF, floated the peso. Despite the flexible exchange rate system, the currency depreciated only moderately during the downturn, which, given the high rates of inflation, led to a substantial appreciation of the real exchange rate. The Philippines made efforts to reform tariffs and import controls under the World Bank structural adjustment loans of the early 1980s, but, following the 1983 debt crisis, it reimposed controls and began a series of major devaluations.

The evolution of exchange rate management and trade policies differs in the two countries as well. Given Thailand's low inflation, that country's real exchange rate did not appreciate during the upturn but, in fact, depreciated slightly. During the downturn, with the nominal rate fixed and inflation accelerating, the real exchange rate appreciated significantly. The degree of overvaluation was, however, less than that in the Philippines, and Thailand tackled it much earlier—in 1980 compared with 1983 in the Philippines. Interpreting it another way, the Philippine government used an overvalued exchange rate along with negative real interest rates more consistently as a covert means of income transfers, whereas in Thailand the government refrained from extensive use of these tools and relied more on explicit fiscal transfers. Because of the country's realistic exchange rates, Thailand's reliance on import controls was consistently low by international standards and, more significantly, declined even during the downturn.

Therefore, although Thailand and the Philippines are geographic neighbors, the pattern of their policy evolution and their responses to similar shocks have been markedly different. Thailand kept its policy parameters steady over time, while the Philippines showed substantially more oscillations. These differences in behavior may be traced partly to the precise composition of their natural resource endowments; rice (in Thailand) and cash crops (in the Philippines) undoubtedly provide different opportunities for generating rents. Nonetheless, the existence of substantial behavioral differences over time between two neighboring countries, yielding marked differences in bottom-line performance to this day, surely provides a fairly robust test of the usefulness of the theoretical framework.

Conclusions for Policy

This chapter has attempted to do two things: to propose an approach to the endogenization of development policy and to begin to test it against the postwar empirical experience of some actual country cases. It has become increasingly obvious to both donors/creditors and LDC policy makers that the issue of changing development policy and the pros and cons of accepting structural adjustment packages are based not so much on an inadequately shared understanding of the technical problems involved as on a more subtle political economy–tinged process. After more than forty years of buildup in human capacity in the third world and forty years of discourse between the donor/creditor and recipient/debtor communities, both parties have become increasingly aware that achieving policy change is a question of responding knowledgeably to poorly understood and partially obscured dimensions of the environment. If such processes can be exposed to the light of analysis and rendered more transparent, the chances of gaining greater mutual understanding and advancing the development process as a positive-sum game would be substantially enhanced.

Obviously, I do not claim to have rendered policy making fully endogenous here. That is much too ambitious an undertaking, given the other factors at work, our inadequate understanding of the role of the state, and other complexities that have not even been introduced. Moreover, rational expectations theory notwithstanding, I do not believe that policy can ever be fully endogenized, since a truly dynamic scenario will always have to leave room for differences in time horizon, individual personalities, and old-fashioned surprises. Rather, I would be quite content if I have succeeded in pointing to a fruitful direction for future policy-oriented research, recognizing, to paraphrase Goethe, that the first step toward self-improvement is self-realization—in other words, transparency. It is political economy in this sense—tracing different policy responses in different types of LDCs rather than tracing the implications of a class struggle among vested interest groups who manipulate a neutral or not-so-neutral government—that is being deployed here.

Specifically, it is my contention that an economic system's initial conditions, given by nature, affect not only its initial level of income and welfare, but also its policy responsiveness and flexibility over time. They influence the extent to which development policies are likely to accommodate or obstruct basic evolutionary changes. The nature and pace of policy changes that alter the nature of government intervention are related to several critical dimensions of the initial conditions; the two most important are the relative initial strength or weakness of what Kuznets called "nationalism," and the relative strength or weakness of the natural resource endowment of the system. The first dimension, which I have referred to but not fully analyzed here, affects the relative mildness or severity of the seemingly inevitable primary import-substitution subphase of transition growth. The second makes itself felt in two ways. First, the larger the initial resource endowment, the more important the rents emanating from the primary sector and therefore the more animated the struggle among contending parties to appropriate these rents for themselves. Second, the larger the natural resource endowment, the more exposed the system is to exogenous fluctuations in the terms of trade. The amplitude and periodicity of such fluctuations in turn affect the rate of secular organizational/institutional change, that is, the shape of the liberalization trend.

Other important dimensions of the initial conditions are country size and the extent of population pressure on the land, or the severity of a system's labor-surplus condition. Although these sources of typological heterogeneity have not been analyzed in this chapter, they are undoubtedly relevant to the evolution of policy and performance over time.[14]

The empirical summaries presented in this chapter have compared the results of applying the framework to three types of developing countries. They have included such extreme cases as the East Asian countries, on the one hand, and the Latin Americans, on the other, with the Southeast Asians as an intermediate group. These types differ in their initial material and human endowments, in their size, and in the strength of their initial organic nationalism. I have tried to analyze the differences in the political economy responses of these systems over time; at the same time I have endeavored to compare countries within given types. If transferable lessons can be learned by examining the different responses of countries with similar systems to similar exogenous terms of trade shocks, it affirms the value of the laboratory in which this study is operating. Such comparative longitudinal analysis is, of course, subject to the criticism that the methodology is still rather casual and imprecise, but this criticism must be weighed against the value, as well as the defects, of the timeless cross-section or optimizing individual-country general-equilibrium models.

This chapter focuses not on *what* development policy change and performance look like but on the more difficult question of *why* they occur the way they do. This is a novel and ambitious task, and consequently the results presented in this chapter should be viewed more as a progress report on a continuing research effort than as definitive findings. Nevertheless, I believe that this approach is a fruitful one and likely to become more so as the analytical framework and empirical testing procedures are refined.

Some conclusions for policy flow from the work reported on in this chapter. First, once an LDC reaches the EO subphase of transition, the government should shift from controlling prices and quantities (through rationing) to controlling quantities and letting prices be determined by the market. In the case of monetary policy, the principle of controlling quantity seems to constitute Friedman-like advice, namely that even the world's most experienced central bankers should monitor the quantity of money (M) and forget about trying to control the rate of interest, which should be determined in the loanable-funds market. This suggests that the growth rate of money should be limited to approximately the growth rate of GNP. In the case of foreign exchange management, the same principle implies moving to a relatively clean float system in which the government monitors the quantity of reserves (R) and no longer views the level of the exchange rate as politically "sensitive." It further implies that the quantity of foreign exchange reserves should be limited to the relatively small, constant amount needed for transactions purposes and that an LDC cannot afford the luxury of a large R.

The simultaneous application of quantity restrictions governing both internal and external monetary management is not accidental. In both cases money should be increasingly interpreted as necessary for transactions purposes: M should be seen as a domestic medium of exchange required for the internal division of labor, and R as a medium of exchange for international transactions purposes to accommodate the international division of labor.

Such gradual liberalization implies the increasing substitution of the market for direct government controls. As the interest rate is liberalized, there is less need for credit rationing by political force, and as the exchange rate is liberalized, there is less need for foreign exchange rationing. Although not all government controls, such as import duties, are eliminated, the most serious ones are. No government, either in a DC or in an LDC, makes daily adjustments in its tariff structure, but it does make daily discretionary decisions about the supply of money and the foreign exchange rate. Distortions by tariffs represent a less important cause of oscillating inefficiency.

The state's exercise of monopoly power to print money and the compulsory purchase of foreign exchange are thus more damaging than the retention of import duties, at least for some time. Movement toward liberalization is therefore coextensive with the acceptance of a new monetary philosophy in which M and R are increasingly regarded as mediums of exchange, instead of as purchasing power that can be artificially created or manipulated to achieve socially desirable goals. This call for relative monetary inactivism constitutes something of a rebellion against the postwar mainstream view in the LDCs that regards the government as responsible for promoting growth through expansionary monetary policies. For, despite the slogan "growth with equity," the postwar growth-promoting policies imply the manufacture of profits by a strategy of income transfer that victimizes less politically powerful social groups—consumers, unorganized workers, and, especially, spatially dispersed rural agriculturists and nonagriculturists. Given a limited government capacity to borrow, a commitment to monetary conservatism also implies fiscal responsibility; that is, covert income transfers by and to the government should increasingly be replaced by taxation with consent, with the costs of growth explicitly calculated and apportioned to various social groups.

More specifically, this analysis suggests that fiscal reforms should move consistently toward an increase in tax revenues to reduce the budget deficit and that tax efforts should shift from international trade-related indirect taxes (indirect import and export taxes) to domestic taxes, both direct (income and property) and indirect (sales). Moreover, on the expenditure side, a reduction in the urban bias of government infrastructural allocation would be highly desirable.

Policy reforms are, of course, difficult because of the political opposition they invite from social groups who have developed a vested interest in the status quo and who would lose from change. Moreover, it takes time for new ideas and organizations to replace the old. In a democratic society, subject to normal political pressures and administrative constraints, a government cannot be expected to do or undo everything at once. Some transition period must be allowed on the path to liberalization, since concessions to political reality must usually be made. Thus, putting all the emphasis on cutting the deficit, for example, though meritorious from the anti-inflationary point of view, may actually be bad (or at least untimely) advice from the political standpoint, because it requires a politically mature social consensus concerning how the new tax burden is to be equitably shared. The Latin American type of developing country, for instance, may have to live with some inflation for a period; in such countries using inflation to partially solve some problems is almost a given, because the political art of consensus formation must be developed as liberalization proceeds.

A three-stage, priority-oriented approach to reform suggests itself. The first stage might involve exchange rate reforms. A relatively clean float would move the system toward an equilibrium exchange rate, and monetary decontrol would move it toward an equilibrium interest rate. At this stage, the printing of money might be permitted at a smooth and steady pace as a concession to government's inability to raise taxes, given the aforementioned political resistance of vested interest groups.

In the second stage a revenue-neutral tax reform, involving a shift from indirect international trade taxes to direct and indirect internal taxes, might be carried out over a number of years, during which the resistance by urban interest groups is gradually overcome. As a consequence, the government would gradually renounce its policy of printing money for growth promotion purposes. In the case of import duties, resistance to such a reduction would gradually soften once urban consumers come to realize that they have been paying for years for the inefficiency of domestic industries. Consumer protests would gather momentum as import liberalization proceeds and as consumers have more opportunity to travel abroad and compare the domestic and world prices of consumer goods.

Indirect nonagricultural taxes and, later, direct income taxes, once installed, usually have a progressive feature that makes them GNP-elastic. Liberalization reform in the first stage should therefore be helpful in producing a sufficiently high GNP growth rate to make it possible for the government to eventually close the budget deficit.

Finally, in the third stage, given its increased revenues, the government could begin to promote growth by increasing nonhousehold, line ministry expenditures on decentralized projects with long gestation periods (related to, for example, education, science and technology, agricultural research, and roads), with an emphasis on rural infrastructure. Such projects, based on the economic principle of externality, are intended to provide a better environment for the operation of private entrepreneurs. Success at each stage is, of course, a prerequisite for keeping the budget deficit down in the following stages.

Such a priority-oriented reform program would help rural producers, who usually constitute the class most discriminated against, gradually to regain the purchasing power taken away from them during the early import-substitution phase. This essential, often neglected ingredient would assure that macroeconomic policies increasingly serve to accommodate rather than obstruct developing countries' transition to modern economic growth.

Comments

PRANAB BARDHAN

I shall first comment on the preceding three chapters and then make some general remarks. Ronald Findlay's chapter is a delightful cocktail of political taxonomy, historical sweep, and trade-theoretic models of the outcome of state behavior. His characterization of the state as overdeveloped in relation to civil society and of the extractive maximization by neopatrimonial rulers will, of course, find nodding recognition from most observers of the state in developing countries. I was reminded of Charles Tilly's theory of the state as organized crime and Douglass North's theory in which a group with a "comparative advantage in violence" captures the state and acts as a revenue-maximizing, discriminating monopolist selling protection and justice. Findlay goes further in focusing on the conflict between the productive and predatory roles of the state and the distinction between surplus- and budget-maximizing behavior.

I think Findlay slightly underestimates the vulnerability of even patrimonial rulers (usually in their search for legitimacy) to pressures from various interest groups in civil society. I have a similar problem in Merilee Grindle's chapter, where I find the distinction between state-centered and society-centered models somewhat overdrawn. I think even authoritarian states are often beleaguered by inexorable interest group pressures.

Findlay traces some useful implications for income distribution and political economy of trade taxes or pricing policies in his three variants of trade-theory models. In these neoclassical mini general-equilibrium models, owners of one factor of production affect the incomes of others, through their influence on the marginal products in the production process. These models obviously cannot capture the effects of strategic interaction among owners of different factors or between them and the state. The analysis by the political sociologist Peter Evans of the triangular strategic relationship between the state, domestic capital, and foreign capital in the context of Brazil is an example that economists might profitably formalize.

Findlay talks briefly about the issue of legitimacy, but if he carried it through his taxonomy of regimes he would have to conduct a more complex analysis of why legitimacy means different things in Latin American military dictatorships compared with, say, a Korean dictatorship or with democratic regimes as in India. This question might have led him to a taxonomy in terms of the composition of civil society and its political culture.

Finally, Findlay, like most other writers in the neoclassical political economy tradition, does not even attempt to explain the change of political regimes, in particular how it is possible for some regimes to negotiate the inevitable political hurdles in the process of shifting from one policy regime to another. This point is part of Grindle's critique of neoclassical political economy. I find her emphasis on the dynamics of policy making and the process of decision making and its changes very welcome. But when one follows her discussion of the various contextual issues that surround any particular decision-making situation, one becomes aware that it is difficult to fit them into a generalizable theoretical pattern. Unless she provides an alternative general theory of these richly textured political processes, her critique of the neoclassical political economy models will remain somewhat unfair, since she is not treating them at the appropriate methodological level.

Grindle correctly points out that neoclassical political economy identifies certain policy outcomes from which it then rashly infers political processes that led to such outcomes. In other words, she brings the charge of methodological functionalism: you cannot explain something just by pointing to the consequences. There is, however, a not uncommon intermediate case that she should consider. Even when a policy's origin may have nothing to do with the pressures of a particular rent-seeking lobby, once it is in place and the rental opportunities open, the activities of that lobby may be responsible for the maintenance and perpetuation of that policy.

I very much agree with Grindle's central message about the inadequacy of the neoclassical political economy's way of treating politics just as "a spanner in the economic works." Politics is indeed often the central means through which societies seek to resolve conflicts over the key issues of distribution and values. The primacy of issues of distribution, rather than of efficiency, was the distinguishing feature of classical political economy.

In the chapter by Gustav Ranis, there is a richly detailed comparative study of macroeconomic policy oscillations and divergences and their effects on covert income transfers. I agree with most of his analysis. I probably would place a somewhat different emphasis on the initial conditions discussed by Ranis. He refers to organic nationalism and natural resource scarcity (or abundance) as important initial conditions in an endogenous analysis of differential development policy. I understand the importance of organic nationalism if it refers merely to social and cultural homogeneity, which makes political aggregation easier. But stretched beyond that the analysis could be tautological: he may end up merely redefining what he needs to explain. I am therefore always a little suspicious of words like "organic" or "mature" in this context.

Similarly, I understand the point about the bracing effect of natural resource scarcity. In situations of resource abundance, there may be a preoccupation with the allocation of resource rents rather than with more pressing matters. Perhaps in some situations in Latin America or Africa the imperatives of policy change would have been driven home much earlier if their natural resource constraint were as binding as in some East Asian cases. But I can also think of many developing countries with acute scarcity of natural resources where the policy regimes would be regarded by Ranis as cases of failure. Obviously we have to look elsewhere for a more convincing explanation.

I do not quite agree with Ranis that political pluralism makes adjustments easier and that a multiplicity of interest groups makes it more likely that the future costs and benefits of government policy are more carefully calculated. Mancur Olson's arguments and my own analysis of pluralist India suggest the contrary. I would also have liked Ranis to go a little deeper into the origins of macroeconomic conservatism in Thailand or Taiwan compared with the Latin American countries or the Philippines.

Finally, his country comparisons would have been somewhat richer if he drew upon aspects of comparative sociology as a background to the macroeconomic policy differences. For example, any comparison of Thailand and the Philippines is seriously incomplete without some analysis of their different colonial history and the differential power of the landed oligarchy over the state. It would be interesting to know if the similarity of the legacy of Filipino history with that of Latin America not only in terms of Spanish colonialism and American hegemony, but also in terms of the dominance of the landed oligarchy, has any connection with the Latin American–style policy oscillations and macroeconomic profligacy in the Philippines.

Let me end with some general remarks on the subject with which these three important papers are broadly concerned. First, in much of the neoclassical literature the emphasis is on the extent of state intervention, particularly on the harmful effects of that intervention. As a matter of fact, almost all states in developing countries, successful or otherwise, are interventionist, and the important issue is not really the extent but the quality of that intervention. The nature and quality of intervention by different states, often commanding similar instruments of intervention and sometimes similar extents of intervention, can be very different. We need to understand why the quality of intervention is so different in the different regimes, why the institutional coherence of the executive is so different, and why its ability to pursue collective goals, even with the same instruments of intervention, is so very different. The neoclassical rent-seeking or predatory state may be applicable to Mobutu's Zaire, where everything, including the highest public offices, is up for sale. But it is certainly an incomplete theory in the context of many other states where there is some institutional coherence in the pursuit of collective goals. What seems to be important in making a difference in the quality of intervention is the extent of centralization of decision making coupled with its flexibility in dealing with changes in technical and market conditions; how much operational space the economic technocrats get in their design and implementation of policy; how meritocratic the methods of recruitment of the bureaucracy are; and how much leeway the state has in restructuring its relationships with labor, business, and the rural sector. It is not, as Findlay says, so much a matter of the distinction between left- and right-wing authoritarian regimes, or between traditional monarchies or dictatorships and democratic states. Once developmental goals are centrally involved in the issues of legitimacy of the regime, I think it is not so much authoritarianism per se that makes a difference, but the extent of insulation that the decision makers can organize against the ravages of pork-barrel politics. For this insulation authoritarianism is neither necessary nor sufficient.

The second general point I would like to make is that it is important to distinguish between two parts of the state structure. The state is often identified in the neoclassical political economy literature with the bureaucracy, whose implementation of policies is supposed to generate all kinds of rental income. I think it is important to distinguish between the top leadership, or the state elite, that makes the general policies and the bureaucratic agencies that implement them. Although there are many examples of a corrupt state elite, there are also many cases where it is simply not enough to characterize the state elite as venal, as is automatically assumed in the neoclassical political economy literature. The impulses that shape major policies and actions by the state elite are fueled not merely by motives of self-aggrandizement, but often also by what can be called its conception of national interest, in a way not captured by the neoclassical idea of the predatory state or the classical Marxist class-driven state. In many dramatic cases of state-directed industrialization over the last hundred years or more (the classic case may be that of Meiji Japan), the state leadership genuinely considered itself the trustee of the nation's collective aspirations and derived its political legitimacy from those aspirations. In a world of international military and economic competition, one form these aspirations often take is the quest for rapid economic development. I think Grindle is right in suggesting that the neoclassical rent-seeking literature is better at explaining failures than success stories (particularly of state-led industrialization).

She is also right in pointing out that for the state, economic development is only one of the major goals. Nation building is often a more important goal, and in its pursuit the state elite may have to make many intricate political compromises that may not be economically rational but may be highly sensible for the regime. In the context of many overwhelming ethnic, class, and regional conflicts that threaten nation building, it is the distributive compromises (in spite of their being second-best or nth-best from the point of view of allocational efficiency) that become primary, and economists, to be of any relevance, should pay more attention to them.

JOHN TOYE

Merilee Grindle has provided an account of the new political economy (NPE) that is fuller and more perceptive than many that have appeared. Her approach is not to get inside the logic of neoclassical political economy, but rather to stand outside it, taking it largely as it presents itself—with fair and representative quotation from its exponents—and to ask how useful this apparatus is in explaining the process of policy change in developing countries in the 1980s.

Grindle brings together a number of important aspects of the new political economy to construct and articulate a coherent statement of its strengths and limitations. I particularly liked five points from the paper.

First, the new political economy has an intellectual pedigree, which includes the pluralist tradition of democratic theory in the United States. It is important to say this because the NPE sometimes presents itself as a pure construction of abstract logic founded on the single idea of the rational individual. It thus presents itself as lacking a history, just as its application to particular contexts is typically ahistorical.

Second, the distinction between society-centered and state-centered versions of the NPE is a helpful one in sorting out the by-now considerable variety of messages and methods among exponents of economic theories of politics. The society-centered analysis tends to take as given a particular constitutional order, usually democratic, and to consider only marginal variations upon it, such as varying the election period or paying candidates' campaign expenses out of public funds. When well-developed political institutions exist, both politicians and bureaucrats have to be more passive and reactive, so their individual motives have less power to affect outcomes. Where political institutions are "thin," it is easier for the state apparatus to embark on autonomous projects—and institutional thinness, as Grindle rightly argues, is the typical case in less-developed countries (LDCs). This is part and parcel of societies that also have thin markets and thin people. But we should note that thinness refers to a range or spectrum of institutional density, not an either-or distinction.

Third, Grindle's emphasis on the closed nature of policy making in LDCs and the satisfaction of group interests during the implementation stage is interesting and reflects the case studies of attempted policy reform. She explains this phenomenon in terms of limited information and the high level of uncertainty, bringing into the discussion two factors that, in my view, are much underemphasized in both political and economic analysis. A classic example of the accommodation of interests through the creation of legislative loopholes *after* the top leadership had decided on reform occurred in the attempts at tax reform in South Asia in the 1950s (Toye 1989). The process of policy making and implementation has to be understood properly if the prospects for sustainable reform are to be gauged.

Fourth, the new political economy easily becomes mechanically pessimistic: "Locked into . . . the notion that existing situations demonstrate an inevitable rationality, it is hard to envision how changes in such situations occur except through catastrophic events." Another assessment of how the new political economy fared when applied to the case of India described it as an "economistic hypothesis of equilibrium unhappiness"—or an EHEU theory (Toye 1987: 122–27). It also concluded, in the spirit of Grindle, that most of the available theories (including the NPE) were static, when what was needed was a dynamic theory of change.

Fifth, I therefore agree with Grindle that to explain and assess individual country cases, one has to understand the historical context and the constraints on possibilities that this imposes, how an issue is placed on the policy agenda, the administrative requirements for implementation, and the specific incidence of policy costs and benefits. Especially pertinent is the suggestion that the "degree of public visibility" was an important factor that influenced whether reform policies would be sustainable. Economically irrational policies often rely on a form of "invisibility" to sustain their popularity. A more rational policy, if highly visible, may prove quite unpopular: an example would be a move from cascading sales taxes at a low nominal rate to a value-added tax at a much higher rate. This may make reform efforts slow, partial, and difficult, without making them always impossible.

Within this general approval of the chapter, I offer some more critical comments. The presentation of the policy implications of the new political economy is a little too neat, and this neatness obscures an important point. Although many, perhaps most, NPE theorists are advocates of smaller government, not all are. Downs, for example, wrote an analysis based on the economic theory of democracy that argued that the government budget in a democracy would inevitably be too small (Downs 1960). His argument turned on the costs to citizens of acquiring information about unlikely events that would cause massive damage if they occurred. A topical example would be an environmental problem, such as holes in the ozone layer. But Downs was actually writing in 1960 about the USSR's space and nuclear capability. This example emphasizes the "tool-kit" function of neoclassical economics. Technically, it can theorize government underspending just as easily as government overspending—although it is usually put to the latter use. An intellectual history of the NPE needs to investigate why one kind of tool is produced from the kit at one time and another kind of tool at another time, often with opposite policy implications.

The chapter nowhere explains satisfactorily why the new political economy is called *new*. We leap straight from the naïveté of the alleged

1960s belief in the do-gooding state to the NPE with its "profoundly cynical view of the political process." The only thing in between is "dis-illusion"—we all just grew older, perhaps, and noticed the real world for the first time? This, in itself, is surely a naive view. As Gunnar Myrdal made clear at least as early as 1968, writing as if developing country governments were do-gooding states was more a matter of diplomacy and hoping-against-hope than of belief (Myrdal 1968: 1839–42). The development economists of the 1950s and 1960s were largely foreigners in the developing countries, where they were operating at the instance of their home governments. They occupied willy-nilly an un-tenable position. Their mandate was to assist their adopted country as professional economists but at no time to meddle in local politics. As professional economists, they assumed the existence of certain institu-tions and attitudes, which were usually not there. But to *say* the institu-tions and attitudes were not there could itself be interpreted as a political act. Myrdal's concept of "the soft state" was so interpreted. As a result of this impasse, visiting economists—as the argument and ex-ample of Dudley Seers (1962) show—knew that they were largely inef-fective and felt morally uncomfortable, but at the same time they loyally respected the diplomatic imperative.

What orthodoxy could not then acknowledge emerged as dissent—the Marxian political economy that Grindle does not mention at all. That "very cynical view" of the political process in developing countries first appeared in the 1950s with Paul Baran, but took hold strongly in the following decade. The "class logic" version of Marxian political econ-omy is quite similar to the society-centered version of the NPE: the key difference is that the former sees the pressures for economic irrationality stemming from an exploitative class—the comprador bourgeoisie—while the latter talks of self-interested groups. That the political process generated and maintained economically irrational outcomes for society was common ground.

Sometime in the late 1970s, at the end of Robert McNamara's time as president of the World Bank, diplomacy no longer seemed to require tact and tongue biting, but instead needed a justification for more active intervention in the local politics of developing countries. Neoclassical economists, then still producing project appraisal manuals with shadow prices and income-distribution weights, went back to the tool-kit and produced instead a sanitized version of Marxian political econ-omy, identical except for being deducible from individual rational self-interest rather than anything so unorthodox as "class." (The Marx-ists were having sufficient difficulty with "class" themselves!)

That is why Grindle's critique of the NPE parallels so closely cri-tiques of the Marxian political economy of development. Both are ex-amples of economic determinism, and hence pessimistic and static in character. The same objections that apply to one apply to the other. And both require a catastrophe (revolution) or a wise statesman (the classless intellectual) to bring about change. Dudley Seers, who wrote in 1979 on "the congruence of Marxism and other neo-classical doctrines," would not have been surprised by this.

When rebutting the NPE's pessimism, Grindle is less than convincing. Many of the examples Grindle cites of "significant policy changes" in LDCs in the 1980s are not quite as promising in advancing her argument against the NPE as they appear to be. Might not the NPE theorists reply, "In most of the cited cases, not only was there a catastrophe, but the catastrophe was the occasion for the introduction into local politics of those wise officials of the International Monetary Fund and the World Bank"? Such a response would neutralize the cases of The Gambia, Ghana, and Mexico as evidence contrary to the NPE view. Most of the cases from the 1980s are contaminated by the political success of the NPE theorists in justifying much more active interventions by external agencies in LDC policy making. We will never know what would have happened if the NPE theorists had *not* cried, "local reform is impossible," and policy reform lending by the international financial institutions had not been launched.

The purely scientific contribution of the NPE has, as Grindle states, not been negligible. But her endorsement of the policy prescriptions of the NPE (if only they could be applied, if only the LDC government had a tabula rasa) seems to me too fulsome. The scientific achievement of NPE has been to explain with some detail and precision how microeconomic incentives continually undermine the design and execution of development projects and programs that would (from an economic viewpoint) be in the best public interest. One example is Robert Repetto's work on irrigation projects, in which he analyzes the coalition of self-interested parties that bias irrigation spending toward new works construction and away from economical management of water supplied through existing works (Repetto 1986). But this successful diagnosis by no means leads to viable policy conclusions that are market-based or rely on correct prices or charges. In irrigation, water pricing is simply not feasible as a solution to the bad management problem, because it implies a control over water delivery that does not exist. Here, as in other cases, an NPE diagnosis may show that new forms of government intervention or new forms of community action are required rather than the standard NPE price-it and charge-for-it prescriptions.

Ranis's substantial and impressive study is not—despite its title—centrally addressed to the NPE paradigm. Rather, it is a long-term comparative study of the macroeconomic performance of three pairs of countries grouped according to initial conditions. Its theme is not so much economic theories of politics (as discussed by Grindle) as a political theory of economic macromanagement—a modern variant of the political business cycle literature. In developing countries, however, the cycle is not self-induced, but something external that has to be adjusted to—with more or less economic skill. The story, demonstrated with a battery of economic statistics, complete with significance tests, is that Thailand's adjustment policies have led to greater growth and stability than those of the Philippines. There are also many subplots and a final set of recommendations aimed at fiscal and monetary transparency and soundness and the liberalization of the credit and foreign exchange markets.

As I understand it, the analysis of the external cycle allows Ranis to treat certain policy changes—in regard to foreign exchange reserves, monetary and fiscal policy, export promotion, and so on—as "required." The respective policy performances are assessed in relation to these "requirements." In this sense, some policy is made endogenous to the analysis. This is an ingenious analytical device, which is thoroughly exploited in the course of the paper. But it does pose problems for an NPE approach to policy making.

How does the paper throw light on the NPE, as defined and discussed by Grindle? It does so obliquely and not head on. The opening sections of the paper present, in effect, a stylized account of macroeconomic mismanagement in developing countries. The forms of economic misbehavior are the "artificial" inducement of industrialization, inefficient trade controls, fiscal laxity, covert redistribution through the inflation tax, the absence of independent monetary policy, repressed interest rates, the discouragement of saving, and a few more. This does not advance us much beyond Little, Scitovsky, and Scott (1970) and the financial repression literature. But it is a skillful synthesis and describes a total syndrome of economic mismanagement.

Ranis places particular emphasis, however, on the power of the state to print money at will as a key source of temptation to economic misbehavior. He avoids suggesting that there is something about states as such that makes irrational policies inevitable. The Thailand-Philippines comparison is designed to show just the opposite—how between similarly placed LDCs, it is possible for one to be less irrational than the other. The final liberalization recommendations also take it for granted that change—albeit gradual—is possible. Despite the endogenization of policy, Ranis avoids the EHEU trap.

This "optimistic" stance thus raises the question of how states—all (except Liberia, which uses the U.S. dollar) endowed with the same source of temptation—eventually come to abstain, rather than indulge in monetary irresponsibility? In answering this central question, the endogenization of policy making is not helpful. It directs us to only one answer—namely, that over the cycle, governments gradually learn that "bad" economic policies are not indefinitely sustainable, and groups gradually learn that all is not as it seems: savings evaporate, rich entrepreneurs are not really productive, growth is unstable, and the system does not provide economic justice to the common man.

This answer is at best partial. The other parts of the explanation are obscured by the endogenization of policy making. First the endogenization approach assumes a unitary state, embarked on a strategy and managing the politics of it quite successfully. In fact, LDCs are fragile and conflict-ridden, something that foreign liberalizers actively try to exploit "for good ends" when persuading important political groups to back economic reforms. The internal vicissitudes of policy making are crucial in understanding how abstinence gets established, and the chapter does not convincingly integrate the endogenization of policy with these political vicissitudes.

Second, the role of external agencies can be important. National policy making is not sealed off from the rest of the world any more than from the economic problems it addresses. International agencies can underwrite "bad" economic behavior. Indeed, it is often said that this explains the macroeconomic performance of the Philippines in the 1970s. The International Monetary Fund (IMF) in the 1970s failed to enforce the normal discipline of stabilization on the Marcos regime, and some observers have suggested that this easy treatment was due to pressure from the United States. I am not here asserting that this was the case; but there is a clear possibility of collusion between self-indulgent LDC regimes and the international financial institutions in response to U.S. geopolitical interests. This consideration needs scrutiny.

Third, neither Thailand nor the Philippines is an example of an LDC that retains the institutions of financial repression—government deficits financed automatically by the central bank, low administered interest rates—and yet has followed policies of financial caution and successfully avoided high levels of inflation. Reading Ranis's very generalized assertions about the economic mismanagement syndrome in developing countries and the need for liberalization of their economic institutions, one gains the impression that developing countries either indulge in financial irresponsibility or they embark on liberalization drives, like Thailand. That inference should not be drawn. India is an example of a third case: a country that retains financially repressed monetary institutions but that has prudently avoided the perils of inflation (at least until recent years, when liberalization moves were also placed on the political agenda, although not pushed forward with much force or persistence).

As Grindle argues, the NPE has at least four different faces, focusing analysis on the behavior of interest groups, politicians, bureaucrats, and the state as a whole at different times. In his chapter here, Ronald Findlay adopts the latter option, having taken some of the earlier ones in his earlier papers. He argues that the choice of the autonomous state as the unit of analysis is particularly relevant when analyzing the political economy of LDCs "because most LDCs are ruled by military juntas or one-party dictatorships of one kind or another." On this basis, he sets out to establish "resoundingly" the relevance of the NPE to understanding LDCs.

This starting point seems problematic. As Findlay says, some sort of agent-principal relationship always exists between the state and civil society. In my view, it is fallacious to believe that this relation can be abolished by military juntas or one-party dictatorships. The abundance of such regimes in the third world does not, therefore, mean that a unitary autonomous state is an especially relevant framework of analysis of the LDCs.

Findlay seems to endorse the concept of neopatrimonialism as having special relevance to third world politics, and indeed it does, especially in sub-Saharan Africa. But the lesson to be drawn from this, in my view, is that neopatrimonial states are deeply entangled in civil society, not independent of it, for the precise reasons indicated by Findlay—the threats of loss of legitimacy, intensification of political competition, and erosion of barriers to political violence. Neopatrimonial behavior could reasonably be argued to be an essentially self-protective device for weak regimes that are going nowhere, rather than a means of purchasing state autonomy.

Even when military dictatorships or one-party states are strong, they are not usually autonomous from domestic political forces. Despite Pinochet's rhetoric about standing above all sections of civil society, it is clear that his regime in Chile relied constantly on middle-class support. In devising its economic policies, the regime had to make precise political calculations to protect the junta's support in civil society. This careful calculus is the price of the power to oppress other groups in the population.

Although in general states that have a specific domestic support base in civil society are strong, and states that have to buy off domestic opposition extensively are weak, one can find interesting exceptions. Ghana under the Rawlings regime, for example, is that curiosity—a state with virtually no support in civil society that is both politically stable and engaged in an autonomous project of economic reform. But it has external support, in the form of substantial capital inflows from the IMF and the World Bank. To look only at domestic politics is partial and misleading. For these reasons, I am skeptical of pinning the relevance of the NPE to LDCs on the existence of autonomous states on a grand scale in the third world. It is more plausible to suggest that the NPE's best case for relevance turns on its ability to throw light on the divorce between the official and the real functioning of the state, its internal fissures and conflicts, and its failure (with some exceptions) to embark on major autonomous projects like reform in pursuit of modern economic growth.

Be that as it may, these issues fade from sight as the chapter's economic models are presented. These models are very general in character, initially without any specific "third world" characteristics at all. We inspect the completely general case of a unitary state's budget making under various constraints. The constraints modeled are familiar economic ones—the decline in productivity that will ensue if the public sector absorbs labor from the private sector beyond an optimal point and the disincentive to the production of exportables caused by the use of tariffs for raising revenue. Such models tell us that the state may or may not choose optimal levels of public expenditure and taxation. States may behave in a predatory or bureaucracy-maximizing fashion, or they may do neither. These models are highly abstract, and they do not predict behavior, or claim to. They therefore avoid the determinacy and pessimism that Grindle sees as a key characteristic of the NPE.

They are only given a definite interpretation by postulating a link between different strategies of public finance on the one hand and different types of third world states on the other. For this purpose the democracies of the third world are left on one side; the two forms of traditional personal rule (monarchies and dictatorships) are characterized by predatory behavior (or surplus-maximization); and the two forms of authoritarianism (right-wing and left-wing) are identified with the maximization of public sector employment.

This interpretation is not meant to be tautological. Real countries are named as examples of the ideal types of states. Yet somehow the whole construction fails to convince. One problem here is that the typology of states is pulled out of the air. Its criteria of classification are alluded to rather than fully discussed. What is the special significance of states that have a single ruler (monarchies and dictatorships)? A state with a single ruler is not the same as one where the boundary between the ruler's or rulers' patrimony and the public realm is ill defined. Some important distinctions are covered over by the unhelpful use of the word "traditional," a concept from which political sociology is still struggling to recover.

The typology seems to assume that traditional, single-ruler regimes do not have an explicit commitment to national development, while authoritarian regimes of both right and left do. It is unclear, however, in what sense monarchical Saudi Arabia is any less committed to national development than authoritarian Burma. Is this meant to be a matter of words or deeds? The chapter itself explicitly distinguishes between the nondevelopmental dictatorships of Haiti and the Philippines and the developmental dictatorships of South Korea and Taiwan. It does not establish a significant correlation between regime type (excluding democracies) and developmental commitment (Robison 1988: 58). Therefore, the postulated link between regime type and public finance strategy itself becomes suspect.

Even if all countries could be allocated unambiguously to one or another of the boxes of the state typology, a further difficulty would arise. The theory of a link between type of state and its management of public finances is not readily open to empirical testing. Until the optimal level of public spending and taxation can be given an operational definition, excessive extraction of revenue and overspending on public employment cannot be pinned down in the real world.

So has the new political economy told us anything that we did not already know? Public finance is limited by economic constraints; within these constraints, states can do a variety of things, of which n minus 1 are suboptimal; dictatorships are kleptocratic or "star performers in the development field." As a resounding demonstration of the relevance of the new political economy to the developing countries, this does not seem quite sufficient.

PART II

APPLYING THE NEW POLITICAL ECONOMY

Foreign Trade Regimes

It is a commonly observed fact that governments, in pursuing their objectives, often choose policies that from an economist's perspective impose an avoidable welfare cost on society. Several examples can be cited: if the objective is to encourage domestic production of an importable good, the least costly way to achieve it is to offer an appropriate subsidy to production rather than a tariff on imports. But import tariffs or quotas are the policies usually chosen. Similarly, if the objective is to reduce the luxury consumption of an importable, a tax on consumption is the best instrument. Yet tariffs or quotas are used. Generally, when there is a choice between an instrument that achieves the objective using market forces (such as tariffs and commodity taxes) and one that uses government controls (such as quantitative restrictions and administrative allocations), governments often resort to the latter. An interesting analytical problem is to explain such a choice.

This chapter aims to provide a positive, political economy–based theory of why developing country governments do what they do with regard to trade policy, as a preliminary step to formulating normative

I thank Jagdish Bhagwati and Gerald Meier for comments on an earlier draft.

statements about what they ought to do. If one takes a hard-boiled equilibrium view, one sees that political, social, and economic processes jointly determine "equilibrium" values for the set of endogenous variables of these processes. Analytical interest (apart from the traditional concern with exploring the existence, uniqueness, and stability of equilibrium) must be confined in such a view to the comparative statics of the equilibrium when it is unique. That is, the only analytical question is how the unique socio-political-economic equilibrium is affected by shifts in the variables that are exogenous to these processes but influence them. Exogeneity of these shifting variables by definition rules out their being influenced by the processes. If all political variables, especially the choice of policy instruments, are endogenous, it is impossible to ask normative questions about them. In Bhagwati's (1989) terminology this is the Determinacy Paradox.

The paradox is easily illustrated by an example from Bhagwati et al. (1984). Consider a world in which the choice of an import tariff is exogenous to the political process. One can then meaningfully rank alternative levels of the import tariff with respect to their effects on any chosen indicator, such as welfare or output of the protected sector. Suppose now that the tariff rate, instead of being set exogenously (so that in principle it could be set at any level), is a unique equilibrium value determined by a political struggle between protectionist and anti-protectionist forces. Clearly, comparing such an equilibrium tariff rate with other rates is no longer meaningful since none of the latter could emerge as an equilibrium rate. One has to look deeper into the exogenous variables that drive the protectionist and antiprotectionist forces and then examine how a shift in one or more of them could affect the politically determined equilibrium tariff. For example, if the exogenous world price of the imported commodity influences the resources spent by import-competing industries to demand protection from the state and by consumer lobbies to protest protection, then clearly one can do a comparative static analysis of the equilibrium tariff rate, welfare levels, outputs, and employment with respect to changes in the world price. If the political struggle determining the tariff is played according to exogenously set rules of the game (for example, limits on contributions to political campaigns), a comparative static exercise with respect to these rules can be undertaken. As Bhagwati suggests, one may be able to rank alternative institutional arrangements in terms of the desirability of the equilibria they produce if they are exogenous variables. More generally, if a subset of social, political, and economic variables can be exogenously set, one can ask normative questions as to the levels at which they ought to be set. Ranking of institutions is one such question.

The literature on the political economy of foreign trade policies is vast, and I do not attempt here to add much that is original to this impressive literature (see, for example, Magee 1984 and Hillman 1989). Instead I propose to review it selectively from the perspective of trade policies and strategies for developing countries, ignoring issues related to developed countries. I shall also ignore the currently fashionable oligopoly models of trade, whose relevance to developing countries is dubious (Srinivasan 1989). I shall first consider the findings of political economy in situations where some of the policy instruments affecting foreign trade, such as tariffs and quotas, are set exogenously. Then I shall review the consequences of making the choice of the instruments endogenous. The next section will be speculative, attempting to explain from a political economy perspective why particular trade policy instruments were in fact chosen in many developing countries, while others that could just as well have achieved the stated objectives were not. In particular, the revealed preference of policy makers for an inward-oriented import-substitution strategy will be discussed. I shall also briefly look at the principles and rules governing world trade, such as the General Agreement on Tariffs and Trade (GATT), from a political economy perspective. I conclude the chapter with a brief summary of the analysis in the previous sections and draw out its policy implications. The final section will also touch on some simulation results on welfare gains when trade liberalization replaces a rent-seeking situation.

Defining the New Political Economy

The distinguished economic theorist, Frank Hahn, once drew the following distinction between "economics" and "political economy":

> The political economist seeks to understand economic events and arrangements in the framework of a comprehensive social theory, or at least as part of a social totality. . . . The economist, by contrast, sets out to study the "economic" in isolation from the "social" not by ignoring the latter but by taking it as given. . . . there is substance to the complaint that economists have too sparse a description of the constraints under which agents act in society, and too narrow a view of the motives of actions. But if forced, I will choose economics and that for two reasons: first, one can understand what it has to say and second, that it attempts to say only those things which have a chance of being understood. That limits what it can claim to know or do. There are many economists who pretend otherwise. To account for them is a task for political economy (Hahn 1985: 1399).

If indeed political economy is simply pretense at knowing what is not knowable given the tools of economics, it should take its rightful place alongside astrology! Clearly, there is more to political economy: it goes beyond the increasingly untenable position that the sociopolitical framework is a "given" for economic analysis and takes into account the two-way interaction between political and economic systems.

The "new political economy" is often defined as the neoclassical economic theory of politics. This, of course, leaves open the question of what is meant by neoclassical economic theory. I define it narrowly by the axiom that agents behave rationally; that is, they have a consistent set of preferences over the outcomes of their actions, and they choose an action whose outcome is preferable to the outcomes of other actions they find also feasible, given the constraints within which they act. It is natural to extend this postulate to all behavior, including political behavior. Thus agents are assumed to behave rationally, whether they are citizens using available information to form expectations about the future, bureaucrats fighting for turf or distributing publicly created rents, or lobbyists and voters. It is also clear that no other assumption can lead to a meaningful, testable theory, because once the postulate of rational behavior is abandoned, any outcome is a priori possible. After all, whereas rational behavior is narrowly circumscribed, irrational or deviant behavior can take a myriad of forms. In this chapter the term "political economy" will be restricted to analyses that are based on the postulate of rational behavior by all agents in economic and political spheres.

I should also add that I do not find persuasive the distinction attributed by Krasner (1985) to Max Weber, namely, that between "formal rationality," concerned with the efficient use of resources to achieve given goals under a given decision environment, and "substantive rationality," concerned with the choice of goals and environments. After all, the latter has to presume the former if it is to make sense at all. For this reason I reject Krasner's distinction between rational power and metapower, the former being associated with the behavior of states to achieve given goals within a given international regime and the latter with behavior that attempts to change the rules of the international game.

It must also be pointed out that the postulate of rational behavior in all spheres need not lead to a theory of political economy. If, say, (1) each agent's preferences are separable in political and economic outcomes, (2) the set of constraints on political and economic actions also can be separated into two sets, one of which constrains only the political actions and the other constrains only the economic actions, and (3) political actions do not affect economic outcomes and economic actions do not affect political outcomes, then one could analyze the political and economic processes independently of each other.

Another preliminary remark is worth making. The rationality postulate is always to be understood as rational behavior given the knowledge and information available to the agent. This condition also means that the analyst must be specific about what information is private and known only to each agent and what is common knowledge in the technical sense. For example, if the government's constraints and preferences are common knowledge, it cannot announce a policy and expect it to be credible, given rational behavior, if the policy violates a constraint or if the government is known to prefer an alternative feasible policy. The credibility problem is one of the most serious barriers to liberalization of foreign trade policies in many developing countries. The reason is that all agents, particularly those in the private sector, understand that there will be serious short-run adjustment problems with liberalization. If they also correctly perceive that the government does not have the political and economic resources to tackle them, any announced liberalization program will fail because agents will not take the actions consistent with a liberalized trade regime (such as invest in industries hitherto penalized by the restrictive regime or repatriate capital invested abroad) because they do not find the government's commitment to reform credible. The austral plan in Argentina and the cruzado plan in Brazil were expected to fail and did fail because there was no credible way in which the governments could commit themselves to the needed change in public policies.

The postulate of rational behavior given available information obviously rules out irrationality and lack of knowledge or information as explanations for behavior, attributed to governments, that contradicts the normative principles of development economics. However, rational behavior by all agents as a working hypothesis does not preclude the emergence of patently undesirable outcomes as equilibria. Thus if a set of individually rational actions leads to outcomes that are nonoptimal— that is, other outcomes exist that would be considered at least as good, if not better, by all agents—the explanation must lie in an externality (that can arise from a number of reasons including asymmetries in information), the existence of agents with significant power in political and economic markets, or the existence of political or economic structures that have characteristics analogous to those of prisoner's dilemma games. Of course, explanations based on power are inadequate unless they explain not only how the particular distribution of power came about but also how it is being sustained.

Political Economy of Exogenous Trade Restrictions

Consider first the rent-seeking model of import quotas in a small, open economy described by Anne Krueger (1974). Economic analysis based on the traditional two-commodity trade model is illustrated in Figure 5.1. P^* and C^* represent equilibrium levels of production and consumption, respectively, under free trade. The imposition of a quota of CD on

FIGURE 5.1   The Effect of Import Quotas in a Two-Commodity Trade Model

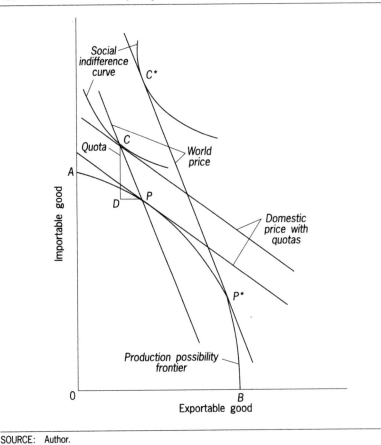

Production possibility frontier

Importable good

Exportable good

SOURCE: Author.

imports of the importable good shifts the production vector from P^* to P and consumption vector from C^* to C. The loss in social welfare caused by the quota is indicated by the shift from a social indifference curve through C^* to a lower one through C. The domestic relative price of the importable increases from that prevailing in the world markets (which equals the common slope of C^*P^* and CP) to a value equal to the common slope of the social indifference curve at C and the production possibility frontier at P. Implicit in this analysis is the assumption that quota rents—that is, the difference between the value of the quota of goods at the domestic price at which it is sold and its value at the world price at which it is bought—are transferred to consumers in lump sums with no resource cost.

The above analysis of course ignores political considerations that Krueger brought to bear. It is very unlikely that import licenses will be auctioned in a competitive market with the resulting revenues distributed to consumers. Rather, import licenses will be administratively allocated so that the quota rent will accrue to the recipient of the allocation. This in turn will provide incentives for importers to attempt to gain the licenses by influencing administrators. If such attempts do not involve any resource costs but merely result in redistribution of quota rents, the results of purely economic analysis remain unchanged, provided we neglect distributional effects. But it is virtually certain that resources have to be spent in seeking the allocation of quota rents. The fundamental insight of Krueger was that resources used this way will not be available for the production of goods and services. This use imposes a welfare loss over and above the primary welfare loss due to the quota that was identified by purely economic analysis. And the cost of this welfare-reducing use of resources identified by insights of political economy may equal the value of quota rents; in other words, rents will be completely dissipated. If the rent-seeking activity is itself competitive, however, any resource used in seeking rents will earn the same return as it does when used in other productive activities. The post-rent-seeking equilibrium is shown in Figure 5.2. The production vector is at P', inside the production possibility frontier, and consumption is at C'. $C'D'$ (equal to CD) represents the import quota. The additional welfare loss due to rent seeking is indicated by the shift in the social indifference curve through C to a lower one through C'.

Bhagwati and Srinivasan (1980) consider the tariff counterpart of Krueger's rent seeking, which they call revenue seeking, in which individuals perceive that the revenues generated by an import tariff are up for grabs and spend resources to get part of it for themselves. The analysis of Bhagwati and Srinivasan shows that the resource-using political scramble for tariff revenues need not always result in an additional welfare loss over and above the primary welfare loss imposed by the tariff and in fact can reduce the latter. Unlike a quantity restriction such as an import quota, a price-based intervention such as a tariff leaves the quantity of imports to be determined by the market. To the extent the diversion of resources to revenue seeking reduces the resources devoted to the production of costlier import substitutes (compared to the situation with tariffs but no revenue seeking), clearly the deadweight loss due to the tariff is reduced. The reduction in the output of import substitutes may even be large enough to bring it below its level under free trade! Thus a tariff that is protective with no revenue seeking may end up disprotecting the import-substituting industry if seeking is present. In such a situation the structure of nominal and effective tariff rates need not have any correlation with the extent of realized protection across sectors.

Krueger (and Bhagwati and Srinivasan for most of their analysis) assume that the entire quota rent or revenue from a tariff will be

---

FIGURE 5.2   The Effect of Import Quotas with Rent Seeking in a Two-Commodity Trade
Model

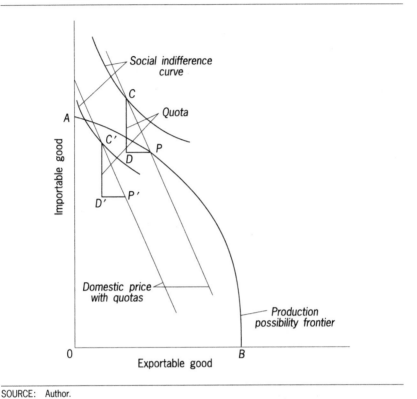

SOURCE: Author.

---

dissipated by competitive seeking activities with free entry. Hillman and Riley (1989) point out that this analysis further assumes that all entrants to seeking activities place the same value on the available rents and are risk-neutral, and the number of potential entrants is sufficiently large to make competitive behavior plausible. Obviously, if the expenditure of resources by a rent seeker does not guarantee his obtaining an import license so that there is some positive probability his expenditure will be wasted, a competitive risk-averse seeker will spend less than a dollar of resources to seek an import license yielding a dollar of rent. Of course, as Hillman and Riley observe, if the rents sought are sufficiently small relative to the seeker's initial wealth, the fall in the marginal utility of wealth in the relevant neighborhood of initial wealth will be negligible, so that the seeker is in effect risk-neutral and will spend close to a dollar to seek a dollar of rent.

If the probability of winning a license by one seeker is a function of the resources spent by his rivals on seeking, so that there is strategic behavior in spending, Tullock (1980) shows that resources spent will be less than the value of the rent. Hillman and Riley, however, quote a result of Hillman and Samet (1987) that reestablishes complete rent dissipation (in the sense that the expected value of resources spent equals the value of rent) in a model where the seeker spending the highest amount wins the right to the rent. They show that if the value placed on, say, an import license is not the same among all seekers and if the highest spender is certain to get the license, only the contenders with the two highest valuations will seek the license and the expected value of their total spending as a ratio of the winner's valuation will equal the ratio of the second highest valuation to the highest. Clearly if the two highest valuations differ substantially, the expected value of resources spent will be much less than the gross rent gained (that is, the valuation of the winner).

In short, the cost of resources spent in seeking may equal or fall short of the rents sought depending on the nature of the mechanism by which the rights to rents are allocated. Since by their very nature seeking activities are often secretive, empirically estimating their cost is extremely difficult if not impossible. To the extent some of the rents are, or have to be, "kicked back" to the bureaucrats and their political masters, the cost of resources spent on seeking will fall short of the rents. Indeed, it has been suggested that in some developing countries with regular elections, the process of allocating governmentally created rights to rents has been used to generate campaign funds for the party in power. Such kickbacks and transfers, while reducing the real resource cost of rent seeking, impose a social cost by subverting the political and administrative process.

In many developing countries non-economic objectives, such as achieving specified output, import, or employment levels that would not occur in a laissez-faire equilibrium, often motivate economic policy interventions. An important insight of political economy is that the presence of competitive seeking with complete dissipation of rents can reverse the conventional ranking of optimal policies to achieve non-economic objectives. For example, in conventional theory a tariff is superior to a production subsidy or a consumption tax in restraining imports to the desired level (Bhagwati and Srinivasan 1969). With competitive revenue seeking, however, the superiority of the tariff need not hold (Anam 1982). As Anam points out, in addition to the distortion created by a tax (such as a consumption tax or a tariff), revenue seeking introduces another distortion by diverting resources from production. The second distortion, however, can attenuate or augment the deadweight loss of the first distortion depending, inter alia, on the nature of the tax. Thus the ranking of optimal policies based on the combined effects of the two distortions can differ from that based only on the first.[1]

Rent- and revenue-seeking activities need not necessarily violate or evade any laws and are often legal. Exogenously imposed policy interventions, however, such as tariffs and quotas also induce illegal activities such as smuggling. Smuggled imports by definition evade tariffs and, because they are not included in officially recognized imports, are not subject to quotas. Bhagwati and Hansen (1973) provided an early analysis of tariff-induced smuggling, followed by Falvey's (1978) analysis of quota-induced smuggling. In the Bhagwati-Hansen model, smuggling to evade an import tariff need not improve welfare. On the one hand smuggled imports cost more than legal imports (at world prices), but on the other hand they are cheaper than domestic import substitutes at domestic tariff-inclusive prices. Therefore, in an equilibrium in which smuggled imports completely replace legal imports, the net change in welfare with smuggling can be either positive or negative, depending on whether the gain due to reduced domestic production of costly import substitutes is more or less than the terms-of-trade loss on smuggled imports compared with legal imports. Anam (1982) shows that with revenue seeking present in the tariff equilibrium this ambiguity disappears. Smuggling improves welfare over the tariff equilibrium with revenue seeking.

A point relevant for policy in developing countries emerges from the above discussion: there is an asymmetry between price-based interventions and quantitative restrictions (QRs) when seeking activities are present. Since QRs are used more commonly than tariffs in these countries, this asymmetry is important to note. As stated by Bhagwati and Srinivasan (1982), whenever the exogenous intervention that triggers seeking activity is the only distortion in the economy, and it is a pure quantitative restriction that remains binding in the presence of seeking, there can be no welfare improvement over the equilibrium with no seeking. If the triggering distortion is a price distortion, however, seeking activity can raise welfare. Since import quotas, rather than import tariffs, are the preferred means of intervention in foreign trade in many developing countries, the above results suggest that rent-seeking activities triggered by such quotas will only exacerbate the welfare loss due to the quotas.

Yet another asymmetry between quantity restrictions and price distortions arises with respect to the shadow prices for primary factors. These prices, representing the social value of the factors, are used in the evaluation of development projects. In the absence of seeking activities, the shadow prices of factors are their market prices if the distortion is a quota but not if it is a tariff. This is because a binding quota turns an open economy into a closed economy at the margin, and therefore the marginal value of an additional unit of a factor is its domestic market reward in the absence of any other distortion. If seeking is present, however, the shadow factor price equals the market price only if the triggering distortion is a price distortion. The reason is once again straightforward. With competitive revenue seeking and complete dissipation of revenues, domestic consumption expenditure equals national income at factor cost, and the relative prices faced by the consumers equal the tariff-inclusive prices. As long as the tariff rates do not change, the commodity prices will not change, nor will the market prices of factors as determined by the commodity prices. Therefore, a marginal increase in the availability of a factor affects welfare only through its effect on national income at factor cost. With unchanged factor prices, this effect is simply the market price of the factor.

Policy Choice and the Political Process

At least since the days of mercantilism, if not earlier, policy making with respect to foreign trade has been heavily influenced, if not completely determined, by the political process. Since policies that hurt no one and help at least some are rare, there will be some gainers and some losers associated with any policy. It is natural to look to the relative political strengths of gainers and losers in explaining the observed policy choices. Sometimes, of course, faith and ideology, rather than the balancing of political strengths of interest groups, may be the dominant factors in the choice of a particular policy (for a discussion of the roles of interest groups and ideology in the repeal of corn laws in Great Britain in 1846 see Irwin 1989). Be that as it may, analytical modeling of foreign trade and of the political process that determines the choice of trade policies has been influenced by the interest-group approach to politics.

In the standard two-factor, two-commodity Heckscher-Ohlin-Samuelson model, it follows from the Stolper-Samuelson theorem that a rise in the domestic price of a commodity, for example through an import tariff or an export subsidy, raises the real reward of the factor that is used intensively in its production and lowers that of the other. Thus if capitalists supply no labor and workers own no capital, the interests of capitalists and workers will be in conflict with respect to the imposition of a tariff. But in the real world, the lobbying for or against a tariff is often industry-based rather than class-based. This led to the formulation of the so-called specific-factor model. In its simplest version, two goods (agricultural and manufactured) are produced using three factors: land, which is used only in agriculture; capital, which is used only in manufacturing; and labor, which is used in both. It can be shown, for example, that protecting agriculture will raise the real reward of landowners while the reward of labor will go up in terms of manufacturing and fall in terms of agriculture. Likewise, protecting manufacturing will raise the real reward of capitalists, and the reward of labor will again be ambiguous. If in the consumption basket of workers, manufacturing figures more prominently, then clearly protection to agriculture will raise the real consumption wage. Therefore, owners of both factors employed in agriculture, labor and land, will be interested in agricultural protection. By identifying agricultural goods as pure wage goods and manufactured goods as including capital goods, Jones (1971) uses this model to show how protection to manufacturing in the United States would raise both the real wage and real interest rate (defined as the ratio of rental price of capital to the price of manufactured goods) compared with, say, Britain, which had access to the same technology but did not protect either sector. Although Jones clarified a debate among economic historians of the United States with this result, he did not delve deeply into the political process.

Findlay and Wellisz (1982) took the next step of explicitly modeling the political lobbying process with the level of protection (in this case, a tariff) as outcome and with production described by the specific-factor model of Jones. They assume that labor remains passive while landowners lobby for, and capitalists against, a tariff on imports of agriculture. Each of these groups hires labor for its lobbying activities, and the level of the tariff increases at decreasing rates as the lobbying labor hired by landowners increases and decreases at increasing rates as lobbyists hired by capitalists increase. The model, if it is interpreted as depicting the steady state of the society, implies that labor hired for lobbying has to be employed in that activity forever if the tariff level is to remain unchanged. Be that as it may, the authors adopt the Cournot-Nash equilibrium concept for determining the extent of lobbying by each group. Since this is a model in which the economic variables (outputs, factor prices, factor employments, commodity prices) and political variables (the tariff, labor employed in lobbying) are determined in a politico-economic equilibrium, the question of trade liberalization or reform does not arise. Interestingly, the tariff level in the political equilibrium could be zero, meaning that there is free trade in commodities. Yet welfare in this economy will be unambiguously lower than in an otherwise identical economy where a free-trade policy is exogenously specified rather than the equilibrium outcome of a resource-using political process.

There is a basic conceptual difference between the deadweight loss imposed by lobbying for rents from an exogenously imposed quota and the welfare cost of lobbying in the Findlay-Wellisz model. One could argue that in the former case, there could in principle be other ways of allocating the quota than those that trigger lobbying activities, while in the latter the lobbying is an aspect of a "pluralist democracy of checks and balances between interest groups," as Findlay and Wellisz view it.

If a democratic system of this type—that is, one in which different groups with legitimate interests are free to organize and lobby in their own behalf—is in itself of social value, then the material welfare cost of lobbying has to be balanced against it.

It would appear that there can be no systemic value to the rent seeking associated with a quota. However, to the extent the allocation system is not based on competitive rent seeking but is instead used covertly by the politicians in power to generate income for themselves or for their party, it can be argued that open and competitive rent seeking may have a systemic value in preventing covert abuse of political power. Of course, this view cannot be taken seriously since an open auction of a quota is a feasible option that avoids rent seeking and political corruption. It has been suggested that in economies such as that of the USSR or India, where administrative allocation of inputs to users is dominant, the reallocation of such inputs from the initial recipients to others through gray markets improves the efficiency of their use. This efficiency gain, however, will occur even in a world of rent seeking, because those who obtain the rights to rents from an allocated input will obviously maximize their rents by selling to those who will pay the highest price for it, thereby ensuring the efficiency of its use. Thus the issues of to whom the rent accrues and whether he or she has to spend resources for the rights to rent must be sharply distinguished from the efficiency of use of the commodity whose allocation creates the rent.

Unlike the models with exogenously set quotas or tariffs and complete dissipation of quota rents or tariff revenues through seeking, the Findlay-Wellisz model shows that as long as the equilibrium tariff is positive, some tariff revenue is available and assumed to be returned to consumers in a lump-sum fashion. Feenstra and Bhagwati (1982) postulate that a benign government will judiciously use part of the revenues to improve welfare by buying off the relevant interest group through an appropriate income subsidy, thereby changing the extent of its protectionist lobbying in the context of a fall in the world price of imports competing with domestic production. They recognize that it may seem strange that the same government on the one hand responds to protectionist lobbying and on the other tries to maximize welfare by trying to offset lobbying pressure. But they point out that in a multibranch government the legislature is likely to be protectionist while the executive will be in favor of liberal trade. Their model makes sense in such a context.

Brock and Magee (1978), in a pioneering approach, used a partial equilibrium game-theory model with two (pro- and anti-tariff) lobbies and two political parties to generate tariffs endogenously. Each lobby contributed to political parties in order to maximize the income of its clientele, while each party took a stand on tariffs suited to maximizing the probability of its winning election. In a subsequent paper Magee and Brock (1983) used the Findlay and Wellisz model but explicitly brought in two political parties, one proposing an import tariff and the other an export subsidy, each of which tried to maximize the chances of its election.

In the models of Findlay and Wellisz, Bhagwati and Feenstra, and Brock and Magee, the conflict of interest over a tariff arises from differences among groups over ownership of factors. Mayer and Riezman (1987) show that factor ownership differences would lead interest groups to lobby not for trade taxes or subsidies but for output taxes or subsidies. A tariff, being both a production subsidy and a consumption tax at the same rate, yields the desired effect on factor prices but at the same time imposes a gratuitous consumption tax. A production subsidy avoids this. In a later paper Mayer and Riezman (1989) allow individuals to differ not only in factor ownership but also in consumption preferences and income tax treatment, and they show that tariffs may yet emerge as the outcome in the political process, rather than the other tax/subsidy instruments. They do not set up an explicit model of the political process but assume that it satisfies "reasonable restrictions" so that a Pareto-dominated choice of policy instruments (that is, one compared to which there is another that makes everyone better off) will not emerge as the outcome. They show that tariffs may not be Pareto-dominated under certain assumptions about procedural rules of policy making, costs of coalition formation, and signaling of group interests. Thus, with Pareto-dominated outcomes excluded, tariffs, not being dominated, cannot be ruled out as the equilibrium outcome of the political process.

The Choice of Trade Policy Instruments

The analysis of Mayer and Riezman in effect relates the political process determining policies to the ultimate effect of such policies on the welfare of individual voters. I will now turn to the narrow issue of choice among policies directly affecting foreign trade—specifically, quotas and tariffs. Any fruitful approach to trade policy, whether purely economic or politico-economic, has to address why protection takes particular forms when other forms are available. Before I speculate on this, let me describe some characteristics of policy interventions in most developing countries. By and large, quantitative restrictions such as import quotas, export targets, and domestic content requirements, and not price-based measures such as tariffs, have been the preferred modes of protectionist intervention in particular sectors or industries. Further, nonselective macroeconomic policies such as monetary, fiscal, and exchange rate policies have been actively used by only a few developing countries (mostly in Latin America) to address imbalances in trade and payments. In the rest of the world, selective QRs have been used to address macroeconomic imbalances as well. In some countries, such as India, selectivity has been carried to extremes. For example, instead of an overall quota that restricts the imports of an intermediate commodity, each individual enterprise that uses the commodity in its production is awarded a quota.

I will not review here some of the standard economic arguments that might tilt the choice toward QRs, most of which are based on the proposition that quantitative restrictions are not equivalent to price-based allocation in a well-defined sense if the relevant market structures are not competitive or if uncertainty is involved (for example, production of an agricultural good may be affected by uncertain weather). Some more or less plausible but ultimately not very satisfactory political arguments have been offered in the literature to explain why QRs are preferred by policy makers. First, it is argued that the protective effect of a quota is not as transparent to losers from it as that of a tariff, because an ad valorem tariff directly expresses the increase in domestic price over imports while the price effect of the quota is less immediate. This is an implausible argument if it is interpreted as implying that losers will oppose a protectionist quota less than they will a protectionist tariff. What matters to the losers is the price increase they face. Whether a 5 percent rise in price relative to landed costs of an import is due to an ad valorem tariff of 5 percent or some quota specified in physical units is not relevant to the losers' political behavior as long as they associate import restrictions of any kind with a domestic price above world price. Of course, if the choice placed before the voter is between a specified tariff level (in ad valorem terms) or a specified quota level (in physical units), clearly the voter will need additional information about demand and supply functions (and market structure) to translate the quota into a price that can be compared with the tariff inclusive price, and in this case, a tariff is transparent. Rarely are voters asked to exercise such a choice.

The relevant issue is why fully informed policy makers choose QRs as protective instruments so often. Put another way, if it were the case that any of a policy maker's potential outcomes, such as getting re-elected, improving the welfare of the members of his political party, and raising public revenues, can be achieved with some set of tariffs or some set of quotas, and if the policy maker's preferences regarding these outcomes are also defined, then it is clear that the policy maker can achieve these outcomes either by a set of optimal tariffs or by a set of optimal quotas. There is nothing in this model to indicate which is preferable. For a genuine first choice between the two instruments to emerge, either (1) some combination of the relevant outcomes must be reachable by one instrument but not the other, or (2) the policy maker's preferences must depend on both outcomes and instruments (at least their type, if not necessarily their values). Of course, explaining a policy maker's choice of a quota through his preferences for quotas is not a powerful theory.

At first blush, the argument put forward in Hillman (1989) that import quota rights are like assignable property rights, and tariff revenue is generally not easily assignable to specific individuals seems to fit in with condition 1 above. On reflection, however, this is not very convincing. After all, there are many historical cases in which taxing rights have been assigned to individuals (for instance, the zamindari system of land revenue collection in British India). Hillman concludes from the observation that revenues are fungible (and as such, revenues from tariffs are indistinguishable from the general pool of revenues) that assignment of revenues (that is, allocation of public expenditures) has to be contested at the level of overall budget allocations. The fungibility argument can be carried too far. Frequently revenues from particular taxes are assigned or earmarked to particular expenditure categories with no transfer across categories permitted. In any case, a determined government can dispose of revenues in ways that benefit particular groups and not others. Any tax that is levied and collected on the basis of individual assessments (such as the personal income tax) usually allows a wide scope for the growth of individual or class-specific favors and exemptions. By reducing the total revenue from such a tax by an amount equal to the revenue generated from a tariff and manipulating these favors and exemptions to achieve any desired incidence of the reduction, revenues from tariffs or any other taxes can be indirectly assigned. This said, it should be added that assigning quotas is likely to be less cumbersome and costly than assigning tariff revenues. Ironically, this ease of assignment may make the distributional effects of quota rents transparent!

The most telling criticism against the property rights view of quotas is that it is in effect no different from a revenue assignment scheme, since it is equivalent to first auctioning the quota rights in a competitive market and then assigning the revenues so generated. If agents in the economy are well informed and rational, as we assume in political economy models, they certainly would perceive this equivalence. If they do, so will rational policy makers. As such, quotas will not have any differential advantage of assignment over tariff revenues.[2]

It is argued that some forms of protection, such as "voluntary export" restrictions (VERs), are chosen over import quotas or steep tariffs because quotas violate GATT articles, and tariffs, once bound in GATT, cannot be raised. This is not the occasion to discuss the fascinating political economy aspects of VERs. Suffice it here to say that this argument is irrelevant in the case of developing countries, since they have been exempted from many of the GATT disciplines.

Another version of the transparency argument is the "optimal obfuscation principle" of Magee et al. (1989). They argue that a policy instrument that obfuscates the identity of its ultimate gainers from the losers yields political benefits by blunting opposition. Because it usually has a higher deadweight loss, however, it has political costs as well. The policy instrument that balances the political benefits and costs at the margin obfuscates to the optimal degree. Although this is an ingenious argument, it does not necessarily suggest that a quota rather than a tariff is always the optimally obfuscating policy instrument. Further, it presumes that obfuscation can be successfully carried out. This assumption is not plausible in a model with rational agents, for, as argued earlier, the lack of transparency of one policy instrument as contrasted with another is not an informational asymmetry arising out of information privately held or signals privately received. It is hard to imagine that rational agents are incapable of informing themselves about the distributional effects of one type of instrument (quotas) but are fully capable with respect to another (tariffs). If the argument is phrased in terms of the cost of acquiring information, it is not clear why the needed information about quotas is consistently more costly to acquire, such that they are chosen as trade restrictions regardless of the characteristics of the commodity imported, the economic and political structure of the countries, and their stage of development. Finally, the obfuscation story is likely to be relevant, if at all, only to the few developing countries with representative governments.

It is often suggested that a quota achieves the intended reduction in imports more quickly and with more certainty than a tariff. The implicit assumption behind the alleged slowness of a tariff must be that the price elasticity of import demand is low in the short run. If this is the case, it means only that a high tariff will be needed to achieve a reduction in imports in the short run. Also, achieving a reduction in the quantum of imports with certainty is not equivalent to achieving a reduction in the value of imports with certainty, if world prices of imports are uncertain.

In the burgeoning literature on the political economy of economic liberalization and its sequencing, the view that policy interventions in developing countries have created "property rights" that are hard to change is common. For example, Lal (1987) argues that such politically created property rights for various groups, including a significant portion of "the bureaucracy, public sector functionaries, [and] industrial labour," are financed by implicit or explicit taxation of the general populace. Sooner or later the financing becomes increasingly difficult, either because large-scale tax evasion and capital flight become serious or because Ricardian rents from the exploitation of natural resources that sustained public spending run out. This view, although it is empirically well supported, does not explain why particular policy instruments are chosen to create property rights in the foreign trade sector. It does not explain why, given fungibility, natural resource rents are different from any other item of revenue in the public budget. All it suggests is that members of some groups (the general populace in Lal's example) are endowed with little political power individually and find it too costly for reasons elaborated by Mancur Olson (1965) to organize collectively to resist other groups until the burdens imposed on them become too heavy. Even then they largely take the Exit rather than the Voice option, to use Hirschman's (1970) terminology, by evading taxes and engaging in capital flight rather than voicing their protests through political action. Of course, political action is not completely ruled out, as street riots in many countries testify.

The Choice of a Development Strategy

It is now widely accepted that in the years immediately following the Second World War the thinking about development was very much influenced by the disastrous experience of a deep depression, defaults on international debt, beggar-thy-neighbor trade policies, and the collapse of trade volumes between the two world wars. Development economists and policy makers did not anticipate rapid growth in world trade, nor did they expect a significant flow of long-term development capital from the financial centers to the developing countries. They therefore identified the shortage of domestic savings and of foreign exchange as the two key constraints on development. This idea, coupled with the belief that there was a long-term secular decline in the terms of trade of primary product exports, led policy makers to choose industrialization through import substitution (IS) as a development strategy. Economists also held that externalities, indivisibilities, and economies of scale were pervasive in the process of development. Markets, therefore, could not be relied on to bring about an efficient allocation of resources, and state intervention in the economy and comprehensive planning were necessary. More important, the perceived success of Soviet planning in rapidly industrializing a backward agricultural economy in a short span of less than four decades influenced policy makers such as Prime Minister Nehru of India to opt for planning. Of course the colossal human and material cost of the Soviet system became evident only later. Thus, given the information then available, one could plausibly argue that the choice of an inward-oriented dirigiste strategy was rational. By the early 1960s, however, it was increasingly clear that world trade had grown at an unprecedented rate after the end of the

war and that import-substitution efforts, far from alleviating the perceived foreign-exchange shortage, had in fact worsened it, for the newly
established industries depended on imports of raw material, equipment, and spares. And Soviet-style planning without a Soviet-style polity was infeasible. Above all, dirigisme, instead of correcting market
failures, led to government failures. Thus from an economic perspective
the dirigiste IS strategy was not yielding the expected results. Why then
did only a few countries (such as South Korea) shift away from import
substitution? Is there a political explanation?

Krasner (1985) embeds the choice of development strategy in the
larger context of the role of developing countries in the international
economic system and the now dead (though perhaps not yet cremated)
demand for a New International Economic Order (NIEO). In his view,
the emergence of a large number of resource-poor, independent nation-
states since the end of the Second World War

> has led to tensions between the material power capabilities of individ-
> ual actors and major international regimes. The most important re-
> gimes governing international economic transactions are infused with
> liberal, market-oriented principles whose consequences can exacerbate
> the political vulnerabilities of many countries of the South. The basic
> objective of the New International Economic Order program has been
> to establish new rules of the game that would legitimate authoritative
> allocation by states acting directly to distribute goods, or indirectly to
> limit the right to alienate private property. This can be accomplished
> either by legitimating national regulation or by creating or transform-
> ing international institutions. This agenda is not rooted in transitory
> ideological preferences, irrational hatred of former colonial masters,
> economic ignorance, or miscalculation of the material consequences of
> existing or proposed regimes. Rather, it reflects enduring political real-
> ities grounded in the international and domestic weaknesses of almost
> all Third World countries (p. 267).

Krasner's analysis leads him to conclude that the most important
motivation of the developing countries is "to reduce vulnerability by
supporting principles, norms, and rules that legitimate authoritative
allocation, rather than market-oriented allocation. . . . Only very large
Third World states, or those which develop political institutions that
can adjust to the perturbations of the global system, will reconcile
themselves to liberal international regimes" (p. 306). India and China
are classified as large countries that are nearly self-sufficient, and the
East Asian Gang of Four (Hong Kong, South Korea, Singapore, and
Taiwan) and possibly Brazil and Mexico are deemed to have domestic
political and economic institutions that make it possible for them to
adjust to external changes. Krasner's thesis, prima facie, not only is
appealing but also appears to provide a convincing explanation of why

an inward-oriented strategy did not lose many adherents when its economic failures were evident.

Unfortunately this political explanation is problematic in many respects. First of all, an outward orientation in a global liberal trading regime certainly subjects a country to shocks of an external origin as pointed out by Krasner, but at the same time it enables a country to offset shocks of an internal origin. Thus, a small country that cannot influence its terms of trade will face terms-of-trade shocks if it trades with the rest of the world, but it can also absorb any increase in domestic excess demand or supply for a commodity it produces, say due to fluctuations in its output due to weather, by importing or exporting that commodity to the required extent without any change in its price. Thus it is not necessarily the case that greater integration with world markets increases risk. Second, Krasner does not make a sufficiently clear distinction between exogenous and endogenous factors. It is not evident whether the East Asian countries' choice of outward orientation is a result of their greater institutional flexibility for adjusting to external shocks or the choice of outward orientation and hence, outstanding performance with respect to foreign trade, enables them to have easier access to external finance, thereby minimizing the extent of painful domestic adjustment to external shocks. Nor is it the case that large countries are reconciled to a liberal trading regime. Third, an outward-oriented strategy is not equivalent to a laissez-faire strategy, and East Asian countries are by no means shining examples of absence of state intervention and a complete reliance on markets. The important point is that they have avoided grossly distortionary interventions by maintaining an incentive structure that is largely neutral between earning a unit of foreign exchange through exports and saving it through import substitution. Finally, the fact that the East Asian regimes (and Brazil during military rule) are authoritarian is neither here nor there. Genuine representative democracies are pitifully few in the developing world. Thus the case that inward orientation and authoritative, nonmarket allocation reduce the vulnerability to and increase the capability for facing external shocks is rather flimsy.

To sum up the argument thus far, political economy explanations based on rational agents for the adoption of an inward-oriented development strategy and the ubiquitous choice of QRs in developing countries are not completely convincing. Abandoning rationality, however, on the part of some or all agents leads to the unfortunate situation that almost anything can be "explained" at a superficial level, but at a deeper level nothing can. It is evident that the description of political processes in the available political economy models is perhaps much too simple, even simplistic. With a more realistic description of political processes one may yet be able to solve the puzzle of QRs.

GATT and Developing Countries

Let me now turn to two important issues related to GATT that are relevant for developing countries. One is the "differential and more favourable treatment of developing countries" embodied in Part IV and other provisions of GATT. The other relates to the principle of reciprocity and most-favored-nation treatment. The essence of special and differential treatment (SDT) of developing countries is that, first, developed countries will provide more favorable access to their markets to developing countries than they do to each other (through, for example, the generalized system of preferences), and second, the developing countries are exempted from many GATT regulations in their choice of trade policies. In addition, they have used Article XVIII, Section B of GATT to impose QRs for balance-of-payments reasons. Although Article XII contains a similar provision applicable to all signatories, Anjaria (1987) points out that after the mid-1960s industrial countries ceased using this article to impose QRs for balance-of-payments reasons and, in any case, the restrictions on the use of QRs under Article XVIII B are much looser than those under Article XII.

It is clear from the actual performance of the generalized system of preferences that improved market access has not substantially benefited developing countries, in part because the developed countries could choose the commodities to which the preferences would apply and to what extent. More important, the acceptance of SDT as a principle meant that developed countries could get away politically with non-GATT-conforming arrangements, such as the multifiber arrangement governing trade in textiles and apparel, the elimination of which would have been extremely beneficial to developing countries as a group. The case for developing countries participating as full members of GATT in the Uruguay Round of trade negotiations does not depend on whether the developed countries would agree to roll back their own non-GATT-conforming trade policies in return for developing countries giving up SDT. As Martin Wolf (1987) points out, it rests in the fact that first of all it will help liberalization at home in the larger, inward-oriented developing countries, and second, it will help discipline and diffuse protectionist lobbies at home. Thus, if the use of quotas for balance-of-payments reasons cannot obtain GATT blessing as easily as at present, it is likely developing countries will make less use of them and will attempt to use appropriate macroeconomic policy tools to address balance-of-payments problems instead—a change that will be beneficial on other grounds as well. Of course, with less use of quotas, fewer resources will be diverted to lobby for quota rents.

The reciprocity principle underlying past GATT negotiations of tariff reductions is that liberalization of home imports is the price of improved markets for a country's exports. From an economic point of view, of course, unilateral removal of import restriction by a small country is in its interest regardless of what its trading partners do. From a political perspective, however, it is natural to think that one's own tariffs are bargaining chips to be exchanged for a trading partner's reducing his tariffs. Yet, by making reciprocity the cornerstone of GATT, the developed countries sent the strong signal that unless a country has a large enough market so that greater access to it through removal of restrictions would be of interest to other countries, it cannot expect to play a significant role in negotiations. Developing countries were thus led on the one hand to believe that they have no role in GATT, which they viewed as a rich man's club, and on the other to argue that equal treatment of unequals (in terms of development) is unfair and succeeded in obtaining SDT.

It can be argued that reciprocity has the virtue of being likely to move the system toward universal liberal trade. Bhagwati (1989) points out that although it is economically sensible for a country to maintain free trade and to let foreign countries subsidize their exports to itself because it will obtain its imports more cheaply, it can also lead to demands for protection by domestic interests hurt by import competition, thus undermining its free trade policy. Therefore, trading import restrictions against the elimination of export subsidies by foreigners will in this scenario lead to universal free trade. Does this path toward universal free trade, however, necessarily constitute reciprocity? The answer is not obvious.

Moreover, most-favored-nation (MFN) treatment, according to purely economic reasoning, does not make sense. For example, if there are multiple sources of imports (with different supply functions) and if for whatever reason imports are to be restricted, the least-cost way of achieving such a reduction will almost surely not be through a uniform tariff.[3] Some of the egregious departures from the spirit if not the letter of GATT rules, such as voluntary bilateral import restrictions, are also ways of evading the MFN treatment that the use of an import tariff would have entailed. Indeed, it has been proposed in some developed countries that departures from unconditional MFN treatment may be worth considering. Yet from a political economy perspective, abandonment of MFN has unpleasant systemic consequences in that it will open the door for a variety of discriminatory trade practices.

Summary and Conclusions

The arguments in the previous sections can be summarized as follows:

1. Political economy, defined as neoclassical theory of politics, has to base itself on rational behavior of all agents in the

political sphere, just as the bedrock of neoclassical economics is rational behavior in the economic arena. Departure from the rationality assumption leads to an untestable theory.

2. If all political and economic variables are deemed endogenous, with their values determined in a unique politico-economic equilibrium that depends on other factors exogenous to the politico-economic system, then only limited comparative static exercises can be performed as to how a shift in one or more exogenous variables shifts the equilibrium. For a meaningful and normative theory of political economy to emerge, there must be some interdependence between political and economic variables in the preferences or constraints or the technology that associates outcomes with actions, and at least a subset of these variables has to be exogenous.

3. Rent seeking and other directly unproductive profit-seeking (DUP) activities triggered by exogenously specified trade policies can have serious economic and political consequences. Often they impose an added welfare loss to that imposed by the policies themselves. Further, they can reverse the welfare rankings of alternative policies that would obtain in the absence of these activities. There is an important asymmetry between quantitative restrictions on foreign trade and tariffs and other price-based interventions. In the presence of DUP activities, the former will never lead to welfare improvement, whereas the latter can in some situations. Also, whether market prices for factors equal their shadow prices to be used for project evaluation depends both on the nature of the intervention and on the presence or absence of DUP activities.

4. A number of models that endogenize the political process in the determination of trade policies are available. Almost all of them are based on balancing interests of the individuals benefited by a policy with those of the individuals hurt by it. To the extent open and free play of interest groups in the political arena is part of a democratic process that has systemic value, the resources spent by individuals and groups in lobbying for their interests cannot be viewed as wasteful. Although from an economic point of view a tariff is an inferior instrument compared with a production subsidy as a production incentive and with a consumption tax as a consumption disincentive, it can still emerge as the

trade-restricting instrument in a multidimensional political process in a polity with heterogeneous individuals.

5. In most developing countries, quantitative restrictions appear to be the policy instrument most often used. Most of the political economy–based explanations offered for this choice do not appear to be plausible. This choice remains a puzzle.

6. The special and differential treatment for developing countries in the GATT has not significantly benefited them. Their full adherence to the GATT system will help domestic liberalization and act as a check on rapacious rent seeking. While the MFN principle of GATT can be questioned on economic grounds, it has a political virtue of preventing the proliferation of discriminatory trade practice. The reciprocity principle, from an economic point of view, is a vestige of mercantilism. Yet, if it leads to universal free trade, it may be justified on political grounds.

I argued that empirically estimating the cost of resources diverted to rent-seeking activities and hence the benefits of removing incentives to rent seeking is difficult. I will close by pointing to a simulation study of the removal of quantitative restrictions on imports in Turkey by Grais, de Melo and Urata (1986). They use an applied general equilibrium model that allows for the endogenous determination of rent-seeking activity levels in the presence of quantitative restrictions on imports of intermediate goods. They assume that quotas on imports of consumer goods do not lead to rent seeking, and they do not consider revenue-seeking activities triggered by tariffs. Short-run effects are captured by treating sectoral capital stocks as immobile, and the long-run effects by allowing free intersectoral mobility. The effects of the following six policy experiments are simulated:

1. removal of quotas on imports of intermediate goods with fixed sectoral capital

2. same as 1 but with capital mobile across sectors

3. removal of import quotas on consumer and intermediate goods with fixed sectoral capital

4. same as 3 but with capital mobile across sectors

5. same as 3, plus 50 percent tariff reduction across the board

TABLE 5.1   Macroeconomic Results of Six Trade Policy Scenarios in Turkey

Indicator	Base-year value	Policy scenario (ratio to base-year value)					
		1	2	3	4	5	6
Real exchange rate[a]	1.0	1.011	1.045	1.073	1.099	1.124	1.145
Value of imports (millions of TL)[b]							
Consumer goods	25	1.000	1.000	1.232	1.227	1.372	1.393
Intermediate goods	71	0.995	1.035	0.979	1.018	0.995	1.037
Other	25	1.085	1.098	1.085	1.096	1.064	1.062
Total	121	1.014	1.040	1.054	1.078	1.088	1.117
Value of exports (millions of TL)[c]	75	1.024	1.065	1.086	1.126	1.142	1.189
Real GDP (millions of TL)	1,281	1.046	1.052	1.048	1.054	1.049	1.055
Real household consumption (millions of TL)	845	1.035	1.038	1.038	1.042	1.048	1.057
Real investment (millions of TL)	313	1.097	1.112	1.097	1.110	1.073	1.071
Rationing-induced rents (% of nominal GDP)							
On consumer goods	0.6	0.7	0.6	0.0	0.0	0.0	0.0
On intermediate goods	5.4	0.0	0.0	0.0	0.0	0.0	0.0
Real value of imports (% of real GDP)	9.4	9.2	9.3	9.5	9.7	9.8	10.0
Real value of exports (% of real GDP)	5.9	5.7	6.2	6.1	6.3	6.4	6.6

NOTE: TL = Turkish lira.
a. The real exchange rate is defined in terms of the domestic price of agricultural goods.
b. Exclusive of tariffs, at base-year prices.
c. At base-year prices.
SOURCE: Wafik Grais, Jaime de Melo, Shujiro Urata, "A General Equilibrium Estimation of the Effects in Reductions in Tariffs and Quantitative Restrictions in Turkey in 1978," in *General Equilibrium Trade Policy Modeling*, T. N. Srinivasan and J. Whalley, eds. (Cambridge, Mass.: MIT Press, 1986).

6. same as 4, plus 50 percent tariff reduction across the board

The results are given in Table 5.1. A striking feature of the results is that if quantitative restrictions and the associated rent-seeking activities are left untouched, removal of tariffs does not lead to appreciable efficiency gains. Major gains arise from the removal of QRs and rent seeking. Experiment 3, involving the removal of quotas on intermediate and consumer goods and rent seeking, leads to a short-run gain of a 4.8

percent increase in real gross domestic product (GDP). Experiment 5, however, which reduces tariffs across the board by 50 percent as well, leads only to a modest 0.1 percent additional increase in real GDP. This example illustrates the serious consequences of QRs and rent seeking in many developing countries.

Comments

SERGIO DE LA CUADRA

I have no comparative advantage to comment on T. N. Srinivasan's paper from an academic standpoint; therefore, my comments are based on personal experience.

On my flight from Chile to Bogotá, the man sitting next to me told me he had a profitable business exporting shrimp in Ecuador. The exchange rate, however, was not good for his business, because it had not been adjusted as much as the rate of inflation. I asked him about credit policies in Ecuador. He said he had a very good loan, at a subsidized interest rate, from the capital market in Ecuador. Therefore, he added, he was compensated for the poor exchange rate with the subsidized loan. (This man was a Chilean doing business in Ecuador, internationalizing rent seeking.)

The point of this anecdote is that most Latin American economies, and maybe most less-developed countries (LDCs), have not just one distortion, in the trade sector, but many distortions: in the capital market, in the labor market, in the large public enterprises that subsidize some sectors of the economy. We often hear about the political crises when there is an attempt to get rid of subsidies in areas such as transportation, food, and education. With this system of many distortions, we must be very careful when discussing one of them not to ignore the others. It is not easy to get a good estimate of the net benefits of reducing this distortion and that distortion, while maintaining others. We really do not know if we are increasing the net social welfare.

The market for rent seeking is broad, and rents are being sought in many places. Moreover, a rent seeker can get favorable treatment in one area and be punished in another. For example, the farmer can be punished with very low prices for his products (common in the case of LDCs when they import food at subsidized prices under the U.S. PL 480 food aid program), low exchange rates, and no tariffs, making subsidies on food imports extremely high. That farmer is compensated, however, by cheap money through subsidized credits. Combined with high inflation, these subsidies can be fantastic.

Therefore, when the government tells the farmer that a market-oriented policy will provide advantages for him, the farmer is afraid. The government is saying, we are going to increase your prices, and at the same time we are going to get rid of all the subsidies you are receiving. It is not clear to the farmer that he will be better off with the market-oriented policy.

Another implication of this system of many distortions is that there can be a second-best equilibrium. When there is a distortion, some politicians react not by eliminating the distortion but by adding a new one to compensate for it. They create a net of distortions that in some way produces a political equilibrium. This system of distortions in the economy gives rise to rent seeking, subsidies, and taxes. In the end it is difficult to determine the net gain of eliminating any of these distortions.

I think this situation also has important implications for international organizations that recommend liberalizing the market. They ask why the capital market or the labor market is not liberalized, implying that liberalization would solve all the problems in the economy. Liberalizing one market, however, while maintaining distortions in all the other markets, will generate only short-lived success. The probability of a successful liberalization is higher when distortions are reduced in many markets at the same time. With a full package of market-oriented policies, it is not clear what rents are being eliminated and what rents are available. Such a policy is much more confusing for rent seekers. From an economic point of view, it makes more sense because it will lead to a more efficient economic equilibrium.

The rent-seeking approach is useful to understand the sustainability of protectionist policies. But in my opinion it is not sufficient to explain the buildup of protectionism. Why does a government move from a free-market policy to a protectionist position? I would say that the business cycle is important in explaining commercial policies in many LDCs and even in countries such as the United States. As we well know, when the United States is in a recession, the claims for compensatory duties multiply by several times. When an economy is facing a recession, it provides fertile ground for rent seekers. They are less successful when the economy is growing and everything is going well.

What are the main forces of these business cycles in many small economies? The concentrated nature of production and the volatility of terms of trade in small economies make expenditures unstable. So recessions are accompanied by balance of payments crises. I do not know of any country with a balance of payments crisis that does not favor quotas or tariffs. For example, the World Bank did a foreign trade study of about twenty countries, all of whom increased their import restrictions in 1982 (even Chile, the most liberal in the study). This increase was not a response to rent seekers but a reaction to a sharp drop in the terms of trade and a high level of foreign debt.

AUGUSTINE H. H. TAN

T. N. Srinivasan has shown very clearly that creating distortions in the external sector will not compensate for or offset domestic distortions. This idea is well established. Second, he has shown that quantitative restrictions are more damaging than tariffs, conducting much of the analysis in static or comparative static terms. I think it would be more useful to look at the dynamics of the analysis, because certain costs become more evident as one takes a longer-term point of view. What was left out of the calculation of the costs of rent-seeking activities was the diversion of scarce, entrepreneurial talent toward rent-seeking activities. The more control a country has, the more entrepreneurial talent is tied up simply getting past the bureaucracy, obtaining licenses, and lobbying politicians to get things done.

In these comments on T. N. Srinivasan's chapter, I will try to answer two questions posed by Merilee Grindle in her chapter. First, why were these quantitative restrictions (QRs) or tariff restrictions (TRs) imposed in the first place? Second, why are they still there, if the economic arguments against them are so strong?

First of all, Srinivasan assumes the existence of rational actors, but I think we have a problem defining rationality. So far we have presumed that everyone knows what is rational politically and what is rational economically. We can adopt a theory-based vantage point and say, because our theory determines this outcome, anything less than this is irrational. Or we can take an empirical standpoint and say, the facts or the outcomes are such that we define them to be irrational because they are undesirable in some sense. Therefore, we face some difficulty in defining rationality in terms of theory and empirical science.

Let me go on to the economic consequences of smallness, which are related to why the QRs or TRs came about in the first place. Here the chapters in this volume exhibit a curious position. On the one hand, the political model is derived from big countries like the United States. On the other hand, the economic models are derived from small countries, whose terms of trade are given and which can do nothing about the international economic order. So how do we resolve these two sets of models?

In terms of political consequences, many people, especially in the United States, do not realize the reduced degrees of freedom that small countries offer. In Singapore, there is only one city-state. If you don't like Singapore, there is nowhere else to go. In America, if you don't like Chicago you can move to New York City. In other words, the sheer size of countries offers greater political freedom, which is not easily available in a small country.

What are some of the important economic consequences of smallness? First, the terms of trade are given. This means that TRs or QRs hurt the economies that impose them; hence, unilateral reduction is beneficial regardless of what happens to the trading partners. In addition, adjusting to shifts in terms of trade requires great internal flexibility, which may not be present. Finally, domestic costs, if they are not carefully watched, can erode competitive advantage. One can see this in runaway wages, runaway prices, and inappropriate interest rates.

The second consequence of smallness is that the law of large numbers does not operate, which implies straightaway that perfectly competitive markets will not prevail. There is a much stronger tendency for monopolies to emerge in small countries than in large countries. This tendency will necessitate, for better or worse, government intervention in the form of regulation.

The third point is that small countries can only realize economies of scale through international trade. At the same time, they face the risk of overspecialization in terms of industry, products, and markets.

Fourth, small countries need flexibility to respond not only to shifts in terms of trade, but also to shifts in international demand.

Fifth, small countries tend to be more dependent upon foreign investment, foreign technology, and foreign markets.

Sixth, small countries cannot readily devalue their currencies, because the real wage rate is immediately affected.

Finally, small countries have no sheltered domestic market to experiment with and to absorb the overhead costs in developing and producing finished goods. Hence, such countries have a greater comparative advantage in industrial products than in finished goods. Furthermore, the cost of a mistake for a small economy is much greater. A miscalculation can have colossal effects.

The smallness of these countries is not usually properly appreciated. As a result, policy makers make faulty assumptions about their country's potential monopoly power in international trade or about the size of the internal market. In many countries with large populations, policy makers think their internal market is large. Therefore, they believe a policy of import substitution will be successful. Their countries, however, do not have adequate purchasing power. Likewise, many countries that export primary commodities have the mistaken notion that they have monopoly power. They may have it in the short term, but it is easily eroded over the long term. These countries may also face retaliation.

The role of ideology has been left out in many of these chapters. Keynes stated that policy makers tend to be "the slaves of some defunct economist." Certainly, when we try to look at why or how QRs or TRs came about in many of these developing countries, we have to look at the intellectual climate in the late 1940s and early 1950s. There was export pessimism, especially after the Korean War, when commodity prices were declining. There was great concern at the United Nations and other organizations about the terms of trade and the over-specialization of developing countries in one or two primary commodities. At the same time, developing countries had a great desire for economic independence upon acquiring political independence. (A certain degree of xenophobia came with the eviction of the colonial powers). In addition, many developing country policy makers attended universities that supported import substitution and central planning. They came back to their country imbued with those ideas, and it is not surprising that such policies were implemented. At the same time the General Agreement on Tariffs and Trade (GATT) rules permitted developing countries to impose QRs and TRs for balance of payments and developmental reasons. The developed countries also tolerated what the developing countries were doing. They did not require reciprocity, for the simple reason that so many developing countries were insignificant on the world stage in terms of shares of export markets, especially in manufacturing. So the developing countries were ignored or allowed to do as they pleased.

Furthermore, we must not forget that bureaucrats have a propensity to control and to regulate. There is a power imperative and a rent-seeking imperative. I think economists tend to focus on the rent-seeking imperative and political scientists on the power imperative. Put the two together, and you see a very powerful propensity toward QRs rather than tariffs or pricing measures.

The export orientation successes of the newly industrializing countries would not have been possible without an expanding world economy dominated by the United States. As the key shock absorber in the system and the largest free market, the United States enabled these countries to become export oriented. Out of n countries, no more than n minus 1 can be export oriented. The United States happened to be the nth country, which did not care much about its balance of payments. Therefore, countries like Singapore could be export oriented. The United States was also the source of capital, technology, and economic aid.

The question now is, are we in a second period of export pessimism, similar to that of the 1950s, in which protectionism is rising and the United States is increasingly unwilling and unable to be the shock absorber for the international system? Can we persuade other countries that are import substituting to consider outward-looking strategies?

Next, I would like to comment on economic liberalization. We should not forget that liberalization can be very traumatic and that societies and people cannot adjust more than a small amount at a given time. At the same time, policies cannot succeed if large portions of the population are simultaneously affected. Some years ago Singapore had a policy called the graduate mothers program. The government was concerned that there were many women university graduates who were not marrying, and those who married were having few children. The government tried to set up incentives for the graduate mothers, giving them preferential treatment in, for example, the allocation of schools. This raised a great outcry among the nongraduate mothers. During an election campaign I met a nongraduate, pregnant woman who said, "I will show the prime minister that I can produce a genius." Policy makers must be careful politically, then, not to affect too many people at the same time. Finally, and most important, economic liberalization leads to demands for political liberalization. This pattern, which we see occurring in China, can suddenly constrain economic liberalization, if there are serious barriers to political liberalization.

When we talk about rent seeking, I believe we need a theory of corruption that deals with the disposal of the ill-gotten gains. I ask myself, why are there so many countries in which corruption is prevalent, and why is it that some countries decline economically and others, like Japan, are still doing well despite the corruption? I have a tentative hypothesis. First of all, I think there is a tolerable value-added tax that corrupt officials can levy. Its level differs among societies. Second, and more important, is the use of that tax or the ill-gotten gain. Does it go to conspicuous consumption or investment? If investment, is it invested locally or abroad? I think the problem with Ferdinand Marcos in the Philippines was not only that much of his wealth went to conspicuous consumption, which irritated a lot of people, but also that much of it was remitted abroad rather than being reinvested within the country. Thus, the cost of corruption can be minimized if rent seekers and those who are corrupt can be put within certain regulations requiring that (a) they do not consume too much of it and (b) they have a healthy reinvestment rate in their own country. Of course the best solution is to have no corruption at all!

Furthermore, in Chapter 9 Stephan Haggard makes the important point that the analyses of rent-seeking activities have nothing to say about fiscal outcomes and overall macroeconomic policy. Yet rent-seeking activities can worsen the fiscal imbalances, necessitating additional taxes, the printing of money, or borrowing from abroad.

My final point is that our assumption of rationality does not help us explain outcomes like depressions, hyperinflation, and revolution. Do we not need some catastrophe theory that can predict some of these outcomes and deal with them? The rent-seeking model operates on the basis of human greed. When human greed is taken to excess, it has very wild and unpredictable results, which we cannot even fathom. We claim to be able to predict everything, but in reality we must make room for uncertainty.

Land Reform

It is well known that agriculture is subject to a high degree of government intervention in its product and input markets. A general tendency for countries to shift, as they develop, from a policy of exploiting agriculture by such means as export taxes, marketing boards, and overvalued exchange rates to a policy of protecting agriculture by means of border protection as well as direct production and export subsidies has been identified and analyzed in terms of the theory of public choice or the economics of politics (Johnson 1973; Schultz 1978; Bale and Lutz 1981; Anderson and Hayami 1986; World Bank 1982, 1983, 1986). Economists have thoroughly documented the inefficiency and inequity caused by those policy interventions and by

An earlier version of this paper was presented at the International Rice Research Institute Saturday Seminar (August 4, 1988). It reports a part of the research conducted at the Agricultural Policy Research Program, University of the Philippines at Los Baños, under the support of the Winrock International Institute for Agricultural Development. All results of the research are compiled in Hayami, Quisumbing, and Adriano (1990). The author gratefully acknowledges collaboration of M. A. Quisumbing and L. S. Adriano, and comments and encouragement from C. C. David, K. Otsuka, and A. M. Tang.

the pervasive accompanying rent-seeking activities in the markets for agricultural products, fertilizer and other cash inputs, and credit (Bates 1981; Adams, Graham, and von Pischke 1984; World Bank 1986; Hayami 1988). There has been relatively little investigation, however, into the causes and effects of government interventions in the markets for agricultural land and labor. In developing economies, intervention in the land and labor markets mainly takes the form of land reform laws and regulations concerning landholdings and tenancy contracts. This chapter aims to shed light on the problems of land reform, which have hitherto been characterized predominantly by ideological discussions in the framework of "traditional political economy," and on the positive theory of "new political economy," drawing mainly on the Philippine experience.

During the early post–World War II years, the governments of newly independent developing nations and foreign aid agencies developed a great enthusiasm for redistributive land reform.[1] A widely held belief then was that the transfer of land to the tillers and tenancy contracts favoring tenants were preconditions not only for attaining an acceptable degree of equity but also for raising productivity in the dominant agricultural sector.[2] Their enthusiasm was fueled by the initial experiences with land reform in Japan and Taiwan.

Subsequent land reform attempts for other countries, however, were repeated failures. Disillusioned national governments and aid agencies shifted the focus of their rural development programs from land reform to other policy measures, such as the integrated rural community development programs and the development of seed-fertilizer technology. Yet the traditional model of land reform survived in the minds of policy makers, and their enthusiasm revived periodically whenever political crises escalated to such an extent that support from the peasantry became desperately needed. During crisis situations, when the ruling order had to compete with radicals and revolutionaries for the support of landless peasants, politicians found it impossible to disregard the magic slogan "land to the tillers." Since it did not introduce fundamental changes in the political market, however, land reform continued to have only limited success. The enthusiasm of politicians usually diminished as soon as the crisis showed signs of receding, often leaving the program with useless plans or adding more regulations to the already complicated and unenforceable reform laws.

A typical example is the history of Philippine land reform. The Philippines inherited from the Spanish colonial regime highly skewed distributions of both land ownership and operational holdings, with the coexistence of small peasant farms and large plantations in the countryside. Such an agrarian structure is rare in Asia and is somewhat similar to those in Latin American countries. Widespread tenancy and a large number of agricultural laborers working in the plantations have led to sharp class confrontations in the Philippine rural sector. To reduce agrarian unrest, successive administrations have tried land reform repeatedly, from the first President Manuel Quezon (1935–1944) to the authoritarian regime of Ferdinand Marcos (1965–1986). The reform programs grew stronger during periods of political crisis, such as in the early postwar years when the economy was threatened by the Hukbalahap (or Huk) revolt and in the 1970s when the country was under martial law. It is fair to say that, in terms of its scope and coverage, Philippine land reform has surpassed most other land reforms in South and Southeast Asia. Yet the reform efforts have been far short of the country's needs, as attested to by the intensified insurgency problem in recent years.

Land reform has revived once again as a highly controversial political issue under the Aquino government, which was installed after the February 1986 "revolution" that ended the twenty-year reign of Ferdinand Marcos. A compelling goal of the new administration has been to restore the social and political stability conducive to private investment and economic growth, without which unemployment and social unrest will continue to deteriorate in a vicious circle. Like past administrations, this government envisions land reform as a means of reducing rural poverty and inequality, thereby minimizing agrarian unrest. After a series of heated debates in the Philippine legislature, Republic Act No. 6657, known as the Comprehensive Agrarian Reform Law, passed and was approved by President Corazon Aquino on June 10, 1988.

The success of the new land reform program in the Philippines, as in any country, will hinge on whether or not its design takes account of the political market reality existing in the country. Programs based on ideological preconceptions or wishful thinking and grounded on the unduplicable success of other countries are likely to be impractical or, if implemented, to produce more negative than positive consequences, especially for rural poverty and inequality.

This chapter intends to search for a new paradigm of land reform that will provide the basis of a program design that is feasible and yet effective in reducing rural poverty and inequality, taking into account the existing political market conditions. For this task, the Philippine experience will be used as a highly relevant illustrative case.

In the following, a model of the political market for land reform is developed to determine the source of failure in past land reform programs. This is followed by identification of the basic contradictions in the traditional model of land reform applied to developing countries in Asia in achieving the dual goals of efficiency and equity. Finally, a new design of land reform is suggested for solving the contradictions under existing political market conditions.

Source of Failure of Past Land Reform Programs

As aptly defined by Alain de Janvry (1981: 264), postwar land reform in the noncommunist third world is "an institutional innovation promoted by the ruling order in an attempt to overcome economic or political contradictions without changing the dominant social relations." It attempts to redistribute property rights on land without changing the basic configuration of the social system and power structure. Although the reform may be beneficial to the ruling elites in general, partly because it assures the continued safety of both their lives and their properties and partly because it spurs economic growth as a result of the political stability that ensues, it is natural for individual landed elites to be free riders in the Mancur Olson (1965) sense by taking maximum efforts to evade reform programs. Given the concentration of wealth and power in the landlord class on the one hand, and the "soft state" defined by Gunnar Myrdal (1968) as a political and administrative system based on personal connection and nepotism on the other, it was inevitable that the reform patterned after the experience of Japan and Taiwan has not been able to achieve the intended goal but rather has produced negative consequences: "Tenants have been evicted, sometimes beaten, their lives have been disrupted, sometimes ended, and they have watched the opportunities for sharecropping dry up and security guarantees from landlords disappear in the train of tenancy reform" (Herring 1983: 48).

What had been overlooked are the major differences between the social and political conditions of the East Asian countries (Japan, South Korea, and Taiwan) and those of other developing countries that severely limit the likelihood of reproducing the land reform experience of the former in the latter. It should be recalled that Japan's reform was executed under the authority of U.S. occupation forces, when the power and confidence of the ruling elites were at their lowest ebb as the result of the great defeat. The reform in South Korea was carried out during the crisis of aggression and destruction by the North. In the case of Taiwan, the reform was enforced by the Nationalist government, which was exiled from mainland China and was therefore alienated from the island's indigenous landed interests. Equally important in these countries was the existence of a relatively well-disciplined bureaucracy coupled with the reservoir of well-documented and accurate data on land ownership and tenure relations accumulated since long before World War II. In addition, Japanese tenants had learned from their long history

FIGURE 6.1   A Model of the Political Market for Land Reform

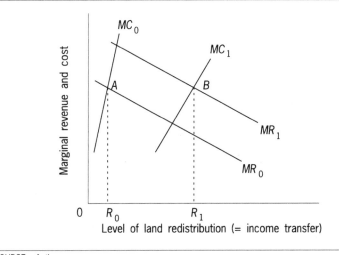

SOURCE: Author.

of cooperativism and tenant unionization how to organize and represent themselves as a unified force. Thus, the success of land reform in Japan and Taiwan was based on the favorable conditions of demand for and supply of that particular institutional innovation in the political market, a situation that has rarely existed in the world's historical experience. It is, therefore, counterproductive to blame a lack of political will for the failure of land reform in other countries without first considering the differences operating in these countries' political markets.

In terms of the economic theory of politics in the tradition of Anthony Downs (1957), James Buchanan and Gordon Tullock (1962), and Albert Breton (1974), the demand for and supply of land reform policies may be seen as the schedules of marginal revenue and marginal cost that political entrepreneurs or leaders expect from programs to redistribute the property rights on land. Figure 6.1 is a model of how the level of redistribution is determined in the political market. In this figure, the horizontal axis represents the level of effective land redistribution, measured by the total income transferred to landless tillers (tenants and agricultural laborers) as a result of land redistribution or tenancy regulations. It should be noted that the income transfer to landless tillers is not equal to the income transfer from landlords, because a part of income deprived from landlords may be dissipated through inefficient resource allocations resulting from government interventions into land and labor markets as well as the rent-seeking activities of reform officials and politicians (Buchanan, Tollison, and Tullock 1980; Tollison 1982). Therefore, increases in the coverage of reform programs over areas, target groups (for example, agricultural laborers in addition to tenants), and property rights to be distributed (for example, from rent control to redistribution of full ownership titles) will, in theory, increase the total income transfer to landless tillers but may not do so in practice if the increased coverage, with more complicated rules and regulations, reduces administrative feasibility and stimulates rent-seeking activities.

The vertical axis represents the marginal gain and the marginal loss that national political leaders expect to incur if they raise the level of redistribution by one additional unit. If we follow Downs (1957) in assuming parliamentary democracy, the gain may be measured by the expected increase in the number of votes in support of the political leaders from the group demanding for reform policies, while the loss may be measured by the expected decrease in votes from the opposition group. More generally, the marginal revenue and the marginal cost curves in Figure 6.1 (MR and MC) may be seen as the schedules of marginal increase and decrease of the probability of staying in office expected by the political leaders, based on expected gains and losses in political support from various interest groups, whether the political framework is democracy or not.

It would be reasonable to assume that the marginal revenue curve is downward-sloping because the intensity of support (including revolt and insurgence) is likely to diminish at a high level of redistribution, while the resistance is likely to multiply, resulting in the upward-sloping marginal cost curve. The subjective equilibrium of maximum expected profit (revenue minus cost) for politicians will be established at the intersection of the marginal revenue and the marginal cost curves.

The effectiveness of reform programs, as measured by the total income transfer to tillers, depends on the factors that determine the locations of these two curves. Essentially, their locations are determined by the power and effort of the groups demanding and opposing the reform. The group demanding reform consists of not only the rural landless, but also urban business and middle-class people seeking social stability and expansion of rural markets for urban goods and services. Landed interests, including not only landlords but also their clients, such as estate managers and overseers, constitute a strong opposition group. In addition, bureaucrats and local politicians tend to join the opposition, through protests and sabotage, if the government tries to increase the transfer to the landless by reducing bureaucrats' opportunities for rent seeking through strengthened supervision and penalties. The budgetary requirement for program enforcement itself is a major factor in determining the location of the marginal cost curve, because it represents the opportunity cost of land reform by reducing the resources available to purchase support from other interest groups by means of various government projects.

In developing countries characterized by a highly skewed land distribution, landless people in the rural sector are large in number. It is typically too costly to organize them for group action, because they are largely uneducated and scattered over a wide area with poor communications and transportation infrastructure, as the Olson (1965) theory predicts. Landed elites, however, find it easy to organize themselves because of their small number and high level of education. They are able to mobilize their wealth and power effectively for political lobbying, including bribery and intimidation. The general inefficiency and corruption of administrative machineries, together with the absence of accurate records on land tenure relations, lower the cost of their resistance at the level of program implementation.

Under such economic, political, and social conditions, the marginal revenue of land reform in most developing countries is likely to be low as represented by MR_0 in Figure 6.1 and the marginal cost is likely to be high as represented by MC_0, with an equilibrium at A corresponding to the very low (often zero) level of effective land redistribution or income transfer to the landless as represented by OR_0.

In contrast, the conditions that prevailed in Japan and Taiwan during the immediate postwar years may be represented by the locations of the marginal curves at MR_1 and MC_1 with the equilibrium at B. In Japan, for example, tenants had learned to organize themselves through cooperative and tenant-union movements that existed long before World War II. In the wake of the crisis situation after the great defeat, urban business and middle class interests also strongly called for land reform as a measure of "democratization" to prevent communist influences in the rural sector. Moreover, pressures from the U.S. occupation forces were decisive in raising the marginal revenue curve of political leaders because their chance of staying in office was small if they did not listen to the directives issued by the Allied headquarters. Landlords' resistance was reduced as their power and confidence waned in the crisis period. The accumulation of administrative experience and accurate data on land tenure relations in the hands of relatively honest and well-disciplined bureaucrats greatly reduced the cost of program design and implementation.

In developing countries, too, the political market equilibrium shifts occasionally to the right during political crises when the ruling order sees the risk that landless people will side with radicals and revolutionaries. In such a situation, the expected marginal revenue for politicians rises because the probability of their staying in office without attractive reform programs for the landless becomes small. The expected marginal cost declines because the landed elites tend to give up resistance to the reform under the threat of guerrilla activity and revolt. For example, since World War II the Philippines has experienced the four major shifts in equilibrium. First, under the threat of the Huk rebellion, the Magsaysay regime enacted the Agricultural Tenancy Act (1954) and the Land Reform Act (1955). Second, for fear of the infiltration of communist influence during the Vietnam War, the Macapagal administration undertook a major advancement in agrarian reform legislation in the form of the Agricultural Land Reform Code (1963). Third, under the martial law proclaimed in 1972 to suppress serious antigovernment demonstrations and disruptions, the Marcos administration attempted to implement the 1963 reform code on an expanded scale with Presidential Decree No. 2. Fourth, the political turmoil after the downfall of the Marcos dynasty forced the Aquino government to enact the ambitious Comprehensive Agrarian Reform Law (1988). Although the outcome of the fourth attempt has yet to be seen, the previous three major reform efforts subsided as soon as the visible crisis situations were over, leaving complicated laws and regulations without much effective income transfer to the landless; this reflects a shift in the political market equilibrium back to A in a normal third world situation.

A major source of failure in land reform programs in developing countries is the application of the Japanese and Taiwanese reform models in entirely different political market conditions. For the reform to be successful, it must be designed so as to reduce the marginal cost of achieving real income transfers to the landless within the existing political market. Of course, the potential for effective income transfer is severely limited under the present configuration of power and wealth distributions in most developing countries. Yet if reform programs continue to be designed according to a model that is incompatible with prevailing political market conditions, future reform efforts will inevitably fail.

Contradictions in the Asian Model of Land Reform

The first step in designing a feasible, effective reform program is to examine past land reform programs in various countries in order to understand why they failed to reduce poverty and inequality in the rural sector.

For this purpose, the Philippines is a useful example. The design of Philippine land reform programs follows the noncommunist Asian model.[3] In general, the noncommunist model of land reform involves redistributing all or some private property rights on land to create and preserve independent property-owning peasants as a stabilizing bloc in the rural society. It differs from the communist model, in which private property rights on land are denied, and lands confiscated from landlords and landowning peasants are consolidated into collective or state farms.

In the Asian noncommunist model, the redistribution of land rights from landlords to tenants is limited; it consists essentially of (1) government purchase from landlords of any land in excess of a retention limit and resale of that land to tenants, and (2) transfer of some property rights on tenanted land from landlords to tenants, resulting in the transfer of a part of the income produced from the land. The latter scheme is achieved by means of government regulations on tenancy contracts such as rent control and by prohibitions on the termination of tenancy contracts by landlords (security of tenure) and on the use of certain tenure forms (especially the prohibition of share tenancy).

Typically, in the Asian model, farm estates, however large they may be, are not subject to reform programs as long as they are managed by landlords themselves using hired laborers. Because land redistribution is limited to that from a landlord to his tenants, the Asian model of land reform is expected to affect the distribution of lands by tenure status but not the distribution of operational landholdings. Indeed, in Asian land reform programs, almost no attempt has been made to subdivide plantations for distribution to laborers; the organization of plantations has remained essentially unchanged, either as private enterprises (as in, for example, Malaysia, Philippines, and Sri Lanka) or as state enterprises when confiscated from colonial planters (as in, Indonesia).

Because of their minimal effect on farm-size distribution, land reform programs based on the Asian model have had ambiguous results at best for agricultural productivity, despite popular expectations. There is no doubt, for example, that the land reform in Japan promoted more equal asset and income distributions among farmers, thereby contributing critically to the social stability of the rural sector. But the farm-size distribution did not change, and the small-scale family farm remained the basic unit of agricultural production. Although land reform contributed to an increase in living standards and consumption levels, its contributions to capital formation and productivity growth in agriculture have not been clearly visible or have not been significant in terms of quantitative analysis (Kawano 1969).[4]

Another variety of the noncommunist model may be called the Latin American model. This model focuses on the transformation of semifeudal estates based on bonded labor (such as corvee and labor rents) into capitalist estates based on hired wage labor and, further, into landowning family farms or free peasantry, even though redistribution of tenanted land and regulations on tenancy contracts are also involved (de Janvry 1981). The contrast between the Asian and the Latin American models reflects the different agrarian structures developed through different historical processes in the two regions. In the old-settled Asia the peasant mode was traditionally dominant and class conflicts emerged mainly in the form of the landlord-tenant conflict; this was especially the case in East

Asia, where the plantation sector was negligible. In newly settled Latin America, however, agriculture was dominated by the large estates of European settlers, created mainly by opening new land or plundering natives' lands, which were then operated using bonded labor of natives and imported laborers. Naturally, class conflicts between estate owners and laborers were a major source of agrarian unrest in Latin America.

Although its agrarian structure combines features of the Asian and the Latin American models, the Philippines has followed the Asian model of land reform, with the programs limited to the redistribution of tenanted lands and regulations on tenancy contracts (Hayami, Quisumbing, and Adriano 1990: ch. 3). Such a design has not only severely limited the coverage of land reform but has created serious hindrances for attaining the very goal intended by land reform.

To achieve the ultimate goal of reducing rural poverty and inequality, the correction of unequal asset distribution by means of land redistribution is, of course, important. Another important source of inequality, however, is the decreasing rate of return to labor relative to the return to land because of strong population pressure on land. It is therefore critically important to increase employment and labor income per unit of limited land area. Indeed, a major source of the failure of land reform programs, including that undertaken under the Marcos regime, seems to be that the design of land redistribution conflicted with the goal of increasing employment and labor income.

First, the limitation of the previous programs to tenanted land created a strong incentive for landlords to evict their tenants and cultivate their land under direct administration. However, per hectare labor inputs, and hence agricultural output and labor income, are usually higher in small family farms than in large farms based on hired labor, because the inherent difficulty of supervising wage laborers in spatially dispersed and ecologically diverse farm operations tends to induce the adoption of labor-saving farming systems in large farms.[5] Therefore, the exemption of land under landlords' direct administration had the effect of reducing labor input per hectare below a socially optimum level, thereby reducing the income of the labor population. Furthermore, the limitation of the reform programs to tenanted land has induced some rich people to keep their lands idle, as often observed in frontier regions like Mindanao, rather than letting tenants cultivate them.

Second, land reform in the Philippines was limited to rice and corn lands, where tenancy arrangements predominate. This limitation has induced landlords to divert their land to other crops, often at the expense of both efficiency and equity. For example, several potentially productive rice lands with higher income-earning and labor-absorptive capacity were converted into farms planting labor-saving crops such as coconuts.

Third, regulations on tenancy contracts (especially the prohibition of share tenancy and the control of land rent) reduced the incentive of large landholders to rent out their land in small parcels, resulting in a reduction in social product as well as labor income.

These evasion practices undertaken by landlords could have been prevented if an honest and efficient bureaucracy, accurate data on land tenure systems and cropping patterns, and countervailing tenant organizations existed at the village level. Also, the distortive effects of those evasion practices were relatively small in economies like those of Japan and Taiwan where the plantation sector had traditionally been negligible and where farm labor could easily find employment in the rapidly growing nonfarm sector. In the absence of these conditions, the application of the traditional Asian model has inevitably created a serious conflict between land asset redistribution and the efficient and equitable utilization of land in the Philippines. Thus, the first step in developing an effective land reform design should be to learn from the past failures arising from the application of a model that was successful in some countries to an environment with vastly different economic, political, and social conditions, or political market.

The second step is to recognize the analytical errors on which the traditional Asian model was built. The first error is the assumption of economies of scale in agricultural production. Since Karl Marx, it has been common to assume that large-scale commercial farms using modern technology and capital equipment are more efficient than semisubsistence peasant producers (Mitrany 1951; Schultz 1964). Economists have thought increasing returns to scale to be especially strong in commercial crops such as sugar and bananas. Recent studies, however, have shown that although increasing returns in agricultural production tend to prevail in high-wage economies that demand large-scale machinery and capital equipment for the purpose of saving labor, agriculture in low-wage developing economies is generally characterized by constant returns or even decreasing returns to scale (Hayami and Ruttan 1985: ch. 6; Hayami and Kawagoe 1989). Our field observations are consistent with the hypotheses that (1) even for commercial crops such as sugar, pineapple, and banana, scale economies exist in processing activities but not in farm production itself; (2) if small producers are properly organized through contract farming with processing industries, there will be no loss in efficiency with the breakdown of plantations into family farm units; and (3) agricultural wage workers in plantations can be transformed into efficient small farmers with adequate support of technical extension and credit if lands will be given to them (Hayami, Quisumbing, and Adriano 1990: chs. 5 and 6).

The second erroneous assumption underlying the design of traditional land reform programs is that share tenancy results in inefficient resource allocation. Because of a misunderstanding of Alfred Marshall's classic statement that a share contract reduces tenants' work incentive because only a portion of additional output accrues to their income, it had been common to assume that a sharecropping contract leads a tenant to apply labor and other inputs at less than optimum levels.[6] Recent empirical as well as theoretical developments, however, have supported the hypothesis that a share contract can achieve the same degree of efficiency as the fixed-rent contract and owner farming, and furthermore, that a share contract can be more beneficial for tenants because of its risk-sharing features and the use of landlord-tenant credit relations.[7] An emerging consensus is that the artificial limitation of the choice of land tenure contracts, such as the prohibition of share tenancy, reduces both efficiency and equity.

If the shortcomings of existing reform laws and regulations are to be overcome, new land reform programs must take these problems into account. Land reform must incorporate incentives for the efficient and equitable use of land in addition to the smooth redistribution of land ownership titles. Especially needed are mechanisms that would penalize landlords who hold land for the sake of hoarding and speculation to the extent that they impede efficient land use.

Redesigning Land Reform Programs

To achieve the goal of reducing rural poverty and inequality, the new reform design must be based on hard calculations not only of economic but also of political and bureaucratic resource endowments in the country. There are three basic considerations for a successful reform in developing economies like the Philippines.

First, the rules of reform must be simple, transparent, and uniform. Complex regulations and numerous exemptions will not only reduce the chance of effective program implementation but also induce rent-seeking activities by the political elites and the bureaucracy at the expense of the poor who have little legal knowledge. This implies that the same reform rules must apply to both tenant farms and plantations.

Second, regulations resulting in distortions in resource allocation must be minimized. Some regulatory policies may have the objective of redistributing assets and income in favor of the poor, but if such policies reduce employment and labor income through the misallocation of resources, the net effect on the target group will likely be negative.

Third, although political commitment is essential to the success of land reform programs, the reform must be designed so that the scope of discretionary government involvement in its implementation is as small as possible to minimize drain on scarce government resources.

The last consideration appears to be critical for the course of land reform in the Philippines under the Aquino government. The new land reform law of 1988 (Republic Act No. 6657) is the first in the Philippine history to stipulate extension of program coverage to the plantation sector, while it maintains the same bureaucratic control and regulation on land redistribution and tenancy contracts as in the previous programs for rice and corn. Extending traditional bureaucratic procedures to the plantation sector, however, presents extreme difficulties. Unlike tenanted land, in which "tillers of the land" can easily be identified, plantations typically have workers organized into teams according to tasks, and thus no specific plot of land is assigned to an individual worker. Moreover, if land assets or incomes of plantations are to be redistributed, who should be considered legitimate beneficiaries? Should clerical workers and technicians, in addition to fieldworkers, be included? Is it fair to exclude casual workers who are employed temporarily and who receive lower wages than regular workers? Is it possible to reorganize large plantations into small, family-sized farms without detrimental effects on income, employment, and foreign exchange receipts? Given these administrative difficulties, one may doubt whether the country has sufficient budgetary and manpower resources.

In light of these three considerations, a mechanism to induce institutional change would be more desirable than a deliberately interventionist and discretionary reform program. Specifically, it would be more effective to establish a mechanism to provide incentives for landlords to distribute their lands to landless tenants and laborers and for agribusiness firms to reorganize plantations into small, family-farm operations linked to a processing and marketing firm than for the government to purchase land directly and sell it to the landless.

On the basis of the above considerations, the following components could serve as the core of the new program design:

1. *Ceiling on aggregate land owned.* The ceiling on landholding must be imposed on the amount of land owned regardless of crops and of tenure status. This will limit the size of farms under landlords' direct administration. The smaller the land ceiling, the greater is the improvement in distribution of income and, probably, the gain in efficiency. The ceiling must be decided, however, in due consideration of political and administrative feasibility. This ceiling should be announced with a notice that land in excess of the ceiling will be confiscated with only a modest rate of compensation at the end of a sufficiently long transition period. Government should encourage landlords to sell the excess land directly

to smallholders within the transition period by eliminating the government as a middleman in the transfer of land. Special long-term credit programs can be instituted to further reduce the cost of acquiring land, especially for the poor.

2. *Progressive land tax.* To facilitate more intensive use of land and to mobilize funds for the government to purchase land in excess of the ceiling after the transition period, as well as to subsidize credit needs of poor farmers for the purchase of land, a progressive land tax according to the size of holding should be instituted. An elevated land tax for large holders will compel them to use land more intensively to raise sufficient agricultural income to pay for the tax. The tax will be a disincentive to those who wish to hold land for the sake of its hoarding value or speculation. As a result, the supply of land will increase and, correspondingly, the sale value of land will decrease. Many large landlords will find it advantageous to subdivide their land into small parcels and rent them to tenants who use the land intensively with family labor rather than managing a large unit extensively with hired labor. The increased tax revenues may be used to support the operation of reform programs as well as complementary services such as technical extension and credit.

3. *Deregulation of land tenure contracts.* To facilitate the subdivision of large holdings into small family farm units, all regulations regarding land tenure contracts, including tenancy forms and land rent, should be removed. However, the rights of leaseholders established by the previous land reform operations in rice and corn, including the regulated land rent, should be preserved and made similar to property rights so that the leasehold titles may be sold, mortgaged, and rented (subtenancy).

4. *Progressive rent on public land lease.* To induce multinational and local agribusiness firms that now operate plantations mainly on leased public land to reorganize into a system of contract farming with small growers, the land rent should be graduated according to the size of holding. The revenues generated by the government from the implementation of a progressive land rent may be used to support the land reform operations as well as the construction and maintenance of local public infrastructure that are now shouldered by the plantations to a significant extent. The progressive rent

would also be effective to induce transformation of under-used public lands such as extensive cattle ranches into productive, family-sized agroforestry farms, thereby increasing employment and income in marginal upland areas.

With the above program design, there is little danger that existing scale economies of modern plantations will be disrupted. If plantations and ranches based on wholly owned land would find it profitable to maintain the present form of organization, the deregulation of land rental contracts would permit them to lease back land in excess of the retention limit. Likewise, plantations leasing public land have the option of either continuing the present system by paying a progressive land rent to the government, thereby remaining profitable so long as the assumed scale economies exist, or developing contract-farming arrangements with small independent growers.

Admittedly, under the suggested framework much of the land owned by large landlords will be purchased by the rural middle class rather than by the landless. The landless, however, will have the chance to ascend the "agricultural ladder" (Spillman 1919) from landless workers to sharetenants, to leaseholders, and finally to owner-cultivators. The likelihood of their ascending the ladder will be increased by government programs aimed at redistributing public land with the support of technical guidance, credit, marketing, and infrastructure. The increased revenue from the progressive land tax on private land and the progressive land rent for public land lease will provide a basis for financing such settlement programs as well as special long-term credit programs to reduce the cost of acquiring land for the poor.

Through such a process the agrarian structure of developing economies will gradually shift from the present bifurcated system (where landless agricultural workers crave land, on the one hand, and landed elites monopolize wealth and power, as is typical in the Philippines, on the other) to a unimodal structure where the middle class is dominant and even rural landless workers have a chance to ascend. The process of transformation will certainly be long and arduous. But if no reform action is taken or if too drastic reform measures based on ideological preconceptions are attempted, class conflicts will intensify and the route to the unimodal rural society will be closed forever.

Ideology and knowledge commonly shared among people in a society are important determinants of the supply of institutional innovation (North 1981; Hayami and Ruttan 1985). Therefore, once policy makers and the general public recognize the source of failure of past land reform programs and the merit of new programs, the configurations of the political market will change so that the equilibrium illustrated in Figure 6.1 shifts from *A* toward *B*. Given this expectation, the establishment of a new paradigm or conceptual framework for land reform design is vital to prevent repeated failures of reform programs.

Conclusion

In retrospect, it is clear that the failure of past land reform programs in the Philippines and in other developing countries to establish social stability by alleviating poverty and equalizing income distribution has stemmed largely from direct application of the traditional reform model to a social environment incompatible with the model. Programs based on the traditional Asian model have had a limited coverage over the property rights on tenanted land to be redistributed from landlords to tenants. Owing to this limitation, the programs have been deliberately interventionist and discretionary, requiring huge bureaucratic resources for the implementation of both land redistribution and tenure regulations.

Such programs were successful in Japan and Taiwan immediately after World War II when the power and confidence of ruling elites were diminished through defeat and occupation by foreign forces. Their success was also based on the existence of a relatively well-disciplined bureaucracy, accurate land-tenure records, and established tenant organizations. The strongly interventionist programs that were barely successful under the exceptionally favorable political market conditions in East Asia were bound to fail in the absence of these conditions when applied to other parts of the third world.

Not only were these programs weakened by resistance and evasion by landlords, but they also resulted in serious distortions in resource allocations. Specifically, the limitation of program coverage to tenanted land created a strong incentive for landlords to use their land less intensively or even to keep it idle under their direct administration rather than to let tenants cultivate it. As a result, employment opportunities were reduced and the opportunity for agricultural laborers to ascend the ladder to become cultivators of their own land was closed. Thus, the limited program coverage resulted in serious inequity as well as inefficiency in the economies where a large plantation sector exists alongside a peasant sector—such as the Philippines—while it posed no major problem in East Asian countries, where the population of agricultural wage laborers had traditionally been negligible.

If the traditional reform design is maintained, the expansion of these land reform programs to cover the plantation sector will likely prove unfeasible both administratively and financially. To be effective in reducing inequality while minimizing distortions in resource allocation, a reform design must replace deliberately interventionist and discretionary programs with a mechanism for inducing institutional and organizational change.

Ample evidence has already been accumulated to convince us that the traditional land reform design is incompatible with the political market conditions of the third world. The shift to a new paradigm is long overdue. It is hoped that this chapter will stimulate the efforts to search for effective reform designs under different political market conditions in different countries that will eventually culminate in the new paradigm.

Comments

ROBERTO JUNGUITO

My comments on Yujiro Hayami's provocative chapter seek to apply some of his hypotheses to the Colombian experience with land reform. Since the 1930s Colombia, like most Latin American nations, has used land reform as a means of reducing the latifundia (large landed estates based on bonded labor). The basic land reform was passed in 1961, but in 1973 it was drastically and regressively reformed. Land reform issues were then of secondary importance until the early 1980s, when political considerations led to the discussion of a new law, which was adopted in 1988.

Colombia, it should be underlined from the start, did not suffer as much as other Latin American countries from landholdings made up of latifundia and minifundia (small estates). Moreover, land reform in Colombia has had social and political goals rather than aiming to increase output. Economically, the major result of land reform has been the accelerated development of the nonreform sector as a means of escaping the reform measures prevailing until 1988.

One of Hayami's hypotheses is that "the traditional model of land reform survived in the mind of policy makers, and their enthusiasm revived periodically whenever political crises escalated." This is exactly what happened in Colombia. The basic land reform law in Colombia was adopted after the 1957 overthrow of the military regime that had come to power in the wake of the political violence of the 1950s. The politicians' renewed enthusiasm in the 1980s stemmed from peace dialogues undertaken with the guerrilla movements and from an express demand by the Fuerzas Armadas Revolucionarias Colombianas (the Colombian Revolutionary Armed Forces).

Land reform decisions, then, according to Hayami, are the result of political entrepreneurs' expectations about the marginal revenue and marginal cost of distributing property rights on land. It is interesting to note that in the 1960s Colombia's two major political parties had serious difficulties settling on a land reform law. As a compromise they adopted Law 135, but the expropriation of lands entailed a very difficult juridical process. This impediment, together with the deliberately insufficient resources provided to the land reform institute, Incora, made the land reform law a political statement with no real economic content. In 1988, however, both political parties rapidly agreed to reform the law and facilitate the juridical expropriation process, although they limited land reform to specific regions of the country. Even the powerful Sociedad de Agricultores de Colombia, representing the agricultural interest groups that had fought so vigorously against the land reform law in the 1960s, showed support for the new progressive reform law.

In the Colombian case, once again, Hayami's hypothesis seems to find support: although in the 1960s politicians and the agricultural private sector did not see land reform as offering special social benefits, in the 1980s guerrilla group demands seemed to create prospective social benefits that led even the strongest traditional adversaries to support the reform.

Hayami points out that supporters of land reform include not only rural landless but also urban and middle-income groups seeking social stability and expansion of domestic markets for urban goods. The wide support of the new land reform law by the Colombian Congress and by public opinion coincides generally with Hayami's views.

Colombian urban groups, however, do not seem convinced by the argument that land reform will lead to the expansion of domestic markets. The Asociación Nacional de Industriales, representing the manufacturing sector, has instead always supported increasing minimum wages, especially in agriculture, to increase domestic markets for the overprotected manufacturing sector.

The budgetary requirements for land reform, Hayami stresses, are important in predicting the success of reform because they represent an opportunity cost in terms of forgone government projects designed to purchase support from other interest groups. In the case of Colombia, the budgetary constraint has acted as a brake to prevent the execution of the land reform, sometimes in a very deliberate way: Incora's lack of resources led to a slowdown in acquiring land and transferring titles to peasants. A major feature of the 1988 law was the establishment of an earmarked fund for land reform, based on a surcharge on the import tax. The new law also authorized Incora to issue bonds for land acquisition, reducing significantly the budgetary outlays required for land expropriations.

To reduce potential output losses, Colombia's regressive land reform law of 1973 had stipulated that "adequately exploited" holdings would be exempt from land expropriation actions. Under the 1988 law, "all rural properties are potentially the subject of acquisition either by direct negotiation or by expropriation for the execution of land reform programs." This more progressive method of expropriation, however, is limited to sections of the country where social conditions and violent actions justify all types of land acquisition.

Finally, in Hayami's view, land reform requires rules that are simple, transparent, and uniform. The description given here shows that the political transaction that led to Colombia's basic land reform law in 1961 resulted in complicated rules that deliberately created severe obstacles to the adoption of true land reform. The 1988 law has simplified the rules, particularly the procedures for expropriation. The Sociedad de Agricultores de Colombia called the new law "a powerful and speedy instrument for redistributing rural land."

In the debt-burdened Latin American countries, the land reform issue has passed to secondary importance on the economic agenda. The central discussion now is whether the adjustment policies designed to correct balance-of-payments and fiscal disequilibria are favorable to agriculture. Two schools of thought seem to be emerging: some economists, under the leadership of the International Food Policy Research Institute, argue that undervaluation of exchange rates and industrial protection worked against agriculture in the past and that more adjustment is needed, while the Food and Agriculture Organization contends that adjustment policies have worked against agriculture and that import substitution and agricultural protection are the way out of the crisis. One could argue that both schools view land reform as merely a compensatory sectoral policy for inadequate macroeconomic policies.

Thomas P. Tomich

A front-page headline from the *Asian Wall Street Journal Weekly* (July 10, 1989) reports that "Corruption Is Bringing Manila's Land Reform Program to a Near Halt" only a year after the policy was adopted. Once again events confirm that pursuit of self-interest through politics—in this case, by landowners and corrupt bureaucrats—can derail a policy that promised to increase equity and economic efficiency.

Rather than simply predicting or explaining failure of "good" economic policy as a result of conflict with political rationality, Yujiro Hayami employs the new political economy (NPE) as a tool in a search for insights that can improve prospects for successful land reform in the Philippines. His NPE analysis is complemented by results drawn from the new land tenure economics (Hayami and Ruttan 1985; Stiglitz 1986), which analyzes land tenure and other rural institutions as ways of coping with imperfect information, reducing transactions costs, and sharing risk. There is even a taste of what Meier (1989: 550) calls the "older" political economy. Such eclecticism is a hallmark of good policy analysis. I will take a narrower view, examining the NPE analysis of the "market" for land redistribution in order to explore the limitations of NPE as a source of political insights for new reform initiatives.

In the NPE component of his analysis, Hayami proposes a "political market" to consider why redistributive land reform programs transfer little land—certainly less than is socially desirable or economically feasible. The supply side of this political market is straightforward: landowners are powerful and use the system to protect their interests, first by fighting policy reform and later by circumventing implementation. Political analysis would yield similar insights, probably with simpler models and fewer implicit assumptions.

For me, the novel insight from the author's application of NPE concerns the way the political market clears (or fails to do so). The prominent role bureaucrats play as policy arbitrators has important economic effects. Unlike Leon Walras's auctioneers or James Clerk Maxwell's disinterested demons, corrupt officials interfere to influence the process to their own advantage. In the NPE analysis, their pursuit of self-interest is as important as opposition from landowners in explaining the failure of reform.[1] These actions by landowners and bureaucrats point to two of the author's policy recommendations: (1) base reform on rules that are simple, transparent, and uniform and (2) minimize the scope for discretionary government action. Beyond these—which might be called the two fundamental theorems of NPE—what does the approach offer? Perhaps additional insights about the uses or limitations of NPE could come from a closer look at the demand side of this political market, which receives relatively little attention in the chapter.

What payoff does land redistribution offer to policy makers? In other words, what is their marginal "revenue" on the demand side of the political market? One possibility, stressed by Hayami, is political survival: threatened with insurrection, rational policy elites in the Philippines may have sought to improve their chances of holding on to power by responding to demands from the New People's Army (NPA) for "Land to the tiller." Another possible payoff, stated in the chapter as the goal of land reform, is the reduction of rural poverty and inequality. Progressive policy makers interested in social welfare would value this result, but NPE has nothing to say about policy preferences. This goal, however, could be described in terms of NPE as the narrow self-interest of policy makers whose supporters include direct beneficiaries or others who value progressive objectives.

Yet there are paradoxes on the demand side of this political market. It seems unlikely that land reform will have much effect on the insurrection. Indeed, the NPA may be able to turn the emerging fiasco to its benefit. Corrupt bureaucrats and other opportunists who exploit loopholes could be the major direct beneficiaries, but it is difficult to conceive of them as important actors on the demand side of the market. Political support from the few peasant families who eventually receive land titles can hardly compensate for the immediate opposition engendered among the oligarchy. Most peasants will not benefit from reform. Either policy makers erred in their political calculus or effective demand for land reform comes from other groups without a direct interest in land redistribution.

Who could exert enough pressure to get land reform on the political agenda in the Philippines and cause so much soul searching among the political elite, yet would not withdraw support even if the reform is botched? The middle class, certain urban business interests, and international organizations all appear to support the land reform concept but lack a direct private stake in redistribution of land.[2] Policy makers might earn support from these groups through the adoption of reformist policy and a good-faith effort at implementation. Even if politicians pursue only their narrow self-interest in retaining power, the broader public interest and ideas on which support is based matter too, whether motivated by widely shared interest in political stability, a preference for social equity, or a combination of the two.

Broad-based political support may well be the driving force on the demand side of the political market for land reform in the Philippines. This possibility raises hope that the political force of other popular ideas could be tapped by progressive policy makers to build support for alternatives that promote social and economic welfare. A political economy perspective such as NPE, however, that stresses narrower, private aspects of self-interest would seem to hold little promise of adding insights in the process of identifying these policy alternatives.

The tragedy of land reform is not so much that redistributive reforms fail to transfer much land, but that the political coalitions that emerge in favor of reform have not been channeled toward more viable policies to promote social and economic welfare. This tragedy is often coupled with another: the policy adopted in many cases as a substitute—land tenure reform—has the effect in practice of reducing equity and undermining efficiency.

Whereas the task for NPE regarding redistributive land reform is to explain why there is so little land redistribution, the task regarding land tenure reform is to explain how politics leads to more land tenancy reform than is socially desirable or economically efficient. Although redistributive land reform and land tenancy reform appear to be good substitutes in political markets, they typically have contradictory economic implications.

Land tenure regulations adopted as part of earlier land reforms in the Philippines and elsewhere (often when significant land redistribution is not politically feasible) are intended to establish rent ceilings, to secure tenure, and to abolish sharecropping. The goal of land tenure reform is to give tenants some, but not all, property rights in land by mandating formal changes in contracts. Within an NPE framework, this solution seems like a nice equilibrating device: tenants (usually the middle-income peasants who have a relatively strong political voice) gain new rights, and landlords retain a portion of their claim to each plot of land. This view of land tenure reform is misleading because it overlooks the range of reactions open to landlords, including eviction of tenants. In practice, land tenure reforms can threaten the interests of most tenants, sharecroppers, and even agricultural laborers.

Like redistributive land reform, land tenancy reform raises the issue of which interests are served on the demand side of the political market for land tenancy reform. It seems much more plausible that political support could be grounded on misguided economic notions held by groups that have a preference for progressive reform but only an indirect stake in the actual outcomes—the middle class, urban business groups, and international organizations—rather than mistaken notions among the peasantry who would bear the burden of bad policy. As Hayami points out, agricultural economists share in the blame because the conventional wisdom among academics once was that tenancy reform was a second-best alternative to redistributive land reform. Although it has been rejected by many academics, it remains a popular notion among policy makers.

There is not enough information at hand to determine which explanation underlies the unfortunate propensity for land tenure reform—political interests or preferences for the wrong policies. If interests are the sole answer, perhaps NPE has something to offer in the search for viable alternatives. To the extent that ideas matter in this political market, however, conventional economic analysis plus persuasion would appear to offer greater hope for improved policy than NPE.

Despite the setbacks suffered by the Philippines' most recent land redistribution program, policy makers' political commitment may have survived along with the broader political support for reform. Although land redistribution is desirable as a means of promoting equity and efficiency, fortunately it is not a necessary precondition for productivity growth or for a broad-based pattern of agricultural development (Johnston and Tomich 1985). Among the economically sensible alternatives, ranging from sector-specific policies like the progressive land taxes recommended by Hayami to macroeconomic policies aimed at stabilization and structural adjustment, some politically viable reforms can no doubt be identified. Unfortunately, few if any of the other standard alternatives can rival land reform as a popular cause. It would be hard to capture the political power evoked by calls for "Land to the tiller!" with a battle cry like "Tax the oligarchs!"—not to mention "Equilibrium exchange rates!" Neither economists nor their tools have a particular advantage in determining which of these "good" economic policies would excite the greatest popular support. Yet broad-based political support for the public interest could once again prove to be decisive in the Philippines, as it did in the "People Power" movement to overthrow the Marcos regime. The public interest and political leadership that made this possible are important blind spots in NPE.

Poverty Alleviation

Much has been written about poverty alleviation, equity, and growth in the developing countries, especially during the 1970s, when the development debate focused on the provision of "basic needs" and "redistribution with growth." Economists concluded that in many countries, particularly the middle-income countries of Latin America, basic necessities could be provided to most of the poor at relatively little cost. Indeed, because of skewed distribution, the incomes of the poor are such a small share of national income that even a substantial increase would represent a small portion of gross domestic product (GDP). For example, a World Bank report showed that during the years of rapid economic growth in Brazil the cost to society of extending the coverage of basic health care, reducing malnutrition, increasing enrollment in basic education, and improving housing, water supply, and sewerage would be an estimated 4 to 6 percent of GDP over ten years. Meeting the basic needs of the poor would cost society less than 1 percent of GDP per year in that country (Knight and Moran 1981: 85).

If the cost of eliminating the worst features of mass poverty is so modest, why haven't the basic needs of the poor been met long ago?[1] The customary response in the 1970s was that countries lacked the political will to alleviate poverty. But when one tries to discover the meaning of "political will," no clear answer emerges. Moreover, the absence of poverty alleviation is not clearly associated with a particular form of government: Costa Rica and Chile both ran effective social programs under diametrically opposed political regimes.

This chapter will use the new political economy to shed light on this apparent paradox. Poverty alleviation is, after all, a bureaucratic/administrative activity that can be viewed through the lens of the new political economy. The chapter will distinguish between the two kinds of poverty that exist in many developing countries. Since the early 1980s, economists have paid a lot of attention to "adjustment poverty"—that is, the poverty created during the structural adjustment process—and to what compensatory measures governments can take. But there is also the underlying problem of "structural poverty," which is the poverty that existed before governments embarked on structural adjustment programs and encompasses the vast majority of the poor. Adjustment poverty is largely an urban phenomenon; structural poverty exists in both cities and rural areas, but in Latin America it is mainly a rural reality.

To help the poor, policy should focus, I believe, on poverty alleviation and not redistribution of income. Income distribution is influenced far more by changes in the shares of the upper and middle classes than by what happens to the incomes of the poor, and is therefore largely irrelevant to them. Also, distribution data are even less reliable than data about the incomes of the poor. Moreover, policies designed to alter the distribution of income often set compensatory forces in motion.

I will sidestep the thorny issue of poverty criteria. Some countries use income or expenditure criteria to determine poverty levels and target poverty programs. Others, in particular the poorer countries in Asia, gauge poverty by food consumption. Colombia and Argentina focus on housing conditions. Targeting criteria for nutrition and health services can be based on geography (focusing on rural residents of northeast Brazil, for example), age (focusing on children and old persons), or health condition. Although each society defines poverty in its own way, there is clearly a nexus of syndromes. And since the statistics are usually unreliable and the poverty line is arbitrary, I believe that how these data are used in trying to target particular poverty alleviation programs is probably more decisive than the choice of a particular criterion. Loose targeting, tight targeting, or indeed mistargeting can occur no matter which poverty criterion is used.

Identifying and Reducing Structural Poverty

In 1979 Richard Webb and I went to Brazil to study income distribution and poverty, and their trends over time (Pfeffermann and Webb 1983).

A major household survey that covered 55,000 households nationwide had just been carried out. The results confirmed all statistics previously gathered for Brazil and for other developing countries, namely that the poorest people live in rural areas. Typically, they own few productive assets and are underemployed. These conclusions sound trite, yet to this day few governments have bothered to gather the information needed to answer the question, who are the poor?

A first step in any effort to help the poor is to convince governments to carry out a household income or expenditure survey capable of identifying poor families by location, sources of livelihood, and so forth. Such surveys have become far easier and cheaper to do than they used to be, owing to computer advances. The World Bank's Living Standards Measurement Study (LSMS) unit has carried out surveys very quickly entirely on personal computers. LSMS is currently involved in a number of African countries, Peru, Bolivia, Jamaica, Morocco, and Pakistan, with discussions going on in Colombia, Guatemala, Nepal, and China. The World Bank is also applying LSMS methods to sub-Saharan African countries through a project on the social dimensions of adjustment. Work on household surveys has begun in eight countries, and another twenty countries or so have signed up. The project focuses on identifying the poor and finding out how they are affected by adjustment policies.

Most programs allegedly designed to help the poor in fact ignore the rural population. Roberto Macedo (1988) wrote a splendid piece on the mistargeting of social programs in Brazil that arises partly from ignorance of the facts. How many developing countries have up-to-date information on who the poor are? Where they live? What they do? Information alone, of course, is a necessary but not a sufficient tool for rational targeting. But surveys and their diffusion by the media may help influence politicians.

The roots of mistargeting are of course political: political power, especially in newly democratic countries, is concentrated in the urban middle classes, and they perceive the poor as the people they see in *favelas* and other slums when they are commuting. Furthermore, the urban poor (or the "relative poor") are numerous, especially in Latin America, and they are the ones, of course, who might overthrow governments. The rural poor remain invisible for a number of reasons:

First, as urbanization gains momentum, the share of the rural poor in the population and therefore their political visibility decreases precipitously; an increase in urbanization from, say, 50 percent to 80 percent may imply a drop in the share of the rural poor from near 40 percent of the population to only 15 percent. Although this is no doubt a welcome trend for formerly rural poor families, it sharply reduces the political clout (which is very small to begin with) of the remaining rural population.

Second, there is physical dispersion and isolation. Many of the poorer rural families live in inaccessible areas such as jungles, remote valleys, or high mountains, far from the highway network. This condition further reduces their visibility.

Third, Robert Chambers (1980) stresses that it requires a considerable effort on the part of professionals to meet the rural poor. Not only do these poor tend to be physically inaccessible, but also visitors to rural areas (which Chambers calls "rural development tourists") tend to meet the more progressive farmers, village headmen, traders, religious leaders, teachers, and paraprofessionals. It is they who articulate the village's priorities for development. The poorer or the poorest usually do not speak up. The poorest are usually women, who are unlikely to engage in conversation with visiting professionals.

Fourth, bureaucracies thrive on an affluent or powerful clientele and are therefore far more likely to bestow their patronage on the urban areas than to dissipate their efforts by promising improvements to the rural poor. Most developing countries have followed the tradition of former colonial administrations in giving low status to the Ministry of Agriculture. This low status might be logical in industrialized countries where relatively few people work in agriculture, but it makes no sense in developing countries. The absence of a strong rural administration may have contributed to the perpetuation of poverty in developing countries. It is also possible, however, that the workings of Parkinson's Law drives institutions into "new markets" for the sake of bureaucratic expansion. For example, many social security institutions in developing countries have expanded their scope, covering not only employees in the formal sector, but also increasing numbers of the self-employed and those in the rural and informal sectors.

It can be argued that migration is the only cost-effective way to alleviate poverty. No doubt it is much cheaper to provide broad social sector coverage where the population is concentrated than in the rural areas. And if urban services encompass the informal sector they certainly can achieve equity goals. The fact remains, however, that the largest numbers of poor people live far from the cities and, at least in Latin America, precious little has been done to improve their condition. This is particularly true of the Indian populations and of rural northeast Brazil.

Incidentally, in Latin America, the Church, which plays a most important social role, seems to have a blind spot for trade-offs between the urban and rural poor. It often supports urban wage increases, programs benefiting formal sector employees, and poverty alleviation programs that directly or indirectly hurt the rural poor.

So what, if anything, works?

First of all, one must ask whether there are examples of successful poverty reduction. There is hardly any doubt that economic development, where it has taken place, has gone hand in hand with a reduction in the proportion of very poor people. In some cases there has been, in spite of continued rapid population growth, a reduction even in the absolute numbers of poor people. This contention is supported by census data and household surveys. David Morawetz (1977) made the point in a book that was a reaction to the pessimistic views of former World Bank President Robert McNamara. If one looks at material conditions—the number of households drinking clean water, the number of people wearing shoes, and, most important, life expectancy at birth—it is difficult to maintain that economic growth has not had a major positive effect on poverty alleviation. I did a back-of-the-envelope calculation a few years ago that showed that, over twenty years, Brazil's poor improved their real incomes far more than India's despite India's improving income distribution, simply because of the much faster growth of Brazilian aggregate income.

Gary Fields (1989) produced an interesting review of "Poverty, Inequality, and Economic Growth," based partly on the twenty country studies included in the research project The Political Economy of Poverty, Equity, and Growth launched in 1985 by the World Bank. Fields tests the hypothesis that poverty tends to decrease with economic growth and finds that, indeed, poverty is nearly always reduced by economic growth. Among eighteen countries with consistent data on poverty over time, only in the Philippines was positive economic growth not accompanied by a fall in poverty. The primary reason, according to Fields, was the nature of that country's economic system (crony capitalism).

The policy conclusion that follows is that trickle down does work to a considerable extent. Or to put it the other way around, economic stagnation and retrogression are highly unlikely to help the poor. On the contrary, the main channel through which trickle down operates is labor mobility and structural change in labor markets, which have drawn family members as well as whole families out of rural neglect into cities where jobs are being created with growth and where social services are far more accessible than in the rural areas.

The case of Chile illustrates the workings of trickle down. During the years of rapid economic growth (1975–1981), the rate of unemployment declined from 14.5 to 11 percent. In 1982, when gross domestic product (GDP) fell by 14 percent as a result of a massive reversal in capital flows, higher interest rates, and a low copper price, unemployment rose to 18 percent. Since then, Chile has experienced rapid economic growth once again, and unemployment has dropped to 6 percent, undoubtedly alleviating poverty. Furthermore, the number of persons in government emergency employment programs fell from 360,000 in 1984 to 8,000 in January 1989. To the extent that trickle down helps the poor, the growth performance of China and India during the past few years must also have helped more of the world's poor than any government poverty alleviation programs. The other side of the coin is the tragic plight of the poor in most of the highly indebted countries where per capita incomes have fallen, or, at best, stagnated during the past six years.

But what about the rural areas?

One can distinguish two kinds of government measures: (1) punctual interventions, such as area development programs that provide inputs to a certain number of villages, and (2) across-the-board measures, such as changes in subsidies. The latter type of measure has, clearly, a much broader compass than the former. Furthermore, such measures take immediate effect, whereas punctual programs take years to show results. An example of across-the-board intervention is the subsidization of those basic foods that have been identified as being consumed mostly by the poorest people. But it is often hard to extend such subsidies effectively to the landless rural poor who most need them.

Area development is one of the main tools used by the World Bank to try to alleviate rural poverty. Area development usually consists of attempts to coordinate the provision of a large number of inputs, such as improved seeds, livestock breeds, irrigation facilities, fertilizers and chemicals, credit, storage, transport, and marketing services. High-quality staff and management are essential prerequisites. Rural development projects such as Programa Integrado de Desarrollo Rural (PIDER) in Mexico and POLONORESTE in Brazil extend the concept to wider geographic areas. Between the mid-1960s and 1986, the World Bank lent US$20 billion for rural development projects. Total project costs were estimated at US$50 billion.

A recent World Bank report, *Rural Development: World Bank Experience, 1965–86,* sheds light on the results. The bank performed an ex post audit of 112 rural development loans targeted at the poor and approved between 1973 and 1978. Altogether these projects benefited fewer than 5 million families worldwide. This is clearly a drop in the bucket. In the rural northeast of Brazil alone, for example, there were about 2 million poor families at the time. And the effort has been very costly—some US$10,000 per family. Furthermore, it is not clear whether such projects do benefit the landless, who are the poorest.

Quite apart from their limited coverage, rural development programs have been fraught with difficulties. Success requires full commitment on the part of the government. It also requires reasonable macroeconomic equilibrium, particularly in relation to prices and exchange rates. A realistic exchange rate is a powerful tool for agricultural development, and therefore also for raising the incomes of the poor. A minimum of fiscal balance is also required; if the fiscal situation is out of hand, the public resources required for successful rural development will not be forthcoming. Perhaps worst of all, there is the administrative nightmare of trying to coordinate in a project area the many different bureaucracies responsible for services such as agricultural extension, access roads, rural credit, irrigation, rural electrification, education, and health. In the end the integrated (or Christmas-tree) approach was abandoned in favor of simpler projects.

The World Bank report suggests that the value of capital-intensive infrastructure in relieving some of the more severe causes and effects of rural poverty have probably been underrated. This is an interesting and important point. Much of the aid rhetoric, particularly that of voluntary aid organizations, favors "soft" approaches to rural poverty alleviation and frowns on components such as power and highways. Yet Judith Tendler (1988) went to northeast Brazil and sought out the views of a great number of people about rural development projects to which the World Bank has committed more than a billion dollars between 1975 and 1988. I quote her opening paragraph: "When asked what impact the POLONORESTE projects had in their regions, people's responses were remarkably similar—whether they were agency directors, department managers, headquarters or field staff, beneficiaries, or outside observers. Almost everyone said the projects had little impact 'except for roads and electrification' and, sometimes, rural water supply." Many people also referred with enthusiasm to the Advance Purchase Program and the Surplus Production Purchase, minor parts of the POLONORESTE programs. The Advance Purchase Program provided operating credit to farmers before the planting season in return for a commitment to sell the crop to the credit-advancing agency, and the Surplus Production Purchase guaranteed the purchase of small-farmer production at the minimum price. Both programs gave priority attention to the basic crops produced by large numbers of poor farmers—beans, corn, manioc, rice, and cotton.

What is interesting are the components that recipients and observers did not mention: long-term investment credit, extension, research, and marketing. Yet these occupied the center stage of POLONORESTE and many other area development projects. Why this discrepancy? The Brazilians saw roads, electrification, and water supply as having the widest distributional effects or the greatest potential for them. Though they saw the agricultural components as having strong distributional potential, they also saw the institutional and political problems of achieving this potential as almost insuperable.

This may well not have been the experience in other countries. And Judith Tendler's observations must be taken with a grain of salt. What people remember long after the event may lack objectivity. Yet the Brazilian experience surely highlights the crucial importance of administrative simplicity as an essential condition for success in countries where administrative talent is rare.

In any case, there is no doubt that the extension of cost-effective social services to the rural areas is a desirable goal. Few Latin American countries, however, have been able to achieve it. Chile and Costa Rica are exceptions, but Chile's rural population is quite small, and Costa Rica's efforts are costly. There are lessons from these two countries that could usefully be applied.

We should not lose sight, however, of the limitations of social services. Food and minimal housing must come first: priority should be given to programs that create or increase access to productive assets, enhance the rates of return on the assets held by the poor, create employment opportunities, and increase income and consumption transfers. Social services can only be a complement, and perhaps one of their main benefits is to improve the chances of upward mobility. There are severe limits to productivity and income improvements in the rural areas that are inherent in agriculture and intertwined with most difficult issues of land tenure. When all is said and done, one must recognize how very difficult it is to help those in the two or three lowest income deciles. For many of the rural poor, particularly the children, migration to the cities may offer the greatest hope for progress.

Approaches to Alleviating Adjustment Poverty

Discussing poverty and adjustment has become a cottage industry. I myself have contributed with *Poverty in Latin America: The Impact of Depression* (World Bank 1986), *Targeted Programs for the Poor during Structural Adjustment* (World Bank 1988b), and *Nutrition and Health Programs in Latin America: Targeting Social Expenditures* (Pfeffermann and Griffin 1989). The common message of these publications is that one need not and should not wait for sustained economic growth to occur before trying to do something to help the poor and that it should be possible to do quite a lot without additional budgetary resources.

When countries adjust, the visible costs (such as unemployment among former government workers and cuts in health and education spending) inevitably precede the resumption of growth and employment creation. I call the interval the "crossing of the desert."

A number of countries have tried to make the crossing of the desert less painful by changing their policies and establishing special programs. Changes in policies usually focus on (1) better targeting of social services (as well as charging those who can afford to share the costs) and (2) more efficient delivery of social services. Chile is an example of a country pursuing both approaches with some success.

To the extent that these policies lead to savings, more funds will be available for special compensatory programs, such as unemployment relief. According to the Bolivian authorities, the establishment of the Bolivian Social Emergency Fund, broadly targeted to the "adjustment poor," was a sine qua non for successful implementation of the stabilization program. Such programs are popular with external aid institutions and have helped mobilize foreign assistance. Actions to alleviate adjustment poverty are usually easier to defend politically than programs designed to help the structural poor. The success of such policies and programs depends on many factors:

- The programs must not be so expensive that they undermine the major adjustment effort that requires reduction of the public deficit, and they should not be allowed to cause major distortions (for example, massive low-cost housing programs must not crowd other borrowers out of financial markets).

- Subsidy programs should be considered against the background of broader fiscal policy. Sri Lanka's food program is reaching many poor families, but increases in taxes on sugar and rice withdraw resources from some of the same families.

- The programs must not be allowed to strain the administrative capacity of governments when the success of the whole adjustment effort hinges on improving performance in nonsocial areas. Yet the success of special programs depends greatly on their being well run. Some private assistance may help resolve this conflict (as it did in the Bolivian program run by former private sector managers with help from nongovernmental organizations).

- The programs must not be allowed to take root and become ever-growing entitlements. Even the United States is finding out that it cannot afford this.

- Again, programs must be based on the correct identification of the poor. In many countries, the poor cannot be accurately identified, and politicians are likely to think of only urban workers as the poor.

Several questions must be answered before effective poverty alleviation is possible:

- How much of the compensatory programs is rhetoric and how much is reality? Only a few countries have set up effective programs. Most programs are established for political reasons and in order to attract aid funds, and they do not achieve their stated purpose.

- How can politicians' perceptions of who the poor are be changed?

- Can and should the structural poor and the adjustment poor be treated differently?

- How much targeting is feasible or desirable? If it is a matter of life and death (especially of children), it is surely wise to err on the side of leakage. Also, will the middle classes support a program that brings no direct benefit to themselves?

- What is the cheapest and simplest way to obtain the statistics needed to design and monitor programs?

- Should the burden of poverty alleviation be on the strongest bureaucracies—for example, social security institutions and power companies—rather than on weaker institutions such as the ministries of health and education?

- Should compensatory programs be carried out by existing ministries and agencies or by a newly created specialized institution?

Another issue to be considered is the role of the private sector. In recent years there has been a substantial increase in the activities of the private sector in social areas (for profit as well as not-for-profit, domestic as well as foreign). The amounts channeled through nongovernmental organizations are in the billions of dollars worldwide. These organizations have focused on needs that were not met by governments either because of administrative incompetence or because of a lack of fiscal resources. A new and encouraging trend is the emergence of corporate philanthropy in countries such as Brazil and Colombia, along the lines of the U.S. experience. There is no doubt that private organizations are playing a vital role, even though few efforts have been subject to an evaluation of costs and benefits. Perhaps one could bring to bear financial mechanisms such as debt-equity swaps to increase funding for corporate philanthropy.

Governments (even those that are not providing adequate services) are not always willing to allow private organizations to step in. Teachers' unions often strongly oppose what they regard as competition from the private sector; yet private organizations, with a strong element of self-help on the part of clients or recipients, can provide comparable or better service at less cost. This privatization is occurring in education in the slums of São Paulo and is certainly worth a great deal of attention. It offers an *otro sendero* (or "other path") for social services for the poor.

I would like to say a few words about the school of thought represented by UNICEF's book *Adjustment with a Human Face* (1987). The authors are persuasive when they discuss health, education, and nutrition. However, they say surprisingly little in this imposing book about bureaucratic demands. South Korea and Chile are rightly included among countries that have set up effective compensatory programs, and they have both managed "adjustment with growth." Yet how many poor countries have anything like the administrative structures of these two countries? The real trick is to find solutions applicable to the countries with the weakest administrations, particularly in Africa. The authors also propose well-intentioned alternatives to traditional stabilization and adjustment policies. Here they are misleading. Several of the countries in the book have not in fact made serious macroeconomic efforts; their experience is therefore irrelevant to the argument. The authors, who wrote in 1986, endorse the Peruvian program as a model of an imaginative use of government policy (macroeconomic as well as microeconomic) to avoid the crossing of the desert and to help improve income distribution while coping with adjustment and growth. In 1990 the Peruvian poor are worse off than ever. This is largely because the García government followed unproven macroeconomic policies that brought about a fall in GDP and extremely high inflation. Recommending such policies is highly irresponsible.

Reasonably good macroeconomic policies are a prerequisite for effective poverty alleviation, not only because, as I said initially, economic growth is a major engine of social improvement, but also because imbalances impede social programs. Since the debt crisis began in 1982 most countries have adopted realistic exchange rates, which have helped generate employment through exports and import substitution and have benefited agriculture and therefore some of the poorest families. The rise of informal labor markets has also eroded unrealistically high regulated wages, and this too has encouraged employment creation. Fiscal problems, however, are far from solved. Many countries are suffering from high inflation, which hurts the poor who do not rely on home production, because, for example, they have to use cash, they are not part of the credit card culture, and they cannot store food in freezers.

Furthermore governments suffering from severe fiscal imbalances and high inflation tend to allow poverty programs to erode; for example, in Argentina school meals are supposed to be served in poor areas, yet the state governments often lack the resources to provide them. High real interest rates, often a side effect of fiscal deficits, also hurt the poor because they inhibit job-creating investment. It is not by chance that the most successful targeted programs in Latin America, those of Chile and Costa Rica, were both associated with reasonably orderly macro-economic conditions. Recent evidence from Uruguay gathered by the Economic Commission for Latin America and the Caribbean illustrates the beneficial effects of reasonably sound macroeconomic policies on the adjustment poor in a predominantly urban country: between 1984 and 1986 the percentage of households living below an arbitrarily defined poverty line went down from 20.5 to 16.4 percent. Of the 4.1 percentage point reduction, 3.3 percentage points were recently poor households. Economic growth, job creation, some gain in wages can be credited for this improvement in the lot of the adjustment poor.

Conclusion

Economic growth sustained over years is by far the surest way to raise the living standards of the poor. The record of punctual interventions such as rural development programs is mixed at best. Such programs are costly, benefit relatively few people, and usually demand extensive administrative resources. Good macroeconomic policies complemented by a safety net of well-designed social programs are essential for long-term poverty alleviation.

Likewise, resumed economic growth is the most effective way to help the adjustment poor. Governments can, as shown by some successful examples, design targeted social programs. But few developing countries have the administrative resources to do so effectively. All too often safety nets capture few of the poorest. There is a great need for developing countries and public and private aid organizations to improve such safety nets in ways that minimize demands on particularly scarce administrative talent.

Lastly, even where the public administration is competent enough to tackle poverty alleviation effectively (this includes industrialized as well as developing countries), there has been little success. The new political economy approach provides useful insights on this problem. Unless the bureaucratic self-interest can somehow be harnessed to the ends of poverty alleviation, it might be better to let private organizations operate as freely as possible. Such freedom, however, is likely to be denied by the very government health and education bureaucracies that are not, at present, doing much for the poor. If the new political economy moves away in the future from its largely normative character and becomes more operational, preferably in an interdisciplinary context, it might help bring about more effective poverty alleviation programs.

Comments

ROBERTO MACEDO

Guy Pfeffermann's chapter is short but filled with many ideas. I agree with most of them, but I will also argue against a few. My comments are based on my experience with similar issues in Brazil.

Let me start with the points we have in common. I share his concern with poverty alleviation and targeting as subjects of fundamental importance in the design of government policies, although I do not think we should neglect the traditional and more general concern with income distribution, a theme to which I will return later.

Pfeffermann correctly stresses that structural poverty is mainly a rural reality. The Brazilian northeast is indeed a typical case. His chapter contains a useful list of the factors that account for the neglect of the rural poor in the design of poverty alleviation programs: the reduced share of the rural poor after urbanization; their physical dispersion and isolation; the social relations between the rural communities and the program officers, which are established in such a way that no voice is given to the poorer or the poorest; the political patronage biased toward the urban areas; and so forth. His analysis is good political economy. To me, it does not matter if it is "old" or "new," as long as it is useful for the design of better policies.

Pfeffermann says that when dealing with the rural areas the government should use across-the-board measures rather than punctual ones. This approach makes sense on the basis of the Brazilian experience. The recent improvements in grain production are to a large extent the result of an agricultural policy that emphasized investment in improved techniques, especially better seeds and equipment, together with an enlarged public infrastructure. Moreover, the boom in the production and export of soybeans and orange juice would not have occurred in the absence of a realistic exchange rate. It is interesting to note that on June 30, 1989, the government undertook a mini-devaluation of 12 percent. The devaluation took place largely because of the pressure of soybean producers who blocked roads with their tractors to show their displeasure with the exchange rate, which was then exceptionally unrealistic after a failed stabilization attempt. Now that Brazil has diversified its exports, the exchange rate is no longer a matter of dispute between a few exporters of major primary products and millions of consumers. Brazil now has more parties on the exporting side, who bring more pressure for a consistent policy.

My work on poverty alleviation has also expressed, as does Pfeffermann, a concern with the obvious and fundamental question, who are the poor? Many policies are mistargeted because of sheer ignorance of the facts. Policies designed to reach loosely defined groups such as "the workers" or even "the population of the Brazilian northeast" are often mistargeted because these groups include some segments that are not so poor or that are even rich. Moreover, the specific design and implementation of policies often neglect the poorer or the poorest among these groups. In Brazil, for example, many social benefits are provided only to workers that have a formal labor contract, thus excluding those in the informal sector.

It is also true that the roots of mistargeting are based not only in an ignorance of the facts, but also in politics. It is not easy, however, to separate these two causes, because the ignorance is widespread. Brazilian politicians, for instance, are fond of proposing measures allegedly in favor of those who live in the *favelas* (slums or shanty towns). The measures they design, however—such as housing loans for those who have a formal labor contract—often do not reach those living in the *favelas*. Is it because an unsurmountable bureaucracy is embedded in the laws, because the politicians do not know the measures are mistargeted, or because they know their votes will come from a middle class that does not want to see the *favelas*? It is easy to answer yes to the last reason, but there are now so many *favelas* and so many voters living in them that the point cannot be taken for granted.

Maybe because I am a teacher, I still believe that ignorance of the facts among both politicians and voters is a major issue. One could say that the politicians are opportunistic, as they usually are. Notice, however, that the Church, an important pressure group for the urban poor, particularly in the city of São Paulo, has not yet shown serious concern for the targeting aspects of poverty alleviation. On the contrary, when the new Brazilian Constitution was voted on in 1988, church leaders pressed hard for the approval of "social rights" in the form of fringe and social security benefits. In practice, however, many of the poorer or poorest groups will not receive these benefits, since some of them are not wage earners and those who are often do not have a formal contract. Moreover, the middle class and the rich usually get most of the benefits.

Pfeffermann asks what, if anything, works. Again I agree with his response: if there is a single answer, it is economic development. It is well known that Brazil has a serious income distribution problem, but when the country was growing fast in the 1970s, trickle-down effects led to poverty alleviation. With the economic stagnation of the 1980s, the poor have also stagnated in poverty.

Pfeffermann did not touch directly on this point, but I think he would agree that now the major poverty problem in Latin America is the lack of growth. Unless Brazil gets out of this mess of high debt, high inflation, and low growth, the situation is hopeless. Brazil has adjusted the external sector and the private sector but has put off the badly needed adjustment of the public sector—a precondition for stabilization and for getting a better deal with the foreign creditors. This is the root cause of our difficulties.

I now turn to the few points of disagreement. Pfeffermann criticized what he calls the "school of thought represented by UNICEF's book *Adjustment with a Human Face*" and its authors by saying that "they propose well-intentioned alternatives to traditional stabilization and adjustment policies." He adds that recommending unproven macroeconomic policies is "highly irresponsible."

As one of the authors, I would say that his comments are mistargeted and apply only to the editors of a book that has many papers. Most of the authors tried, with varying degrees of success, to show the costs of adjustment among the vulnerable groups, children in particular. Most authors, including myself, did not address the issue of an alternative macroeconomic policy.

The lesson of the book as a whole is that adjustment has a major social cost in developing countries because their institutions are ill prepared to cope with the adjustment poor. Those countries that have urbanized very quickly, such as Brazil, have not yet developed the social safety nets, even the cheapest ones, such as soup kitchens, to cope with the undesirable effects of adjustment. Therefore, I agree that countries should accept the need for adjustment and stabilization, but they should also design policies for establishing or improving essential safety nets. This strategy would give adjustment a human face.

I share Pfeffermann's concern with the adoption of unproven macroeconomic policies. After three failed stabilization experiences in the past four years, it is not necessary to be an economist to realize that the versions of the heterodox shocks adopted in Brazil did not work because they neglected the orthodox component of the heterodox menu. In other words, wage and price freezes can help in stopping inflationary inertia only if the fundamentals of the stabilization plan—that is, the fiscal and monetary policies—are also set right. I would also add that any program, to have a chance of success, must tackle the foreign debt problem, which is a source of major fiscal, monetary, and exchange rate disturbances. The foreign creditors, with their irresponsible lending policies, also bear some of the blame for the crisis and should share some of the sacrifices, although in the Brazilian case I think the crisis is 70 percent homegrown.

If Brazil could put its house in order, it would be in a position to obtain better terms from outside lenders.

In a recent paper I sketched out my version of adjustment (and stabilization) with a human face (Macedo 1988). The plan should include a strong and consistent attack on the fundamental causes of inflation, in particular a restructuring of the Brazilian public sector, and a new design for making government social expenditures according to targeting criteria. Since the amount of these expenditures in Brazil is considerable—19 percent of a gross domestic product (GDP) of roughly $300 billion—and they are essentially mistargeted, shifting their focus to the poorer would give the plan a human facelift without compromising fiscal policy by lavishly increasing social expenditures. In other words, my idea is to use targeting as a compensatory policy. Moreover, even the social expenditures that now reach the poor could be made more cost-effective (cost and effectiveness are still foreign words in the vocabulary of our bureaucracy). In addition, the plan would contain measures designed to foster investment, in order to avoid or mitigate a recession.

Let me now move to a point that has more potential for discussion. I refer to Pfeffermann's comment that "poverty alleviation and not income redistribution should be the focus of policy." As far as social expenditures are concerned, poverty alleviation and income redistribution mean the same thing. With regard to the tax revenues that support these expenditures, income distribution emerges as the basic issue, because as a whole the government's social policies would be consistently targeted only if the tax system were structured on equity grounds. In Brazil it is not. The tax system is based mostly on indirect taxes on consumption and not on direct and progressive taxes.

I now come to the final point of disagreement. Pfeffermann says that poverty alleviation has not been particularly successful in the industrialized countries and it may even be easier to alleviate poverty in traditional societies such as Sri Lanka than in the United States. We know, however, that in 1987 Sri Lanka had a per capita GDP of only US$400, while per capita GDP in the United States was US$18,430 (World Bank 1988). The United States therefore has a lot more resources to make poverty alleviation easier. In my view, this comparison again shows that when dealing with poverty alleviation, one cannot lose sight of the income distribution problem, and Pfeffermann's statement about Sri Lanka and the United States might make sense for income redistribution. In other words, income redistribution might be easier in Sri Lanka, but it is hard to believe that poverty alleviation would be more difficult in the United States.

JOAN M. NELSON

Guy Pfeffermann has offered important insights on an issue of great current concern. With respect to the political economy aspects of poverty alleviation, I would like to emphasize his distinction between the structural poor, who normally have almost no political influence, and the adjustment poor, who often have considerable clout.

Much of the discussion and debate about "adjustment with a human face" has been muddled by the variety of concepts of the poor used by different agencies and groups. (The varying concepts are distinct from the technical arguments about poverty criteria—where and on what bases to draw poverty lines.)

- Many humanitarian organizations give highest priority to reaching the poorest of the poor.

- UNICEF, in accord with its mandate, is concerned with an overlapping but different category: the vulnerable poor, above all young children, who may suffer irreversible damage from even temporary deprivation.

- The World Bank has recently been using a rough guideline in its analyses and discussions of "the poorest 30 percent," although many of its concrete programs and projects clearly address broader (and much less heavily rural) groups.

- Most politicians, and most politically relevant public opinion in developing countries, define the poor (or the popular classes) much more inclusively. They usually have in mind less the bottom third than the middle deciles, including especially the semipoor and working classes who comprise most of the urban population.

It is often suggested that adjustment programs that are more sensitive to the needs of the poor would also be more politically sustainable, that is, less likely to provoke protests that may derail the adjustment effort (such as the maize meal riots in Zambia in December 1986). Whether that is true depends on which poor are protected. Programs that help the poorest or most vulnerable—which are most attractive to external donors—are only marginally relevant to political sustainability. Measures that help the urban popular classes are highly relevant, but they also run a much higher risk of being incompatible with the financial and economic requirements for stabilization.

Compensatory or relief programs for the adjustment poor are spreading rapidly. These programs pose few political problems to governments: they are mainly externally financed, temporary, and usually do not focus only on the very poor. In contrast, switching from broad and financially unsustainable food subsidies to more tightly targeted programs, or reorienting education and health expenditures to better serve the poorer strata are measures that are permanent and require obvious redistribution of resources from the better-off. Such measures are extremely difficult (often explosive) politically, and there are very few success stories.

In short, although I agree with Pfeffermann's message that more can and should be done to protect poorer groups, particularly the adjustment poor, in the course of adjustment, I want to underscore another message in his paper: the task is much harder politically than is often assumed.

MIGUEL URRUTIA

Guy Pfeffermann has written a very informative and stimulating chapter. I question only one of his arguments.

Pfeffermann states that poverty alleviation has not been particularly successful in the industrialized countries. Later he discusses mistargeting because of political factors, especially in newly democratic countries. I would like to qualify these broad conclusions somewhat.

First, some state programs in industrialized countries have had a dramatic impact on poverty alleviation. There is now a broad literature in the industrialized countries on the frustrations of social programs and poverty alleviation. That literature is unfortunately misleading, and in Latin America we should analyze more closely the successes of social policy in industrialized countries.

According to the U.S. Bureau of the Census, before state intervention (that is, before government transfers) it appears that 45 percent of the people over sixty-five in the United States are below the poverty line. After benefits from social security and government programs, about 9 percent remain below the poverty line. This is a spectacular success rate for a loosely targeted program. So we should take some of the things that are being recommended to us, such as the emphasis on tightly targeted programs, with a grain of salt.

There is no question, however, that in the industrialized countries government programs for black unwed mothers in the ghettos have not been effective. Scholars are doing a lot of interesting work on the new political economy and on the theory of pressure groups to try to understand why these programs fail and how these tragedies can be prevented. Nevertheless, there is no question that state intervention does have an effect on poverty in the industrialized countries and in some cases can significantly increase the welfare of the poor.

I would argue that some poverty alleviation has in fact taken place in the democracies of Latin America. Authoritarian governments in Latin America have no legitimacy and are therefore more vulnerable to middle-class pressures than democracies. Why? First, the military is part of the middle class. Second, students are more dangerous to regimes with legitimacy problems than disaffected peasants. The poor, through the vote, can obtain and have obtained some state benefits. In Colombian urban areas, government expenditures truly redistribute. In Costa Rica government expenditures also probably redistribute income.

I would also like to note some political aspects of Colombian development. In Colombia, four out of the five administrations since 1970 have made redistribution the major objective of government expenditure policy. Colombia is very unusual among Latin American countries: it runs a fairly orthodox macroeconomic policy and a redistributive fiscal policy. Coincidentally, there is now clear evidence that from the early 1970s to 1988, income distribution in Colombia has improved significantly. Many factors other than government policies explain this improvement, such as the demographic trends. But there is no question that government intervention helped. Expenditure is in fact targeted to the poor, at least in part because of the political process.

I agree with Pfeffermann that in Latin America import-substitution policies created a middle class that has been the crucial political actor and has also received many of the benefits of the state. Interestingly enough, however, in Colombia the improvement in income distribution that has taken place since the late 1970s has been at the expense of the middle class. The poorest 50 percent of the population has gained, and there is some evidence that those in the upper ranges have also gained. So there is clear evidence that in Colombia the middle class has not gained most from the development process.

In summary, the imperfect democratic structures in some Latin American countries, including Colombia, Costa Rica, and Venezuela, have generated pressures for poverty alleviation and for institutions to implement those policies. These societies seem to have many of the characteristics of pluralist societies in industrialized countries, and therefore some of the U.S. and European literature on the new political economy may be more relevant than is at first apparent.

The Latin American democracies are full of surprises. Pfeffermann asks, who ever heard of the minister of agriculture becoming president? Well, Virgilio Barco, recent president of Colombia, was minister of agriculture. Even more interesting, former president Alfonso López won office in 1974 promising economic support for agriculture and the dismantling of import substitution. In addition, during the campaign he committed himself to decreasing urban bias. As always happens in Colombia, and I suppose in all democracies, the political promises were only partially achieved or implemented, and there was only a small decrease in protection. With respect to urban bias, however, since 1974 Colombia has not provided any subsidies for the city of Bogotá, and the various fiscal redistribution systems have not benefited the city. Not surprisingly, Bogotá's rate of growth decreased, and some cities in Colombia are growing faster than Bogotá. So Colombia has a clear policy against urban subsidies that has not been reversed for over a decade.

There is no question that in the Colombian political system, as in most democracies, the rural population is overrepresented. Furthermore, in Colombian political parties, the weakest region is the Bogotá area. The power of the provincial representatives within the parties is immense. Thus the decrease in urban bias is related to the democratic political structures.

I agree with Pfeffermann that rapid economic growth is the best means of diminishing poverty. Colombia, however, has experienced constant and unspectacular growth and an improvement in income distribution. This occurred during a period in which economic policies produced measures and institutions that can and have generated rent-seeking activities. There is a marketing board for the country's major export, quantitative controls on trade, interest rate controls, and many of the other demons of the new political economy. Yet there has been economic growth and improving income distribution since the 1970s, with mild interventionist policies. Although the growth rate has not been spectacular, it is the highest in Latin America.

It is also true, however, that since the late 1960s, the demons have not been well fed. There has been a gradual dismantling of some of these types of intervention, in a period in which democracy has also been strengthened and income distribution has improved. At the same time guerrilla terrorist activity has increased, and the drug trade has generated a very wealthy minority that threatens the political institutions in an unprecedented manner. To Colombians, most of these latter outcomes are unexpected, and it would be interesting to try to apply the tools of the new political economy to understand how these outcomes came about.

LEROY P. JONES, INGO VOGELSANG,
AND PANKAJ TANDON   CHAPTER 8

Public Enterprise Divestiture

The 1980s appear to have been the decade of privatization. From the Thatcher revolution at the start of the decade to the dramatic announcements of impending privatization in Eastern Europe, it seemed as if the frontiers of the state were being rolled back in virtually every country in the world. Sober reflection, however, reveals that the experience was not so uniform. Particularly in the less-developed countries, there has been far more rhetoric about privatization than there have been tangible results. The question naturally arises, why this difference? We believe that the answer to this puzzle lies in an analysis of the political economy of public enterprise divestiture.

Our approach to "political economy"[1] is this: first, we identify winners and losers from a particular policy; second, we assess the relative political strengths of each group; and third, we use this information to either explain outcomes or modify policy. We use a benefit-cost approach,

We thank conference participants for useful comments and the International Center for Economic Growth and Banco de la República de Colombia for financial support.

199

meaning that we measure gains and losses in the applied welfare economics tradition.

We therefore apply an intermediate level of technology and examine only a piece of the divestiture pie. The whole pie would include, on the one hand, the rich and diverse tapestry of the verbal tradition as represented by the volumes edited by Vernon (1988) and by Suleiman and Waterbury (1989). On the other hand, it would include the narrow technical virtuosity of the formal modeling tradition as represented by the works of Bos (1988a, 1988b) and of Shapiro and Willig (1989).

We begin by developing our analytic framework, giving separate attention to the efficiency and distributional effects of divestiture. We then note that the most relevant use of the resulting framework is for ex ante or ex post analysis of actual cases, something we do not at present have to offer. Instead, we use the framework at a more aggregate level to examine the genesis of the current wave of privatization. We conclude by analyzing factors that contribute to the contrasting levels of divestiture in less-developed and more-developed countries (LDCs and MDCs).

Analytic Framework

Two trade-offs. Before trying to figure out who wins and who loses, we first need to identify what is won and lost—that is, how is economic welfare altered by divestiture? To answer this question, we present in this section a simple version of other work (Jones, Tandon, and Vogelsang 1990). We want to capture two distinct effects of divestiture: a behavioral effect resulting from the fact that the enterprise is presumably run differently before and after divestiture, and a fiscal effect resulting from the fact that buyer and seller exchange asymmetrically valued streams of income. Each effect embodies a trade-off such that divestiture can on balance either enhance or reduce welfare.

Behavioral effects. The economics of divestiture become interesting only when enterprise conduct is altered as a result of sale. On this, opponents and proponents can agree. On the one hand, private management is said to improve static operating efficiency and dynamic entrepreneurial innovation. On the other hand, private motivation is said to lead to exploitation of consumers, workers, and the environment. In short, there is a trade-off between the possibility that private objectives are less desirable socially and the possibility that the private sector will pursue these objectives more efficiently. This is the fundamental trade-off of divestiture.

The resulting change in welfare (ΔW) is decomposed into a change in consumer surplus (ΔS) and a change in enterprise profits ($\Delta\Pi$). In the public enterprise context the role of providers of inputs (such as labor, credit, and permits) is critical and the change in their rents (ΔM) must also be included. That is,[2]

$$\Delta W = \Delta S + \Delta \Pi + \Delta M.$$

Now this equation is valid only if consumer surplus, profits, and input rents all have equal weight. To allow for the possibility that they may not, we choose to introduce weights for profits and rents, implicitly measuring their importance relative to consumer surplus (the numeraire). Thus our expression for the change in welfare is

$$\Delta W = \Delta S + \lambda_\Pi \Delta \Pi + \lambda_m \Delta M \tag{8.1}$$

where λ_Π and λ_m are the respective weights for profits and input rents

Fiscal effects. If $\Delta \Pi$ is positive, then there is a positive-sum game between buyer and seller. The benefits from this game are distributed by the negotiated strike price (Z) at which the enterprise is sold. The private buyer gains to the extent that his maximum willingness to pay (Z_p)[3] exceeds what he actually pays (Z). Therefore, the private buyer's share of the gain = $Z_p - Z$. In the unlikely event that government negotiators are able to drive such a hard bargain that the buyer gains nothing beyond the opportunity cost of his resources, then $Z = Z_p$. The buyer gets none of $\Delta \Pi$, and the government gets it all. To the extent that Z falls short of Z_p, the government's share is reduced. So the government's share of the gain = $\Delta \Pi - (Z_p - Z)$.

We now need to recognize that society's valuation of these flows may be asymmetric, requiring the introduction of shadow multipliers. A staple of the project evaluation literature is the notion that a dollar of government revenue may be worth more than a dollar of the numeraire consumption good by a factor termed the government revenue multiplier (which we will call λ_g). Assume that public goods exist and must be financed by taxes. Taxes impose a deadweight welfare loss or excess burden, meaning that at the margin a dollar of taxes results in a loss of consumption of more than one dollar, and λ_g is greater than unity. What is less widely recognized is that a dollar of profits can also be worth more than a dollar of consumption, creating a private profit multiplier (λ_p). Assume that capital income is taxed or that other distortions in markets for capital or entrepreneurship drive a wedge between the return to capital and the present value of the consumption stream it generates. Then, insofar as profits are used for investment, λ_p also exceeds unity.

The fiscal trade-off is now clear. One common motive for divestiture is government revenue. However, this can come only at the expense of the private buyer who diverts funds and entrepreneurial talent from other investment activities. The trade-off is between what society gains from the application of those energies to the divested public enterprise and what society would have gained had they remained in the private sector. We incorporate this trade-off by evaluating the welfare effect of the profit change as the respective profit shares weighted by their respective multipliers:

$$\lambda_\Pi \, \Delta\Pi = \lambda_g[\Delta\Pi - (Z_p - Z)] + \lambda_p(Z_p - Z).$$

Rearranging the equation yields

$$\lambda_\Pi \, \Delta\Pi = \lambda_g \, \Delta\Pi - (\lambda_g - \lambda_p) \, (Z_p - Z). \tag{8.2}$$

Welfare equation. Substituting equation (8.2) in equation (8.1)[4] yields our basic accounting framework for calculating the change in welfare:

$$\Delta W = \Delta S + \lambda_g \Delta\Pi + \lambda_m \Delta M + (\lambda_g - \lambda_p)(Z_p - Z). \tag{8.3}$$

We will say more about the interpretation of this framework after extending it by introducing income distribution and identifying specific actors and what each wins or loses.

Analytics of Distribution

The equations in the previous section were derived using an implicit assumption of distributional neutrality in consumption. An incremental dollar of consumption was of equal worth regardless of who consumed it (so long as it was not a foreigner). Dollars were different insofar as they were used for different purposes (for example, investment rather than consumption), and this led to efficiency multipliers. In this section we incorporate distributional considerations, leading to multipliers that reflect both equity and efficiency.

Income distribution. The mechanics of introducing income distribution is a four-step process:

1. Redefine the numeraire to represent a dollar of consumption accruing to a particular group. Ideally, we would like to use as numeraire an allocation that does not change the distribution of consumption. A simpler and more pragmatic possibility is a dollar accruing to the "average"[5] consumer, as utilized in Squire and van der Tak (1975: ch. 10).[6]

2. Calculate the multipliers. Discrete multipliers may be assigned to some groups (for example, foreigners equal zero) or regions. For the rest, we need a continuous distribution as

a function of consumption. This is commonly captured in a single parameter for the consumption elasticity (n) of the marginal social utility (δU) of consumption (C) (for example, in Squire and van der Tak 1975):

$$\delta U_c = C^{-n}$$

If n = 0, then the marginal social value of consumption is independent of the level of consumption, we do not care about distribution, and the shadow multiplier for consumption (λ_s) equals unity. Greater levels of n yield exponentially greater levels of redistributional weight. For example, if the target group's consumption is half of the median, then their consumption is twice as valuable if $n = 1$ and four times as valuable if $n = 2$.

3. Insert the consumption multiplier thus calculated in the consumer surplus term in equation (8.3).

4. Reinterpret the existing multipliers in equation (8.3) to incorporate both the previous efficiency effect and the new distributional effect.[7]

There is a bit more to it than this, but the first two steps are a staple of the cost-benefit literature and the last two are straightforward. Before proceeding to interpret our basic distributional equation, we will identify the actors in our story.

Actors. We identify seven classes of actors. The first four share the costs and benefits of divestiture:

1. Citizens are the ultimate beneficiaries of funds accruing to the government, whether in the form of reduced taxes, greater consumption of public goods, or reduced inflation.

2. Consumers are affected insofar as divestiture alters the price/quantity/quality bundle offered by the enterprise.

3. Purchasers of the enterprise benefit from the sale in so far as the actual sales price falls short of their maximum willingness to pay.

4. Providers of inputs lose insofar as divested cost-cutting efforts reduce rents previously accruing in forms such as excess

wages, overbilling for intermediates or construction contracts, excess profits to middlemen, kickbacks to providers of credit, and side payments to signers of various official pieces of paper. They may also gain if, for example, profit shares and incentive payments are offered to employees after sale.

The remaining three sets of actors are involved in the decision-making process:

5. Patrons are broad-minded political agents who make the ultimate decisions about public enterprises, taking into account both their ideological requirements and explicit effects on the general interests of citizens and the narrower interests of various special-interest groups.

6. Technocrats are narrow-minded economic agents who attempt to influence patrons to act in the interest of citizens.

7. Clients are the special-interest groups of providers, consumers, and purchasers who attempt to influence patrons to act in their interest.

This morphology is imperfect in that the categories are neither mutually exclusive nor exhaustive. In part, this imperfection is trivial: for example, almost all actors are citizens, but if a provider gets one-hundredth of the benefits, we can safely ignore the fact that as a citizen he also pays one-millionth of the costs. In part, it is by design: patrons can also be providers, and therein lies a portion of the story. In part, it is a simplification designed to draw attention to certain fundamentals: for example, providers are a rather heterogeneous group encompassing selected unionists, capitalists, and bureaucrats, among others. Depending on the political bargains struck to gain support for divestiture, some may gain while others lose. Their interests will therefore ultimately have to be separated, but as a starting point it is useful to call attention to their common interest in opposition to simple divestiture. The proof of the pudding, however, is in the eating, so let us see how this particular classification works as a starting point.

Distributional equation. Given our choice of actors and the introduction of the new multipliers,[8] a simple rearrangement of equation (8.3) yields our basic distributional equation (8.4), completely allocating the change in welfare resulting from divestiture:

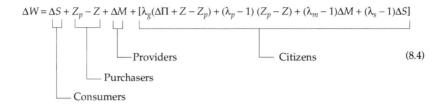

That is:

1. Consumers receive the change in consumer surplus. This is positive to the extent that greater efficiency or competition reduces prices and negative to the extent that prices rise because of exploitation of market power or abolition of price subsidies.

2. Purchasers benefit to the extent that their willingness to pay (Z_p, the present value of future profits) exceeds the price actually paid (Z). Since they are not coerced into buying, the expected value will be nonnegative.

3. Providers receive any change in rents accruing to suppliers of inputs. This will most commonly be negative but can be positive for particular subgroups if facilitating side payments are agreed to in advance or their bargaining power is maintained and they receive a share of increased enterprise rent after divestiture (witness the increased returns to labor after divestiture raised profits at Jaguar).

4. Citizens' returns are somewhat more diffuse and harder to interpret. The first term says that in the unlikely event that bargaining extracts the purchaser's full willingness to pay ($Z = Z_p$), citizens receive the entire stream of enhanced profitability, evaluated at the shadow price of government funds. To the extent that the strike price falls short of the buyers' willingness to pay, this benefit is reduced. The next three terms follow from the definition of the respective multipliers. Recall that a λ_p greater than one might mean that a dollar of investment is worth more than a dollar of private consumption because of capital market distortions. This excess accrues to citizens in the form of government revenue or greater investment creating more jobs and ultimately leading to higher aggregate consumption levels. The same

holds for the efficiency component of λ_m. For λ_s (and the equity components of λ_p and λ_m) the interpretation is that although the individual consumer gets the extra surplus, society as a whole benefits from living in a more egalitarian society.[9]

This gives us a brief outline of the candidates for positions as winners and losers from divestiture. The next step is to get to know them better.

Distributional Realities

Where do the different actors fit into the income distribution of a country? Where do they fit into the power distribution? This section addresses these questions in turn. Particular attention will be focused on the role of providers, a group we view as central to the political economy of divestiture.

Divestiture and the poor: LDCs. Where do the various actors appear in the income distribution? Mechanically, are λ_s and the distributional components of λ_p and λ_m likely to be greater or less than one? We focus attention on the case of the LDCs.

Who consumes public enterprise products? Consider electricity. Some goes to consumers who are disproportionately wealthy: the rich have air conditioners and stereos, while the poor have one light bulb dangling on a wire or are not served at all. The rest of the output is sold to industry as an intermediate input, and, depending on the degree of competition in their output markets, is shared between the owners (rich, obviously) and the consumers of energy-intensive projects (also relatively well-to-do). A similar analysis applies to the bulk of public enterprise products, which are capital and energy intensive. Even for foodstuffs, which do not fit this mold, relatively little goes to rural areas where the bulk of poverty lies, and even within urban areas the well-to-do consume more than the poor.[10]

Exceptions may occur. Lifeline pricing in electricity may direct benefits to the poor. Profits from luxury housing may be used to subsidize low-income housing; the same may occur between first- and third-class rail or bus service. Even in these cases, it is by no means certain that the subsidized consumer is significantly below the median. While allowing for the possibility of such special cases, it seems that in general λ_s will be less than one in LDCs.

What of providers? Obviously, suppliers of inputs, contractors, and approvers of credit, licenses, and other documents are disproportionately at the top of the income distribution. At first blush labor would seem to be less well off, but studies in a variety of countries shows that even the lowest-paid worker in a public enterprise is typically in the seventieth percentile of the income distribution and certainly in the top half. The distributional component of λm will generally be less than one.

What of purchasers? Sale to a single individual, family, or closely held corporation obviously affects only the very top of the income distribution. Sale of shares on the stock market moves down the distribution somewhat but still affects primarily the top decile. Even sale to employees involves only the top three deciles. The distributional component of λ_p will certainly be considerably less than one.

What of citizens? Here, of course, the poor are represented. If, at the margin, additional government funds are used to benefit the lower half of the income distribution and if divestiture is implemented in such a way that the government captures a share of the benefits, then the poor can gain. How likely is this? Not very. As we shall argue below, an environment facilitating extensive divestiture is likely to be characterized by fiscal stringency and an ideological predilection for less government, not more. Under such conditions, then, additional government revenues are more likely to reduce taxes than to increase services to the poor. If so, the segment of citizens benefiting at the margin from additional government revenues is likely to be taxpayers, whose mean position on the distributional scale is well above the median. In sum, the distributional component of λ_g could in principle be greater than one but in the environment of extensive divestiture is likely to be lower.

In LDCs, then, divestiture is a game played primarily between the rich and the upper middle class. This is not to say that divestiture cannot improve income distribution. Transferring resources from those in the ninety-ninth percentile to those in the seventieth may be worthwhile. If the bottom half of the population is to gain directly, however, one must look at the benefits to citizens and not those accruing to consumers, purchasers, or providers. For divestiture to help the poor, the primary route is indirect: the government must get a substantial share of the gain from divestiture and then use it to provide services to the poor.

Rent seeking. Rents are gravy: that is, returns to the actor in this activity exceed those available to him elsewhere. It is therefore hardly novel to suggest that people seek rents. What the burgeoning literature on rent seeking contributes is the insight that a lot of the gravy gets sopped up in the process.[11]

Is a rational economic agent willing to pay something for $100,000 in rents? Of course. He will pay in two fundamentally distinct forms. First, as a client (or potential client) he will make transfer payments to the producers and distributors of discretionary rents—patrons who protect a monopoly position or convey tariff, tax, credit, licensing, or other privileged position. Note that these payments need not, and often will not, go to the individuals themselves but to political parties, charitable causes, or other worthy endeavors espoused by the patron. Second, he will incur real resource costs to find out who these people are, gain access, acquire their trust, and fend off competing bidders.

What are the relative magnitudes of the two components? Focusing on a single transaction, it might be thought that transfer payments would be the dominant element. However, two other considerations greatly increase the role of real resource costs. First, the recipients of the transfer payments also are receiving rents as a result of their official position, and they are willing to pay a price for this. Governors, policemen, and other officials have been known to pay for so-called wet positions in some countries at some times, and politicians almost always pay for theirs. As the original transfer payment passes through successive hands, more and more of it leaks into real resource costs. The second source of real resource expenditures are other rent seekers pursuing the $100,000. Although few will succeed in gaining rents, many will expend resources seeking them.

What might the resulting resource costs total? In the extreme, if markets for rents and patrons were both perfectly competitive, then competitive pressures would ensure that no one would receive more than their opportunity cost and all potential rents would be eaten up in the quest. This is patently absurd, but extremes serve to make the point.

In sum, the fundamental contribution of this literature is that some—and in the extreme, all—potential rents are dissipated in the quest to obtain them. This would suggest, for example, that the traditional argument minimizing the deadweight loss due to monopoly is wrong. The argument is that monopoly profits are merely a transfer from consumers to the monopoly firm, leaving only a small "triangle" of deadweight loss. In the extreme rent-seeking case, however, real resources are used in the acquisition of those monopoly profits. Thus all of the monopoly profits should be included as deadweight losses, substantially increasing our estimate of the evils of monopoly—and of any other rent-generating market imperfections.

Now, one may or may not agree that this constitutes "one of the most stimulating fields of economic theory in recent years" (Tullock 1987: vol. 4, 149), but it is clearly a handy notion. It offers two benefits. First, it provides a properly pedantic euphemism that allows academics to talk about patronage, kickbacks, and other forms of corruption without sounding like journalists. Second, in forcing us to take a hard look at the distinction between "neutral" transfers and "evil" deadweight losses, it leads us to new calculations of the benefit-cost ratios of various public policies. Typically, this means that since the costs of discretionary market failures are understated, the returns to reform are likewise understated. Sadly, the reverse can be true in the case of divestiture.

Inefficiency and rent seeking. Briefly, the argument is this. If seekers find rents in public enterprises, then those rents are entered on the books as a cost. A major perceived benefit of divestiture is improved efficiency, but a portion of that is rent reduction and a portion consists of transfers. Some—we will argue a considerable portion—of the ostensible benefits from divestiture are therefore not deadweight gains, but transfers. This has two central implications for our analysis. First, technocrats must not neglect to deduct the change in rents (ΔM) when calculating the change in welfare (ΔW). Second, since there is no danger that clients will ignore ΔM and neglect to convey this awareness to patrons, any divestiture strategy must give explicit attention to dealing with the interests of clients. In this subsection we therefore examine in more detail the relationship between rents and inefficiency.

Public enterprise inefficiencies can be thought of as reflecting potential rents and quasi-rents that do not accrue to capital. An analysis of sources of inefficiency is then a description of the existing distribution of those rents. Improvement of efficiency means returning those rents to the owners of capital. As usual in a rent-seeking context, we must be careful to distinguish two sorts of inefficiency: first, inefficiency whose removal merely involves a transfer of existing rents; and second, inefficiency whose removal creates rents through real resource savings. For example, on the output side price may be too low, amounting to a subsidy to users. If price is raised, enterprise profits will rise, but much of this is a transfer from users who were previously receiving the subsidy. The same distinction must be made on the input side, where costs can be lowered either by reducing input prices or by reducing quantities. As a first approximation, endogenous input price changes can be thought of as transfers, and quantity changes as real resource savings.[12] The price category includes, among other things:

1. wages, benefits, and perks above opportunity cost[13]

2. markups on contracts and intermediates

3. sales at below market price to privileged middlemen who resell at market

4. contributions to political parties and designated charities

On the one hand, if cost reductions are achieved by reducing or eliminating such distortions, then rents are not created but merely transferred from one recipient to another. On the other hand, if costs are reduced by decreasing the quantities consumed (pure technical efficiency improvement), then it would seem that rents are created.

In the strictly neoclassical view, no such pure rent creation can occur. The argument is that costs can be reduced only by the actions of individuals—especially managers—who work harder or smarter. The cost reduction is thus accompanied by a reduction in the welfare of the persons putting out more effort, in the form of sacrifice of alternative output, leisure, or psychic utility. If, in the extreme, all cost reductions are interpreted this way, then the net output (or welfare) of society is unchanged but is redistributed from employees to the enterprise. Either employees were previously earning a rent, which is now being taken away, or some market imperfection makes labor immobile, allowing the divested firm to reduce employees' welfare below their opportunity cost and thus charge a negative rent. This might be called the neoclassical theory of the exploitation of the masses. If X or cost inefficiency does not exist, then no real cost savings can result from reducing slack.[14]

Note the symmetry with the rent-seeking extreme: in the perfect neoclassical world, all rents disappear in the cost of seeking; but cost-saving efficiency changes become rent redistribution. As already noted, we do not espouse either extreme view as a reflection of the world of imperfect markets, but merely note that some ostensible quantity savings may have nonmonetary resource-cost offsets.

Where does this leave us regarding inefficiency and divestiture? On the one hand, some apparent efficiency improvements (ostensibly cost savings) turn out, on closer examination, to be rent transfers. On the other hand, there are some apparent rent transfers (which therefore do not appear to be efficiency improvements), which in fact are reduced costs of rent seeking. The relative size of the two components is presumably a case-by-case empirical issue. Here we only note that, in an imperfect world, some of what appear to be cost savings from the point of view of the enterprise are really rent transfers, and the resulting negative ΔM creates opponents to divestiture.

Why Divestiture Now?

There is a marked discontinuity in postwar world economic history: until the 1980s the public enterprise sector expanded or remained the same in almost all countries in almost all subperiods; after that it contracted or remained the same in almost all countries.[15] The generalization is surprisingly robust across the world's two-hundred-odd countries.[16] The question is, why the discontinuity?

One class of answer focuses on the role of ideological change and "great men and women":

> Most analysts trace its beginnings to proposals stumbled onto and subsequently pushed with great zeal by the Thatcher government after 1979. In just a very few years, similar types of experiments could be found in dozens of countries and on every continent (Ikenberry 1989: 1).[17]

A different class of answer is stressed by Vernon and his colleagues:

> Thus, in interpreting the significance of the surge of divestiture programs all over the world, my colleagues and I have been strongly inclined to discount the possibility that the movement represents a basic ideological shift among the countries concerned. Instead, we see the programs as the result of a learning process stretching over two or three decades, a process that has given the governments involved a keener appreciation of the costs and benefits associated with their ownership and management of various enterprises (Vernon 1988: 18–19).

Being wishy-washy middle-of-the-roaders, we see merit in both explanations. In our framework, there are three stylized classes of change precipitating divestiture:

1. Technocrats' views may change because ΔW has changed as a result of real exogenous shifts in the costs and benefits.

2. Clients' effective views may change, either because their own net benefit position has changed or because their political power has changed.

3. Patrons' positions may change, either because the previous two viewpoints have changed or because they themselves have changed their weightings.

We consider these possibilities in turn.

Change in technocrats' position. We have argued that there are two broad sets of changes determining the welfare effects of divestiture: behavioral and fiscal. Both have changed in ways that might increase returns to divestiture. For behavior, a secular trend of increasingly competitive markets is the dominant factor, potentially increasing the various components of ΔW. For the fiscal effect, increased fiscal stringency potentially increases λ_g and the efficiency component of the other multipliers (λs). These, and other, contributing factors are discussed below.

Increasing effective market size. The potential number of firms in a market depends on the size of that market relative to minimum efficient scale. There are two distinct sources of increasing market size and therefore increased potential competition. The first is economic growth. In the three decades from 1959 to 1989, the world economy—and therefore the average economy—has roughly tripled in size.[18] An economy that was large enough to support only three cement plants in the late 1950s might have been able to support nine in the late 1980s.

The second source of increasing market size is increased openness. The fact that there are only one or two domestic producers of a commodity is not terribly significant if the bulk of production is freely imported.[19] Increasing openness therefore increases competitive pressures. Casual evidence indicates that both technological change (decreasing transport and information costs) and policy change have contributed to increased openness over the long-term at the global level. Indeed, this is true not only for the developed countries, but also for the developing countries since 1980.[20] As a special case of the foregoing, the creation of a single market in Europe is important enough to warrant separate attention. After 1992, an inefficient European producer of tradables will die or require huge subsidies; inefficient producers of nontradables may survive but make it difficult for domestic producers of tradables to compete. For both reasons, anticipation of 1992 should have produced major technocratic pressures for public enterprise reform.

Decreasing minimum efficient scale. Whereas effective market size has clearly grown, economies of scale seem to have grown at a lesser pace, or even declined. This is of course highly variable across industries, but seems to have been particularly pronounced in the public utility sphere where public enterprises are concentrated. One reason for this has to do with a trade-off between the two-thirds rule[21] and the strain on materials as machines or containers become larger and larger. This trade-off is said to explain the failure to build reliable thermal electricity–generating units with a capacity greater than 600 megawatts. In telecommunications, the natural monopoly argument has lost much of its validity largely because of technological advances such as microwave transmission, cellular radio, and satellite technologies (although fiber optics may recreate part of the natural monopoly). Another important development is the use of computers as inputs in production processes. The ubiquity of personal computers and off-the-shelf hardware has reduced returns-to-scale across a large range of products requiring information, coordination, and control.

In sum, it seems safe to conclude that in the majority of countries for the majority of public enterprise products, the rate of growth of market size has substantially exceeded that of minimum efficient scale and that competition has accordingly been increasing dramatically. How does this affect the technocratic divestiture decision?

Competition and the change in welfare (ΔW). Since competition is the economist's grail, it comes as something of a shock to inspect equation (8.4) and find that competition is a mixed blessing in terms of ΔW.[22] The positive side is obvious: the more competition in the output market, the less likely that the divested firm will exercise market power and create a negative ΔS. The neutral side is that the more competitive the output market, the less likely that any cost savings from divestiture will be passed on to consumers. The negative side is that under competition there is less likely to be any cost savings to pass on: $\Delta M + \Delta \Pi$ approaches zero. Why is this?

Given that monopolies are inefficient and public enterprises are often monopolies, is the observed inefficiency of monopolistic public enterprises due to imperfect control from the market or to imperfect control from the government?[23] A substantial volume of empirical work tends to support a dominant role for the market, failing to find evidence of efficiency differentials between public and private firms after adjusting for the degree of competition in the market.[24] The literature is far from unanimous on this point, however, and it is not our intention to resolve the issue here. We only note that, to the extent that some of the observed public enterprise inefficiency is due to absence of market pressures, increasing competition alone will improve performance, and the efficiency returns to divestiture will be smaller than otherwise.

In sum, the effect of competition is to reduce the range of ΔW: the downside potential is reduced, but so is the upside. Consider an extreme case in which the fundamental trade-off is the only issue (meaning, among other things, that fiscal effects can be ignored). Then competition means that one cannot lose from divestiture (ΔS will be nonnegative), yet the potential gain from efficiency improvements will be small, to the extent that competitive pressures have already, or will in the future, determine public enterprise behavior.

Improving organizational technology. In addition to technical change, organizational change also needs to be considered. Two forms can be distinguished: internal, affecting the ability of large organizations to control themselves; and external, affecting the ability of governments to control enterprises (regulation for private enterprises and oversight methods for public enterprises).

On the one hand, it can be argued that internal organizational change (such as the M-Form structure emphasized by Chandler 1977) and the use of computers have reduced managerial diseconomies of scale associated with very large organizations. On the other hand, it can be argued that changes in communications, information management, marketing, and globalization combine to make markets more dynamic and thus penalize the slower decision making that characterizes large mechanistic organizational structures. How these two offsetting forces net out we leave to others, since it does not seem to be critical in the current context. Unlike technical change, these organizational changes would not seem to be of sufficient magnitude to alter significantly the number of potential producers unless the number is already large (that is, a change from ten to eleven participants is a reasonable expectation, but from one to two is not). If so, then the innovation does not alter market structure, but only cost efficiency. The issue then becomes the relative speed with which organizational innovations are accepted by private as opposed to public firms. To the extent that public enterprises tend to be slower in adopting such innovations, divestiture may be a way to speed up their diffusion, and correspondingly ΔW increases.

With regard to external organization, changes that increase W under both private and public operation can be identified, making the ΔW from divestiture unpredictable. On the private side, reforms of regulatory mechanisms make possible increased W under private regulated monopoly. Considerable advances have been made in regulatory theory in recent years.[25]

Public enterprise control mechanisms have similarly been improved. Broadly speaking, the reforms involve a philosophy of management by objectives in which managers are granted increased autonomy over methods in return for greater accountability (through incentives) for results. Examples include the program contract system popular in Francophone countries (Nellis 1989a), the recent memoranda of understanding in India (Trivedi 1988), and the highly regarded Korean reform (Park 1985).

To summarize the trend in external control mechanisms: two imperfect mechanisms for dealing with imperfect situations are being modified imperfectly, albeit for the better. To the extent that the rate of imperfection reduction under regulation exceeds that under public ownership, ΔW is enhanced. Although the difference may be significant in some countries, we doubt that it has much explanatory power at the global level: the sign may well be wrong and the magnitude of the difference is probably small.[26] We now turn to a more robust candidate for a causal factor.

Fiscal stringency and the government revenue multiplier (λ_g). In many, if not most, countries, divestiture programs correlate with periods of fiscal stringency. Considerations of theory and fact lead many observers to attribute causality:

> The fact that so many countries showed signs of . . . [divestiture] . . . in the early 1980s, we believe, was a reflection largely of the drying up of

cash in that period, a reaffirmation of the soundness of Samuel Johnson's observation that the prospect of being hanged in a fortnight wonderfully concentrates the mind. The pronounced slowdown in the growth of the world economy at that time, when coupled with the drying up of the international credit markets, provided the functional equivalent of a sentence of hanging (Vernon 1988: 19).

We do not question the conclusion that fiscal stringency played a major role, but rather ask whether this role was due to economic or political factors or both. That is, to what extent do tough fiscal times increase technocrats' ΔW and to what extent merely patrons' perceptions?

At first blush, the technocratic answer would seem clear. Consider an exogenous fiscal shock such as a fall in oil prices for an oil exporter. A rational government in equilibrium would respond either by eliminating lower-valued public expenditures or by raising money at greater cost. In either case the value of government funds (λ_g) rises at the margin and, as shown by equation (8.3), [27] other things being equal, so does ΔW. That is, when times are tough, at the margin a government will spend only on highly valued items and obtain funds at higher cost. Under such conditions, the technocratic valuation of ΔW will rise simply because the marginal value of funds is higher for a poorer government.

In disequilibrium, of course, anything is possible. The government might respond to fiscal duress by spending more on tear gas and riot police to keep the masses quiet; if the technocrat evaluates this as a lower-yielding activity, then λ_g will fall.

Diminishing returns to government and the government revenue multiplier (λ_g). Diminishing returns is as robust a law as economists have. Apply it to the well-documented expansion of government worldwide from the 1950s through the 1970s. Other things being equal, expanding expenditures means undertaking progressively lower-yielding projects while expanding revenues means using increasingly high-cost alternatives. To the extent that this process has continued into disequilibrium, marginal benefits from government expenditure are below the marginal costs of financing it.

Under these circumstances, how would a technocrat value λ_g? At the low value implied by looking at expenditure? Or, at the high value implied by looking at revenue? The answer depends on whether he believes the government will use an extra dollar (obtained from the divestiture) to cut high-value taxes or expand low-value expenditures. What government does is probably a function of the nature of the government in power. It would not be unreasonable to expect a conservative government to reduce taxes and a liberal government to increase services. If so, in a disequilibrium context of excess government, a change of regime from liberal to conservative would raise λ_g and increase the returns to divestiture. Thus a trend toward conservative governments might explain why divestiture actually becomes more rational from the economic (or technocratic) point of view. We will therefore shift toward consideration of political issues.

Change in technocratic influence. The foregoing factors alter the judgments of technocrats. Are there any factors that might change the degree of influence they have on patrons? Two come to mind. First, in LDCs postindependence leaders typically focus on problems of nation building over economics, leading to economic decline, and a second generation of leaders typically focuses on growth. Sukarno and Syngman Rhee ignored technocrats; Suharto and Park Chung Hee did not. The second factor follows from our discussion of fiscal stringency: when times are tough, patrons are more likely to listen to technocrats. It is a common observation that in oil-rich countries a decline in oil prices might be a long-run boon because it facilitates needed reforms.

Summary of technocratic change. We have identified a number of factors that over time have on balance altered the benefit-cost calculation in favor of divestiture. Two stand out. First, as a long-term trend, increasing competition reduces the possibility of exploitation of market power by the divested firm, thus increasing returns to divestiture. Second, fiscal stringency can both enhance the returns to divestiture and increase the probability that it will be carried out.

Change in clients' position. Over time, clients' effective position on divestiture may change for two reasons. First, their own net benefit position may change. Second, their power to force patrons to consider their views may change. Both reasons are considered in turn for the three classes of clients: providers, purchasers, and consumers.

Providers: employees. We have already stressed that providers are major potential losers from divestiture and that what they stand to lose is not their total compensation, but only its rent component. If rents decline over time in the public sector, then providers have less to lose and their opposition might be expected to decline. We therefore first look for changes in the rent component of employees' wages. The following hypotheses seem relevant:

1. *Secular decline in rent component.* If we are correct that unskilled public enterprise workers in LDCs receive a far larger rent component than their counterparts in MDCs, and if

cross-section data can be used to infer intertemporal change, then the rent component might decline over time.

2. *Unemployment*. The greatest rents accrue to those whose alternative is unemployment. If the probability of unemployment declines over time with economic development, then the rent component declines.

3. *Social insurance*. Similarly, the spread of unemployment insurance or other forms of welfare payments decreases rents to public enterprise employment.

4. *Changing skill mix*. It can be argued that rents are highest at the bottom end of the public enterprise pay scale and lowest (if not zero or negative) at the top. If so, then changes in technology that shift the mean employee toward the top will lower the mean rent. An example might be the replacement of telephone operators by computer operators.

5. *Deteriorating enterprise financial position*. Rents must be paid from somewhere, either from a favorable enterprise market position or a sympathetic government. As markets become more competitive and as particular companies enter their geriatric phase and become less competitive, the capacity of enterprises to yield to union demands declines. Increasing fiscal stringency yields the same result.

In sum, we have a testable hypothesis: over time, the share of rents in total employee compensation declines. If so, then the intensity of labor opposition to divestiture also declines.

For a given level of intensity of preference, how has employees' ability to influence patrons changed? One factor might be the declining share of unions in total employment, thus reducing the need for patrons to pay attention to the demands of particular unions.

Providers: other. Rent extraction is facilitated by imperfect markets. Thus, suppliers of inputs to public enterprises will likely enjoy less rent as they face more and more competition. A single bidder on a government supply contract is much more likely to extract rent and keep a large share than when there are multiple bidders. Subsidized interest rates by definition give someone a rent, but this is much less likely under what passes for market-clearing rates. Increasing competition therefore reduces net rents over time.

Development of journalism also plays a major role. It is one thing to find rents; it is quite another to have the discovery announced on the six o'clock news. Development of pluralistic political institutions plays a similar role. The existence of multiple competing centers of political power makes it more likely that rent finding will be publicized and, in any case, causes the proceeds to spread more widely.

In sum, the development of political, economic, and journalistic competition reduces the magnitude of rents and also spreads their benefits more widely, in both cases reducing the intensity of providers' resistance to divestiture. This is by no means to say that rents disappear with development. Readers of the *New York Times* are daily treated to announcements of rent finding in the U.S. government, and this is, if anything, more pronounced in many U.S. state and local governments. The argument is only that rent seeking is reduced in the process.

Purchasers. Purchasers present a puzzle. Barring bad judgment on their part, they can only win from divestiture. One therefore expects them to be pro divestiture and to be in the vanguard of the movement. Surprisingly, both the literature and the oral tradition are silent on their role.[28] One exception occurs when previous owners of nationalized firms clamor for reprivatization. Otherwise, divestiture leaders tend to be politicians, technocrats, and academic scribblers, with businessmen playing at most a supporting role. Accordingly, what needs to be understood first is not the trend in their interest or influence, but its level.

One possibility is that evidence on the purchasers' position exists and that we and others have missed it. If so, we would like to be informed. If not, then brilliant academic hindsight can be brought to bear using hypotheses such as the following:

1. *Dispersed benefits in MDCs.* Insofar as sale is through public share offerings to a dispersed public, or insofar as sale is to a publicly held company with similarly dispersed ownership, then there are the familiar free-rider obstacles to coalition building. Purchasers, then, are much like the other set of potential winners—the citizens.[29]

2. *High opportunity cost in LDCs.* In LDCs it is more likely that sale will be to individuals or narrowly held family groups. In a number of countries, however, divestiture advocates have been disappointed at the distinct paucity of enthusiasm among potential buyers. Unsystematic interviewing of this group in various countries yields a composite response as follows: "When making an investment I expect to get my money back in three years, but there's no way I can do this

by buying a public enterprise; the opposition is already ac-
cusing the government of 'selling the national patrimony,' so
the deal will be scrutinized very carefully; besides, the last
thing I need is the hassle of dealing with such a work force."
In short, there are plenty of ways for well-connected entrepreneurs to make money, and, at first blush, taking over a
public enterprise does not look high on the list.

In any event, we detect little evidence that increasing returns to, or
increasing influence of, purchasers has much to do with the divestiture
wave.

Consumers. As a first approximation, whether consumers are likely to
win or lose from divestiture is likely to have little effect on patrons'
decisions because of the dispersed benefit problem. The most elaborate
application of this line of thinking is due to Olson (1965), who emphasizes the difficulty interest groups face in overcoming their internal free-
rider problem: any political gain achieved by the group is a public good
from which all people with similar interests can benefit without necessarily having to pay their dues. One corollary is that small groups form
more readily than large groups both because the costs of organizing and
policing the free-rider problem are lower and because the per member
benefits are greater. As a result, inefficient policies whose costs exceed
the benefits may nevertheless be adopted when the costs are dispersed
over a large group while the benefits are concentrated on a small group.
Public enterprise consumers are generally a large group relative to providers, and therefore their interests are liable to be subordinated.

One major exception occurs if the product has been heavily subsidized and an increase in prices approaching market levels accompanies
divestiture. Riots in the streets are a common result of such price increases in LDCs even without divestiture, and such occurrences certainly
gain patrons' attention. A further corollary of Olson's work comes into
play: "On balance, special-interest organizations and collusions reduce
efficiency and aggregate income in the societies in which they operate
and make political life more divisive" (1982: 47). Riots over price rationalization would seem to qualify. Further, one wonders how many purchasers would buy under such conditions. Accordingly, we would
expect enterprises whose prices are hugely out of line not to be candidates for divestiture.

A second exception occurs when output is subsidized to only a
moderate degree, but the bulk of output is sold to a small number of
downstream users who in turn sell in imperfectly competitive markets.
In this case the benefits of the subsidies are concentrated in a few hands
and opposition to divestiture is likely to be communicated to patrons.

A third possible exception occurs if, as Olson (1982: 41) also argues, more and larger interest groups can be organized in stable societies through innovation and reduced organizational costs. Is it possible that some of the observed increase in divestiture in MDCs represents the rise in the power of consumer groups relative to providers?

Change in patrons' position. In the previous two sections we identified a number of reasons why the returns to divestiture may have increased over time and why the coalitions opposing divestiture may have become weaker. There is, however, a fundamental flaw in attributing causality to these factors because we would be using a set of largely continuous phenomena to explain a discontinuous event. That is, most of the factors were rooted in an evolutionary process of growth and development, and they would have led to a smooth process of divestiture rather than the jump that occurred in the 1980s. It may be that the causal factor is the one important discontinuous event on our list—fiscal stringency. This is also less than perfectly satisfying since in previous decades most countries went through tough times without divesting,[30] and in the 1980s countries such as South Korea divested even though they were by no means suffering from fiscal stringency. This would seem to leave a change in patrons—the Reagan-Thatcher[31] bandwagon—as the dominant explanatory variable. However, this explanation too has its problems.

Ideology and divestiture. A number of authors have stressed the striking lack of correlation between ideology and divestiture or nationalization. Bermeo is worth quoting at length:

> . . . periods of expansion and contraction of public enterprise are not related in any simple way to whether the ruling party is socialist or non-socialist. Spain's public enterprise sector was initiated by a right-wing authoritarian regime, expanded by a democratically elected center-right government and then successfully challenged, for the first time in history, by a democratically elected Socialist party. In Greece, New Democracy, a democratically elected center-right party, expanded the much smaller public sector during the mid 1970's and the Socialist PASOK expanded it further in the 1980's. In Portugal, the Socialist Party supported the nationalization of banking and industry and then maintained tacit support of a massive state enterprise sector, for at least twelve years. For these cases, at least, a ruling party's position on the ideological spectrum tells us little about national policy toward public enterprise (Bermeo 1989: 9).

The only problem with this statement is its modesty in confining the conclusion to those cases. Boneo documents a similar phenomenon for Argentina, noting that the share of public enterprise in the economy does not fluctuate with dramatic political change, but steadily increases. His explanation is that liberal regimes add enterprises while conservatives add value added through pricing and management reforms, but neither divests (Boneo 1986). Turning from time series to cross-section, Jones and Mason (1982) begin by documenting the remarkable similarity in the size, structure, and growth of public enterprise in ideologically diverse India and South Korea. They go on to identify similar patterns across a broad spectrum of LDCs and attribute this to common responses to common problems of market and organizational failure.

A synthesis. The question then becomes, if ideology was impotent elsewhere at other times, what made Reagan, Thatcher, and others different? Our answer is timing.

Our story hinges on the dialectics of diminishing returns to government. As described earlier, expansion of government involves increasing costs and decreasing benefits. This process continues well past equilibrium and into disequilibrium because of inertia; discontinuous political change; the time necessary for a problem to build to such a magnitude that citizens become aware of it; and the fact that any change involves substantial economic, political, and psychological costs. The process of diminishing returns to government thus creates the internal contradictions that lead to its own destruction, spawning Thatcher and Reagan, who then appear not as exogenous causal forces but as endogenous trigger mechanisms.

LDCs and MDCs

Rhetoric and reality. In LDCs we find a striking gap between rhetoric and reality. On the rhetoric side, many—perhaps most—LDCs have announced ambitious divestiture programs. A comprehensive World Bank listing identifies more than seventy LDCs with divestiture platforms (Candoy-Sekse 1988). On the reality side, developments are somewhat less impressive. First, some LDCs with the largest public enterprise sectors have not even indulged in the rhetoric of divestiture to any major extent; India, Indonesia, and Egypt spring to mind.[32] Even more important, among those who have announced programs, there has been considerably more smoke than fire.

The experience of the World Bank is instructive since it is one of the alleged transmission mechanisms for the Reagan-Thatcher bandwagon effect. Nellis (1989b) has examined 101 different structural and sectoral adjustment loans with public enterprise components signed by the bank from 1978 to 1988. On the rhetoric side, divestiture was the most common single element of conditionality, appearing in 40 percent of the

cases. On the reality side, Nellis provides details for nine countries selected for intensive study. Among these, four are identified as relatively
successful: Jamaica sold a half-billion dollars' worth of enterprises; Togo
leased four, shut down five, and has twenty awaiting sale; Niger divested three companies fully and eight partially; and Panama sold five.
Even the successes represented only a small fraction of the total number
of public enterprises in the respective countries and a far smaller fraction of total sector sales or value added. Further, in many cases the sales
were accompanied by conditions that considerably reduced any positive welfare effect: for example, in Guinea five of fourteen divested
firms maintained monopoly positions and a sixth was granted the right
to import oil duty-free for fifteen years (Nellis 1989b: 16). Considerably
less happened in the other five countries.

Turkey is perhaps prototypical and certainly well documented.[33]
Divestiture was a major component of Turkey's liberalization program
as early as 1980. By 1986 a US$2 million master plan was developed with
World Bank assistance. As of 1988, all that had been accomplished was
sale of the first tranche of a portion of the government's minority share
holding in Teletas, the telecommunications company. How can this
slow going be explained? It has been suggested that the rhetoric-reality
gap results from the fact that the divestiture announcements do not
reflect the true beliefs of the nation's leaders, but are merely intended to
placate and gain funding from alleged transmission mechanisms of the
Reagan-Thatcher bandwagon, such as the U.S. Agency for International
Development and the World Bank. Although this may indeed have been
a factor elsewhere, it was not so in Turkey, where divestiture had the full
support of Turgut Ozal, first as senior civilian in the military government and later as elected prime minister. Further, many other elements
of the liberalization program were implemented, and Turkey has generally been considered a success story of economic rationalization. Why
not in the field of divestiture?

Turkey is not alone. In which LDCs has divestiture been significant
enough to reduce the size of the public enterprise sector by, say, 10
percent of its GDP share? It is a measure of our ignorance that the
literature is largely silent on this sort of question. We know how many
firms are involved, and occasionally how much their sales are, but seldom have a sense of the basic empirical magnitude: just how much of
the sector are we talking about here, anyway? We would hazard a guess
that as of 1989, the number of LDCs passing the 10 percent test are few
and may consist only of Chile and Mexico.

Regardless of the accuracy of this last guess, the basic question
remains: why, in the LDCs, has there been far more rhetoric than reality?
Asking this question should not obscure the fact that previous decades
had not even witnessed much rhetoric. That programs were widely

announced; that some divestitures actually occurred; and that others are likely to follow in the future still represents a clear break between the 1980s and previous decades. What needs to be explained is why the process progressed so little, or at least so slowly, in the LDCs as opposed to the MDCs.

Time-series arguments. Our answer to the question, why has so little divestiture occurred in LDCs, is simple. In the previous section we argued that as economies grow, markets become more competitive. On the one hand, this increases the technocrats' estimate of ΔW; on the other, it lowers rents and spreads them more widely, thus reducing clients' opposition to divestiture and their ability to impose that opposition on patrons. This class of arguments is especially applicable to the LDC–MDC comparison. Using per capita GDP as a proxy for market forces, we see about a threefold growth in market development in LDCs over three decades, whereas we see nearly a fortyfold difference in market development between MDCs and LDCs.[34] If the time-series argument has any explanatory power, then the cross-section variant has much more.

Fiscal stringency in LDCs. The fiscal stringency argument would seem to predict more, not less, divestiture in LDCs. If it seems Thatcher faced fiscal problems, imagine being a Latin American finance minister in the 1980s.

The fact that little divestiture has occurred suggests at least two possibilities. The first is that the fiscal effect is dominated, at least in LDCs, by the behavioral effect. This is consistent with Leeds's report that sixteen senior government officials ranked revenue generation last of fourteen possible divestiture objectives in Turkey (Leeds 1988: 163–64). A second possibility is that the fiscal effect primarily benefits citizens and that citizens' interests are poorly represented in LDCs as opposed to MDCs.

Capital markets. Observers of LDC divestiture are virtually unanimous in identifying capital market imperfections as a major obstacle (for example, Commander and Killick 1988). Equity markets are thin, characterized by few participants, low volume, and impacted, or incomplete, information. Debt markets are fragmented, with many sub-markets clearing by executive decision rather than price. The magnitude of these imperfections is sometimes hard for Westerners to appreciate. One manifestation is the São Paulo exchange (Brazil's largest), where prices tripled in six months, then plunged 61 percent in a week, allegedly because of the manipulations of one individual whose transactions accounted for half of the market during the run-up and involved a major play on Val do Rio Doce, a public enterprise (*New*

York Times, June 20, 1989). Are there any LDC markets without similar episodes in their history? The point is not that this is any different from the early history of Western exchanges or that things will not improve over time. Rather, the point is that only rather special individuals willingly participate in such a market, the information imparted by share prices is limited, and the discipline imposed by being responsible to a market is suspect.

Capital market imperfections have a number of implications for divestiture. First, it is hard to sell large enterprises: if British Telecom had to be split into two tranches to avoid disrupting the capital market, imagine the problem in LDCs where the 1988 trade volume in twenty-seven LDCs as a group was only one-tenth that of London (International Finance Corporation 1989: 16–17).[35]

Second, selling parts of the large enterprises will not produce "people's capitalism." Several writers see major political-social-economic externalities of divestiture from broadening stock market participation (for example, Hanke 1987). In the United Kingdom divestiture led to significant expansion of share ownership among workers and the middle class. In LDCs, however, shares would go only to a minority at the top. If the government tries to sell shares to workers, they might prefer to buy food; if it induces them to buy by offering a premium, they are likely to resell quickly, because at their income levels the demand for savings for old age is modest. If it forces them to keep the shares (commonly, through sales to a workers' pension plan), it may well have accomplished something, but still only among the top third of the distribution.

Third, if the government does manage to sell parts of any enterprise to a dispersed public, there may not be much change in behavior. In an MDC, selling some shares on the market is thought to provide an element of market discipline to offset bureaucratic indiscipline: managers will be more attentive to the movement of share prices and to the elected representatives of the shareholders and less attentive to the minister. In many LDCs, the thought that a manager appointed by the government—who remains the dominant shareholder—would respond to minority shareholders rather than to the minister who appoints him is humorous.

Fourth, if the government does manage to sell parts to a dispersed public, it will likely do so by underpricing the sale, thus reducing the return to divestiture (assuming $\lambda_g > \lambda_p$).

Fifth, if the government sells to an individual or corporation, it is likely to go to a minority: foreigners, an ethnic minority, or the wealthiest fifty families. This may be objected to on non-economic grounds: in Indonesia, a standard explanation for the lack of enthusiasm for divestiture is that the only buyers are Chinese. It also may be objected to on Jeffersonian grounds: that is, concern for the effect of concentrations of wealth on a free society. It may also be objected to on economic grounds: concentrations of wealth lead to privileged access to credit, protection, licenses, and other scarce commodities, and this distorts behavior across many markets (more on this in the next subsection).

Sixth, if the government prohibits any one group from getting a controlling interest, it may well get it anyway. In South Korea, the government prohibited any group from amassing more than a small percentage of the shares in any divested bank. The use of friends, dummies, and relatives, however, has reputedly led each of the biggest business groups to obtain a controlling interest in a different bank.

Seventh, although the government may want to sell to smaller buyers, they may not have the capital and may be unable to raise it on the stock market, so government or other banks might have to loan it to them. If these lenders are unaccustomed to making careful creditworthiness evaluations, the result may be a bankruptcy. The first wave of Chilean divestitures were heavily debt-financed and subsequent widespread failures led to renationalization of the banks and with them most of the companies (Marshall and Montt 1988). In Bangladesh, oral tradition has it that divested firms were typically purchased with 10 percent or even less in effective equity, giving substantial motivation to mine the firm of its assets and declare bankruptcy for a tidy profit.

Eighth, if the government does sell to an individual and he does not go bankrupt but turns a tidy profit, then it will be accused of corruption and giving away the national patrimony. Absent a stock market to set the price and a fully functioning press to disclose any side deals, questions about favoritism or collusive bidding are going to arise, whether or not they are true.

We do not contend that these bold assertions hold for all countries and all times. Markets in NICs and Latin American countries with per capita GDP in the thousands of dollars are far different from those in countries with per capita GDP in the hundreds. Public enterprises have been divested and more will be as clever people create clever ways of overcoming the sorts of problems enumerated above. Our only purpose has been to suggest that capital market problems exist, that they are more severe in LDCs than in MDCs, and that therefore somewhat slower progress is to be expected.

The private "alternative." Not only capital markets, but also private firms are imperfect in LDCs. Manual Tanoira, former undersecretary for divestiture to Argentina's Raúl Alfonsín, makes this point clear in the context of divestiture. He begins by quoting a colleague of a colleague: "First, we've got to privatize the private sector" (1987: 54).

Tanoira elaborates on this theme, and the following quote conveys the essence of his argument:

> . . . privatization might mean no more than an expansion of not-so-private enterprise, or an expansion of government by another name. This is the best reason I can offer for the perpetuation of unprofitable state-owned enterprises (SOE's) in Argentina. To the people, privatization is less likely to be seen as a means for *eliminating* the enormous subsidies received by SOE's than as a means for *transferring* the protection of the state to private (in other words, not-so-private) firms (p. 56).

In terms of our framework, we interpret this statement as stressing the importance of ΔW: welfare under public operation is suboptimal, but so also is welfare under private operation. In particular, both public and private enterprises operate in a highly imperfect environment in LDCs, reducing the technocratic return to divestiture. Transfer of rents from citizens to patrons is by no means confined to the public sector.

Competitive enterprises. Although the foregoing arguments help explain the slow pace of divestiture of enterprises that are large relative to product and factor markets, they do not explain the reluctance to divest small-scale competitive establishments. It is difficult to construct a technocratic argument for a negative ΔW for Venezuela's love motel, Peru's pornographic movie house, or any of the other small-scale establishments that litter the public enterprise rolls in many LDCs. Divesting these firms not only would have a positive welfare effect, but also would free bureaucratic and technocratic resources to concentrate on the 20 percent of the companies that generate 80 percent of the value added and involve real trade-offs.

Conclusion

Like the public investment decision, the public disinvestment decision cannot be understood simply as an economic phenomenon and should not be understood simply as a political phenomenon. Economics tells us which decision should be taken to maximize welfare. Politics tells us which decision will be taken. Our approach to political economy links the normative and the positive by assigning economic costs and benefits to particular classes with differential political influence. Ex post, this approach helps us understand why particular economically suboptimal outcomes occurred. Ex ante, it allows us to evaluate the distributional impact of alternative modes of divestiture, thereby helping us to achieve political feasibility with the minimum sacrifice of economic desirability.

Comments

ALICE H. AMSDEN

Leroy Jones, Ingo Vogelsang, and Pankaj Tandon do an excellent job of presenting a sober view of some of the supposed benefits of privatization. They also do a splendid service in forcing us to think about privatization's distributional consequences. It is very tempting to discuss their work in detail because it provides rich avenues for further research. I will, however, resist this temptation and not discuss the body of the chapter. Instead I will focus my remarks on an issue of general interest for the new political economy. It is an issue that these contributors alone raise and that I would like to take further. The issue challenges the conventional wisdom of this volume: the notion that privatization by its nature increases economic efficiency.

The challenge arises from the fact that countries at various stages of their development often find their entrepreneurs engaging more in what could be called *private rent seeking* than in productive activity. Such rent seeking was prevalent in many developing countries in the 1950s and early 1960s, and thereafter has flared up in periods of external shock. Private rent seeking lies at the root of LDCs' interventionist states.

It is indisputable that many public enterprises throughout the world are poorly managed because their budget constraint is soft. They often suffer from inefficiency, overinvestment, and inadequate attention to marketing and incremental productivity improvements. Despite public enterprise mismanagement, however, one cannot assume that performance is invariably better in the private sector.

The new political economy has made efforts to enter the black box of politics and to incorporate public rent seeking into its analysis. It has not gone far enough, however, into the black box of the private firm. The private firm still tends to be idealized and its activities placed above suspicion. There have, however, been some very important institutional changes over time in the nature of the firm, in terms of both how it is managed and how its owners behave.

By private rent seeking I mean what Adam Smith meant by buying cheap and selling dear, or realizing profit "upon alienation" rather than through investment in new plant, equipment, and human resources. Rent seeking becomes private when private individuals or institutions are involved and has nothing to do with the government. Private rent seeking connotes speculation and arbitrage in stocks of existing assets rather than investment in production flows of new goods or services, where production is defined to include all activities necessary to bring a product or service to market, ranging from design to distribution. Rents are involved insofar as stocks of old (existing) assets are, by definition, restricted in supply over some time period, and returns to assets whose supply is insensitive to price changes are defined as rents (or quasirents, depending on how long supply is fixed).

Private firms may be imagined as holding diversified portfolios, with some of their capital tied up in new assets (production) with a rate of return of R_N and some in old assets with a rate of return of R_O. One might begin to conceptualize rent seeking by supposing it to be present when R_O exceeds R_N. (When R_O equals R_N, the holders of old assets may be regarded as earning merely capital gains.) For simplicity, it may be assumed that the rate of return on new assets (productive investment) has been equalized across all producers, that different forms of rent seeking yield the same return, and that all rates of return have been adjusted for differences in risk. In periods when firms are preoccupied with exploiting new technology or markets, the ratio of R_O to R_N may be very small. In periods when, for various reasons, including external shocks, it is easier for firms to make money by buying cheap and selling dear than by investing long term, R_O/R_N may be expected to exceed unity.

One meaning of competition, perfect knowledge, is anathema to rent seeking: if knowledge were perfect, the intrinsic value of old assets would be apparent, and no one, therefore, would pay more than a single price. With perfect knowledge, there would be no rent seeking. But another meaning of competition, a large number of buyers and sellers, perversely stimulates private rent seeking: the more buyers and sellers are active in markets for old assets, the greater will be rent seeking. Additionally, the more buyers and sellers there are in product markets—say, for steel or soybeans—the more the rate of return to these activities will tend to be driven down, making rent seeking more attractive.

Activity in markets for old assets covers a multitude of sins. The least objectionable forms of private rent seeking relate to reorganization and rationalization associated with, say, conglomeration or divestiture. These activities may increase efficiency even if no new assets are created in the process. The buyers of old assets may even improve upon them with fresh injections of capital. When old assets are improved, the distinction between earning profits and earning rents is blurred. The least productive forms of private rent seeking include hoarding (say, of fine art) and creating scarcities in the process of speculation. Charles Kindleberger refers to insiders who "destabilize by driving the price up and up, selling out at the top to the outsiders" (1978: 32). Nevertheless, during the stage of rent seeking before prices fall (if ever), rent seeking in general tends to absorb financial resources that might otherwise be invested in new plant, equipment, and human capital. Moreover, international competition has become so intense that a firm that diverts resources away from manufacturing to speculating and misses a single stage in the product life cycle risks being unable to catch up.

Private rent seeking was rampant in the U.S. economy in the 1980s and is by no means a rarity in LDCs. Many owners of family enterprises—small or large—often prefer to speculate for extended time periods in land, urban real estate, commodities, and financial stocks at home or abroad rather than to make long-term investments in capital accumulation. If we return to T. N. Srinivasan's question of why exorbitantly high rates of tariff protection in the manufacturing sector exist in Latin America, part of the answer is that high rates of protection are necessary to inflate profits and induce private entrepreneurs to invest in manufacturing activity instead of in real estate or scarce commodities.

Now the question is, why are these entrepreneurs so reluctant to invest in manufacturing? One reason is that in the past, undoubtedly because of state intervention, the investment climate became uncertain and risky. One must go back even further in history, however, to appreciate that governments intervened initially because many entrepreneurs, instead of investing in productive activities other than those related to primary products, made their business the buying and selling of existing assets. To induce private entrepreneurs to invest in manufacturing, governments had to provide them with elaborate financial supports as well as high rates of protection.

Extensive government support has been necessary, even for investments in labor-intensive industries, to help entrepreneurs overcome the penalties of industrializing "late." By late industrializers I mean companies that grow by borrowing technology rather than generating new technology, the hallmark of leading firms in the industrial revolutions of the eighteenth and nineteenth centuries. Without the competitive asset of novel products or processes, late industrializers have to compete on the basis of low wages. Yet in all but the most labor-intensive industries—say, Christmas tree lights, wigs, and wallets—low wages are an insufficient weapon to wield against more experienced and productive firms from economically advanced countries. In South Korea in the late 1960s, for example, even cotton spinners and weavers required tariff protection and large financial incentives from the government in order to compete against Japanese textile companies, notwithstanding that existing prices of foreign exchange and intermediate inputs in South Korea closely approximated their shadow or international prices. Therefore, the Korean government provided its "leading sector" with extensive supports.

The nature of late industrialization, or growth without novel products or processes, has required that governments intervene with subsidies. Otherwise, manufacturing investment stagnates and rent seeking blooms. Subsidization has occurred in Japan, South Korea, and Taiwan as well as in India, Brazil, Turkey, and other late-industrializing countries. Extensive support has been necessary to enable firms to import foreign equipment and technology, accumulate experience, raise productivity, improve quality, and thereby compete against more experienced firms from economically advanced countries.

Elsewhere I suggested that the above-mentioned Asian countries have grown faster than the other late industrializers for reasons related to discipline (Amsden 1989). In countries like Mexico, Brazil, and Turkey, the power of big business has been such that subsidies have been allocated as giveaways. In Japan, South Korea, and Taiwan, by contrast, the power of the state has been such that subsidies have been allocated in exchange for performance standards. The state has disciplined big business to use subsidies productively, not for speculative purposes but for efficient manufacturing activity. The market has been protected, but subsidy recipients have had to export. The cost of capital has been subsidized, but capital flight has been prohibited. In South Korea the penalty for illegal capital flight has been a minimum of ten years' imprisonment and a maximum of death. Discipline over business by the state has helped to lower the rate of return at which the private sector is willing to invest, as well as raise the productivity of investment. In turn, lower expected returns and higher productivity have enabled tariff protection and subsidies to be smaller than otherwise.

Many states are neither as powerful nor as capable of disciplining business as the states of Japan, South Korea, and Taiwan. Nevertheless, recognizing the problem of private rent seeking is a step toward understanding economic development among late industrializers. Given private rent seeking, success in economic development depends not just on how well the private sector controls the rent-seeking activities of the state, but also on how well the state controls the rent-seeking activities of the private sector. Without such recognition, the analysis of public rent seeking is one-sided, to the jeopardy of policy making.

Once it is appreciated that private rent seeking often stands in the way of the most socially efficient use of resources, then greater efficiency and privatization are not necessarily synonymous. It consequently becomes desirable to widen the policy menu of how to deal with poorly run public enterprises. Privatization may not be the best remedy. I would have liked to see Leroy Jones and his coauthors apply their considerable analytical skills to the possibility of, say, leasing rather than privatizing public firms, because leasing helps to ensure that public enterprises taken over by the private sector are efficiently run and work in the public's interest.

Finally, returning briefly to the chapter by Jones, Vogelsang, and Tandon, I suggest qualification of their conclusion that the distributional effect of privatization is likely to be inconsequential because "privatization is a game played among the high-income earners." To see that it is not just a game played among high-income earners, one need only look at one of their examples, the provision of electricity. Although, as they note, the rich are more likely than the poor to receive electricity in LDCs, some poor people still receive it; if electricity is privatized, that service may cease. If Jones, Vogelsang, and Tandon wish to maintain that the distributional effect of privatization is likely to be negligible, they must state more clearly the assumptions on which their argument is based.

STEPHAN HAGGARD   CHAPTER 9

Inflation and Stabilization

Why have some middle-income developing countries had histories of
high inflation over the past two decades, while others have pursued
stable macroeconomic policies? Among countries experiencing inflation,
why do some governments move to stabilize with alacrity, while others
postpone the adjustment decision, often with disastrous costs? Once the
decision to stabilize is taken, why are some countries capable of sustaining stabilization policies while others falter and reverse course?

A wide array of economic factors is important in understanding
particular national experiences with inflation, including the severity of
exogenous shocks. Nonetheless, inflation often has political roots, and
whatever its causes, stabilization poses profound political dilemmas.

This chapter reviews some current thinking about the political
economy of fiscal policy and advances some hypotheses about differences in inflation and stabilization efforts among middle-income developing countries. The rent- and revenue-seeking approach of the new
political economy is useful for understanding the political incentives to

I would like to thank William Easterly, Robert Kaufman, George Kopits, and
other participants at the conference The New Political Economy and Development Policy Making for comments on the first draft of this chapter.

government spending and explains why subsidies and state-owned enterprises become politically entrenched. This approach, however, does not explain cross-national *differences* in fiscal performance and inflation. Such variation can be accounted for in part by pressures for government spending that result from interest group and partisan conflict. The organization of urban labor and its incorporation into the party system appear to be important factors. The developing countries with histories of high inflation, mostly in Latin America, have been those in which urban "popular sector" and labor groups have been mobilized into populist parties within relatively polarized party systems. Such high-conflict countries also had the greatest difficulties stabilizing in the 1980s, particularly where stabilization episodes overlapped with transitions to democratic rule. It is difficult to disentangle lines of causality because the size of external shocks and initial disequilibria posed greater difficulties for the large Latin American debtors, but the vulnerability to external shocks was itself partly the result of previous policy choices.

The structure of interest groups and the nature of the political regime are, of course, not easily changed. Other political factors affecting fiscal outcomes may offer greater scope for reform, though. The political difficulties of macroeconomic adjustment appear to be less severe where decision making is relatively centralized within the government and insulated from rent-seeking pressures. This suggests the importance of institutional reform for sustaining credible macroeconomic policy.

The Political Economy of Inflation and Stabilization

Albert Hirschman has pointed out that "the explanation of inflation in terms of social conflict between groups, each aspiring to a greater share of the social product, has become the sociologist's monotonous equivalent of the economist's untiring stress on the undue expansion of the money supply" (1985: 57–58). To construct a political theory of inflation and stabilization demands an explication of the precise mechanisms through which political variables contribute to increases in the price level and difficulties in stabilization.

In studies of the advanced industrial states, cross-national variations in inflation have been traced to differences in wage-setting institutions and relations among business, organized labor, and government.[1] Wage policy has played a role in efforts to control inflation in the developing world, but a growing body of evidence suggests that fiscal policy is a more appropriate focus for an examination of the political economy of inflation in developing countries (Cooper and Sachs 1985; World Bank 1988). Since developing country governments generally have limited scope for domestic borrowing, financing fiscal deficits usually involves recourse to foreign borrowing and the inflation tax. There appear to be few cases of severe and prolonged inflation in the developing world that were not associated with fiscal deficits financed by money creation.

Fiscal policy also helps explain the accumulation of debt and the subsequent vulnerability of debtor countries to external shocks. When net capital inflows ceased abruptly in the early 1980s, debtors were unable to cut expenditures and raise revenues quickly. They thus relied on instruments that constituted implicit taxes on financial intermediation, with adverse consequences for investment (Easterly 1989).

Not surprisingly, fiscal policy has been central to stabilization efforts. International Monetary Fund stabilization programs invariably target some monetary indicator as the key performance criterion, but the focus on monetary policy reflects the availability of data and the political problems of appearing to interfere in sensitive allocational decisions rather than a belief in the primacy of monetary measures. The actions required to meet monetary targets are usually fiscal: some combination of increased taxes or nontax revenues and cuts in expenditures. The principal political dilemma is that no matter how beneficial these measures may be in the long run for the country as a whole, they entail the imposition of short-term costs and have distributional implications for particular groups.

Contributions and Limits of the New Political Economy

The new, or neoclassical, political economy relies heavily on interest group models that seek to explain policy, including taxation and expenditure, as the result of political exchanges between welfare-maximizing constituents and support-maximizing politicians (Krueger 1974; Colander 1984). On the demand side of the political market are constituents, conceptualized as individual voters, interest groups, or even bureaucratic groups within the state itself. The political process consists of spending by these constituents to influence the size and direction of fiscal redistribution.[2] Rational constituents will expend resources—on lobbying, political contributions, demonstrations, and so forth—until the marginal cost of their influence efforts equals the expected marginal return from securing their desired policy outcome. Where rival constituencies have conflicting interests, groups expending the most on the influence attempt will prevail.

Politicians constitute the supply side of the market, though the real "suppliers" are those groups from whom income and wealth transfers are ultimately sought. The key insight of the new political economy into fiscal policy is that politicians view expenditures to their constituents not as costs, but as benefits.[3] They will thus seek to increase expenditures to constituents to the point at which the political return is offset by the economic and political costs, including the inflationary consequences of high budget deficits. The lure of deficits is strengthened by fundamental asymmetries between spending and taxing decisions: the means of financing deficits—inflation and borrowing—are less visible than taxation, spread more widely across the population (inflation), or pushed onto future generations (borrowing).

The new political economy underlines the incentives facing politicians to spend and explains puzzles such as the bias against least-cost alternatives and the tendency for projects to assume unnecessary scale. Ultimately, however, this rent-seeking approach cannot predict whether central government accounts will be in surplus, balance, or deficit. Put differently, there is a problem in getting from the microlevel of a particular expenditure or tax to the macrolevel of aggregate fiscal outcomes.

Discussions of subsidies and state-owned enterprises that draw on rent-seeking models illustrate this difficulty. Subsidies give politicians an instrument for building electoral or clientele support (Bates 1982). Because they can grow into virtually open-ended government commitments and are seen as entitlements by their recipients, subsidies have been a major factor contributing to fiscal deficits in a number of middle-income countries. Their reduction or elimination has been a central component of most stabilization plans and is one of the most difficult to carry through because of the vulnerability of most governments to urban consumer groups (Bienen and Gersovitz 1985; Nelson 1984). Yet not all governments have fallen into the subsidy trap, and some have managed to reduce subsidies.

A related example is provided by the growing literature on state-owned enterprises (SOEs) (Aharoni 1986; Vernon 1988). SOEs played a major role in contributing to fiscal deficits and external borrowing in a number of developing countries over the 1970s and 1980s. Some of this expenditure was no doubt for legitimate purposes; viewed politically, however, SOEs represent powerful constituencies within the government because of the resources under their control and their importance in generating employment. In many cases, SOEs are more powerful than the ministries that presumably oversee their activities; state-owned oil enterprises, such as Mexico's PEMEX, are important examples. Governments have also been politically vulnerable to pressures from customers, contractors, and suppliers to maintain purchases of goods and services, limit price increases, raise wages, and retain employees. Again, the puzzle for the new political economy is in explaining variance. In some countries, SOEs have mushroomed and been a major drain on national treasuries, while in others their role has been limited or subject to effective control.

One way of bridging the gap between the micro- and macrolevels of political analysis is through the political business cycle. This literature argues that regardless of the party in power, economic policy will change over the electoral cycle as politicians seek to manipulate the short-run Philipps curve (showing the trade-off between unemployment and inflation) to electoral advantage. The evidence for a political business cycle remains weak for the advanced industrial states (Alt and Chrystal 1983: chap. 5). The model assumes short voter memory concerning past performance and myopia concerning future inflation, or, as Brian Barry has put it, "a collection of rogues competing for the favors of a larger collection of dupes" (1985: 300).

Many of the political and institutional characteristics that mitigate political business cycles in the advanced industrial states are absent, however, in the developing countries. These include, among other things, informed publics; independent media coverage of economic policy; institutionalized forms of consultation between business, government, and labor; and welfare systems that cushion the costs of unemployment. Given lower levels of income, extensive poverty, and the insecurity of political tenure in a number of polities, it is plausible that politicians' time horizons in the developing world are oriented toward the delivery of short-term benefits for electoral gain.[4]

A second way of joining the micro- and macrolevels is through models emphasizing partisan conflict. In one such model, the economy is divided into two groups, "workers" and "capitalists," each with its own political party (Alesina 1987; Alesina and Tabellini 1987). The party in power seeks to redistribute income in favor of its constituency: right-wing governments pursue policies that favor profits; left-wing governments, those that favor wages. In designing fiscal policy, each party will seek to tax its opponents to the maximum feasible extent, while redistributing to its own constituency. Governments in power have a strong incentive to borrow, knowing that the full cost of servicing current obligations will be borne by political successors.

Two hypotheses result from this line of inquiry. First, a high level of political instability, measured by frequent changes of government, is likely to generate higher fiscal deficits, since politicians will have particularly short time horizons. Second, a polarized political system in which the objectives of the competing parties are highly incompatible will generate higher fiscal deficits than those systems in which the objectives of the competing parties overlap and are less zero-sum in nature.

Bringing Institutions Back In

Economists who have branched into political economy tend to think of the polity in terms of economic cleavages. Workers have different interests than capitalists; holders of financial assets have different inflation preferences than debtors; urban consumers have different preferences regarding agricultural prices than rural producers. As the partisan-conflict model suggests, economists assume a close "mapping" between economic cleavages and political organization, and see the state and politicians as relatively passive registers of social demands.[5] With this approach, every policy that has a distributional consequence could be explained on the grounds that it favored some group. The more demanding task is to explain why some polities are riddled with revenue seeking, while others have developed mechanisms of fiscal control.

Answering such questions requires greater attention to organizational and institutional factors. First, different types of economic activity may be more or less amenable to political organization and collective action (Shafer forthcoming). The agricultural sector may loom large in the economy, but peasants are difficult to organize and rural influence on policy can easily be offset by smaller, but better organized urban forces. It is therefore important to have information not only on economic cleavages, which provides good clues about policy preferences, but also on which social groups are in fact capable of effective organization.

Second, party organization can aggregate interests in different ways. In some polities, the party system reinforces societal and economic cleavages and conflicts, for example, pitting populist or labor parties against conservative and middle-class parties, or urban-based parties against rural-based ones. In other countries, broad, catchall parties cut across class or economic divisions and tend to mute them. These organizational differences can have profound influence on the political appeals parties make, on the demands on public finance, and consequently on the conduct of macroeconomic policy. Macroeconomic stability is more likely in two-party systems with broad, catchall parties than in those that pit class-based parties against one another or in multiparty systems that foster more ideological parties.

It is not enough to know how groups are organized for political action; equally if not more important is the question of how social demands are represented in the decision-making process. The new political economy has focused its attention on the advanced industrial states, and thus assumed the existence of political processes such as general elections. Elections are not relevant for policy making in authoritarian regimes, and may not be relevant for policy making in some arenas even under democratic conditions. For example, monetary policy and the details of budgeting may have more to do with internal bureaucratic politics or the independence of the central bank, than with electoral or party constraints.

The absence of democratic processes in the developing world may help explain the attraction of lobbying and rent-seeking models, which can presumably be applied to both democratic and authoritarian regimes. Democracy may not be ubiquitous, but lobbying is. Yet interest group pressures constrain authoritarian rulers less than they do democratic rulers. It is thus plausible that the political regime can be an important factor in explaining the ability to impose stabilization costs.

These observations suggest the importance of combining interest group and partisan explanations with an analysis of the overall institutional context: the nature of the party system, the budget process, and the type of regime.[6] This analysis can be illustrated, though not definitively tested, by examining some hypotheses about the variation in inflation and stabilization efforts among the middle-income countries.

Politics and Inflation in Middle-Income Countries

Although the debt crisis of the 1980s has had global implications, its effects have been felt quite differently in various geographic regions.[7] Among the middle-income countries, Latin America has been the hardest hit. Twelve of the seventeen countries designated by the World Bank as the most heavily indebted are in the Western Hemisphere. The most severe problems with inflation are found in that region as well. By contrast, the middle-income countries of East and Southeast Asia—South Korea, Taiwan, Indonesia, Thailand, Malaysia, and the Philippines—have largely been immune from devastating inflations.

Table 9.1 suggests that differences in inflation are not simply the result of recent events. Before the onset of the debt crisis, Latin America consistently had higher levels of inflation than other developing countries, though there are important contrasts within regions. Brazil, Chile, and Uruguay all have histories of comparatively high inflation. The current hyperinflations in Brazil and Argentina are outside the range of those countries' historical experience, but both have experienced severe inflations before. Other Latin American countries, including Colombia, Venezuela, and Mexico, have not had chronically high levels of inflation, though all have suffered increasing inflationary pressures in recent times. Peru, historically a low-inflation country compared with the Southern Cone nations (Argentina, Chile, and Uruguay), is now veering toward hyperinflation.

In Asia, Thailand, Taiwan, and Malaysia have had histories of low inflation and all largely escaped the debt crisis of the 1980s. Indonesia had a near hyperinflation in the mid-1960s, but its fiscal and monetary policy have been conservative since. South Korea has had high levels of debt and inflation by Asian standards but adjusted relatively smoothly in the early 1980s. The Philippines, by contrast, had painful problems of adjustment in 1984, though by comparison to the Latin American debtors, that country's difficulties appear relatively mild.

TABLE 9.1   Inflation Rates for Selected Developing Countries, 1965–1980

Country	Average annual inflation (%)
Latin America	
High-inflation countries	
Argentina	78.3
Brazil	31.3
Chile	129.9
Uruguay	57.8
Low- and moderate-inflation countries	
Colombia	17.4
Mexico	13.1
Peru	20.5
Venezuela	8.7
Asia	
Indonesia	34.3
South Korea	18.8
Malaysia	4.9
Philippines	11.7
Taiwan	7.6
Thailand	6.8

NOTE: Inflation rates for all countries except Taiwan are measured by the growth rate of the GDP implicit deflator. For Taiwan, the rate given is the average annual change in the consumer price index.
SOURCE: World Bank, *World Development Report 1988* (New York: Oxford University Press, 1988); *Taiwan Statistical Data Book 1988* (Taipei: Council on Economic Planning and Development, 1988).

Recognizing that economic circumstances vary across cases as well, what political factors help account for these long-term patterns? The new political economy would suggest that differences in the density and composition of interest group organization should be a starting point. Through most of the postwar period, the Latin American countries can be differentiated from the Asian cases in terms of the size and organization of urban-industrial interest groups, including the so-called popular sector, which has played a crucial role in Latin American politics.

Mexico, Brazil, and particularly the countries of the Southern Cone had longer histories of industrialization, larger urban-industrial populations, and comparatively small agrarian sectors at the outset of the borrowing boom of the 1970s than the East and Southeast Asian countries. These conditions have implied denser and more established networks of unions, white-collar associations, and manufacturers' groups linked to the import-substituting industrialization (ISI) process in Latin America.

This density of urban-industrial groups, in turn, had two implications for economic policy. The first concerns overall economic strategy. There have been important economic barriers to shifting the pattern of incentives toward export-oriented strategies in Latin America, including the problem of setting exchange rates where there is a strong comparative advantage in natural resource export. The number and extent of groups linked to import-substituting industrialization have also been significant factors (Haggard 1990). Even authoritarian governments with preferences for market-oriented policies, such as Brazil after 1964, faced constraints from groups linked to the ISI process. The well-known balance of payments problems associated with ISI were, in turn, one factor in the expansion of foreign borrowing during the 1970s and the subsequent macroeconomic policy problems.

In South Korea and Taiwan, by contrast, industrialization, and particularly ISI, were of shorter duration, and there were consequently fewer interests opposed to the crucial exchange rate and trade reforms that launched export-led growth. Elite concern with rural incomes may also have had some effect on policy, constituting a political counterweight to ISI forces (Sachs 1985). This constellation of interest groups may help explain the ability of the Philippines, Thailand, Malaysia, and Indonesia to maintain realistic exchange rates and to shift, though to varying degrees, toward the promotion of manufactured exports.

The second consequence of the density of urban-industrial groups relates more immediately to macroeconomic policy. The political mobilization of urban groups and unions, particularly in a context of high income inequality, is an important factor in explaining the appeal of populist economic ideologies in Latin America. As Dornbusch and Edwards (1989) and Sachs (1989) have argued, there is a remarkable similarity in populist economic programs across countries. Their main political objective is to reverse the loss in real income to urban groups that results from traditional stabilization policies or simply from the business cycle.

Populist prescriptions include fiscal expansion; a redistribution of income through real wage increases; and a program of structural reform designed to relieve productive bottlenecks and economize on foreign exchange. Populists reject the claim that deficit financing is inflationary, arguing that the mobilization of unused spare capacity, declining costs, and, if necessary, controls, will moderate inflation.

Populist experiments go through a typical cycle, usually triggered by orthodox stabilization efforts:[8]

Phase 1.   Policy makers enjoy a honeymoon as their prescriptions appear to be vindicated. Output grows and real wages and employment improve. Direct controls are used to manage inflation. The easing of the balance of payments constraint and the buildup of reserves under the previous orthodox program provides the populists a crucial cushion for meeting import demand.

Phase 2.   Strong domestic demand starts to generate a foreign exchange constraint, but devaluation is rejected as inflationary and detrimental to maintaining real wage growth. External controls are instituted. The budget deficit widens because of the growth of subsidies on wage goods and on foreign exchange.

Phase 3.   Growing disparity between official and black market exchange rates and general lack of confidence lead to capital flight. The budget deficit deteriorates because of continuing high levels of expenditure and lagging tax collections. Inflation soars.

Phase 4.   Stabilization becomes a political priority, and the principal political debate concerns whether to pursue a more "orthodox" or "heterodox" policy mix.

Why do such cycles appear in one political setting and not in another? Stop-and-go macroeconomic policies themselves are partly to blame, since they carry particular costs for urban workers. One determinant of such populist cycles is the way urban political forces are initially organized—in other words whether historical partisan alignments mute or reinforce sectoral and class cleavages.

In Argentina, Peru, Chile, and Brazil, antioligarchical parties of the center and the left recurrently sought the support of urban workers and small manufacturers by appealing to class and sectoral interests. These appeals produced the kind of political polarization and macroeconomic policy outcomes predicted by the partisan-conflict model outlined above. In Colombia and Venezuela, by contrast, such conflicts were discouraged by the electoral dominance of broadly based patronage parties. In Uruguay, the traditional Colorado and Blanco parties also tended to discourage class and sectoral conflicts that lead to expansionary macroeconomic policies, though by the mid-1960s, the influence of these parties had come under challenge from a coalition of center-left parties with strong bases of support in Montevideo.

Mexico provides an important example of the significance of institutions in determining the ability of new urban-industrial groups to formulate effective demands on the state. Under the leadership of President Lázaro Cárdenas in the 1930s, the ruling Partido Revolucionario Institucional (PRI) encompassed peasant, middle-class, and working-class organizations. Mexico experienced structural changes comparable to those in Brazil and Argentina in the 1950s and 1960s, but under stable macroeconomic policies. This regime of "stabilizing development" was achieved following a painful devaluation in 1954. The government was able to withstand short-term protests to this crucial reform because of the special relationship it enjoyed with state-sanctioned unions. Not until the early 1970s did deepening social problems and the populist political strategy of President Luis Echeverría combine to break the pattern of stable monetary and fiscal policies. Nonetheless, Mexico still managed to pursue more "orthodox" stabilization policies in the 1980s under Presidents Miguel de la Madrid and Carlos Salinas than either of the other two large Latin American countries, Brazil and Argentina. This is due in large part to the PRI's continuing ability to engineer political compromises and exercise discipline over urban workers (see Kaufman 1989).

Even when populist forces surfaced in East and Southeast Asian countries, they never succeeded in gaining a political foothold. A larger proportion of the population remained outside the framework of urban interest group politics altogether than in Latin America, and patterns of political organization also differed. Broad, anticolonial movements muted class and sectoral conflicts. Generally, the most serious political challenges came not from the urban areas, but from rural insurgencies. When and where urban working-class politics did emerge, it was either assimilated into corporatist structures or suppressed.

In the Philippines, two diffuse political machines dominated the electoral system before the announcement of martial law by Ferdinand Marcos in 1972. Pork-barrel conflicts were more important than programmatic differences, but elite domination of the political system resulted in extremely low levels of taxation. Beginning in the late 1960s, urban-based leftist organizations grew, but they were crushed following the declaration of martial law. Even when political liberalization provided new opportunities for the left to organize, its influence was counterbalanced by that of the old political machines and the new middle-class democratic political movement, headed finally by Corazon Aquino, which owed little to the left.

In Malaysia, politics was dominated by a single nationalist party and its minor coalition partners, but class and sectoral conflicts were secondary to ethnic rivalries. Indonesia remains a single-party system, with very limited pluralism. Thailand, despite periodic democratic openings, has shown a continuity in economic policy thanks to the central role of the bureaucracy and the continuing influence of the military.

South Korea and Taiwan once again provide sharp contrasts to the Latin American cases. Until the transition toward more pluralist politics in the two countries in the mid-1980s, both South Korea and Taiwan (beginning in 1972 and 1949, respectively) were ruled by strong, anticommunist, authoritarian regimes that limited the possibilities for interest-group organization. Taiwan's one-party system effectively organized and controlled the unions and disallowed opposition parties. The South Korean government combined informal penetration of the unions and periodic repression to keep labor and urban-based opposition forces in check. The recurrence of urban-based opposition among students and workers may explain the Korean government's greater tolerance for an expansionist macroeconomic policy, but the opportunity for open political organization and populist appeals was severely limited. Both countries showed a continuity in government unparalleled in any of the Latin American governments except Chile.

This discussion suggests that the middle-income countries of Latin America and East and Southeast Asia can be arrayed on a continuum from very high to low levels of group and party conflict. Argentina, Chile, Brazil, Uruguay, and Peru appear at one extreme, with relatively large popular sectors, and with political movements and party structures that historically tended to reinforce sectoral and class conflicts; these countries have historically also had higher levels of inflation. At the other pole are Indonesia, Taiwan, and Thailand, where the popular sectors were smaller, and both political alliances and party structures less conducive to the emergence of populist movements; these countries have also generally had lower levels of inflation. The other Latin American and Asian countries fall between these two polar types, with varying degrees of urban and working-class mobilization and organization.

The Politics of Stabilization

These stylized patterns of political conflict also help explain variations in the political management of stabilization over time. Stabilization efforts have encountered the greatest difficulties in those countries where intense group conflicts and persistently high levels of inflation have fed on each other over long periods of time. In these circumstances, the capacity to impose stabilization has in the past been linked to the nature of the political regime, suggesting once again the importance of institutional variables in explaining policy outcomes.

There are examples of populist military governments: Bolivia in 1970–1971, the Peruvian experiment in the early 1970s, and the first year of South Korea's military rule in 1961–1962. Typically, however, militaries have seized power in the midst of political-economic crises characteristic of the later stages of the populist cycle outlined above. They have initially pursued policies designed to impose discipline and rationalize the economic system, in part by limiting the demands of leftist, populist, and labor groups. This general pattern was followed, with varying constraints, in Brazil (1964), Argentina (1966, 1976), Indonesia (1965), Chile (1973), Uruguay (1973), and arguably South Korea (1980–1981).

As the initial crisis is brought under control, military regimes begin to face new problems of consolidation or transition. Old political forces resurface, and regimes face pressure to build support and moderate the militancy of the opposition. Brazil provides an example. The government's decision to pursue high-growth policies during the oil shocks coincided closely with the military's decisions concerning the opening of the political system.

The transition to democratic rule in such systems is likely to pose particular problems for stabilization efforts. The transition opens the way for well-organized and long-standing popular sector groups to reenter politics, groups that had been controlled or repressed under military rule. High inflation and erratic growth make the distributional and political costs of fiscal restraint appear particularly formidable, but these costs are compounded by the uncertainties associated with the transition itself. New political leaders are necessarily preoccupied with securing the transition, and thus have relatively short time horizons. Those political forces that have been in opposition, or simply suppressed, are eager to press new demands on the government. As political leaders attempt to accommodate these strongly conflicting demands, it becomes difficult to maintain macroeconomic stability.

It could be argued, however, that the transition process is less important in explaining macroeconomic policy than the nature of the economic problems these governments inherited from their authoritarian predecessors. First, in countries with chronically high inflation, both authoritarian and democratic governments have accommodated conflicts over income shares through indexing. Indexing itself generates inertial inflation and complicates the conduct of monetary and fiscal policy. Second, the severity and speed of external shocks, particularly the withdrawal of external lending, severely narrowed the range of economic policy choice (see Easterly 1989). Economic legacies, rather than political constraints, matter; Argentina simply inherited greater difficulties than the Philippines or South Korea.

Yet in the transitional democracies that faced high inflations, political constraints do appear to be significant in the making of macroeconomic policy. The three experiments with heterodox adjustment strategies—Argentina, Brazil, and Peru—occurred in systems with a high level of popular sector mobilization. Brazil under José Sarney and Peru under Alán García responded to high inflation with heterodox policies in the mid-1980s that included wage-price controls and currency reforms. In contrast to Mexico, however, neither new democratic government placed a high priority on containing wage pressures, reducing subsidies, or controlling spending, and both experiments ran into difficulties. Raúl Alfonsín's middle-class government in Argentina also pursued a heterodox shock policy to manage high inflation, but initially placed greater emphasis on negotiating wage restraint and bringing deficits under control. Nonetheless, fiscal policy remained a source of inflationary pressure, stabilization efforts faltered, and political competition with the Peronists and the anticipation of a change of government ultimately undermined the coherence of macroeconomic policy.

The interesting exception is Uruguay, one of the most economically successful of the new Latin American democracies. The return to constitutionalism in Uruguay restored the dominance of the two, broad-based centrist parties that had dominated political life until the coup in 1973, providing a framework for elite negotiation and accord much like that in more established democratic systems such as Colombia and Venezuela. Negotiations between the Blanco and Colorado parties led to an economic policy agreement in early 1985 that emphasized controlling budget deficits and inflation, promoting exports, and undertaking structural reforms.

The transition to democracy has played a less important role in explaining macroeconomic policy in countries with a lower level of popular sector mobilization and a greater institutional continuity in political and decision-making structures. Not coincidentally, these countries also faced less daunting economic problems, and it can once again be argued that economic circumstance rather than political factors account for the variance. It nonetheless appears plausible that politics had at least an intervening effect on policy choices and outcomes.

In Thailand, the new political order ushered in by parliamentary elections in 1979 might be labeled semidemocratic. In 1980, General Kriangsak was forced to resign over economic mismanagement in the face of rising protest and pressure from within the military. Another general, Prem Tinsulanon, was elected by a large majority in both houses to replace him. Prem moved to incorporate opposition parties into a broad-based coalition, yet in Thailand's "bureaucratic polity," power continued to reside in the army and bureaucracy. There were no fundamental discontinuities in business-government relations and technocrats even gained in influence.

In South Korea, General Chun Doo-hwan's handpicked successor, Roh Tae-woo, was forced to widen the scope of political liberalization and constitutional reforms in the wake of widespread urban protests in 1986 and 1987 that included students, workers, and middle-class elements. Running against a split opposition, Roh captured the presidency with just over one-third of the popular vote. Though the conservative ruling party subsequently lost control of the National Assembly and has been forced to make a number of economic concessions, including those to labor and farmers, the executive and bureaucracy maintain comparatively tight control over fiscal policy.

In the Philippines, Aquino was brought to power by massive middle-class demonstrations against fraudulent elections in February 1986. This "revolution" did not rest on popular sector mobilization;

indeed, the left made the tactical error of not supporting Aquino's presidential candidacy. Subsequent development planning focused greater attention on rural problems in an effort to counteract the insurgency, and the government pursued a mild Keynesian stimulus through a public works program. But Aquino also moved quickly to cement ties with those portions of the private sector disadvantaged by Marcos' cronyism, and Aquino's economic cabinet was dominated by businessmen-turned-technocrats. The reconvening of Congress in 1987 provided new opportunities for pork-barrel politics, but as in Thailand and Korea, fundamental political and institutional continuities limited political pressures on macroeconomic policy.

More generally, in those countries where underlying class and sectoral cleavages are less intense, or where class and sectoral cleavages have been muted by integrative forms of party organization, the political stakes of stabilization appear lower. This has two further implications. First, the capacity to carry out stabilization programs in these cases is not closely influenced by the type of regime. Democratic governments in Venezuela and Colombia have done as well or better at maintaining fiscal discipline as systems dominated by one party such as Mexico.

Second, where the parties are less polarized and the process of political succession is institutionalized, changes of government should not be expected to produce major shifts in policy. In such cases, unlike in high-conflict societies, newly elected governments do not usually represent previously excluded groups that expect immediate material payoffs. The time horizons of political leaders are therefore likely to be longer.

Democratic governments of this sort may be subject to political business cycles, but they are also in a better position to capitalize on the honeymoon effect by imposing stabilization programs early in their terms. This, too, is related to the time horizons of politicians in more institutionalized systems. With greater expectations that they will be able to reap the political benefits of stable policies, politicians will be less tempted toward unsustainable expansionist policies.

Conclusion: Is Political Theory Relevant for Policy Making?

I have drawn on insights from the new political economy to suggest some hypotheses on the variation in macroeconomic policy in middle-income countries. The relevance of political theory for policy making, however, cannot be assumed. Prescriptive policy analysis aims to identify policies that are optimal given some criterion such as efficiency, stability, or growth. Positive political analysis, by contrast, often takes the form of suggesting why economically optimal policies are unlikely to be adopted. It is hardly useful from a policy perspective to suggest that long-term patterns of inflation are the result of deep-seated historical factors, such as the density of urban working-class organizations, the structure of the party system, or the nature of the regime.

If economists tend toward a voluntarism that explains political constraints in terms of lack of will, political economists can be overly deterministic. Many of the neoclassical models in the rent-seeking tradition fail to openly confront their own determinism and as a result fall into the following paradox. They seek to use political economy to demonstrate the venality of politicians. Once exposed, such venality can be undercut by reform of the policies and institutions that encourage rent- and revenue-seeking in the first place. But constituents, particularly if they are the beneficiaries of politicians' venality, are not interested in seeing it exposed. Moreover, both institutions and policy interventions are themselves the products of political processes and must be wholly endogenized if the new political economy is to fulfill its analytic goals.

Does this mean that the new political economy has nothing to offer to policy makers? In fact, the scope for political maneuvering is wider than thought. The variable that is hardest to manipulate in the policy equation appears to be the overall balance of interest groups, but interests are not in fact fixed. Actors may not be aware of their interests on a particular policy issue, such as fiscal policy, and may be myopic with reference to the longer-term consequences of their own preferences. If stabilization is not merely a technical exercise, but a political process that demands the building of coalitions, it is crucial that potential beneficiaries be identified and persuaded of their interest in the success of the program. Research on the distributional consequences of stabilization programs is important not only to identify the economic gains and losses, but also to identify political winners and losers. For example, it is important for economists to stress that populist policies frequently have the effect of doing the most harm to precisely those groups that they purport to assist.

Such research might provide as much ammunition for groups opposed to fiscal reform as for supporters. There are, however, three other areas where political economy may be of use to policy makers designing stabilization programs. One is the importance of devising compensatory schemes for those negatively affected. Compensating losers, even those that are relatively well off, may prove less costly than political opposition that undermines programs. The costs of political failure should be fully taken into account in designing particular programs.

A second area of policy advice, not addressed in detail here, concerns processes and institutions internal to the government itself. Deficits result when governments confront pressures to spend that exceed the ability to extract resources. Politicians and bureaucrats may have an interest in fiscal responsibility, but they have a competing interest in policies that provide benefits for constituents. Such situations present collective action dilemmas—conflicts between individual and group rationality. These conflicts can be overcome by institutions that limit the ability of politicians to pursue individual political interests or that provide information on the costs of political decisions. Many developing countries could benefit from reforming the budgetary process by centralizing spending decisions, moving them away from autonomous units such as state-owned enterprises, ministries, or legislative subcommittees. Multilateral organizations might focus more attention on designing institutions that will guarantee compatibility between the incentives for optimum political and economic behavior.

The final insight from the new political economy that might be of use for policy making concerns timing and the structure of conditionality. In some circumstances, a program that is likely to raise expectations and fail may be worse than no program at all. Providing external assistance may only allow countries to continue to pursue misguided policies. Conditionality that demands action prior to the disbursement of loans remains crucial for gauging the political capacity of countries to undertake successful reforms.

Comments

WILLIAM EASTERLY

I do not envy Stephan Haggard's task of reviewing the implications of political economy theory for macroeconomic stabilization. He is attempting to draw policy implications from a body of theory that is still in its infancy. Nevertheless, he does an admirable job of providing insights into macroeconomic policy choice in developing countries. I particularly like his discussion of the role of the urban working class in populist economic policies.

Since space is brief, however, I will concentrate on where his chapter seems to fall short, which I believe reflects more the shortcomings of

The views expressed here are those of the author alone and not of the World Bank.

existing theory than any lack of intellectual diligence on Haggard's part. I have four principal questions to raise:

1. What is the causal relationship between politics and economics?

2. What are the policy implications of his analysis?

3. Does his political economic theory fit the facts?

4. How does his theory of inflation compare to other theories?

The first point is the most fundamental and has already been discussed under various guises in this volume. Haggard's central hypothesis is that politically polarized societies are more likely to experience high public deficits, high inflation, and macroeconomic instability than societies with broad-based political parties that either incorporate or repress the urban "popular sector." However, it is difficult to sort out which direction the causality goes. The idea that inflation itself leads to class conflict and polarization is an old one, as Haggard admits in the chapter. Political and economic stability therefore seem likely to be simultaneously determined. If this is so, we cannot define a unique relationship between them. We need to identify the exogenous variables in order to predict both political and economic outcomes.

Even if we accept that causality is from political polarization to macroeconomic instability, what does it imply for policy making? Perhaps the main contribution would be simply a greater realism about the feasibility of programs in conflict-ridden societies. Even so, it is not very appealing to imagine, for example, the multilateral institutions' refusing to support an economically sound stabilization program on the grounds that a society is too polarized. There may be some obvious examples of severe polarization (like a civil war), but there will also be plenty of borderline cases. Are the multilateral institutions the best judges of political stability in these cases?

Does the political economy theory underlying the relationship between political polarization and inflation fit the facts? Allow me to summarize the theory somewhat crudely—when a society is highly polarized between two groups (such as labor and capital), each group will try to have a fiesta during its time in office, leaving the other group to foot the bill. According to political business-cycle theory, the fiesta is also supposed to be timed to prolong the period in office. The problem with this theory is that there are numerous examples of populist regimes that were forced to pay the bill for their own fiesta and then lost power prematurely.

Some names that spring to mind are Alfonsín, Manley (in his first incarnation), Allende, Isabel Perón, Alán García, and Daniel Ortega.

Even more important, the group that was supposed to benefit from the populist policies, the urban working class, in fact usually lost out in the long run. This is abundantly clear in the paper by Dornbusch and Edwards to which Haggard refers. Capital is internationally mobile; labor is not. As a result, labor gets stuck with the bill for the fiesta.

The self-defeating nature of populist policies does not support a theory of rational politicians pursuing such policies to their political advantage and to the economic benefit of their working-class constituents. It instead supports economists' rather arrogant, old-fashioned idea that policy makers often do not know enough economics to act in their own best interest.

I want to suggest a simpler political economy theory of inflation, which is the old idea that inflation is a fiscal phenomenon. Stated simply, money creation (and thus inflation) is the last-resort way for a government to finance spending after it has exhausted conventional means such as taxing or foreign borrowing.

This simple theory explains one of the phenomena mentioned in Haggard's chapter, the upsurge in inflation after the debt crisis. In a recent paper, I argue that a broadly defined inflation tax was a common means of financing the fiscal deficit after the outbreak of the debt crisis (Easterly 1989). This inflation tax includes both money creation and the tax implicit in government borrowing from the financial system at negative real interest rates. This tax is implicitly paid by users of financial intermediation services, in other words, depositors and borrowers.

I call this broadly defined inflation tax the "tax on financial intermediation." As shown in Table C9.1, this tax was important for five out of the seven debt crisis countries considered. In contrast, countries that did not experience a debt crisis largely eschewed the tax on financial intermediation.

Of course, the taxation of financial savings in the debt crisis countries contributed to further capital flight and financial disintermediation in those countries. The result was a severe squeeze on credit to the private sector and thus on investment. In the noncrisis countries, however, financial savings and investment performed well.

Why did countries attempt to finance their fiscal deficits in this costly and self-defeating way? Here the fiscal theory of inflation gives useful insights. I suggest in the paper that the abruptness with which external financing disappeared in the crisis countries forced very rapid adjustments. Taxing financial assets is quicker than raising new conventional tax revenues or restructuring spending. More fundamental measures require the assent of the legislature or at least of large segments of

TABLE C9.1   Tax on Financial Intermediation in Crisis and Noncrisis Developing Countries, 1976–1986 (percentage of GDP)

	Average[a]							
	1976–78	1979–81	1982–86	1982	1983	1984	1985	1986
Crisis countries								
Argentina								
NF	n.a.	5.70	15.24	7.90	29.18	26.00	7.36	5.75
NRI	n.a.	2.73	10.22	7.47	17.09	17.15	6.09	3.29
Brazil	n.a.	n.a.	2.27	1.25	3.27	2.54	2.03	n.a.
Chile								
NF	n.a.	2.16	1.49	2.72	0.91	0.84	n.a.	n.a.
NRI	n.a.	0.80	n.a.	1.82	0.63	0.64	n.a.	n.a.
Mexico								
NF	n.a.	3.52	11.64	16.42	13.63	8.32	6.95	12.90
NRI	n.a.	0.83	7.12	12.74	8.23	3.95	1.76	8.90
Morocco	n.a.	2.32	1.24	0.93	2.50	1.20	1.63	–0.07
Philippines	0.56	1.20	0.89	0.18	2.11	3.69	–0.85	–0.70
Yugoslavia	n.a.	7.12	10.87	6.35	12.12	10.63	12.49	12.77
Noncrisis countries								
Colombia	1.70	2.48	1.21	2.09	0.76	0.74	1.26	n.a.
Indonesia	0.85	1.01	0.28	0.50	0.52	0.24	–0.28	0.42
Korea	1.12	1.82	0.23	0.33	0.29	0.29	0.23	0.03
Thailand	n.a.	1.31	–0.74	–0.61	–0.38	–1.25	–0.74	–0.70
Turkey	n.a.	7.32	2.80	2.48	2.79	3.82	3.28	1.66

NOTES: n.a. = not available.
NF = including nominal flow of bank reserves.
NRI = including only negative real interest rate paid on reserves.
a. Period average for years for which data are available.
SOURCE: William Easterly, "Fiscal Adjustment and Deficit Financing during the Debt Crisis," in Ishrat Husain and Ishac Diwan, eds., *Dealing with the Debt Crisis* (Washington, D.C.: World Bank, 1989).

the bureaucracy, whereas taxing financial assets can be done by fiat through the central bank. In line with the fiscal theory of inflation, money creation is the last resort when other means of financing public expenditure are unavailable in the short run.

What policy implications follow from the fiscal theory of inflation? At the most optimistic, the theory implies that allowing more time for adjustment might lead to more rational means of adjustment, such as broadening the tax base. According to this view, payment schedules on debt should be altered to give debtors time to generate new revenues through tax reform.

A more pessimistic interpretation is that the revenue and expenditure structure cannot be altered even in the long run. Some countries seem to have much more difficulty broadening the tax base than others.

Why do only 8,000 people pay income tax in Argentina? To judge whether the pessimistic or optimistic view is correct requires a political judgment on the viability of tax reform. Although the fiscal theory of inflation tells us more about money creation and inflation than monetarist platitudes, it still does not explain the political economy determinants of the tax and expenditure system.

FRANCISCO X. SWETT

Stephan Haggard has produced an insightful review of several hypotheses developed to explain variations in macroeconomic policies in the middle-income developing countries. His critical treatment of the different explanations is probably shared by those whose knowledge of the subject has been gained through experience in those countries. Finally, and this is not insignificant, he provides a fair and representative assessment of the literature, presenting a balanced view of the arguments and positions taken by different schools.

This said, there are a number of points that deserve consideration. First is a problem of imprecise terminology. Haggard tends to use such terms as economic stabilization, fiscal policies, neoclassical economics, and political theory interchangeably. Fiscal policy, for instance, may or may not be the most important component of a stabilization effort. Furthermore, economic stabilization is a global concept that describes the whole gamut of policies designed to deal with inflation, unemployment, stagnation, uneven income distribution, and, in general, economic problems that weaken the fabric of society. Stabilization should not be viewed as simply an effort to lower inflation or to apportion fiscal resources. Neither should the relevance, or lack thereof, of political theory be equated with the effectiveness of the tools of economic analysis to provide an adequate framework for understanding and explaining the real world.

Second, Haggard states that he is partial to decision-making, business-cycle, and partisan-conflict models for understanding political outcomes. In his view, rent-seeking and interest-group models are good ex post explanations of the interplay of support-maximizing politicians and welfare-maximizing constituents, but they do not help explain the jump from the microlevel of a particular rent, expenditure, or tax to the macrolevel of political outcomes. The new political economy is therefore limited by its inability to explain the variance of outcomes.

If this synthesis does justice to Haggard's views, and if such views are correct, one may be tempted to say that the tools of political theory, and presumably those of neoclassical economics, are better for writing good history than for forecasting political outcomes based on current observations. Haggard's skepticism regarding the predictive value of the new political economy therefore presents an important challenge. But, at the risk of taking his views out of context, I hasten to add that sound economic policies, based on sound economic theory, do make a significant difference in determining acceptable economic and political outcomes. To put it another way, bad economics is at the heart of poor politics.

Third, the models reviewed in Haggard's chapter present a mechanical view of society; the equations of the empirical models were specified to choose the independent variables that have greatest explanatory power. This type of exercise is useful, but to understand political outcomes it is necessary to go beyond such measurements. The actors and driving forces—decision makers, institutions, exogenous factors, ideologies, and the interplay of political and economic events—have to be identified and understood in order to make what Haggard has called the jump from the microlevel of specific interests to the macrolevel of political outcomes.

A case in point is the analysis of the differences in development patterns over time between Asia and Latin America. According to Haggard, the new political economy suggests that different patterns emerge from the "density and composition of interest group organization." He further says that, in contrast to the Asian countries, the Latin American countries have had longer histories of industrialization, larger urban-industrial populations, and smaller agrarian sectors. This, he concludes, implies denser and more established networks of unions, white collar associations, and manufacturers' groups linked to the import-substitution process.

This is a description of some Latin American conditions, but it overlooks the causes behind those conditions. A number of relevant questions must be raised: How were the coalitions formed? What types of policies were adopted and why? What were the results of such policies? The answers to such questions deserve careful treatment, and we now turn our attention to them.

Latin America has been dominated by a structuralist model of development that was born as an expression of political and intellectual autonomy at the end of World War II. The intellectual influence of the Economic Commission for Latin America (ECLA) and Raúl Prebisch, its first secretary general, who warned of the pitfalls of the "secular deteriorating terms of trade," was enormous throughout the region, and no effort was spared in the design and application of his Latin doctrine of development.

Asia, however, had no Prebisch- or ECLA-style intellectual leadership; rather, its heritage was closer to the British and American doctrines of vigorous free trade and export expansion. In Asia it was understood very early that local markets could not sustain high rates of growth. Asian countries developed on the basis of their comparative advantage and factor endowments, whereas in Latin America development strategies turned inward. When economic integration schemes such as the Central American Common Market and the Andean Trade Pact were attempted, members made no effort to coordinate macroeconomic policies, but instead placed the entire emphasis on trade policies. The result was that such schemes promoted trade diversion, not trade creation.

The political economy of structuralism was an important factor in explaining why the model was widely adopted in Latin America and why coalitions were formed to sustain it. Politicians hold nationalism in high regard, and structuralism stressed protection of local productive powers and national resource endowments. Those politically inclined to favor an interventionist state felt that structuralism required the government to actively exercise the tools of fiscal, monetary, exchange rate, financial, and pricing policies, as well as public investment strategies. Local entrepreneurs found that factor price distortions, market segmentation, and administrative practices associated with structuralism worked for the most part in their favor, except when public investment became aggressive and the state began carving out its own areas of economic competence. Finally, organized labor in both the public and private sectors managed to reap wage and subsidy packages worth more than the shadow price of labor and thereby appropriated excess rent.

Asian states also became powerful, but unlike their Latin counterparts they put a premium on productive efficiency. Whereas the structuralist model promoted consumption, and political instability and negative expectations caused capital flight in Latin America, Asians emphasized the virtue of frugality and eventually achieved the world's highest national saving rates. While highly protective labor legislation was one of the costly results of the adoption of the structuralist model in Latin America (some would argue this was a way to achieve a measure of positive income redistribution), no such labor codes were enacted in Asia, and labor mobility was, except in Japan, more fluid than in Latin America.

Structuralism was based on the active manipulation of factor prices. Distortions were most evident in exchange rate and financial policies. Overvalued exchange rates and financial repression were needed to sustain industrial development and to finance industrial investment growth. Such manipulations caused important shifts in intersectoral terms of trade (between industry and agriculture, for instance). Those realignments, almost always contrary to the countries' comparative advantage, caused massive migration from the countryside to the cities where politicians' priorities lay and thus where jobs were being created.

With the first oil shock in 1974, the Asian countries adjusted and managed to curtail aggregate demand, but the Latin countries did not. The recycled petrodollars that financed the region's external debt from 1974 to 1982 postponed the day of reckoning for the oil-importing countries. It also twisted the Latin American oil exporters' perception of the future, with regard to both oil prices and capital flows. The artificial conditions created by external savings allowed those countries to maintain price subsidies across the board, to embark on overambitious projects of physical infrastructure, and to live well beyond their means while lagging in their fiscal effort.

The Latin economies became addicted to foreign capital. Therefore, the cessation of credit and the reversal of capital flows that resulted from the onset of the debt crisis wreaked havoc in countries that followed the structuralist model. In Asia, the control of aggregate demand, the endogenous generation of savings, and the export diversification drive sustained high levels of economic growth without significant foreign indebtedness. The Asian economies achieved financial development; industry became highly competitive by world standards; and eventually some, such as South Korea and Taiwan, reached capital surplus positions. The Latin American economies, by contrast, found themselves with substantial liabilities and insufficient productive capacity to deal simultaneously with the debt problem and the promotion of growth. The new priorities then became export diversification, correction of factor price distortions, reduction and elimination of subsidies, and financial development. The evolution of the debt crisis and the need to accommodate the conditionality imposed by the multilateral institutions, the Paris Club, and the commercial banks played a major role in undoing the region's traditional structuralist practices. The last salvos of its practitioners were the so-called heterodox adjustment programs in Peru, Argentina, and Brazil. Because they did not correct price distortions and thereby limited the chances of achieving monetary and fiscal equilibrium, such exercises and policy initiatives were bound to fail. And they did.

In Latin America, therefore, the structuralist model led to a development strategy characterized by aversion to adjustments and a greater dependence on external financing. Industrial development did take place, but it was costly, it failed to generate sufficient employment, and in extreme cases it minimized local value added. The success of the model was dependent on the distortion of factor price, and this caused a misallocation of economic priorities.

In Asia such widespread distortions did not take place. The Asian economies imposed fiscal discipline and actively encouraged competitive exports. The state did not become directly involved in productive processes. Policies promoted labor mobility and labor absorption. Saving and frugality became collective virtues. A high premium was placed on productive efficiency. And adjustments took place along the way, as circumstances warranted, to check inflation and to achieve maximum levels of real growth.

A fourth and final point is that Haggard, as stated, expends considerable effort in reviewing the different models for explaining political outcome variations. Even though that is the objective of his paper, the effort to define which model is best appears unproductive: it is wasteful to seek to build elaborate explanations based on self-evident truths. Each model offers a partially valid explanation of the real world. There are such things as political compromises (as stated in the decision-making model); politicians do behave differently over the life cycle of their stay in power, always anticipating who may come next (as predicted by political business-cycle models); and finally, politicians do seek to favor their specific constituencies (as the partisan-conflict models would indicate).

Thus, although each model has a measure of validity, it is a mistake to think that the real world admits only one explanation to the exclusion of all others. Political decisions concerning economic policy are subject to a number of factors that determine the degree of freedom of decision makers. Such factors include the balance of political power and the need to achieve a working order with the opposition forces, the relative state of the economy, the technical design and efficiency of the policy, the distribution of benefits and costs of a given set of policies across different groups and over time, the technical and political objectives of decision makers and, obviously, the results obtained over time. In essence, time factors, distributional aspects, and the efficiency as well as effectiveness of the decisions are at the core of the political economy of adjustment.

The balance of power refers to the degree of fragmentation of political power and to its relative distribution among different agents. Such balance is never static, and it is seldom stable over time. In a democratic setting, it is important to identify the centers of power: for example, political parties, the military, the legislature, the executive, labor, students, and, at election time, the electorate. Any master political plan has to assess how the different centers of power will be affected by political decisions and what their reaction will be. Haggard is right when he states that adjustment processes may not be viewed as purely technical exercises, lest policy makers find themselves faced with their own demise.

Policy makers are thus confronted with the need to build coalitions, and that process is the origin of compromises, which may consist of power-sharing arrangements, joint policy design, or outright payoffs. In presidential regimes, the executive will seek a majority in Congress and will threaten the use of veto power as a countermeasure against legislative pretensions. The minister of the interior therefore becomes a key figure in the communication between the centers of

power and the executive. The cabinet, finally, has to become fully at-
tuned to presidential decisions, to carry them out, and to bear responsibility before Congress.

Haggard states that a task of economic and political analysis is to
identify the different groups affected by decisions. He notes that political economy considerations should be helpful in devising compensatory schemes for those negatively affected. Such schemes, however, may
be possible only to a very limited extent, if at all. Moreover, the trade-off
between economic and political choices may preclude introducing loopholes, to prevent the whole policy design from being affected adversely.

It should also be noted that the temporal variables—the timing,
sequencing, and duration of policies—are of critical importance in the
design of stabilization policies. In any administration there are always
at least two schools of thought: one that favors shock measures and
another that favors gradual change. A general rule of thumb, which
contradicts a criterion expressed by Haggard, is "the sooner and the
harder, the better." In the early stages, a government can benefit from its
honeymoon period with the electorate, if not with Congress. Also, the
results of stabilization efforts are always a function of the degree of
comprehensiveness and efficacy in policy design. Half-baked and partial measures create their own slack, which may make further adjustments more difficult both economically and politically.

As recently as the mid-1980s, ideology played a central role in determining policy makers' choices. In the early 1990s, when the tenets of
ideologies contrary to market practices are being challenged every-
where, reassessing the fields of study that are at the core of social relations and policy making becomes imperative. Insofar as the new
political economy can increase our understanding of the economic, political, social, and ethical consequences of the different choices available
to policy makers, it fulfills its function as a tool for analyzing the real
world.

PART III

PERSPECTIVES ON THE NEW POLITICAL ECONOMY

ROBERT H. BATES,
STEPHAN HAGGARD,
AND JOAN M. NELSON   CHAPTER 10

A Critique by Political Scientists

ROBERT H. BATES

I am a political scientist who specializes in the political economy of development. Recognizing full well that governments decisively affect the performance of developing economies, I am convinced that to understand and to abet the process of development, analysts must better understand the behavior of governments. I therefore deeply want the new political economy to succeed. But as someone who specializes in the study of politics, I cannot help but feel that much of the work that economists refer to as the new political economy is deeply flawed. In addition, as a political scientist, I am aware of alternative approaches to the study of politics. Models of politics based on the assumption of rational individual behavior have long existed in political science. Indeed, they represent one of the major thrusts in contemporary political research. A major objective of these notes is to motivate development economists to investigate this literature, virtually none of which is cited in the chapters in this volume.[1]

I wish to acknowledge the helpful criticism of Joan Nelson, Stephan Haggard, and Anne Krueger.

261

The central paradigm of the new political economy is simple: scholars see states as mounted, as it were, upon markets; they then analyze forms of governmental intervention that take place, infer or impute the objectives that lead to them, and evaluate their effects on efficiency and distribution.[2] The new political economy assumes the existence of perfectly competitive markets and builds its analysis upon the market distortions introduced by governments. These distortions are used to measure the power of private interests and political forces.

An important contribution of this approach has been to document the high costs of forms of market intervention commonly found in the developing areas and to show not only the losses in terms of efficiency and growth but also the social costs of patterns of inequality. Indeed, the new political economy has led to a comprehensive reevaluation of the relative merits of governments and markets in the developing areas. Traditionally, development economists stressed the failure of markets and advocated an active role for governments. The new political economy instead emphasizes the failure of governments and advocates a wider role for markets. Given that ideological divisions traditionally center upon the relative roles of governments and markets, highlighting the positive role of markets has made the new political economy controversial—and important.

Problems with the Economics

The new political economy draws almost exclusively upon market economics. In this, I would argue, it has chosen too narrow a base.

Not all economics is market economics. Indeed, contemporary frontiers in microeconomics focus on environments where the conditions for markets to operate do not hold (for reviews, see Willamson 1985; Putterman 1987). A major lesson in much of this literature is that nonmarket forms of organization enable welfare-enhancing exchanges to take place—exchanges that could not take place in market environments. The presumption of market-oriented economists is that nonmarket forms of intervention impose economic costs; the presumption of these alternative approaches is that they promote gains in welfare.

It is difficult for the new political economists to deal with the literature on nonmarket economics.[3] The market imperfection and market failure paradigms provided much of the justification for the activist prescriptions they seek to overturn. Clearly, however, the new political economists have gone too far. Indeed, as has been learned from the forms of economic management employed in the most successful of the developing economies—those in Asia—organizations and bureaucracy can indeed promote efficiency and growth in national economies.

It would appear, then, that the time is long overdue to reemphasize the distinction between the macro- and microlevels of economic analysis. The condemnation of market distortions that figures so prominently in the new political economy may indeed be correct at the macrolevel. But clearly organizations and bureaucracies may promote economic welfare when used to encourage the development of particular industries or the performance of particular markets.

Problems with Politics

Although I am troubled by limitations in the kinds of economic theory brought to bear by the new political economists, I am most bothered by their analysis of politics. It is my conviction that if the goal of the new political economists is to explain the policy choices of governments—and thereby to learn how to alter governments' behavior—then they must change the ways in which they study politics. In particular, I would strongly urge the abandonment of the concept of the political market and of the notion of the government or the state as maximizer. Instead, I would advocate a form of political analysis that draws upon such economic concepts as rational choice and equilibrium analysis but avoids applying forms of market analysis to nonmarket institutions.

The political market. Some political economists approach the study of politics while positing the existence of political markets. This form of political analysis is misleading.

Underlying the appeal of the notion of the political market is the existence of a demand and supply of public policy. Citizens have preferences for policy outcomes, and political entrepreneurs propose alternative packages of public policies when competing for public favor. It is therefore tempting for economists to view the creation of public policy in marketlike terms. The power of such early works as Downs's *An Economic Theory of Democracy* (1957) reinforces such temptations.

I too endorse the application of economic reasoning to the study of politics. Indeed, much of the literature I commend to the attention of development economists interested in politics was written by the followers of Downs. But it is important to underscore that Downs developed an economic analysis, not a market analysis, of politics. He assumed rational behavior and applied methods of equilibrium analysis to account for the policy choices of governments. But in so doing, Downs found it necessary to abandon conventional market analysis and to adopt models of imperfect competition.

In politics, citizen preferences do aggregate (albeit, often perversely) into collective outcomes, and competition on the supply side helps to generate equilibrium bundles of public policies. But these truths do not imply that the political process can be analyzed in the same manner as markets. Although there are citizen demands, the political arena does not operate in a way that relates prices to quantities demanded. And although competing packages of public policies are presented by political entrepreneurs, the political arena does not generate alternative volumes or mixes of public programs for each set of prices, nor do prices form and adjust in such a way that political demands equal supplies, thereby generating an equilibrium. Price theory simply does not go through in political settings. As a consequence, political equilibria are not market equilibria, and market analysis therefore provides little insight into political outcomes.[4]

In response to these arguments, some economists may contend that the political process should operate more like markets. They might advocate, for example, changes in political processes that make citizens aware of the opportunity costs of particular public policies, so that the selection of public programs can be made "more rational." There may be much validity to these arguments. Nonetheless, they do not constitute an adequate reply to the position adopted here. Although conceiving of politics as a marketlike process provides a foundation for reformist proposals, it does not provide insight into how citizen preferences actually translate into public policies. Though possibly powerful as a normative tool, the analogy fails to provide a positive theory of politics.

Much contemporary political analysis is powerful because it applies economic reasoning to politics, but this is not the same as conceiving of politics as a political market. Rather, as will be argued below, political analysis entails studying how rational actors—citizens and public officials—respond to the incentives generated by political institutions. The analysis of politics requires locating the equilibrium generated by the choices of rational actors in nonmarket settings.

The unitary state. Alongside the political market approach to the analysis of governments, there exists a second tradition. Political economists often posit a single objective function for something they call the government or the state, as in the chapter by Ronald Findlay in this volume. In the case of the new political economy, this objective function often embodies goals other than the welfare of the whole society. It includes objectives relating to the state itself—such as the maximization of public revenues—or to particular sectors or interests in the greater economy.

This kind of analysis again represents an extension of an analytic tradition in economics to the study of politics. It is traditional in economics to analyze public policies by examining the policy choices that would result from the maximization of social welfare functions. The new political economy often simply substitutes "more realistic" objective functions for the traditional social welfare functions, and thereby seeks to account for the actual behavior of governments, and, in particular, their tendency to impose welfare costs upon society.

To treat the state as an actor that maximizes some objective function is to anthropomorphize the state. Even though journalists and financial commentators may speak of the market as a single agency with its own objectives, professional economists do not. Rather, they view the market as an institution in which choices are made by individuals and in which the formation of prices leads to the formation of equilibria that determine collective outcomes. It is surprising, then, that when economists turn to politics, they tend to anthropomorphize nonmarket institutions, such as governments. Instead, we should expect them to analyze how competition among political claims and preferences aggregate into collective political outcomes.[5]

Arrow's theorem provides another reason the new political economists should abandon a theory of politics based upon the notion of a state that maximizes some coherent objective function (Arrow 1951). As Arrow indicated, it is not meaningful to speak of society as if it possessed a well-behaved social welfare function unless there is a dictator. Arrow's requirements for a dictator, however, are extremely restrictive; the dictator must be able to secure as the social choice the ordering he prefers, even if it is opposed by all other members of society. As underlined by experiences in Chile and the communist world, neither dictators on the right nor dictators on the left are able to fulfill these conditions. And although the objective functions attributed to governments by the new political economists look more like social illfare functions than social welfare functions, surely Arrow's impossibility result—and the host of other related impossibility theorems that have grown from it—should impel economists studying politics to avoid a method that begins with the maximization of some overarching objective function for an entire polity.

The new political economists are right: governments often do end up with policies that constitute an ordering of choices for their societies. These policies, however, do not represent the preferences of some single actor. They represent the outcome of a political struggle, in which competing interests with rival visions of the social good seek the power to impose policies that are consonant with their preferences upon the collectivity. To account for government policy choices, then, we must study how competition among these preferences is structured and thereby leads to choices by governments.

The approach advocated here represents a call for the new political economists to be what they claim to be: truly neoclassical in their approach to politics. Neoclassical economics starts with the individual and assumes that each person can rationally choose so as to maximize his own interests. It has long been embarrassing to neoclassical economics that on the sides of both demand and supply aggregates rather than individuals stood at the foundations of their analysis: the household on the demand side and the firm on the supply side. The creation of a theory of the household and the firm based on the premise of rational choice by individuals was significant precisely because it extended the neoclassical program. When turning to the study of politics, economists should attempt no less. They should disaggregate such concepts as the state and construct a theory of political outcomes based upon the choices of individuals.

Some Suggestions

In this section I provide a sense of the kind of analysis that can be applied to politics. Rational individuals constitute the unit of analysis. In seeking to secure as society's choice the policies that they prefer, they compete within a set of political institutions. The structure of these institutions shapes their interactions to determine the outcome that will hold in equilibrium.

Figure 10.1 illustrates the spirit of this kind of analysis. Consider the page a two-dimensional issue space, with defense spending on the horizontal axis and domestic spending on the vertical. Say that the level of spending on domestic programs rises as one ascends up the page and the level of defense spending increases as one moves from left to right. Each point on the page then represents a level of spending on the two kinds of programs, with very little spending on either taking place at points low and to the left hand side of the page and large amounts of spending on both on points high on the page and to the right.

Figure 10.1 shows the bliss- or utility-maximizing points of three individuals. The three vertices—labeled I, II, and III—represent the ideal points of three people (call them legislators). Each represents the combination of spending on defense and domestic programs that that legislator most prefers. At points distant from his ideal point, each legislator experiences a loss in utility that increases with the distance from the legislator's ideal spending package. Level curves can then be drawn connecting combinations of defense and domestic spending that yield equal amounts of utility. Three such curves have been drawn, one for each legislator. The curves have been traced through a point that represents the status quo. Each individual prefers all points that lie closer to his ideal point over the status quo; all points on a given curve yield equal amounts of loss, by comparison with the level of utility experienced at the legislator's ideal point. The figure thus constitutes a model

FIGURE 10.1 The Effect of Institutions on Outcomes in a Three-Person Legislature

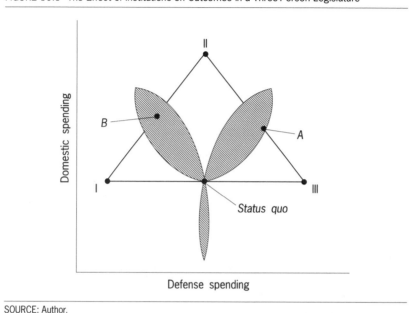

SOURCE: Author.

of a social choice problem. Given this three-person society, what will be the collective outcome?

The result will depend upon the institutions through which these preferences are aggregated into collective choices. If the market is the institution, then we can predict that the collective outcome will fall within the Pareto set. That set is represented in the diagram by the triangle.

The institutions through which these preferences are translated into collective outcomes may also be political in nature. In particular, social outcomes may be selected by majority rule. Then the set of potential outcomes would correspond to the "lenses" or "petals" in the figure. Points falling with those sets lie closer to the bliss points of two of the three members of this society and so would be preferred by a majority to the status quo.

It may be noted that the new political economists are fond of showing how illfare-maximizing states generate efficiency losses. In this disaggregated model, in which individual preferences translate into social choices through political rules, we can easily get the same result—but on more defensible analytic foundations. As the figure shows, many points in the lenses lie outside the Pareto set; as noted above, any of these points could be attained as a consequence of an agreement by a majority. Rational individuals, in the context of this political institution, may well make political choices that are economically inefficient.

This form of analysis can yield fairly determinate results. The more we know about the structure of the institutions, the greater insight we get into the nature of the likely outcome. For example, the political rules could specify not only that policies would be chosen by majority rule, but also that player III could propose policies for the collectivity and that those proposals could not be subject to amendment.[6] Player III would prefer any outcome lying closer to his or her bliss point. The points that offer such improvements and the prospects of a majority coalition lie in the lens formed by the intersection of the utility surface of player III with that of player II. Player III is able to make take-it-or-leave-it offers and, behaving rationally, would be expected to offer point A. As point A is closer to the bliss point of player II than is the status quo, player II, behaving rationally, would accept it. Point A is thus the expected policy outcome, given the institutional rules.

A change in the rules will yield a change in this outcome. Say that player III is still given the power to initiate policy, but that the institutional rules allow subsequent amendments. Then the predicted outcome becomes the status quo. If player III offered to form a coalition with II and proposed policy A, then player I—who is left out of this coalition—could counter by offering player II policy B, which both player I and II would prefer to policy A and the status quo. Player III would thus do best using his power to prevent the introduction of any new policy proposals, for fear of being left out of the subsequent political maneuvering and having to live with an outcome, such as policy B, that he likes less than the status quo.[7]

Clearly, this analysis is largely heuristic, but it does offer several important lessons. One is that such nonmarket concepts of economic analysis as individual rationality and equilibrium analysis can be used to study politics. Another is that the institutional rules within which political games are played can strongly shape the nature of policy outcomes. A third is that a deep understanding of the structure of political institutions can enable us to understand policy choices. Finally, changes in policy outcomes can be achieved by modifying the institutions that structure political choices. Indeed, one of the most promising features of this literature is that it offers the analytic tools with which to design nonmarket institutions or to suggest modifications in existing institutional frameworks to alter—and improve—policy choices by governments.

These points can be illustrated by examining agricultural price setting. For purposes of illustration, we can characterize the preferences of three interests: those of economic "technocrats" or policy planners, consumers, and producers. Also for purposes of illustration, we can assume that these three interests are attempting to determine the basic philoso-

TABLE 10.1   Price System Preferences of Planners, Consumers, and Producers

	Policy planners	Consumers	Producers
First choice	A	B	C
Second choice	B	C	A
Third choice	C	A	B

A = Border parity pricing.
B = Price stabilization through buffer stocks.
C = Cost-plus pricing.
SOURCE: Author.

phy the government should employ in price setting; the alternatives are free trade, price stabilization, and cost-plus pricing.

The technocrats, we assume, prefer the use of border pricing: they wish the government to set domestic prices equal to the import or export parity price for the commodity on world markets. As a second-best alternative, they would agree to government intervention to stabilize prices by manipulating buffer stocks, engaging in world trade only when necessary to replenish or dispose of price-stabilizing inventories. The technocrats would least prefer that the government commit itself to a cost-plus pricing scheme, arguing that this would lead to the separation of domestic prices from world market prices and so prevent agriculture from finding its comparative advantage.

In this example, consumer interests prefer a price-stabilizing scheme. They would least prefer that domestic prices follow world prices, and would agree to cost-plus pricing as a second-best measure, because it would provide greater price stability.

Producers, by contrast, want the government to set prices so as to guarantee a return over and above their costs of production. Failing that, they would prefer border prices to the procurement of buffer stocks, fearing that government inventories would overhang the market and depress prices.

The preferences of the three groups are portrayed in Table 10.1, the most preferred alternative being placed highest in the preference ordering. In this table it is clear that no alternative is unanimously preferred by the three interests; none emerges as the most preferred policy for this society. In the face of such disagreements, how the interests are incorporated into the decision-making process will determine the policy outcome. The structure of this rule will matter.

Assume, for example, that decisions are made in stages by a council that contains representatives of each of the three interests. One way of organizing the proceedings would be to require the council to choose initially between the proposal of the economists and a proposal emanating from one or the other of the "special interests." If the three interests are represented equally, that is, if they control the same number of votes, the final result would be the defeat of border pricing. For if the representatives first choose between the most desired outcome of the policy planners and the consumers, the technocrats would prevail in the first round: A is preferred to B not only by the technocrats but by the producers as well. But the technocrats would lose in the second round, where both consumers and producers prefer cost-plus pricing to free trade. And if the preference of the technocrats was first matched against the producers' demand for cost-plus pricing, their proposal would lose in the first round. The council would then be left with a choice between the positions of the two special interests, and price stabilization, which is preferred by consumers and technocrats, would be chosen over cost-plus pricing. When economic advice is incorporated into the first round of policy planning, given this structure of preferences, it fails to influence policy.

But let us consider a different procedure. Say that the technocrats' advice entered decision making not at the beginning but rather at the end of the deliberations. According to this procedure, competing proposals from special interests would be processed in the initial round, and the recommendation adopted at that stage then paired off against the advice of the economists. In this case, the technocrats would prevail, and border pricing would become the policy of the government. For when the most preferred alternative of the consumers (B) was paired against that of the producers (C), the council would choose B over C by two to one. And when the council then deliberated the merits of the technocrats' preference as opposed to the winner from the "interest group round," it would choose A over B, with the producers joining the technocrats in support of free trade.

This example illustrates the significance of institutional procedures in determining policy outcomes. The configuration of preferences constitutes a "cycle," in the sense Arrow used the term (1951). There is no clear winner—no alternative that could, when matched against any other, command the consent of a majority. Political economists have shown that in such circumstances, any outcome is possible; a sequence or agenda can be devised so as to secure the selection of any of the alternatives. Clearly, then, the procedures themselves become determinants of outcomes. And those in control of the design and structuring of governmental decision making gain control over the making of policy.

The mode of analysis employed above was developed to study the politics of advanced industrial countries; indeed, it is based to a great degree on an analysis of the U.S. Congress (Shepsle and Weingast 1987). It is legitimate to ask whether a literature so grounded can offer much insight into economic policy making in the developing world and, in particular, into the reasons for the political preference for economically damaging public policies. In response, it should be noted that much of this form of political analysis was developed to understand why politicians in the United States chose economically costly policies—for example, unbalanced budgets and rates of public spending that generate trade deficits, high interest rates, and high rates of domestic inflation (see, for example, Fiorina 1977). The literature is motivated precisely by a desire to comprehend the political sources of economic indiscipline.

If political economists are to explain—and influence—policy, then they should examine the steps in which policy gets made and the procedures that structure the councils of government. It should also be noted that many of the most important allocational decisions in developing countries are in fact made by committees. These decisions would include the allocation of import licenses, credit, and foreign exchange, as well as the setting of agricultural prices (Bates 1981). Committees exists within bureaucracies as well as in legislatures, and the decisions made by such committees are of the greatest significance in developing countries. Although perfected in the advanced industrial countries, the mode of analysis outlined herein is thus relevant to the developing world as well.

A brief illustration may further suggest the relevance of this approach to the developing areas. Donald Lien and I (Bates and Lien 1983) once analyzed the economic effects of political rules on the export earnings of developing nations that were members of the International Coffee Organization. As is well known, for nearly thirty years the International Coffee Organization operated to defend the price of coffee in international markets. It did so by limiting the exports of producer countries, assigning to each a quota that it was entitled to place upon world markets. Quotas were assigned by majority rule. Each member country possessed a quantity of votes that was determined by its historical market share; for an allocation of quotas to member nations to be officially binding, that allocation had to secure a majority of the votes of the member nations. Using analytic techniques to model the behavior of the institution that are closely related to those described above, Lien and I were able to determine what allocations were politically sustainable under these rules and thereby to assess the effects of the political process upon the export earnings of the member countries. Indeed, we were able to predict which quotas would be politically viable and which would not, and thereby to understand why Brazil's effort to increase its quota in 1982 was defeated by an alternative championed by Colombia, its major rival in world coffee markets.[8] Given the value of coffee to the economies of the developing countries, we were able to document and to measure the effects of political rules upon the economic well-being of the coffee exporting nations.

Granted, there are few other applications of this approach to the study of the politics of economic policy making in third world nations.

But then, as its title suggests, the new political economy has just begun. Then, too, the paucity of examples has more to do with the nature of the training of those who are interested in economic development than with the merits of the approach itself. Politics is rarely placed at the center of economic research.

Those interested in development must study the role of governments and must better understand why they make the choices they do, if only to change their behavior. Governments are not markets; nor are they unitary actors. The conventional techniques of policy analysis employed by market-oriented economists therefore offer little help in understanding political behavior. Rather, analysts must employ an approach that views policy choices as the result of a political process that takes place within institutions other than markets. Those of us interested in understanding economic policy making in the developing areas must probe more deeply into this political process. Knowledge of how policy making is structured is necessary if we are to understand how political incentives shape the economic behavior of politicians and if we are to be able to modify those incentives in ways that will lead them to make choices that are consistent with the public good.

STEPHAN HAGGARD

The economists and political scientists contributing to this volume are operating with somewhat different conceptions of the state. At one extreme is the model provided by Ronald Findlay: the state as a unified rational maximizer of some social welfare (or "illfare"!) function. At the other extreme, the state is conceived as a relatively passive register of social demands. Policy is supplied in response to pressures from rent seekers or constituents operating in a political market.

Such conceptions operate with very spare assumptions about institutional structure; this is their strength. For political scientists, however, the state is conceptualized as a field of rules, institutions, and organizations that structure the incentives to politicians and social groups. The ability of groups to organize and press their interests and the capacity of executives to act are constrained by this institutional structure.

If the purpose is to explain variations in policy choice, such a conception is likely to be of more use than a very general model. Variations in institutional structure should be important in determining policy outcomes, even where the configuration of group interests is held constant. Four examples will illustrate this point.

First, as T. N. Srinivasan points out, authoritarianism does not appear to be a good predictor of economic success since regimes as different as Korea and Uganda both fall under the broad authoritarian rubric. But as I have pointed out elsewhere, this may simply reflect a failure to differentiate adequately among various types of authoritarian structures (Haggard and Kaufman 1989). It is clear that important reforms in a number of countries were possible only after authoritarian regimes took power: Chile after 1973, Brazil after 1964, Turkey after 1980, and Korea after 1961, to cite just a few.

Second, coherent fiscal policy rests on the ability to reconcile spending and taxing decisions so as not to exceed optimal levels of borrowing. This is more likely where budget authorities have a veto over spending than where spending and borrowing decisions are decentralized across ministries and state-owned enterprises.

A third example comes from American trade policy (Haggard 1988). Before 1934, tariff schedules were written by Congress. Portions of the schedules were farmed out to subcommittees on the basis of legislative interest. This institutional structure provided the opportunity for logrolling. With the Reciprocal Trade Agreements Act of 1934, authority over tariff making was transferred to the executive. The president still had to take into account the interests of various groups, but under the new structure, import-competing interests were counterbalanced by export-oriented ones and broader foreign policy concerns. Moreover, protectionists faced an administrative filter of liberal trade policy officials in the State Department. The ability to lobby effectively was fundamentally altered.

A final example comes from recent stabilization efforts. New democracies have had particular difficulties stabilizing. The reasons are, of course, in large part economic; new democracies, particularly in a number of Latin American countries, have inherited tremendous difficulties from their authoritarian predecessors. These have been compounded by the particularly short time horizons of newly elected officials seeking to consolidate the transition. Ex post, these efforts have proven self-defeating. Ex ante, however, politicians faced difficult choices between consolidating their rule and sensible policies that had long-term benefits but severe short-term costs.

The point of these examples is a simple one. Interest-group and rational-actor models of the state are useful, but their results may be highly sensitive to institutional variation.

JOAN M. NELSON

Contributors to this volume share an intellectual agenda: we seek a better understanding of the factors shaping governments' choices of economic policies and the degree to which they implement these policies. We would like to be able to explain more fully both the evolution of economic policies in individual countries over time and the contrasting choices made by governments in different countries facing roughly similar situations.

We also share a second less analytic and more operational objective. We would like to improve communication between economists (as analysts and as policy advisers) and policy makers, to narrow the gap between economists' consensus views on what is economically rational and politicians' perceptions of what is politically rational or feasible. As part of this second set of concerns, we are interested in the short-run tactics available to governments to reduce the political risks of desirable economic measures. Short-run tactics to manage political opposition (for example, deliberate obfuscation) may sometimes conflict with policy characteristics that increase economic efficiency (for example, transparency). The fascination of short-run tactics should not be permitted to shoulder aside another set of important issues: the economic and political conditions crucial to sustaining at least a critical minimum of support for adjustment over time.

The concept of rent seeking and models developed to trace its implications for particular economic sectors or for whole economies have contributed a good deal to our understanding. Some other approaches illustrated in this volume, such as Gustav Ranis's more inductive framework for understanding evolving policy patterns and Yujiro Hayami's analytic framework for understanding land reform decisions, explicitly incorporate other kinds of political factors or forces. To further integrate economic and political factors into explanations of policy choice, several considerations should be taken more fully into account.

The simplifying assumption that the state is a unitary actor with one or more relatively clear goals finesses some crucial issues in most real-world cases. Usually, much or most of the political struggle over policy choice and (equally or more important) over implementation takes place among different state agencies and actors, rather than between the state and nonstate actors. Much of the struggle turns precisely on the priority of goals that at least partly compete with each other (though they may also have important long- and even short-run complementarities).

Analytic schemes for understanding policy choice, regardless of whether they are heavily deductive or inductive, quantitative or qualitative, would fit reality more closely if they incorporated assumptions of very incomplete information and great uncertainty shaping the behavior of many groups. Several of the policy makers' contributions underscore this point. Roberto Junguito, for instance, described the sharply contrasting views of different groups within Colombia regarding the effects of economic adjustment on export-oriented agriculture. Sergio de la Cuadra remarked that the effects of pervasive and layered distortions in the economy made it difficult for those most immediately affected to gauge the probable effects of reducing or removing some of the distortions. Rapid and accelerating or fluctuating inflation also makes it hard for groups to judge the probable effects of specific policy proposals on their interests. And it is well recognized that uncertainty alters behavior, leading individuals and groups to hedge using the various means at their disposal.

Several of the analytic approaches presented in this volume assume (or could readily be modified to assume) coalitions of groups supporting or opposing particular policies. To better capture the determinants of policy choice, it would be helpful to move from a static array of winners and losers to more dynamic conceptions of coalition formation and modification. From the decision makers' perspective, not only the current array of coalitions but also the best opportunities for strengthening support coalitions are highly relevant. Stated in oversimplified form, do these opportunities lie to the right (including the potential support of international financial institutions) or to the left?

Overarching most of the points already noted is the role of political institutions in shaping policy choice and implementation. Institutions shape processes of interest aggregation. For example, both the behavior and the political influence of labor unions are strongly affected by how they are linked into party systems. Are unions incorporated into one dominant party? As a major or minor partner? Into both of two major competing parties? Are they linked instead with one or more radical parties that can make trouble but stand little chance of forming a government? To take a different example, the power of central executive institutions ranges widely, even within the same type of regime: Costa Rica and Jamaica are both long-established democracies, but the Jamaican prime minister has far greater scope for autonomous action than the Costa Rican president.

Taking these factors more fully into account in our analytic approaches to explaining policy choice is a challenge both for economists and for political scientists. For instance, how shall institutional factors be incorporated into our analyses? Within the economic discipline, institutional analysis (for example, of labor markets) has a long and honorable tradition, but there is not much precedent for incorporating explicitly political and bureaucratic factors. Political scientists, for their part, have only begun to sort out which aspects and dimensions of institutional variation are most crucial for explaining governments' choices and implementation of economic policies. A good deal of attention has been focused on regime type, but the contrasts between democratic and authoritarian regimes may be less important than some more precisely specified institutional variables that cut across types of regimes. Political scientists have also studied the effects of electoral cycles, but as Stephan Haggard discusses in greater detail, some other dimensions of institutional variation, such as executive autonomy, remain largely unexplored. Before we can develop better analytic schemes that capture the political economy of policy choice both parsimoniously and realistically, we probably need more extensive empirical studies of the institutional variables we suspect are important.

Experiences of Policy Makers

Economists are gaining an increased role in policy making and contributing to improvements in economic policy and performance throughout the world, especially in developing countries. These policy-making economists have useful insights into the decision-making process—especially how policy choices are made—thanks to their own experiences, which in many ways resemble the conclusions of the new political economy (NPE). This chapter considers the value and limitations of the NPE for policy-making economists by addressing several broad questions: What is the role of the economist in policy making? How can the policy-making economist gather sufficient political support for effective policies to ensure that they are adopted and maintained? What is the role of the economist in educating the public and the political elites about appropriate policies? How does the policy-making economist penetrate the political institutions and processes of a country to influence perceptions and promote change?

To answer these questions, I draw on my own policy-making experience and on the experiences of other policy makers, mostly from Latin America, who offered their reflections in a symposium at the 1989 conference in Lake Paipa.[1]

Before considering each major area of discussion, I should cite the distinction in the terms of reference generally used by economists and political scientists participating in the conference. On the one hand, the political scientists generally considered the evolution of political institutions and their role in fostering or limiting the application and effectiveness of economic policy. Naturally, the variables they discussed were political institutions and the interplay of politics and policy making. On the other hand, the economists generally considered political institutions as given, and focused their discussions on how to make effective economic policy in practice. The two perspectives are obviously complementary, since the evolution of political institutions and of economic policy are means to the wider end of serving the needs and aspirations of individuals, groups, and nations in the developing world. The understanding of how peoples organize themselves and establish rules and institutions to carry forward their economic and political activities is the basic ingredient in successful economic policy making.

The Role of Economists as Policy Makers

Whether as advisers or policy makers, economists bring a number of skills to the decision-making process. They bring a framework of analysis and values based on their knowledge of the workings of economic activity and policy. They are trained to distinguish between social and private benefits and costs of specific actions. For example, how economic policy affects private gains and losses of business and labor is one part of the analysis, which is normally evident to pressure groups that influence policy. But economists look beyond that to identify the total short- and long-term gains and losses, including those caused to the rest of society and to the functioning of the economy. Their contribution, then, is valuable in defining the parameters of the policy trade-offs between the groups that influence policy. Often political negotiations among such groups concentrate on how to split the existing "pie" among them (a frictional position), but the economist's role is to clarify where the pie can grow—how there can be more wealth and income for everyone (a cooperative position).

Policy-making economists also serve an educational function that is important both to the immediate success of policy and to its long-run stability. By helping stabilize economic activity over the business cycle, maintaining a growth environment with a robust balance of payments and with flexibility that allows innovation and the adoption of new technologies, and making economic growth and efficiency compatible with distribution, the economist can gain support.

The capacity to identify hidden costs of actions taken to benefit bureaucrats, political constituencies, pressure groups, and others has increased the role of professional economists in economic policy making in most developing countries, especially in Latin America. This does not guarantee that economists are always successful either technically or as policy brokers, but their role in policy making in developing countries is much more accepted today than it was thirty years ago. This acceptance is higher when economists incorporate into their analysis and actions the needs and desires of the powers-that-be while also educating them about undesirable actions that are detrimental to them and to everyone else, immediately and in the long run.

As Roberto Junguito pointed out in the panel discussion on the experiences of policy makers, policy-making economists played a significant role during the economic adjustment process of Latin American countries in the 1980s, often by explaining the policy options and consequences to different groups of politicians. The cases of Chile, Mexico, Colombia, Costa Rica, Uruguay, and, more recently, Venezuela are outstanding examples. In some cases, an economist has even served as president (for example, Mexico's Carlos Salinas de Gortari and Miguel de la Madrid are professional economists).

The acceptance of professional economists in policy making in Latin America began to increase in the late 1950s and early 1960s. The influence of the United Nations Economic Commission for Latin America (ECLA) and the Alliance for Progress made economic development an increasingly important item on the political agenda. The need for improved economic performance and solutions to the economic aspects of political problems enhanced the importance of economists to politicians. The economic ideas and policy prescriptions of ECLA and the structuralist economists—including import-substitution industrialization, subsidies, fiscal incentives, regulations, and deficit financing—gained wide support in the early years, because they matched the perceptions of economic realities held by politicians and pressure groups. These strategies were influenced by the experience of the Great Depression when exporters of raw materials and primary goods were clearly at a disadvantage in international markets. The resulting preferences for centralized decision making and guidance of the economic process regardless of market forces, the lack of attention to severe resource and budget constraints, and the overwhelming presence of social inequalities had a strong influence on economic policy making in the political arena. The strategies often appeared to be successful in the first stage, and the hidden costs to the international competitiveness of their economies did not become apparent until much later. The results ranged from orderly and regulated inward-oriented growth in Mexico and the Caribbean Basin countries to oscillating inward-oriented growth, inflation, balance of payments crisis, massive devaluations, and financial problems in South America during the 1950–1980 period.

Since the early 1960s an increasing number of Latin Americans have obtained postgraduate economics training in the major academic centers of the United States and Europe, and professional knowledge of the development process has improved. These economists have played an increasing role in training, research, and policy-making positions throughout the region since the late 1960s, and many countries are showing the effects of their advice and guidance. The results are uneven and often discontinuous, but several countries made a turnaround in policy making during the debt-ridden decade of the 1980s. An evolution in perceptions seems to be taking place. Political leaders, constituencies, and pressure groups who originally believed that economics did not matter or that it could be reinterpreted and rechanneled, free of costs, to fit political and cultural preconceptions now accept the implications of market forces and price mechanisms for economic performance. Concrete results and the explanations of modern economists[2] are creating an improved climate for modern growth policies in many countries. The debt crisis and the more successful experiences of countries elsewhere (mainly in East Asia) have also opened opportunities for modern economists to play an important role in policy making.

Gathering Political Support for the Design of Strategies and the Implementation of Policies

The comments of the policy-making economists at the Lake Paipa conference dealt largely with the gathering of political support for strategies and plans, and their discussion is summarized here. Political support must be sought both within government and from the public at large; the two processes reinforce each other. Achi Atsain of the Ivory Coast, for example, stressed the importance of wide-ranging consultations in the process of building consensus on strategies and plans for different sectors of the economy. Consultations with leaders outside the government are useful to discussions within the government that lead up to a presidential decision.

Roberto Junguito elaborated on the relationship between the economic cabinet member and the president. Often the president, as the leading political power broker, takes policy recommendations but awaits the proper timing to act. Other times he changes the proposals to some extent to make them politically feasible, catering up to a point to the political constituencies that may be the greatest opponents to the policy.

Leopoldo Solís stressed that economic advisers have to protect the president from poor advice resulting from faulty information or perceptions. They have to keep economic analysis honest, well informed, and rational. Economic advisers are most effective when they maintain professional credibility by publishing a good deal, especially outside their own country; by sticking to their advice; and by being willing to be fired. There are occasions when their position within a group making a collegiate policy decision will permit them to tilt a close decision.

Augustine Tan explained that having development high on the political agenda and obtaining professional economic advice were important to the success of Singapore. Consistent leadership, the flow of information and ideas up and down the levels of decision making, and the participation of different political groups in the decision-making process stabilized economic policy making. For example, labor leaders were among the top advisers on economic policy. The political leadership also gained credibility by producing results and by being able to match expectations and realizations.

Francisco Swett explained the elements that allowed the Ecuadoran government to successfully implement adjustment policies when it did not have majority control of Congress. The government implemented stabilization and adjustment policies in a series of steps designed to neutralize opposition as much as possible and achieve credibility by showing results. It preceded each policy application with an information campaign aimed at educating the public. It identified potential beneficiaries of the new policies and drove home the message about their forthcoming gains. For example, a new gasoline tax in this petroleum-producing country was made more acceptable by publicizing the number of houses, schools, public lunches, health facilities, and roads that would be provided to the people with the proceeds of the tax.

The discussants spelled out the political differences between stabilization, which deals with distributing the costs to society of a lower level of economic activity and may have the benefit of stabilizing prices, and adjustment, which is meant to accelerate economic growth by increasing efficiency, savings, investment, and exports, and may over time compensate some groups for their losses with the benefits of growth and employment generation.

Policy implementation, the discussants agreed, is generally most effective when the power to make decisions about the use of policy instruments is centralized. However, fiscal and monetary policies can be defined and implemented more easily at the Ministry of Finance and the central bank than many sectoral and trade policies, which may depend on a more decentralized group of actors that are harder to reconcile.

Guillermo Perry pointed out that the combined economic and political process often leads to the adoption of second-best economic policies. In Colombia, for example, the level of funds for education was not determined in the political process, but was earmarked. This second-best system worked well, however, notwithstanding the built-in inflexibility, because the assigned quota was high and allowed dynamic growth in the sector despite some inefficiencies in resource use.

Sergio de la Cuadra explained the successful implementation of the trade liberalization policies in Chile and the not-so-successful application of financial liberalization policies. The trade policy had clear objectives that were technically sound and politically viable. The government identified "winners" and "losers" from the policies and established temporary compensation patterns for the losers. For example, importers of capital goods, whose import tax exemptions were being eliminated to create a common tariff level, were given credits to cover their taxes for a brief period, until they could adjust their internal financial operations. The credibility of the policy was maintained by not allowing any exemptions and by applying the policy quickly and firmly at the beginning. The existence of a military government added considerable strength to the application of controversial policies that, nonetheless, had to be formulated so as to minimize political opposition that would threaten the regime.

Initially the new policies were controversial. But trade liberalization, as a consistent and sustained policy, gave exporters the opportunity to develop their markets and take advantage of the lower production costs, thereby serving the educational process. It also benefited consumers with a wider range of cheaper and higher-quality goods. Eventually, as exports were increased and diversified, leading to economic growth and employment generation, other groups in society accepted the policy because they saw that their initial losses were compensated in different ways by a more robust and sustainable development process.

The examples cited by the policy makers involved an interplay between leadership and political forces opposed to the new economic policies. When governments, such as in Chile and Singapore, had the political power to implement and sustain the policy until the positive effects became evident to the majority of the powers-that-be, then the new policies became firmly established. When the initial political support of the government implementing the reforms was fragile, as in Ecuador, the road to successful policy change was more difficult. Even though in Ecuador there were clear successes in the implementation of stabilization policies during the first two years, the almost irreconcilable political battles between opposing and delicately balanced political forces stopped the progress in policy reforms. Power politics between Congress and the president, and exogenous factors, such as the international price of oil and an earthquake that broke the oil pipeline, caused the policy effort to collapse, and the government had to fight for survival until the end of its term. Nonetheless, the succeeding government was forced, by inflation and fiscal and balance of payment deficits, to initiate the same policy reforms all over again, even though it had previously opposed them.

The comments of the policy makers show that the policy changes required to regain growth and generate employment imply a change in the value systems and preferences of powerful political groups within each country, such as protected industrialists and labor unions, and entrenched workers of public enterprises and other urban organizations that benefit from subsidies. Political leadership can start policy changes and has to be able to sustain them long enough to achieve an educational process that shows that most groups are better off with a "growing pie" for all than with bigger slices of a "shrinking pie."

There is a difference between economic policy making within a basically sound policy framework, when one has to tinker at the margin to correct a course of action, and policy making to effect fundamental changes in the policy framework. In most of Latin America the latter is occurring in the 1980s and 1990s. Liberalized trade, smaller governments with balanced budgets, unrepressed financial systems, and unregulated and flexible microeconomic policies that can help restore sustainable growth have not been standard practice for the past three decades. Over time, import-substitution policies have created sheltered positions for many sectors in the economy and have led to slow growth in the midst of fast-growing social demands due to burgeoning populations and rising expectations. Since the problem could not be resolved by greater international indebtedness in a hostile international environment of shrinking markets for raw materials and primary goods, the Latin American countries are being forced to make the most fundamental changes in policies in forty years.

The Role of the National Learning Process for Policy Stability

Marginal policy changes can be made within an established policy framework and institutional structure. More significant policy changes implied in a restructuring of the economy or of institutions are much harder to make because they directly affect the benefits perceived by various groups within the existing structure and the value system (that is, the culture) that sustains and provides a rationale for the existing policies and structure. If the country in which the structural changes are to be made is in crisis—that is, the majority of the people perceive high costs and therefore express a need for change—then many policy changes can be introduced. If the country is not in crisis, then success will be achieved slowly. In all cases, the changed policies need to produce explicit results that can maintain or increase the support of the groups that benefit from the changes. A learning process is required first to perceive the problem and its causes and then to accept the early cost of the solution and to see the benefits of the new situation. The latter is normally the most difficult part, since business, labor, and political groups will not readily buy a costly conceptual solution unless they can be shown practical results.

Ideally, the objective should be to achieve for the new policy a position "above politics," that is, a level of generalized acceptance such that no political party or group would attempt to change it without incurring severe political costs. For example, peoples in the Organization for Economic Cooperation and Development countries have a deep distrust of inflation, understand its causes in general terms, and are in most cases unwilling to put up with a monetary and fiscal policy that produces it. Governments have been ousted from office when inflationary pressures rise above even relatively low levels. By contrast, in many Latin American countries there is insufficient understanding of the causes and effects of inflation, a sense of helplessness about it, and a higher tolerance for it in electoral politics. Many economic policies can be raised to an above-politics level of acceptance through a learning process stimulated by sustained policies and successful experiences.

The effect of agricultural research and extension on agricultural production is an example of the learning process. In countries where new agricultural technology has brought dramatic productivity increases known as the Green Revolution, early skepticism and low valuation of such endeavors have turned to wide acceptance of their usefulness. Many changes follow from such changes in perception: not only the acceptance of improved seeds, fertilizer, and cultivation practices, but also a new respect for agricultural scientists whose salaries and esteem increase. In many countries Green Revolution policies have achieved a status above politics and are simply accepted practice.

Agricultural policies may meet less resistance than trade liberalization or sound fiscal policies, because they do not impose early costs on powerful groups in society. Nonetheless, a new policy that will create early costs but increase medium-term benefits for the powers-that-be or for the people at large needs to be sustained beyond early resistance or skepticism until the results are evident and accepted. The critical change in perception and reevaluation of expectations happens as different economic groups accommodate themselves to the new policy, find that they can work with it, and understand its rationale. Perhaps macroeconomic policies leading to a stable and predictable framework are most likely to achieve the status of "motherhood" (in the sense that this is a concept that enjoys wide support and high esteem in most cultures) because of their generalized positive effects.

Some microeconomic policies can also be so rated, especially when they are positive for one sector (such as agricultural technology) and mostly neutral to the rest. But most microeconomic policies that benefit a given sector do so at the expense of others and remain politically contentious, unless they espouse free, unregulated markets.

Conceptually, then, a given set of economic policies (for example, trade protection) can be beneficial to some social groups, such as industrialists and industrial workers, and costly to other groups, such as consumers or agricultural exporters who do not have a competitive exchange rate. It takes wide-ranging leadership to institute policies favoring more open trade and more dynamic economic growth and employment generation. Leaders must demonstrate the case through research, education, and dissemination of ideas; persuade policy makers and political forces that change is desirable for all even though it may have costs at the beginning for some; put together the coalition of political forces that will support the change and neutralize the power of the opposing forces; negotiate with the opposing forces; and sustain the policy until it achieves results that fulfill the original expectations. Leaders can enhance the chances of success by maintaining a clear view of the ultimate objective; by effectively transmitting such a view to the biggest possible audience, especially to the powers-that-be; and by yielding ground on the less fundamental aspects of the policy if necessary during the participation of various groups in the negotiations process. Nothing contributes as much to successful policy change in a democratic environment as participation by different groups in the negotiation and formulation process. Perhaps the most fundamental part of the education process is the definition of a set of general objectives that is broad enough to envelop some objectives of most of the contending economic groups in the country. Thereafter, trade-offs of partial benefits and costs can bring around sufficient forces to implement the policies.

The national learning process occurs naturally. It is most important among elite groups that strongly influence the making of national policies and public opinion. Ideally, the national learning process takes place in a democratic setting where there is freedom, competition of ideas, and dialogue. But it may also bear fruit in more restricted political environments, for the learning process for economic policy ultimately involves recognizing the social and private benefits derived from the new rules of the game implied by modern economic policies. Such benefits should be greater for most groups than in the previous situation, and the perception of gains should be common to all groups or to the majority of the most influential in making and implementing decisions. They accept the new policy, however, not just because it provides a clear national benefit, but also because it establishes an acceptable procedure for pursuing their self-interest. In this sense, it differs from a learning

curve in a business because gains do not come from increasing profi-
ciency in the application of an accepted new way of doing things but
from changed perceptions about how to achieve desirable goals within
redefined rules of the game.

The national learning process as a vehicle for economic policy
change and stability is most useful when there is a national memory of
past economic policy performance. Documented records of the failures
or inadequacies of past policies are powerful teaching devices to support policy changes, especially when they are accompanied by the rationale for the new policies. When pressure groups that benefit from the
present policies are exposed and the limitations caused by such policies
to the rest of society and to the economy at large are made evident, the
chances of gaining support for the new policies are increased.

The communication and dissemination of the policy proposals and
their effect on economic performance are critical aspects of the education process. Each economic group has to see clearly how the new policy
affects it in the short and the long run; all have to be able to perceive the
benefits for society of a more dynamic economy. The complexities of
economic logic and analysis need to be expressed in language amenable
at least to the groups capable of influencing the political process and
policy making.

The restructuring of a value system upon which a set of economic
concessions is based, however, is no easy matter. In Latin America, for
example, favoritism or a form of mercantilism seems to be more deeply
ingrained than in many of the modern OECD economies. Insufficient
openness and competition, unsatisfactory information and accountability, and smaller national economies are among the main factors that
sustain this value system. As a result, the system is structured to dispense economic favors to all groups that have a claim on power. The
business and investor groups get concessions on protection and various
incentives for capital formation and savings; the populist groups get
concessions on wages, social security, and price subsidies. These concessions are expected, and political coalitions are formed to work for them.
The consequence is an economic system of second- and third-best policies that blur the connection between efforts and rewards, increase the
gap between high private returns to investment and low social returns,
take flexibility away from the economy, and reduce the capacity to compete in international markets and to adapt to technological changes that
reshape the economies in the medium term. Such systems also tend to
overload the public administration with regulatory functions that often
lead to corruption, inefficiencies, and delays. The dismantling of these
concessions and the creation of a more competitive, flexible, and open
economic environment therefore requires both a major educational effort and a restructuring of institutions and political processes.

In democracies, political parties participate in elections to win political spoils that enable them to govern. But political spoils in modern and Latin American democracies differ in degree and quite often in kind. For example, one uses a modern civil service; the other dispenses patronage. One awards benefits through competitive bidding; the other without competitive bidding. In Latin America political institutions that permit both stability and flexibility must be strengthened. The perception of an almighty state that dispenses political and economic favors to its members and supporters must be replaced by the perception of a state that supports political competition in democracy and economic competition in development, that permits as much equal opportunity and participation as possible from all groups and individuals in the nation, and that provides some social safety nets to protect the equal opportunity of the disadvantaged.

Such a restructuring of perceptions also entails a restructuring of institutions. It takes a strong government to divest itself of the tools of power that make it a dispenser of favors. That is why it is so difficult to achieve. Politicians have to be shown how the source of their power in the new, more competitive, open, and less paternalistic system will compensate them for their loss of power in the old system.

In sum, the national learning process may achieve for the new economic policies a degree of acceptability within the old structures, but greater advances can be achieved only with changes in value systems and in institutions that will create new avenues for achieving economic growth and human development objectives.

Political Processes and Institutions in the Implementation of Economic Policy

Here I will consider the process by which modern economics and economists penetrate the policy-making machinery and, in so doing, change the perceptions and actions of the political actors that shape economic policy.

Latin America has historically experienced a drive toward modern democratic institutions checkered by intermittent military governments. The political pendulum has swung between democratic governments and military dictatorships. Many explanations have been advanced for this political experience, but let me offer one that is broad and impressionistic. In Latin America, the concept of the state as a rational institution based on constitutions, laws, and organizations was neither amenable to nor consistent with the value systems of the nations—that is, the peoples with their traditions and communities. The central constitutional objectives of freedom, equality, and fraternity did not coincide with the semifeudal practices of the times or with the built-in discriminations among ethnic and racial groups in most of the countries. The law was one thing; the practice of the community was quite another. Slowly most countries found ways of giving operational content to the law, but the political processes evolved discontinuously. Democratic and military governments alternated in power as each failed to match the requirements of the state with the demands of the community. During the 1980s most of Latin America swung toward democracy, and most people in the region are supporting the transition to make it as permanent as possible. Today all countries have democratic systems, some stronger than others.

The Latin American countries are also confronting an economic crisis characterized by high external debt and insufficient investment, savings, exports, and productivity. Chile, Mexico, Bolivia, Costa Rica, Uruguay, and other countries are achieving substantial degrees of economic adjustment. Chile did it with a military government in control; Mexico is doing it with a quasi-democratic, one-party political system; Bolivia and Costa Rica have been doing it with democratic governments; Uruguay started the adjustment with a military government and is continuing with a democratic system. In all these cases, modern economists have contributed significantly to the changes in fundamental economic policies.

Two cases are outstanding examples of the educational process brought about by modern economists who have been there when the national needs were critical: Chile and Mexico.

In Chile, systematic training programs, started in the late 1950s by several Chilean universities with counterpart universities in the United States, produced a significant number of trained modern economists, most of whom went back to teach in their local university. Outstanding among those efforts was that of the Catholic University of Chile and the University of Chicago. Those economists were present in large numbers when the military government decided in 1973 to turn to an open and flexible economy guided by market forces, after the chaotic drive toward socialism. For sixteen years the new economic policies produced remarkable growth, efficiency, and poverty alleviation, as well as some failures. The new democratic government, elected in 1989, has kept most of the policy in place, strengthening the social development programs. The prominence given to modern economists by the military government caused the main political parties in the opposition (now in government) to increase the number of their own modern economic advisers. As a result, economic debate and policy has reached a new plateau. Time will tell whether all the gains will prevail.

In Mexico, the Banco de México (Mexico's central bank), under the strong leadership of Rodrigo Gómez, began in the 1950s and 1960s to send bright Mexicans to study graduate economics at the major U.S. and

British universities and to place them in key technical positions in the Ministries of Finance and Commerce and Industry and at the central bank. Given the Mexican one-party system, the strong institutionalized bureaucracy, and the rotation and upgrading of public officials every six years, the modern trained economists began to occupy higher positions until finally Miguel de la Madrid (a Harvard graduate) reached the presidency in 1982. Today President Carlos Salinas and his whole economic team hold Ph.D.'s in economics from the main academic centers in the United States. In the span of eight years these economists have transformed the economic policy of Mexico. So far they have dealt satisfactorily with pressure groups of different types, having the full backing of the party's political machinery.

Costa Rica, Uruguay, Bolivia, Venezuela, and Colombia are also making use of modern trained economists to transform their policies. Other countries, such as Argentina and Brazil, have used modern economists, but they have not made as many lasting policy changes perhaps because of insufficient identification between economists and politicians or the inability of politicians to persuade strong pressure groups to stay the course.

In some of the more successful cases, professional economists are not only technicians but also participate in the political parties. The leaders of political parties often become government officials in either the executive or legislative branches. They need to be well informed and advised on modern economic policy matters. It is critical, then, to have trained and capable economists who are willing to participate in the institutions that make and influence policy—that is, political parties, public administration, and representative organizations of organized production groups.

The characteristics of the political institutions also influence the outcome. For example, when the democratic system is made up of ideological political parties that stand far apart in the political spectrum, then one of the requirements for a successful democracy, compromise on policy, tends to be derailed, often resulting in wide swings in economic policy from left to right and from consumption-oriented to production-oriented policies. When political parties are structured on a broader social base (including businessmen, laborers, professionals, and rural and urban groups) with fewer ideological underpinnings, compromise is easier to achieve. More stable, predictable policies are the result.

Colombia is a good Latin American example of the latter case. For the past thirty years two strong, traditional, broad-based political parties have honored a commitment to rebuild democratic political institutions and achieve development. As a consequence economic policy has been relatively predictable and stable, resulting in, among other things, one of the lowest levels of external debt in the region. Both parties have had modern trained economists participating in policy formulation, quite often cooperating with each other.[3] A good deal of policy making has been characterized by second-best solutions, because of the influence of powerful economic sectors that have taken advantage of their positions to advance their sectoral development. Having suffered relatively little economic stagnation in the 1980s, Colombia now increasingly debates the degree of economic liberalization it should have. Economists have made advances in modernizing macroeconomic policy, but they have achieved only gradual progress in the microeconomic area, perhaps because of the degree of stability achieved and the power of traditional groups within the political parties. The need for more drastic changes has simply not been felt.

In other Latin American countries, such as Argentina, Chile (before the military government), Peru, and Brazil, political parties have followed a different pattern. The more leftist or consumption-oriented groups have prevailed in populist parties, and the more rightist or production-oriented groups have done so in conservative parties. The common denominator is that both groups perceive the state as a favor-granting structure. In these cases as well, economic policies represent second-best solutions. In the best situations favors and subsidies are granted to all groups, and in the worst, volatile macroeconomic policies swing between inflationary measures and external sector distortions on the one hand and stabilization policies emphasizing austerity, savings, investment, and reduced consumption on the other. Neither extreme is sustainable in such political environments: one is technically inconsistent and unstable; the other lacks support among powerful political groups, such as labor unions, which demand higher levels of consumption expenditures. Modern economic knowledge has not been available in sufficient doses to the populist groups to change their perceptions and to teach them about how better to achieve their economic objectives.

Political parties, as representatives of social forces in a country, reflect the objectives, values, and perceptions of reality of groups. The question then is whether such groups can learn to pursue their economic and political objectives in a more competitive environment in which rules and policies apply equally to all instead of one in which favors and privileges are traded.

Development experience is demonstrating that competitive and flexible market economies, with a strong outward orientation, tend to be more efficient and grow faster. Market forces can be oriented but not disregarded. The system should be decentralized, with economic decisions being made by thousands of separate agents on the basis of a close relationship between effort and reward. Economic policy is successful when it recognizes these facts and provides a stable macroenvironment with a flexible and open microenvironment and a good deal of economic information for decision making.

A democratic political system implies fair competition for political power, open discussion and negotiation of ideas and policies, and compromises over policy. Obviously such compromises need not be, and often are not, optimal for economic growth. Therefore, trade-offs exist between economic and political objectives in policy making. This is one of the main reasons why a centralized economic system in a decentralized democratic political system does not produce desirable levels of growth and human development. The distribution of economic resources on the basis of political spoils is inefficient. Sometimes centralized political systems (such as in Chile, South Korea, Taiwan, and Singapore) produce more decentralized and market-oriented economic development. But there are as many examples with opposite results. Besides, Lord Acton's famous axiom that "power corrupts and absolute power corrupts absolutely" is a permanent reminder of the excesses that may occur with centralized political systems. The best hope for the protection of basic freedoms and for economic development is found in decentralized, democratic political systems with decentralized, market-oriented economies.

Miguel Urrutia of Colombia noted that local and regional governments, can play an important role in building structures that would allow more participation in the development process by people at the regional level. Several Latin American countries, such as Mexico, Chile, Colombia, and Venezuela, are evolving in that direction.

In democratic and decentralized market economy systems, policy compromises are made with the participation of political parties and the groups they represent. Often those organized groups (such as, business, labor, and farmers) have more direct influence on policy than do the political parties. The transactional nature of their compromises has been well explained in several chapters of this volume. The challenge for the policy-making economist, once again, is to demonstrate to these groups that they gain more individually and collectively from a dynamic growth policy that maintains stability and competition than from a shrinking or stagnant economy. This is true even in most cases in which a given group increases its share of the market. Policy should provide incentives to increase total saving and investment and the social and private returns on investment as well as total productivity.

In Latin America the greatest difficulties in achieving such objectives are related to income distribution issues and to populist perceptions that consumption levels can be increased easily (that is, by printing money) without equivalent increases in production. The objectives of improved income distribution and higher levels of consumption are valid. Populist solutions, however, do not work. Experience, economic logic, and demonstration effects are the tools the economist has to persuade political parties and pressure groups about the policies that can achieve these objectives. The appropriate policies involve moving away from favoritism, fostering equality before the law, and giving equal treatment to equal functions. They involve investing in the human and physical capital of the poor. And they involve transferring resources to the poor and the disadvantaged in ways that are neutral to savings and investment and the efficient allocation of resources. To the extent that there is professional agreement on some of these basic policies, the persuasive process can be more effective. But the change of perceptions ultimately requires leadership in the political and economic arenas, and leadership requires people that are aware they want something different but are persuaded they do not know how to get it. Political and economic leadership can then show them the way.

The Policy-making Economist and the New Political Economy

The new political economy (NPE) has provided sensible answers about how political decisions on economic policy can be both rational and socially nonoptimal. The maximization of individual or group utility by interest groups and policy makers leads them to nonoptimal (or irrational) economic policy choices. In society-centered political systems, such as the United States, recognition of this public choice behavior has led economists to conclude that the economy functions more efficiently with a smaller government. In a system that can be described as state-centered because of the power of politicians, bureaucrats, or the state in general, the policy-making process is more autonomous and less dependent on the actions or influence of pressure groups. In such cases politicians make use of state resources for their own ends. Here, the NPE conclusion is the same: the government should participate in the economy less, and economic decisions should be decentralized.

The Latin American experience is full of examples of decisions made in response to pressure groups or initiated by policy makers to protect or expand their political power base. The cases of favoritism cited by both the right and the left illustrate the point. Both democratic governments and military dictatorships have made many economic policy decisions to maximize the interests of pressure groups or policy makers, as predicted by the NPE analysis. As was mentioned, the concept of the state as a regulator and favor-dispensing organization is deeply ingrained in the cultural traditions of most Latin American countries.

One of the most common examples of politically influenced, nonoptimal policy decisions is the combination of high protection for import-substitution industrialization, overvalued currencies, and price regulation and export taxes for agricultural exports. As a result powerful urban groups of industrialists and laborers are protected in their industries, imports, and jobs, while agriculture pays the subsidy that makes it possible. During a good deal of the past fifty years, economic theories provided a rationale to support such policies. In the period 1900–1936, however, countries in the region practiced liberal trade policies that supported exports of foodstuffs, raw material, and minerals. In each period the groups most influential on policy had an economic rationale to support their preferences.

In the 1936–1950 period economic policy making in most Latin American countries faced a turning point. Another such turning point may have begun in the late 1980s and early 1990s. It is more than a change in the balance of political forces and the power of pressure groups that explains such changes. In both cases economic circumstances and needs changed, and leadership groups have been pressed to provide answers to the emerging social and economic problems. The search for solutions has often led to policies that served a perceived national objective as well as the self-interests of the leadership groups. Quite often, though, the long-run consequences of a given policy have been unknown, since many of the potential costs of the new policy were hidden even to the economists of the time.

The new political economy can be useful to predict policy outcomes within a static situation. In a given environment of policies, knowledge, and values, pressure groups and politicians seek their advantages to the margin, and they tend to disregard maximization of national utility if it is in conflict with their preferences. But the NPE needs to be expanded to cover more dynamic situations, in which there are changes in the available policy "technology." In a system where no new technologies or information are being incorporated into economic activity, the economy will tend toward an equilibrium. With recurrent technological changes in production and markets, disequilibria are introduced into the economy and open opportunities for growth in investment, output, and productivity.

The national learning process for economic policy making can be viewed in an analogous way. Knowledge of modern economics and policy performance opens up opportunities to rechannel economic activity and social values in ways that will lead to greater production and well being. The policies will be adopted if the perception that they increase net benefits or reduce net costs to society and the leadership groups can be substantiated. Economic policy need not remain, and in many developing countries it has not remained, in the hinterland of old perceptions and prescriptions, determined solely by the pursuit of self-interest by pressure groups.

The dynamics of Latin American development in the past twenty-five years have been quite dramatic. With populations growing first at over 3 percent per year in twenty countries and more recently at 2.4 percent, problems related to employment generation, the needs of the population under twenty years old (who make up 50 percent of the total), and the fast rural-to-urban migration have been staggering. Part of the attention of self-seeking pressure groups, politicians, and policy makers has been turned over to ways of coping with such social demands and expectations in order to keep the stability they need to achieve their objectives. In several cases, regimes in power have misunderstood or ignored the implications of these social circumstances, only to see themselves voted or thrown out of power. In others, governments have tried to cope with the social demands while helping themselves with the benefits resulting from policy.

Often leaders did not understand that the policies of the past thirty years have aggravated such social trends. Price distortions against agriculture, protection for import substitution, subsidies for capital formation and excessive payroll charges, and growth of the productive apparatus of the state in unproductive ways tended to accelerate migration, generate less productive employment, and overburden the state with functions it could not carry out. When the traditional favoritism for the urban business and labor elites overloaded state regulatory functions, the cities were surrounded by large sectors working at the margin of the formal economy, "the informals," who carry on their economic activities outside the legal system. The use of external debt during the 1970s and 1980s temporarily covered up the inadequacies of the entrenched policies. But the crisis of the 1980s forced a shift toward new economic policy directions.

Ultimately, elites that hold power or influence policy making consider trade-offs between the perceived national interest and their interest when evaluating policy options. If a new policy is favorable to both, then it is easily adopted. If a new policy entails losses to them, even though it may produce a national gain or prevent a future problem, they may postpone it. When the national problem worsens to the degree that it threatens the political power or the economic gains of the elites, they may change policies to "cut their losses short." If a new policy implies short-term losses and a perceived long-term gain for them or for other groups, careful political coalition building may permit the change. The situation is most difficult when a new policy entails new ways of perceiving reality and a change in the value system. In such a case the national learning process needs to be complemented by a crisis or by persuasive, concrete evidence that a new scenario may indeed produce better results for the nation and for elite groups.

A broader version of the NPE would permit clearer evaluation of those different circumstances and help economists and policy makers to structure the trade-offs among national benefits of the new policy, the temporary costs and compensatory mechanisms for the losers, and the gains to the winners. We do not need to interpret the insights of the NPE only in terms of developing countries burdened with second-best, rent-seeking solutions that can never be changed to bring the economy up to higher plateaus of performance through leadership.

The development process is driven by knowledge, technology, and information. Science and technology have been the engines of permanent change over the past four hundred years, introducing new ways of doing things and of perceiving ourselves in the world. Such knowledge is forever widening our choices and expanding our horizons. It appears that nations that maintain a competitive and flexible economic and political environment can more easily introduce new information and technology and benefit from it. In many cases policy elites prefer not to develop such an open system of economic and political competition, because they see it as a threat to their power and benefits. There are sufficient countries in which policy reform is occurring, however, to indicate that a national learning process can take place that brings together social goals and self-interest with new perceptions, values, institutions, and ways of pursuing transactions among social groups. The policy-making economist can contribute a good deal to accelerate that process.

PART IV

EXTENDING THE NEW POLITICAL ECONOMY

The Political Economy of Policy Reform

The previous chapters have emphasized the importance of economic policy in determining development performance. A major theme has been that government failure—as explained by the new political economy (NPE)—results in deficient performance. But to understand non-market failure is not to forgive: the new political economy does not serve simply as apologetics for inappropriate policies in the developing countries. Instead the positive analysis of past behavior of governments may allow economists to anticipate other cases and to acquire insights into needed policy reform. To accomplish policy reform, it is necessary to do more than say that the state must exercise "political will" (whatever that is). Once the NPE explains why a government does what it does, advisers should see if this explanation can itself be an instrument for change and improvement by suggesting how economics must adapt to politics.

This final chapter will therefore assess the strength and limitations of the NPE for indicating how state performance can be improved. It can best do this in the context of policy reform—the widespread need to avoid government failure.

As stated in the World Bank's report *Sub-Saharan Africa: From Crisis to Sustainable Growth*, there is a need for good governance, a public service that is efficient, a judicial system that is reliable, and an administration that is accountable to the public. The report argues that without political change, economic reforms will be less effective. But does the NPE provide guidelines for political change and economic reform? Does the NPE merely illuminate the instances of government failure ex post, or does it also have predictive and normative value? Does the NPE instruct on how state performance can be improved?

Some of the chapters in this volume contain elements of normative analysis (Ranis; Hayami; Pfeffermann; Jones, Vogelsang, and Tandon; Haggard) whereas others are confined to positive analysis (Findlay, Srinivasan). Even those chapters that focus on positive analysis, however, are valuable as the foundation for normative statements because such statements must be based on illuminating positive theory that draws inferences about the consequences of different public policies.

We may now summarize the strengths and limitations of the NPE to answer the overriding questions raised in chapter 1: Does the NPE adequately explain why governments choose the policies they do—especially economically irrational policies? Does it provide insights for the undertaking of policy reform?

All the contributors to this volume agree with the NPE thesis that political factors influence the selection of economic policies and that political objectives frequently have economic consequences contrary to the economist's objectives. What they do not agree on is how best to analyze the politics of development policy making.

The particular strength of the NPE lies in its use of economic method to open some windows in the black box of the state. In addition to society-centered explanations of public policy, the NPE recognizes state-centered explanations. It throws light on the rational basis for the politics of policy making. It offers insights on why the differential development performance among nations has resulted from different public policy choices. In so doing, the NPE elucidates certain types of government failure, especially those associated with quantitative controls and inflationary measures.

It may, however, be argued that the NPE attempts to explain too much. A methodological dilemma in using the NPE for policy prescriptions arises when the model of the rational choice political economist endogenizes the policy maker—when the model allows for no outside or exogenous influence on policy choice.[1] For if there can be no exogenous influence on the policy maker, how then can the economist as adviser ever influence the policy maker to undertake policy reform? If the NPE makes policy decisions fully deterministic, of what relevance is the economist's normative analysis?

There is, however, still room for economic advice insofar as the NPE takes the preferences of decision makers as given by influences outside the model, but does not explain what shapes the preferences in the first place. If the preferences for various policy measures can be shaped by economic information and economic advice, then there is an active role for the economist as adviser. In a state-centered analysis of this sort, economists as advisers may exercise some influence directly on the policy makers. Or in a society-centered analysis, economists may learn from the NPE that certain pressure groups or interest groups should be mobilized in support of their prescription. Ranis and Haggard addressed this in their discussions of liberalization and stabilization, respectively. It is also possible for the economist to rank-order alternative institutional arrangements that bear on policy change (Bhagwati 1989: 32–33).

It would also be a misreading of the NPE to conclude that neoclassical political economists can advocate only a minimal state, a return to the protective state of classical liberalism. It is true that public choice theorists who have concentrated on the more-developed countries have advocated a diminution in the scope of the public sector and constitutional constraints to control government expenditure, revenue, and debt. Grindle observes that "limited government is the neoclassical solution to this problem [of distortive state policy]. . . . In this formulation, less politics generally means better economics." But Grindle's chapter is designed to demonstrate that the NPE "is weakened as an approach to understanding policy making in developing countries and as a policy analytic tool by the assumption that politics is a negative factor in attempting to get policies right."

If the NPE misrepresents or is inadequate to explain the dynamics of political processes that have led to certain policy outcomes, then we need not subscribe to its cynical conclusion that politics is a negative factor in policy choice. Indeed, Grindle argues that politics should not be viewed "as a spanner in the economic works, but as the central means through which societies seek to resolve conflict over issues of distribution and values. In such a perspective, politically rational behavior would not be viewed as a constraint on the achievement of collectively beneficial public policy." The final section of Grindle's chapter presents an alternative approach to political economy that leaves more room for a constructive role for positive government action and policy reform. The implications of the NPE need not be limited to those of public choice theorists. For the less-developed countries (LDCs) a strong case can still be made for public policy measures devoted to improving development performance.[2] The issue is the quality of government policy and the role of politics in determining that quality.

If more appropriate policies are to be realized, it is necessary to understand the process of policy making. As Grindle argues, it is not sufficient simply to describe economically irrational outcomes; it is necessary to draw correct inferences about how those outcomes were generated: "Understanding how policy is made and implemented makes it possible to assess how and when policy changes come about and, thus, how policy reforms can be introduced and sustained." Some would argue, as have the political scientists in chapter 10 and the policy makers in chapter 11, that the NPE is too limited for this task and that other elements of the older political economy must be incorporated into the analysis of the politics of policy making.

It is also true that to date the major contributions of NPE have been for the more developed countries in which political participation is high, voters play a major role, legislative bodies are major actors, and elections have importance. Much of the NPE is based on a pluralist model in which public policy is the result of the pressures placed upon decision makers by large numbers of competing groups in society. The state provides a more or less neutral institutional and procedural framework in which conflicting groups form coalitions, and policy change occurs because different coalitions of interests manage to gain power and impose their preferred solution on society.

Grindle argues, however, that this model has limited transferability to most of the developing countries. In these countries, "policy making tends to be more closed, less visible, and more centered in the political executive. . . . Lobbying activity is consequently difficult to identify in many developing countries." Furthermore, "In developing countries . . . it cannot always be assumed that the rules of the game are established or agreed upon. Where this is the case, the use of society-centric political economy models is misleading."

Political parties, Grindle concludes, may be more important as mechanisms by which elites control mass followings than as means by which interests are articulated from below to government leadership. This is particularly true in regimes in which single or dominant parties direct the political state. Elsewhere, parties may be vehicles for the personal ambitions of individual politicians who are divorced from any real commitment to achieving goals beyond acquiring control of government jobs and distributing them to loyal followers. In other countries, technocratic military regimes have abolished parties.

"Interest groups may be similarly ineffective as structures for presenting collective demands to political leadership. Interest associations frequently are captive organizations of ruling parties, exist only at the sufferance of the government, or, like parties, are formed for the single purpose of protecting the political interests of their leadership" (Grindle 1980: 16).

If, however, a state-centered perspective is adopted, another difficulty with the formal models of the NPE lies in the specification of an appropriate utility function. To say that the state is a rational maximizer of its own utility, without further specification, is vacuous, but the possible variety of utility functions is extensive, and many cannot be predicted but only identified ex post. Moreover, in view of external pressures from overseas donors and international agencies it cannot be said that the government always acts according to its own interests and preferences.

Although objectives may vary, the NPE always views government as a rational maximizer. This raises serious questions about the role of rationality. As Sen (1987: 74) distinguishes, "We have to make a clear distinction between (1) what type of behavior might be described as *rational* and (2) what rational behavior models might be useful in making predictions about *actual* behavior." Although no more so than for other neoclassical models, the rational choice models of the NPE can be criticized for their reliance on instrumental rationality by policy makers. Instead of a unitary state, however, there is in reality an aggregation of preferences. And the preferences may not be "given," but constructed. Moreover, choice may involve resolution, not maximization. The rationality assumption is questionable for economic man—let alone political man. "Bounded rationality"[3] may prevail, and the decision maker will then not attempt to optimize but will be content instead merely to "satisfice" (Simon 1957: 198). These possibilities suggest that social-psychological elements in decision-making need to be considered more extensively than they are by the NPE.

Simon (1986: 210) also contrasts rationality in economics and psychology as follows: "The rational person in neo-classical economics always reaches the decision that is objectively, or substantively, best in terms of the given utility function. The rational person of cognitive psychology goes about making his or her decisions in a way that is procedurally reasonable in the light of the available knowledge and means of computation."

Recognizing this difference, North (1990: 20) has stated that

> The implications of procedural rationality as opposed to instrumental rationality are far reaching for our understanding of economics and economic history. Institutions are unnecessary in a world of instrumental rationality; ideas and ideologies don't matter; and efficient markets—both economic and political—characterize economies. Procedural rationality on the other hand maintains that the actors have incomplete information, limited mental capacity by which to process that information and in consequence develop regularized patterns of exchange to structure exchange. There is no implication that the consequent institutions are efficient. In such a world ideas and ideologies play a major role in choices and transaction costs result in imperfect markets.

The importance of institutions and organizations is also recognized by another commentator on the economics of politics who states,

A perspective which is exclusively geared to the individual is ill-equipped to get to grips with organisations, power, class, and a variety of other social facts that are the very stuff of politics. Because economists have traditionally focused on the individual consumer and entrepreneur, they have no history of concern with organisations *as* organisations— with an existence over and beyond the particular individuals who are within them. Instead, they have sought to reduce all issues of organisation, including political organisation, to the individual's confrontation with alternatives (Dearlove 1987: 8).

Emphasizing the relevance of institutions, Coase (1984: 230) has stated that

Until comparatively recently, economists tended to devise their proposals for economic reform by comparing what is actually done with what would happen in an ideal state. Such a procedure is pointless. We can carry out the operations required to bring about the ideal state on a blackboard but they have no counterpart in real life. In the real world, to influence economic policy, we set up or abolish an agency, amend the law, change the personnel and so on: we work through institutions. The choice in economic policy is a choice of institutions. And what matters is the effects that a modification in these institutions will actually make in the real world.

A behavioral perspective may be more illuminating than the rationality hypothesis if it incorporates concepts and hypotheses from the older political economy. Like its ancestor, neoclassical economics, the new neoclassical political economy may have gained rigor by narrowing the questions asked and by reducing the number of variables examined. The broader but less precise approach of the older political economy should not be forgotten. We might better explain policy choices by examining the role and consequences of ideology, nationalism, classes, elites, power, status, and political culture. All this goes beyond rational choice political economy.

Moreover, the models of the NPE focus only on decision making with respect to policy choice. Analysis should focus initially, however, on the problem of agenda formation. In this regard, Hirschman has distinguished between "pressing" and "chosen" problems. Pressing problems are those "that are forced on the policymakers through pressure from injured or interested outside parties." Pressing problems are generally marked by a perception of crisis. In contrast, chosen problems are those that decision makers "have picked out of thin air" as a result of their own perceptions and preferences (Hirschman 1963).

After the policy choice comes implementation. The models of the NPE analyze political activity at the input stage of the policy process, when interest groups influence the policy choice. In contrast, as Grindle emphasizes, in developing countries it is at the output stage—at the stage of implementation and enforcement—that a large portion of individual and collective demand making occurs, interests are accommodated, and conflicts are resolved. Implementation activities are closely tied to regime maintenance goals.

Furthermore, the credibility and sustainability of a policy—attributes that are essential for policy reform—are determined during the implementation phase. If policy reform is to succeed, it is then that conflict, resistance, and reversibility must be avoided. Given the concentration of political activity in the implementation process, it is much more difficult to predict the efficacy of policies than would be indicated by the NPE's confinement to decision-making at only the level of policy choice.

With its emphasis on government failure, the NPE also tends to ignore the successes of government policy. In particular it gives inadequate attention to what Grindle has termed the "critical moments" when policy changes occur. Why, for example, has a government changed its trade strategy from import-substitution industrialization to export promotion? From inflationary policies to stabilization policies? From financial repression to financial liberalization?

Grindle rejects the notion that change depends on the introduction of enlightened technocrats or statespeople who are somehow liberated from the pursuit of self-interest and thus able to see beyond short-term goals to long-term public interests. Grindle states that "in the general context of negative politics predicted by neoclassical political economists, change is explained exogenously by benign leadership or disinterested advice." Rejecting this, Grindle instead sees change emerging through a more constructive role for the political process—a role that emphasizes such political values as "the compromise of conflicting interests, the search for more equitable solutions to public problems, the achievement of social and political stability based on a reasonable set of rules about how collective problems are best resolved, the creation of public trust based on a shared sense of legitimate authority, the search for basic consensus on the nature of the public interest, the definition of an agreed-upon role for government to perform."

In a state-centered perspective, a change from a weak state to a strong state also results in policy change. For instance, Jones and SaKong (1980) have concluded that the crucial impetus behind South Korea's emergence from slow growth under Syngman Rhee to fast-track industrialization under General Park Chung Hee was leadership change. The autocratic Rhee ran a weak state: interventionist, but lacking coherent industrial priorities and flabby and corrupt in its administration of controls and subsidies. The dictatorial Park ran a strong state that was able to plan more coherently, choose industrial exporting sequences, and implement them more effectively than its predecessor regime.[4]

Others have looked to catastrophic learning experiences or dramatic performance failures as the explanation of change to more appropriate policies. Lal's interpretation of the change from inflationary policies to stabilization programs incorporates this approach (Lal 1987). A government may liberalize its economy during a crisis to regain control when the growth of the "transfer state" has led to generalized tax resistance, avoidance, or evasions. The "withering of the state" occurs as parallel markets arise to erode state control; dramatic policy change is then necessary.

Similarly, Ranis adopted as his basic hypothesis in chapter 4 "that relatively linear policy change occurs not when the role of government atrophies but when government actions become explicit rather than implicit. Policy oscillation occurs when covert policies adopted for short-term political convenience self-destruct because of the unexpected and delayed adverse effects on some groups whose income is being transferred in the absence of a clear political consensus."

Elsewhere Ranis and Fei (1988: 108) have observed that the liberalization process may result from "a natural organizational evolution, companion to the transition toward the epoch of modern economic growth. As the economy becomes increasingly complex, sooner or later the idea seems to surface that command by political forces is cumbersome and that economic decisions must be decentralized in order to achieve economic efficiency."

In a society-centered perspective, a political pact among various interest groups may become undone, thereby causing a change of policy. Thus, considering agricultural policies in Africa, Bates (1983: 357) argues that

> the pattern of price interventions represents the terms of a political pact among organized political interests, the costs of which are transferred to unorganized interests who are excluded from the price-setting coalition. Members of the pact are labor, industry, and government; small-scale farmers constitute its victims; and large-scale farmers stand as passive allies, politically neutralized through subsidy programs. . . .
> No member of the winning coalition possesses an incentive to alter its political dimensions unilaterally. In the short term, then, the coalition and the price structure that supports it appear stable.
> Over the longer run, however, the structure of the payoff achieved by the coalition changes. Farmers adjust; in response to pricing policies, they produce less. The result in food markets is lower supplies at higher prices. The result in export markets is fewer exports and less foreign exchange. The costs which once were externalized upon the unorganized agrarian sector are now internalized, through the operation of markets, onto the dominant coalition. The farmers have transferred the costs of the political settlement to the intended beneficiaries. And as these costs mount, the pact among them becomes less stable.

As the payoffs from this basis for governance in Africa erode, opportunities arise for the introduction of new pricing policies. And as the
costs of the present policies are disproportionately borne by one of the
more influential of the coalition partners, the governments themselves,
the likelihood of policy changes is enhanced.

The general problem for explaining "turning points" is to determine what forces induce political innovations. Policy reform requires
political entrepreneurship. But a theory of political entrepreneurship is
not to be found in the NPE.

As North (1990: 26–27) observes,

Political markets are characterized by high transaction costs. The literature on efficient markets has not only blinded us to the fact that
they are rare in economic markets and entail stringent information
and institutional requirements but also prevented us from appreciat-
ing that they are far rarer in political markets precisely because the
necessary conditions do not exist even in the most favorable political
markets for such efficiency—democratic polities. Rational voter ignorance, substantial agency problems but particularly incomplete com-
prehension of the real consequences of political decisions makes for
high political transaction costs.

The consequent imperfection of political markets can result in re-
inforcing persistently poor economic performance but, paradoxically
enough, it can result in political entrepreneurs, on occasion, having
sufficient degrees of freedom to alter paths (by enacting rules that
induce increased competition—tariff reductions for example). Such
reversals can only occur in periods of stress that reduce, at least in
part, the bargaining power of those groups that stand to gain by the
persistence of the existing institutional framework. In such circumstances political entrepreneurs may be in a position to encourage the
creation of, or foster the expansion of, organizations with different
agendas. While this conjecture is compatible with the kind of casual
empirical observations we possess of the alternation or even reversal
of institutional paths, it lacks theoretical grounding. To my knowledge, however, there is no existing body of political theory that provides insight into such problems.

Given the limitations of the NPE, we must seek a more eclectic approach that combines the old and new political economy. From the perspective of the older political economy, we should give special attention
to the influence of historical tradition, social structure, ideologies, and
institutions. An explanation of the motivations of policy makers is then
too mixed to be understood by only rational choice models of the NPE.

Going beyond the NPE, the political scientists in chapter 10 emphasize the role of political institutions in shaping policy choice and
implementation.[5] Nelson observes that "contrasts between democratic and authoritarian regimes may be less important than some

more precisely specified institutional variables that cut across types of regimes." Haggard also states that "variations in institutional structure should be important in determining policy outcomes, even where the configuration of group interests is held constant. . . . Interest group and rational actor models of the state are useful, but their results may be highly sensitive to institutional variation."

The organization of political life makes a difference.[6] Instead of taking preferences of individual actors as given, an institutional perspective insists that past choices constrain present options, that the preferences and capabilities of individual actors are conditioned by institutional structures, and that historical trajectories are path dependent (Krasner 1988: 66).

A central question is how can institutions be changed to perform better according to criteria of evaluation. Normative assessment should take account of not only the impact of governmental and other institutions on economic outcomes, but also of the impact of economic change on the evolution of institutions (Van Arkadie 1989). Fundamental to a country's development are such economic institutions as markets, property rights, types of contracts, third-party enforcement, and absence of corruption. These institutions constitute sets of rights and obligations that affect people in their economic lives.[7]

State-centered approaches should also be modified by recognizing the interaction between the state and society, for the structure of society affects state capabilities. As Migdal (1988: 180) argues: "Too often, especially in the new social science literature reviving the state as a major actor and unit of analysis, the state has appeared as a given—autonomous, impenetrable, the ultimate independent variable. That view ignores too much of the dynamic of state-society interactions, certainly in Asia, Africa, and Latin America. The impact of society on the state is as important as the effect of state on society for understanding the sometimes surprising patterns of continuity and change in the Third World." Social structure and the strength of social organizations influence the priorities of state leaders and ultimately the ability of state agencies to implement policies.

Migdal therefore claims that the starting point for analysis should be the environment of conflict: there is a struggle between state leaders, who seek to mobilize people and resources and impose a single set of rules, and other social organizations applying different rules in parts of the society (1988: 261). Accordingly, a major distinction between states lies not in their type of government but in the degree to which the government really governs (Huntington 1968: 1–2). In new states, political instability, state ineptness, and the fragmentation of social control are especially relevant for the failure to implement policy choices.

Political Economy of Trade Policy

As an illustration of this broader but necessarily more informal analysis of the combined new and old political economy, let us now consider the behavior of a developing country's government with respect to trade policy—in particular its attraction to import-substituting industrialization (ISI).

Development economists can certainly present logical arguments for protection of import substitution industries. Technical analysis could shape rational economic policy. There is merit to the infant industry argument under certain conditions—namely, the industry enjoys dynamic learning effects that generate irreversible technological external economies that cannot be captured by the protected industry; the protection is limited in time; and the protection enables the industry to realize sufficiently lower costs such that the initial excess costs of the industry will be repaid with an economic rate of return equal to that earned on other investments.

There are also economically sound arguments for industrial protection when there is factor price disequilibrium in a dual labor market such that the urban wage in industry is greater than its social opportunity cost. Further, if a country can exercise international market power it might protect an import-competing industry in order to improve its commodity terms of trade.

Rarely, however, has protection been instituted because of these logical arguments, let alone applied by a government in a technically correct fashion. In practice, protection has been adopted for reasons best explained through a political economy perspective.

Trade policy is usually placed on the agenda as a pressing problem. Balance of payments crises and the need to relax the foreign exchange constraint require the state to take some action. As Hirschman (1975: 389) expresses it,

> the state loses its august character of a sovereign purusing its own objectives and initiating policies to this end; rather, it is seen as coping, as best it can, with a variety of emergencies, as constantly plugging holes, and stopping a wheel from creaking by applying a bit of grease in a hurry. Note that this conception of the coping state goes farther than the interest-group or bureaucratic-politics approaches; these are still concerned with improving our understanding of the state's action, rather than affirming that most of the time the state does not act, but reacts.

This pressing problem of the balance of payments also becomes a privileged problem, in the sense of gaining the attention of the policy maker, because it is reinforced by the ideology of nationalism and the appeal of economic independence. In a newly emergent country the economics of development may initially be an economics of discontent as the politically independent government seeks to overcome its colonial legacy and is attracted to the values of modernization and to the correlative policy of industrialization from the top downward.

As suggested by the society-centered perspective of the NPE, governments also respond to political demands of various interest groups. In some countries ISI is promoted by a development coalition composed of industrialists, urban wage earners, bureaucrats, and intellectuals. In others, there is what Peter Evans (1979) calls a "triple alliance" of multinational corporations, elite local capital, and the "state bourgeoisie."

To illustrate the relationship between interest groups and the state, Wellisz and Findlay (1984) have created an NPE-type model of lobbying, which is discussed in this volume by Srinivasan. The trade regime is determined by the government, which has a "restriction-formation function" reflecting its own preferences—that is, its ideology, the self-interests of the governing group, public support considerations, international obligations, etc. Lobbying expenditures by pro- and antirestriction factions enter the restriction-formation function as arguments and link the political with the economic system. The political system is thus viewed as an institutionalized market in conflict resolution, and the endogenous tariffs that emerge are the terms of trade reflecting the lower organizational costs of the particularized (protectionist) interests relative to the generalized (free trade) interests (Magee 1984: 46).

Moreover, economic resources are used in seeking politically created rents. The restriction of manufacturing imports raises the marginal product of labor in manufacturing, leading to greater rent on capital. For the government, much or even most of its revenue is derived from tariffs. An implicit alliance between a revenue-maximizing or surplus-maximizing Leviathan and protection-seeking manufacturers would then lead to a tariff that is higher than one that maximizes revenue but that falls short of outright prohibition. In this analysis, tariffs can be interpreted as "prices" that clear political markets. With uncertainty, however, the risk-avoiding manufacturers would prefer a quota to a tariff. The government could then gain revenue through the sale of import licenses, but rarely is this done. Instead the government uses the import-licensing regime to dispense patronage within the ruling bureaucratic and political elite (Findlay and Wellisz 1986: 225–26).

This model views the government as soft—that is, vulnerable to group pressure—and the trade system as highly distorted. Under these circumstances, favor seeking flourishes. To the extent that real resources are used in lobbying for trade restrictions or in revenue or rent seeking, such activities may redistribute income within the economy, imposing costs on some sectors and bringing benefits to others. The general conclusion is that high levels of protection in LDCs, which are "irrational" in terms of the conventional theory of trade and welfare, are perfectly explicable in terms of the "rational" self-interest of the relevant pressure groups in the economy (Wellisz and Findlay 1984: 148–49, 151).

Although protectionist policies may coincide with the interests of dominant groups in society, this is not necessarily the result of a weak state being dominated by societal interests but may be the result of other forces that determine the policy preferences of state elites. Instead of reflecting clear domination of the state by specific interests, policies may be influenced by the development ideologies of state elites, by the leadership ("political entrepreneurship") of specific individuals, or by the political accommodations and bargains that are struck between state elites and various social groupings (Grindle 1986: 18–19).

In societies with strong states, the government may impose policy over the objection of particularistic interests. From this viewpoint, Findlay has shown in chapter 2 how the NPE may explain the relationship between the fiscal behavior of the state and international trade.

For a variety of reasons, therefore, a number of developing countries have adopted a host of protectionist policies in an ad hoc and indiscriminate fashion, resulting in a restrictive trade regime that is quite different from an economically rational system of protection. For a Leviathan that seeks revenue, tariffs are appealing. But while imports of the final commodity face high tariffs or quantitative restrictions, the intermediate inputs have low or no tariffs, thereby giving high effective rates of protection on the domestic value added. The final assembly of imported components may also be subsidized by low rates of interest, easy access to credit, foreign exchange allowances, provision of industrial estates, low public utility rates, and favorable tax allowances. At the same time, the subsidization of the import-competing industries tends to be embedded in a general environment of inflation and the maintenance of an overvalued exchange rate that becomes a covert way to tax the agricultural sector.

Whether weak or strong, governments have not adopted the first-best policies in the policy hierarchy of a neoclassical economist. From the syndrome of policies associated with ISI, private profits in local currency and rents have been high but the domestic resource cost to the economy has been excessive, and domestic value added may even be negative at world prices. At the same time, inequalities in income distribution have been aggravated, and employment creation in the urban import-substituting industrial sector has not kept pace with the rural-urban migration. Further, overvalued exchange rates have encouraged capital flight, and foreign borrowing by governments has often gone to finance the private sector's accumulation of foreign assets rather than to an increase in export capacity: the foreign exchange constraint has not been relaxed.

For some countries a turnaround from ISI to industrial export promotion (EP) has occurred after the first easy stage of industrial import substitution.[8] For purposes of policy appraisal, it is important to consider why this turnaround occurs. It is not simply because of a retreat to laissez-faire on the part of the government. For export-led development has generally been state-led, but in a selectively effective manner. Thus, Ranis rejects not only a pure laissez-faire interpretation but also the recent revisionist view that the East Asian success stories resulted from the activity of a highly intrusive government. Instead, he emphasizes the role of institutional and organizational changes orchestrated by a government that was sensitive to the importance of setting the stage for the fullest possible participation through markets of large numbers of dispersed private actors. "The East Asian NICs recognized that a strong government was essential, but that its willingness to exercise self-restraint in selecting the areas in which it could or could not effectively intervene represented the key to building an accommodating institutional structure" (Ranis 1989: 1453).[9]

True, economists have certainly emphasized the deficiencies and adverse effects of ISI and have advocated a change to EP. Their advice has been effective at some times in some countries. But there have also been other reasons for the turnaround in policy making—to be explained by both the new and the older political economy.

Actual experience may itself be more telling than the economists' prescriptions. As Bhagwati observes, "Many developing countries learned [the policy lessons] the hard way by following ISI policies too long and seeing the fortunate few pursuing the EP strategy do much better. Perhaps learning by others' doing and one's own undoing is the most common form of education!" (Bhagwati 1988: 41).

There is indeed an international demonstration effect in government policies, and governments may be tempted to emulate policies that have been demonstrated as successful in other countries. Under international leverage through the elites of the World Bank, International Monetary Fund, or the Organization for Economic Cooperation and Development there may also be some pressure to adopt EP policies.

In a formal sense, we can of course say that a government adopts EP policies when the costs to the government of not doing so become excessive. A major reason for the shift to EP, therefore, lies in the perception by the Leviathan state that its organic interest in autonomy is better served by the outward-orientation policy (Findlay 1988). The ISI policy eventually founders on the shortage of foreign exchange, as requirements for intermediate imports and capital goods rise more rapidly than domestic production can replace imports of final goods. Foreign aid and more external borrowing become necessary to relax the foreign exchange constraint. Thus, instead of continuing along the ever more difficult path of

ISI, the Asian newly industrializing countries turned to EP to capitalize on the unprecedented world trade boom of the 1960s and early 1970s. Diversification of export markets and supply sources could actually ensure that increased participation in the world economy, as measured by higher trade ratios, would result in less dependency and more autonomy, contrary to dependency ideology (Findlay, 1988).

A switch to EP, however, involves not only a change in trade policies, but also exchange rate adjustment and stabilization measures. In addition to Asia's exchange and trade regimes, there is another force that helps make EP policies more effective in Asia than in Latin America—namely, the long-term balance of power between urban and rural interests. Latin American governments have found their most important constituencies among urban workers and capitalists. The relative power of the agricultural sector has declined since the Great Depression of the 1930s, with peasants only loosely organized. Moreover, political unrest is most dangerous in the cities. Trade restrictions therefore tend to shift income from the agricultural and mineral producing sectors toward the industrial and service sectors.

In contrast, governments in Asia have felt the pressing need to win support of, or at least to appease, the stronger rural sector (as in South Korea, Taiwan, Malaysia, Indonesia, and Thailand) (Sachs 1985: 555). Linking rural influence with export promotion has been the first step in instituting an export program. Once export-promoting policies get under way, however, urban-industrial exporters begin to lobby for such policies, eventually becoming the dominant political force in favor of an undervalued exchange rate, and rural interests lose their relative influence.

The switch to EP does not appear to be a function of any particular type of political regime. The switch has occurred in regimes as different as those of South Korea, Thailand, and Brazil (in the 1960s). On the one hand, the policy shift from ISI to EP has taken place in some countries with essentially unchanged political regimes. On the other hand, ISI has been pursued continually in some countries despite radical changes in their political regimes; for example, Egypt and Turkey (until 1980) pursued ISI for more than half a century.

More generally, it should not be concluded that it somehow requires military or authoritarian regimes to have appropriate economic policies. As Harberger states, "The linkage of good economic policy to authoritarian government is certainly overdrawn, if not basically incorrect. It is closer to the truth to say that good economic policies require governments that are reasonably strong and confident, that do not have to tremble at the thought of offending almost any interest group, and that are capable of taking the long view" (1989: 29).

Regardless of the type of political regime, it is striking that a turning point toward an outward-oriented trade strategy is also likely to bring about reform in other policies. Krueger (1990: 110–11) hypothesizes that "one of the reasons for the success of the countries adopting outer-oriented trade strategies is that an export orientation imposes a discipline and set of constraints on all economic policies that prevent the adoption of very many measures severely antithetical to growth." The reform of trade policy leads, in turn, to pressures for realistic exchange rates and budgetary policies and for restraint in attempting to decide which industries should be developed. A World Bank empirical study of nineteen developing countries also confirms that the group of countries that have undertaken trade liberalization have had more stable real exchange rates and have exercised more fiscal prudence (Michaely 1989: 3). Macro- and microeconomic policies become more appropriate because the openness of the economy makes the cost of an inappropriate policy highly visible quickly. The political penalties for adopting inappropriate policies are greater in the context of an ongoing outward-oriented strategy. To the extent that policy reform usually requires a *set* of policy changes, the turning point from ISI to EP thus tends to be pivotal in achieving reform in a wide range of policies.

Conclusion

Of special interest should be the influence that economists might exercise by advising on policy reform—particularly when the reforms involve large, innovative changes. In such cases, the policy issues differ from those susceptible to ordinary economic analysis. The economist is most knowledgeable about the policy-making process in situations of incremental policy changes involving a chosen problem. This type of policy problem is subject to more technical analysis and hence a low degree of politicization (that is, politics-as-usual). It involves instrumental rationality (in other words, the economist identifies technical policy instruments to be used to achieve policy objectives). The perspective is from a society-centered polity, with government as a clearinghouse or broker among interest groups. And institutions are given or ignored. This policy space is represented by the northwest quadrant in Figure 12.1, characterized as the application of ordinary economic analysis with a high understanding of the policy-making process on the part of economists.

In contrast, in situations involving large, innovative policy changes, economists are called upon to advise in a political economy context in which they have a lower understanding of the policy-making process. In this policy space, represented by the southeast quadrant of Figure 12.1, the problems are pressing. They are not amenable to as much technical analysis but instead are highly politicized. The rationality in-

FIGURE 12.1 Types of Analysis in Different Policy Situations

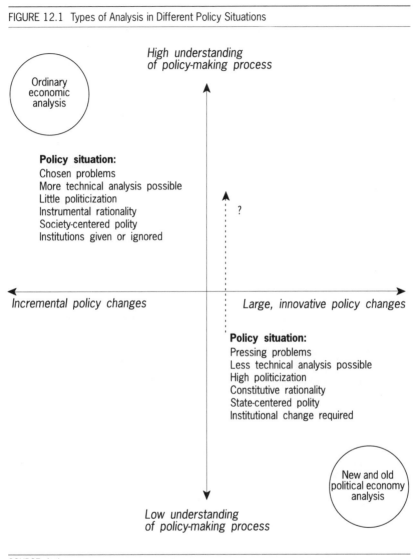

*High understanding
of policy-making process*

Ordinary
economic
analysis

Policy situation:
Chosen problems
More technical analysis possible
Little politicization
Instrumental rationality
Society-centered polity
Institutions given or ignored

?

Incremental policy changes

Large, innovative policy changes

Policy situation:
Pressing problems
Less technical analysis possible
High politicization
Constitutive rationality
State-centered polity
Institutional change required

New and old
political economy
analysis

*Low understanding
of policy-making process*

SOURCE: Author.

volved is constitutive (that is, decisions have to be made about how decisions are to be made—a constitution is needed and an institutional context for decision making has to be established). The policy-making process is more state centered. And institutional structures need to change.

If economists are to become more influential in advising on how to correct nonmarket failures and overcome resistance to policy reform, they will have to give more attention to the policy situations represented by the southeast quadrant in Figure 12.1. It is especially necessary to make policy changes transparent by identifying the distribution of not only the economic but also the political costs and benefits of policy changes, and by identifying the gainers and losers.[10] It is then necessary to examine possible ways to compensate the losers, discover the possibilities for building supportive coalitions, and consider the scope for alternative institutional arrangements.

The upshot is that economists should not view the giving of economic advice as merely a technical exercise; instead, they must integrate it with knowledge of the country's political process. To determine the feasibility and desirability of various policy reforms, economists first need to learn the underlying reasons for government failure. The NPE—although still new—may help economists do this.

Nonetheless, the relationship between economists' knowledge, economic policy, and development performance remains more elusive than it should be. We still need more insights from both the old and new political economy. The challenge is still to move policy problems represented by the southeast quadrant of Figure 12.1 to the northeast quadrant, where understanding of the policy-making process is greater. (The dashed line in the figure indicates a research agenda for the future.)

Economic ideas can matter; they can shape reality. But ideas are like seeds that must fall on fertile ground to germinate. Attention to the political economy of policy reform can help discover the fertile ground. If development economists are to exercise more influence, they will have to achieve greater understanding of pressing problems that are less amenable to technical analysis, more politicized, involve issues of constitutive rationality, and require institutional change. They will then better understand the causes of differences in development performance and how to institute policy reform.

Notes and References

Chapter 1　Gerald M. Meier, "Policy Lessons and Policy Formation"

Notes

1. Lal (1989: 105) refers to the "predatory state" as "a state run by a self-serving ruler, such as a monarch, dictator or charismatic leader. This sovereign . . . is autonomous, insofar as the constellation of domestic interest groups has little direct effect on his/her policies. For analytical purposes the selfish predatory sovereign is assumed to maximize either net revenue (treasure) or courtiers (bureaucrats)."

For a more extensive discussion and model of a predatory state that maximizes the "profits of government," see Lal (1988: 294–306).

2. For a comprehensive survey, see Robert P. Inman (1987).

References

Alt, J. E., and K. A. Chrystal. 1983. *Political Economics*. Brighton: Wheatsheaf.

Bhagwati, Jagdish N. 1982. "Directly Unproductive, Profit-Seeking (DUP) Activities." *Journal of Political Economy* 90 (October): 988–1002.

Buchanan, J., and G. Tullock. 1962. *The Calculus of Consent*. Ann Arbor: University of Michigan Press.

Buchanan, J. M., and R. D. Tollison, eds. 1984. *Theory of Public Choice.* New York: Garland.

Downs, A. 1957. *An Economic Theory of Democracy.* New York: Harper and Row.

Evans, P. B., D. Rueschmeyer, and T. Skocpol, eds. 1985. *Bringing the State Back In.* Cambridge: Cambridge University Press.

Harberger, Arnold, ed. 1984. *World Economic Growth.* San Francisco: ICS Press.

Inman, Robert P. 1987. "Markets, Governments, and the 'New' Political Economy." In A. J. Auerbach and M. Feldstein, eds., *Handbook of Public Economics.* Vol. 2. New York: Elsevier.

Jasay, A. de. 1985. *The State.* Oxford: Basil Blackwell.

Keynes, J. M. 1923. *Tract on Monetary Reform.* London: Macmillan.

Krueger, Anne 0. 1974. "The Political Economy of the Rent-Seeking Society." *American Economic Review* 64, no. 3: 291–303.

Lal, Deepak. 1988. *The Hindu Equilibrium.* Oxford: Clarendon Press.

———. 1989. "After the Debt Crisis: Modes of Development for the Longer Run in Latin America." In Sebastian Edwards and Felipe Larraine, eds., *Debt, Adjustment and Recovery.* Oxford: Basil Blackwell.

Little, I. M. D. 1982. *Economic Development.* New York: Basic Books.

Magee, Stephen P. 1984. "Endogenous Tariff Theory." In D. Colander, ed., *Neoclassical Political Economy.* Cambridge, Mass.: Ballinger.

Mueller, Dennis C. 1974. *Public Choice.* Cambridge: Cambridge University Press.

Niskanen, William A. 1971. *Bureaucracy and Representative Government.* Hawthorne, N.Y.: Aldine.

North, Douglass C. 1981. *Structure and Change in Economic History.* New York: Norton.

Olson, Mancur. 1965. *The Logic of Collective Choice.* Cambridge, Mass.: Harvard University Press.

———. 1982. *The Rise and Decline of Nations.* New Haven: Yale University Press.

Ranis, Gustav, and T. Paul Schultz, eds. 1988. *The State of Development Economics.* Oxford: Basil Blackwell.

Riker, William H. 1962. *The Theory of Political Coalition.* New Haven: Yale University Press.

Sandbrook, R. 1986. "The State and Economic Stagnation in Tropical Africa." *World Development* 14, no. 3 (March): 319–33.

Schaffer, B. B. 1984. "Toward Responsibility: Public Policy in Concept and Practice." In E. J. Clay and B. B. Schaffer, eds., *Room for Manoeuvre.* Cranbury, N.J.: Associated University Press.

Stigler, George. 1971. "The Theory of Economic Regulation." *Bell Journal of Economics and Management Science* 2, no. 3: 3–21.

Timmer, Peter. 1973. "Choice of Technique in Rice Milling in Java." *Bulletin of Indonesian Economic Studies* 9, no. 2.

Vincent, Andrew. 1987. *Theories of the State.* Oxford: Basil Blackwell.

Chapter 2   Ronald Findlay, "The New Political Economy: Its Explanatory Power for LDCs"

Notes

1. The flavor of the new political economy research is perhaps best conveyed by the volumes of readings edited by Buchanan, Tollison, and Tullock (1980), Colander (1984), and Stigler (1988). Analytical surveys of essential issues and results are provided by Bhagwati (1982), Srinivasan (1985), and Wellisz and Findlay (1988).

2. See Skocpol's Introduction to Evans, Rueschmeyer, and Skocpol (1985).

3. Discussions of the autonomy of the state from the Marxist perspective can be found in Miliband (1977) and Elster (1985), while Anderson (1974) is the most impressive application of the Marxist approach in a specific historical context, the "absolutist" states of early modern Europe. A stimulating and original conceptual analysis of the state is Jasay (1985).

4. The subsequent discussion draws on Badie and Birnbaum (1983) and Poggi (1978).

5. The model presented here is a significant extension over an earlier version contained in Findlay and Wilson (1987), since the tax rate is now endogenous, with the labor supply an increasing function of the after-tax wage instead of being perfectly inelastic. The model draws on the insights into the "productive" character of the state contained in North (1981), chapter 3, on "A Neoclassical Theory of the State" and into its "predatory" aspect by Brennan and Buchanan (1980). The predatory nature of the state is also stressed in Lal (1985) and Tilly (1985). None of these authors however have attempted to embody their ideas in a formal general equilibrium model, even a very simple one such as is given here.

6. On modern Argentine economic history see the classic study by Díaz Alejandro (1970). A convenient summary of political developments in relation to the economic background is provided in chapter 3 of Skidmore and Smith (1984). The present effort at attempting to model this historical experience is also indebted to Lal (1986).

7. See Myrdal (1968). For a brief but incisive evaluation of Indian economic performance and policy see also Bhagwati (1987).

8. For a penetrating summary of African experience with respect to marketing boards see Bauer (1987).

9. See the chapter on the Ivory Coast in Dunn (1978).

10. See O'Donnell (1979), Collier (1979), and Evans (1979) for analyses of the role of the state in Latin American development.

11. See Findlay (1988) and references cited therein on the political economy of export-oriented growth.

References

Anderson, P. 1974. *Lineages of the Absolutist State*. London: New Left Books.

Badie, B., and P. Birnbaum. 1983. *The Sociology of the State*. Chicago: University of Chicago Press.

Bardhan, P. K. 1984. *The Political Economy of Development in India*. New York: Basil Blackwell.

Bates, R. H. 1972. *Markets and States in Tropical Africa*. Berkeley: University of California Press.

———. 1983. *Essays in the Political Economy of Rural Africa*. Berkeley: University of California Press.

Bauer, P. T. 1987. "Marketing Boards." In J. Eatwell et al., eds., *The New Palgrave: A Dictionary of Economics*. New York: Macmillan.

Baumol, W. J. 1952. *Welfare Economics and the Theory of the State*. Cambridge: Harvard University Press.

Bhagwati, J. N. 1982. "Directly Unproductive, Profit Seeking (DUP) Activities." *Journal of Political Economy* (October).

———. 1987. "Indian Economic Performance and Policy Design." Thakurdas Memorial Lecture, Indian Institute of Bankers. Delhi.

Brennan, G., and J. Buchanan. 1980. *The Power to Tax*. Cambridge: Cambridge University Press.

Buchanan, J. M., R. D. Tollison, and G. Tullock, eds. 1980. *Toward a Theory of the Rent-Seeking Society*. College Station: Texas A & M University Press.

Clapham, C. 1985. *Third World Politics*. Madison: University of Wisconsin Press.

Colander, D., ed. 1984. *Neoclassical Political Economy*. Cambridge, Mass.: Ballinger.

Collier, D., ed. 1979. *The New Authoritarianism in Latin America*. Princeton: Princeton University Press.

Díaz Alejandro, C. F. 1970. *Essays on the Economic History of the Argentine Republic*. New Haven: Yale University Press.

Dunn, J., ed. 1978. *West African States*. Cambridge: Cambridge University Press.

Elster, J. 1985. *Making Sense of Marx*. Cambridge: Cambridge University Press.

Evans, P. B. 1979. *Dependent Development*. Princeton: Princeton University Press.

Evans, P. B., D. Rueschmeyer, and T. Skocpol, eds. 1985. *Bringing the State Back In*. Cambridge: Cambridge University Press.

Findlay, R. 1988. "Trade, Development and the State." In G. Ranis and T. P. Schultz, eds., *The State of Development Economics*. New York: Basil Blackwell.

Findlay, R., and S. Wellisz. 1982. "Endogenous Tariffs, the Political Economy of Trade Restrictions and Welfare." In J. Bhagwati, ed., *Import Competition and Response*. Chicago: University of Chicago Press.

———. 1983. "The Political Economy of Trade Restrictions." *Kyklos* 36, no. 3: 469–81.

Findlay, R., and J. D. Wilson. 1987. "The Political Economy of Leviathan." In A. Razin and E. Sadka, eds., *Economic Policy in Theory and Practice*. New York: Macmillan.

Gruen, F., and W. M. Corden. 1970. "A Tariff That Worsens the Terms of Trade." In I. A. McDougall and R. H. Snape, eds., *Studies in International Economics*. Amsterdam: North-Holland.

Jasay, A. de. 1985. *The State*. New York: Basil Blackwell.

Keyder, C. 1987. *State and Class in Turkey*. London: Verso.

Krueger, A. O. 1974. "The Political Economy of the Rent-Seeking Society." *American Economic Review* (June).

———. 1977. *Growth, Factor Market Distortions and Patterns of Trade among Many Countries*. Princeton Studies in International Finance, no. 40. Princeton: Princeton University Press.

Lal, D. 1985. "The Political Economy of the Predatory State." Washington, D.C.: World Bank. Mimeo.

———. 1986. "The Political Economy of Industrialization in Primary Product Exporting Countries." Washington, D.C.: World Bank. Mimeo.

Macpherson, C. B. 1962. *The Political Theory of Possessive Individualism*. Oxford: Oxford University Press.

Mayer, W. 1984. "Endogenous Tariff Formation." *American Economic Review* (December).

Miliband, R. 1977. *Marxism and Politics*. Oxford: Oxford University Press.

Myrdal, G. 1968. *Asian Drama*. New York: Pantheon.

Niskanen, W. 1971. *Bureaucracy and Representative Government*. Hawthorne, N.Y.: Aldine.

North, D. 1981. *Structure and Change in Economic History*. New York: Norton.

O'Donnell, G. 1979. *Modernization and Bureaucratic Authoritarianism*. Berkeley: University of California Press.

Parkinson, C. N. 1958. *Parkinson's Law*. London: John Murray.

Poggi, G. 1978. *The Development of the Modern State*. Stanford: Stanford University Press.

Raeff, M. 1983. *The Well-Ordered Police State*. New Haven: Yale University Press.

Skidmore, T., and P. M. Smith. 1984. *Modern Latin America*. Oxford: Oxford University Press.

Srinivasan, T. N. 1985. "Neoclassical Political Economy, the State and Economic Development." *Asian Development Review* 3, no. 2.

Stigler, G., ed. 1988. *Chicago Studies in Political Economy*. Chicago: University of Chicago Press.

Tilly, C. 1985. "War Making and State Making as Organized Crime." In P. B. Evans, D. Rueschmeyer, and T. Skocpol, eds., *Bringing the State Back In*. Cambridge: Cambridge University Press.

Wellisz, S., and R. Findlay. 1988. "The State and the Invisible Hand." *World Bank Research Observer* (January).

Chapter 3   Merilee S. Grindle, "The New Political Economy: Positive Economics and Negative Politics"

Notes

1. In this chapter I adopt a Weberian notion of the state as an enduring set of executive and administrative organizations whose role it is to control a given territory and to make authoritative decisions for society (see Grindle 1986).

2. In an often-cited article appearing in 1976, Tony Killick discusses the implicit notions of politics held by development economists in the past.

[E]conomists have adopted a "rational actor" model of politics. This would have us see governments as composed of public-spirited, knowledgeable, and role-oriented politicians; clear and united in their objectives; choosing those policies which will achieve optimal results for the national interest; willing and able to go beyond a short term point of view. Governments are stable, in largely undifferentiated societies; wielding a centralized concentration of power and a relatively unquestioned authority; generally capable of achieving the results they desire from a given policy decision. They are supported by public administrations with ready access to a very large volume of relevant information which can be processed efficiently (p. 171).

3. In this chapter, the terms neoclassical political economy and the new political economy are used interchangeably. Neoclassical political economy has been developed by both economists and political scientists; in this chapter, work on politics by economists is stressed. A very broad literature exists on political economy; this chapter deals with only a part of it (see Keech, Bates, and Lange 1989 for a review; see also Alt and Chrystal 1983). Moreover, even within neoclassical political economy, there are important differences in approach. As indicated in this chapter, a critical difference among them is whether they approach issues from a society-centered or a state-centered perspective. What unites these models, however, is their basis in assumptions about the primacy of individual self-interest in political behavior.

4. "Bad" policy, as used here, refers to a policy that neoclassical economists consider economically irrational in a general sense. As used in this chapter, a "good" policy, from the perspectives of neoclassical economics, is one that promotes the efficient function of economic markets.

5. Riker and Ordeshook (1973), for example, define politics as "the selection of the preference of some person (or the potential preference of some person) to be the choice of society" (p. 2).

6. For Buchanan, Tollison, and Tullock (1980: ix), rent seeking is the "resource-wasting activities of individuals in seeking transfers of wealth through the aegis of the state." Bhagwati (1982) demonstrates that under some conditions, rent seeking is not welfare reducing. The general consensus among economists, however, is that rent seeking is inefficient for society.

7. Larger organizations will emerge, according to Olson, only if there is some coercive means to force them to join or if there is some incentive other than the achievement of collective goals (see Olson 1965).

8. Pluralist theory is generally traced to the group model of government associated with David Truman (1951). Its roots in democratic theory are found clearly in the writings of James Madison and Alexis de Tocqueville. Robert Dahl (1961, 1971) is perhaps the best known exponent of democratic pluralism in the United States.

9. Although neoclassical theory is largely silent on the issue, pluralists differ in terms of the equity outcomes of interest-based political decision making. Some have argued that virtually all interests have the capacity to organize and attempt to influence government and thus, the actions of government are

just in the sense that they represent the outcome of an open competitive market of ideas (see Truman 1951; Dahl 1961; Lane 1959). Others, however, have noted the extent to which social class, education, money, and access give privileges to certain groups and gain them preferential treatment by government (see Lowi 1969; McConnell 1967). In this view government action is usually biased in favor of the interests of the middle and upper classes and against the poor, the disorganized, the unorganized, or the disenfranchised.

10. Pluralist scholars differ over the passivity of public officials in the face of interest group pressures. In some perspectives public officials almost mechanistically register the aggregation of interests upon them; in most cases, however, they are seen to play more active roles, arbitrating among groups, negotiating compromises, and even pulling together winning coalitions of interests.

11. Political elites seek to maximize support not only in terms of votes but also in terms of rewarding groups whose support is essential when votes are irrelevant or when there is no agreement that voting will determine the outcome of conflict. Thus, public resources that flow to the military, large industrialists, important ethnic or regional groups, or religious leaders are resource transfers by political elites to buy the support of these groups even in nondemocratic settings. Among the most interesting work in this regard has been the effort to deduce the political logic of support coalition formation from analyses of government expenditures (see Ames 1987).

12. T. N. Srinivasan has suggested that society-centric explanations focus on the demand side of politics, while state-centric approaches reflect supply-side dynamics. The important point of distinction for political analysis, as with economic analysis, is the reversal of independent and dependent variables in these two perspectives. Demand-side approaches (society-centric) assert that social groups initiate policy and politicians respond to pressure. In supply-side perspectives (state-centric) politicians initiate policy and citizens respond with support (personal communication, August 1989).

13. Riker (1982) argues that under simple majority rules, there is an ongoing formation and dispersion of minimum winning coalitions around specific issues. "Each coalition gains by dispossessing the losers; the ultimate result is that everyone has victimized everyone else, and everyone is probably worse off" (Koford and Colander 1984: 212).

14. For the policy analyst, cataloging the organized interests that are affected by a particular policy reform—a standard procedure in much Western policy analysis—may be an unproductive exercise unless there is concomitant appreciation of the real capacity to exert influence and the real impact of informal processes of power in a given country. Findlay and Wellisz (1984) distinguish between a society-centric democratic lobbying model and a more state-centric authoritarian model in which "'the prince' is driven to justify his rule by maximizing the output of his regime. . . ." Even in democratic developing countries, however, a purely society-centric model may misrepresent the dynamics of policy making and state leadership.

15. What the new political economy explains is not new to students of politics. Political scientists studying developing countries have long known of and dissected the political logic of clientelism, corruption, and policy choice as ways of achieving not economic rationality but political stability, support, or power.

16. I am grateful to David Abernethy for this formulation of the limits of neoclassical analysis.

17. "The tragedy of the commons" refers to a theoretical construct of a generic common property problem in which each person's short-term advantage works to all people's long-term disadvantage unless a cooperative solution is arranged.

18. Many have pointed out that some of the most dynamic developers in the third world have not adopted this clear policy advice. South Korea is an example of a highly interventionist state that through a highly centralized decision making system effectively orchestrated policy in coordination with politically insulated state technocrats and a captive private business sector (see Haggard and Moon 1983).

19. Many such policy changes are discussed in papers appearing in Perkins and Roemer (1991).

References

Alt, James A., and K. Alec Chrystal. 1983. *Political Economics*. Berkeley: University of California Press.

Ames, Barry. 1987. *Political Survival: Politicians and Public Policy in Latin America*. Berkeley: University of California Press.

Anderson, Kym, and Yujiro Hayami. 1986. *The Political Economy of Agricultural Protection*. Sydney: Allen and Unwin.

Bacha, Edmar, and Richard E. Feinberg. 1986. "The World Bank and Structural Adjustment in Latin America." *World Development* 14, no. 3 (March): 333–46.

Balassa, Bela, Gerardo M. Bueno, Pedro-Pablo Kuczynski, and Mario Henrique Simonsen. 1986. *Toward Renewed Economic Growth in Latin America*. Washington, D.C.: Institute for International Economics.

Bardhan, Pranab. 1984. *The Political Economy of Development in India*. New York: Basil Blackwell.

———. 1988. "Alternative Approaches to Development Economics." In H. B. Chenery and T. N. Srinivasan, eds., *Handbook of Development Economics*. Vol. 1. Amsterdam: North Holland.

Barry, Brian, and Russell Hardin, eds. 1982. *Rational Man and Irrational Society: An Introduction and Sourcebook*. Beverly Hills: Sage Publications.

Bates, Robert. 1981. *Markets and States in Tropical Africa*. Berkeley: University of California Press.

———. 1988. *Toward a Political Economy of Development: A Rational Choice Perspective*. Berkeley: University of California Press.

Bennett, Douglas C., and Kenneth E. Sharpe. 1985. *Transnational Corporations versus the State: The Political Economy of the Mexican Auto Industry*. Princeton: Princeton University Press.

Bennett, James T., and Thomas J. DiLorenzo. 1984. "Political Entrepreneurship and Reform of the Rent-Seeking Society." In David C. Colander, ed., *Neoclassical Political Economy: The Analysis of Rent-Seeking and DUP Activities*, 217–27. Cambridge, Mass.: Ballinger.

Bhagwati, Jagdish N. 1978. *Foreign Trade Regimes and Economic Development: Anatomy and Consequences of Exchange Control Regimes*. Cambridge, Mass.: Ballinger.

———. 1982. "Directly Unproductive, Profit-Seeking Activities." *Journal of Political Economy* 90, no. 51: 988–1002.

Bratton, Michael. 1980. *The Local Politics of Rural Development.* Hanover, N.H.: University Press of New England.

Brock, William A., and Stephen P. Magee. 1984. "The Invisible Foot and the Waste of Nations." In David C. Colander, ed., *Neoclassical Political Economy: The Analysis of Rent-Seeking and DUP Activities,* 177–85. Cambridge, Mass.: Ballinger.

Buchanan, J. M. 1980. "Rent-Seeking and Profit-Seeking." In J. M. Buchanan, R. D. Tollison, and G. Tullock, eds., *Toward a Theory of the Rent-Seeking Society.* College Station: Texas A & M University Press.

Buchanan, J. M., Robert D. Tollison, and Gordon Tullock, eds. 1980. *Toward a Theory of the Rent-Seeking Society.* College Station: Texas A & M University Press.

Buchanan, James M., and Gordon Tullock. 1962. *The Calculus of Consent: Logical Foundations of Constitutional Democracy.* Ann Arbor: University of Michigan Press.

Carr, Barry, and Ricardo Anzaldúa Montoya, eds. 1986. *The Mexican Left, Popular Movements and the Politics of Austerity.* Center for U.S.–Mexican Studies, monograph no. 18. La Jolla: University of California, San Diego.

Colander, David C. 1984a. "Introduction." In David C. Colander, ed. *Neoclassical Political Economy: The Analysis of Rent-Seeking and DUP Activities,* 1–13. Cambridge, Mass.: Ballinger.

———. 1984b. *Neoclassical Political Economy: The Analysis of Rent-Seeking and DUP Activities.* Cambridge, Mass.: Ballinger.

Colander, David C., and Mancur Olson. 1984. "Coalitions and Macroeconomics." In David C. Colander, ed., *Neoclassical Political Economy: The Analysis of Rent-Seeking and DUP Activities,* 115–28. Cambridge, Mass.: Ballinger.

Conybeare, John A. C. 1982. "The Rent-Seeking State and Revenue Diversification." *World Politics* 35, no. 1 (October): 25–42.

Dahl, Robert. 1961. *Who Governs? Democracy and Power in an American City.* New Haven: Yale University Press.

———. 1971. *Polyarchy, Participation, and Opposition.* New Haven: Yale University Press.

Downs, Anthony. 1957. *An Economic Theory of Democracy.* New York: Harper.

Findlay, Ronald, and Stanislaw Wellisz. 1984. "Toward a Model of Endogenous Rent-Seeking." In David C. Colander, ed., *Neoclassical Political Economy: The Analysis of Rent-Seeking and DUP Activities,* 89–100. Cambridge, Mass.: Ballinger.

Fishlow, Albert. 1985. "The State of Latin American Economics." In Inter-American Development Bank, *Economic and Social Progress in Latin America,* 1985 Report, 123–48

Flatters, Frank. 1988. "Trade Policy Reform in Indonesia." Paper prepared for a Harvard Institute for International Development conference on Economic Systems Reform in Developing Countries, Marrakech, Morocco, October.

Grindle, Merilee S., ed. 1980. *Politics and Policy Implementation in the Third World.* Princeton: Princeton University Press.

———. 1986. *State and Countryside: Development Policy and Agrarian Politics in Latin America.* Baltimore: Johns Hopkins University Press.

Grindle, Merilee S., and John W. Thomas. 1989. "Policy Makers, Policy Choices, and Policy Outcomes: The Political Economy of Reform in Developing Countries." *Policy Sciences* 22: 213–48.

Haggard, Stephan. 1987. "Korea: From Import-Substitution to Export-Led Growth." Unpublished manuscript.

———. 1989. "The Political Economy of the Philippine Debt Crisis." In Joan Nelson, ed., *Economic Crisis and Policy Choice: The Politics of Adjustment in Developing Countries*. Princeton: Princeton University Press.

Haggard, Stephan, and Chung-In Moon. 1983. "The South Korean State in the International Economy: Liberal, Dependent, or Mercantile?" In John Ruggie, ed., *The Antinomies of Interdependence*, 131–89. New York: Columbia University Press.

Hamilton, Alexander, James Madison, and John Jay. 1961. *The Federalist Papers*. New York: Mentor Books.

Hampson, Fen. 1986. *Forming Economic Policy: The Case of Energy in Canada and Mexico*. New York: St. Martin's Press.

Hardin, G. 1968. "The Tragedy of the Commons." *Science* 162: 1243–48.

Hirshleifer, Jack. 1985. "The Expanding Domain of Economics." *American Economic Review* 5 (December): 53–68.

Hyden, Goran. 1983. *No Shortcuts to Progress: African Development Management in Perspective*. Berkeley: University of California Press.

Johnson, B. L. C. 1983. *Development in South Asia*. Harmondsworth, England: Penguin.

Jones, Christine, and Michael Roemer, eds. 1989. *Modeling and Measuring Parallel Markets*, special issue of *World Development* (December).

Keech, William R., Robert Bates, and Peter Lange. 1989. "Political Economy: An Approach to the Study of Politics within Nations." Paper prepared for the Annual Meeting of the Midwest Political Science Association, Chicago, April 13–15.

Killick, Tony. 1976. "The Possibilities of Development Planning." *Oxford Economic Papers* 28, no. 2 (July): 161–84.

———. 1988. "A Reaction Too Far: Contemporary Thinking about the Economic Role of the State, with Special Reference to Developing Countries." Paper prepared for a Harvard Institute for International Development conference on Economic Systems Reform in Developing Countries, Marrakech, Morocco, October.

Koford, Kenneth J., and David C. Colander. 1984. "Taming the Rent Seeker." In David C. Colander, ed., *Neoclassical Political Economy: The Analysis of Rent-Seeking and DUP Activities*, 205–16. Cambridge, Mass.: Ballinger.

Krueger, Anne O. 1974. "The Political Economy of the Rent-Seeking Society." *American Economic Review* 64, no. 3: 291–303.

Kuczynski, Pedro-Pablo. 1988. *Latin American Debt*. Baltimore: Johns Hopkins University Press.

Lal, Deepak. 1983. *The Poverty of "Development Economics."* London: Institute of Economic Affairs.

———. 1984. *The Political Economy of the Predatory State*. Development Research Department, Discussion Paper DRD 105. Washington, D.C.: World Bank.

Lane, Robert E. 1959. *Political Life*. Glencoe, Ill.: Free Press.

Lindbeck, Assar. 1976. "Stabilization Policy in Open Economies with Endogenous Politicians." *American Economic Review* 66, no. 2 (May): 1–19

Lindenberg, Marc. 1989. "Managing Winners and Losers in Stabilization and Structural Adjustment: Politics and Policy Implementation." *Policy Sciences* 22: 359–94.

Lowi, Theodore J. 1969. *The End of Liberalism: Ideology, Policy, and the Crisis of Public Authority.* New York: Norton.

Magee, Stephen P. 1984. "Endogenous Tariff Theory: A Survey." In David Colander, ed., *Neoclassical Political Economy: The Analysis of Rent-Seeking and DUP Activities,* 41–51. Cambridge, Mass.: Ballinger.

Mallon, Richard, and Joseph Stern. 1988. "The Political Economy of Trade and Industrial Reform in Bangladesh." Paper prepared for a Harvard Institute for International Development conference on Economic Systems Reform in Developing Countries, Marrakech, Morocco, October.

Maxfield, Sylvia, and Ricardo Anzaldúa Montoya, eds. 1987. *Government and Private Sector in Contemporary Mexico.* Center for U.S.–Mexican Studies, monograph no. 20. La Jolla: University of California, San Diego.

McConnell, Grant. 1967. *Private Power and American Democracy.* New York: Knopf.

McPherson, Malcolm. 1988. "The Gambia's Economic Recovery Program." Paper prepared for a Harvard Institute for International Development conference on Economic Systems Reform in Developing Countries, Marrakech, Morocco, October.

Meier, Gerald. 1989. "The New Political Economy and Development Policymaking." Stanford University. Typescript.

Olson, Mancur, Jr. 1965. *The Logic of Collective Action: Public Goods and the Theory of Groups.* New York: Schocken Books.

———. 1982. *The Rise and Decline of Nations.* New Haven: Yale University Press.

Perkins, Dwight. 1988. "Economic Systems Reform in Developing Countries." Paper prepared for a Harvard Institute for International Development conference on Economic Systems Reform in Developing Countries, Marrakech, Morocco, October.

Perkins, Dwight, and Michael Roemer. 1991. *Reforming Economic Systems in Developing Countries.* Cambridge, Mass.: Harvard University Press.

Popkin, Samuel L. 1988. "Public Choice and Peasant Organization." In Robert H. Bates, ed., *Toward a Political Economy of Development: A Rational Choice Perspective,* 245–71. Berkeley: University of California Press.

Radelet, Steven. 1988. "Economic Reform in the Gambia: Policies, Politics, Foreign Aid and Luck." Paper prepared for a Harvard Institute for International Development conference on Economic Systems Reform in Developing Countries, Marrakech, Morocco, October.

Riker, William H. 1982. *Liberalism against Populism.* San Francisco: Freeman.

Riker, William H., and Peter C. Ordeshook. 1973. *An Introduction to Positive Political Theory.* Englewood Cliffs, N.J.: Prentice Hall.

Roemer, Michael. 1988. "Macroeconomic Reform in Developing Countries." Development Discussion Paper no. 266 (March). Cambridge, Mass.: Harvard Institute for International Development.

Rudolph, Lloyd I., and Susanne Hoeber Rudolph. 1987. *In Pursuit of Lakshmi: The Political Economy of the Indian State*. Chicago: University of Chicago Press.

Runge, C. Ford. 1986. "Common Property and Collective Action in Economic Development." In *Common Property Resource Management, Proceedings of a Conference*. Washington, D.C.: National Research Council and National Academy Press.

Russell, Clifford S., and Norman K. Nicholson, eds. 1981. *Public Choice and Rural Development*. Washington, D.C.: Resources for the Future.

Sachs, Jeffrey. 1985. "External Debt and Macroeconomic Performance in Latin America and East Asia." *Brookings Papers on Economic Activity*, vol. 2. Washington, D.C.: Brookings Institution.

Samuels, Warren J., and Nicholas Mercuro. 1984. "A Critique of Rent-Seeking Theory." In David C. Colander, ed., *Neoclassical Political Economy: The Analysis of Rent-Seeking and DUP Activities*, 55–70. Cambridge, Mass.: Ballinger.

Sandbrook, Richard. 1986. "The State and Economic Stagnation in Tropical Africa." *World Development* (March): 319–32.

Srinivasan, T. N. 1985. "Neoclassical Political Economy, the State and Economic Development." *Asian Development Review* 3, no. 2: 38–58.

Tendler, Judith. 1983. *Rural Projects through Urban Eyes*. Staff Working Paper no. 532. Washington, D.C.: World Bank.

Thomas, John W., and Merilee S. Grindle. 1990. "After the Decision: Implementing Policy Reforms in Developing Countries." *World Development* 18, no. 8: 1163–81.

Thomas, Vinod, and Ajay Chibber. 1989. "Experience with Policy Reforms under Adjustment." *Finance and Development* (March): 28–31.

Truman, David. 1951. *The Governmental Process: Political Interests and Public Opinion*. New York: Knopf.

Usman, Marzuki, and Marguerite Robinson. 1988. "Banking Deregulation and Rural Financial Markets in Indonesia." Paper prepared for a Harvard Institute for International Development conference on Economic Systems Reform in Developing Countries, Marrakech, Morocco, October.

Wellisz, Stanislaw, and Ronald Findlay. 1984. "Protection and Rent-Seeking in Developing Countries." In David C. Colander, ed., *Neoclassical Political Economy: The Analysis of Rent-Seeking and DUP Activities*, 141–53. Cambridge, Mass.: Ballinger.

World Bank. 1984. *Toward Sustainable Development in Sub-Saharan Africa*. Washington, D.C.: World Bank.

———. 1988. *Report on Adjustment Lending*. Country Economics Department. Washington, D.C.: World Bank.

Younger, Stephen D. 1989. "Ghana: Economic Recovery Program—A Case Study of Stabilization and Structural Adjustment in Sub-Saharan Africa." EDI Development Policy Case Series no. 1. Washington, D.C.: World Bank.

Chapter 4   Gustav Ranis, "The Political Economy of Development Policy Change"

Notes

1. One leading example of this is, of course, a policy of monetary expansion that seems to solve an immediate growth or unemployment problem but leads to inflation after a time lag, culminating in conflict among various constituent groups within the body politic.

2. Shifting from covert to overt policies clearly does not necessarily mean a diminished role for government but merely a different role; its indirect functions may actually increase with the continued process of liberalization, even as its direct functions diminish.

3. This mainly externally induced cause of instability in LDCs is basically different from the mainly internally induced cause of instability in developed countries (DCs). Thus, while aggregate demand management in the DCs is largely directed at internally induced instability, demand management in LDCs is mainly directed at maintaining growth in the context of externally induced instability. This does not, of course, exclude the possibility of major business cycle effects on the typical DC or domestic shocks of the crop failure variety in the typical LDC.

4. To refer to this approach as purely Keynesian is somewhat misleading since it is an expansion of the money supply meant to create a "liquid asset" in the Cambridge tradition to meet the demand for liquidity; no such roundabout way of thinking is needed in the LDC, where monetary expansion is a convenient way to create purchasing power to allow the beneficiary (the government or favored private entrepreneurs) to "costlessly" acquire goods and services from the market. As long as money must be accepted, involuntarily, as a medium of exchange, this convenient method of finance can be practiced extensively.

5. The multiple exchange rates, the import-licensing system, the differential interest rate structure, and the availability of bank credit to favored public or private sector industries are typical examples. This contrasts sharply with the normal directional neutrality of macroeconomic policies in the DCs where, under the U.S. Federal Reserve System, for example, the monetary authorities only control the overall levels of new bank lending, generally leaving the market system—banks and the money market—to determine the precise direction of individual allocations.

6. Even contemporary socialist LDCs such as China have rationalized their own brand of liberal reform (post-1979) by tracing it, with considerable justification, to what they now call the "fundamental teachings of Marx," according to which "forces of production" will always be liberated from institutional constraints. The party only expedites the process. The general trend toward liberalization, especially in the wake of the LDC debt crisis, seems unmistakable.

7. Whereas effective demand fluctuations are the root cause of instability in the developed market economies, it is these exogenous fluctuations that cause substantial instability in the LDCs, the more so to the extent that they are small and to the extent they are less diversified and rely on the export of only a few primary products.

8. Treatment of the more complicated and, luckily, less likely nonharmonic case (see C_4, C_5, C_6) is not attempted here.

9. In this chapter $\eta_x = (dx/dt)/x$ stands for the growth rate of the time variable $x(t)$.

10. It is a historical misfortune that the elementary fact that bank loans must be repaid becomes almost an irrelevant minor detail in the liquidity preference theory of interest. To put the emphasis on the total money stock (M) rather than the flow of its creation (dM/dt) renders the Keynesian theory almost entirely irrelevant to the political economy of LDCs. Far more relevant are the Swedish and the forced-saving schools of thought based on the loanable-funds theory in which the obligation of the repayment of a bank loan is formally recognized.

11. There is always a tendency to refer to the informal free market as "black" because it threatens not only the official savings institutions but also the entire manufacture-of-profits mechanism based on the exploitation of savers.

12. It is at this juncture that the government also begins to think about export promotion (by means of, for example, an export bonus scheme) to partially compensate for the overvaluation of the currency. Such selective export promotion schemes are bound to fail because of the basic contradiction between the government's desire to discriminate against existing exports and to promote or diversify into new, potentially profitable exports, which is quite beyond the ability of civil servants to accomplish.

13. Although capital inflows were negative for most years in Taiwan during the 1970s, in Korea they accounted for at least a quarter of gross capital formation, on average.

14. Thus, for example, the importance of foreign trade varies markedly depending on the country's overall size in terms of both population and geography and, along with the endowment of unskilled labor relative to land, helps determine a system's options for mobilizing land- or labor-based vents for surplus through different, policy-tinged subphases of transition growth. Moreover, international shocks, whether terms-of-trade or business-cycle related, are of a smaller order of magnitude in a relatively large economy like India or Brazil than in a small system like Sri Lanka or Costa Rica, to take some extreme cases.

John Toye, "Comments"

References

Downs, Anthony. 1960. "Why the Government Budget Is Too Small in a Democracy." *World Politics* 12, no. 4 (July).

Little, Ian, T. Scitovsky, and M. Scott. 1970. *Industry and Trade in Some Developing Countries*. London: Oxford University Press.

Myrdal, Gunnar. 1968. *Asian Drama*. Harmondsworth: Penguin.

Repetto, Robert. 1986. *Skimming the Water: Rent-seeking and the Performance of Public Irrigation Systems*. Washington, D.C.: World Resources Institute.

Robison, Richard. 1988. "Authoritarian States, Capital-Owning Classes, and the Politics of Newly Industrializing Countries: The Case of Indonesia." *World Politics* 41, no. 1 (October): 52–74.

Seers, Dudley. 1962. "Why Visiting Economists Fail." *Journal of Political Economy* 70, no. 4 (August).

Toye, John. 1987. *Dilemmas of Development.* Oxford: Basil Blackwell.

———. 1989. "Tax Reform in South Asia: Yesterday and Today." *Modern Asian Studies* 23, no. 3 (October): 797–813.

Chapter 5   T. N. Srinivasan, "Foreign Trade Regimes"

Notes

1. Bhagwati, Brecher, and Srinivasan (1984) discuss this and other seemingly paradoxical consequences of directly unproductive profit-seeking (DUP) activities, of which Krueger's model of rent seeking is one example.

2. According to Jagdish Bhagwati, at a meeting of the policy makers of a Latin American country in the 1960s, Arnold Harberger proposed devaluing the currency by a certain percentage to correct external imbalances. He was heavily criticized. At a subsequent meeting he suggested that there be an ad valorem import duty by the same percentage on all imports to keep in particular "Yanqui" goods out and an export subsidy (also at the same percentage) to help the country to sell its goods in Yanqui and other markets. This proposal, which is formally equivalent to a devaluation, was enthusiastically received. This example shows that some policies are more transparent than other equivalent policies, but in the long run Lincoln was surely right: one can fool some people all the time, all people some of the time, but not all people all the time.

3. The reason is that supply elasticities need not be the same for all sources. The result is an analogue of the Ramsey tax rule: to collect a given amount of revenue with the least deadweight loss, the government must make the tax rate on a commodity inversely proportional to the elasticity of its demand. When elasticities differ, tax rates will differ.

References

Anam, Mahmudul. 1982. "Distortion-Triggered Lobbying and Welfare: A Contribution to the Theory of Directly Unproductive Profit-Seeking Activities." *Journal of International Economics* 13, nos. 1–2 (August): 15–32.

Anjaria, Shailendra J. 1987. "Balance of Payments and Related Issues in the Uruguay Round." *World Bank Economic Review* 1, no. 4 (September): 669–88.

Bhagwati, Jagdish. 1989 "Is Free Trade Passé After All?" *Review of World Economics* 1, no. 125: 17–44.

Bhagwati, Jagdish, and Bent Hansen. 1973. "A Theoretical Analysis of Smuggling." *Quarterly Journal of Economics* 87 (May): 172–87.

Bhagwati, Jagdish, and T. N. Srinivasan. 1969. "Optimum Intervention to Achieve Non-Economic Objectives." *Review of Economic Studies* 36, no. 1 (January): 153–63.

———. 1980. "Revenue Seeking: A Generalization of the Theory of Tariffs." *Journal of Political Economy* 88 (December): 1069–87.

———. 1982. "The Welfare Consequences of Directly Unproductive Profit-Seeking (DUP) Lobbying Activities: Prices versus Quantity Distortions." *Journal of International Economics* 13 (August): 33–44.

Bhagwati, Jagdish, Richard Brecher, and T. N. Srinivasan. 1984. "DUP Activities and Economic Theory." In D. Colander, ed., *Neoclassical Political Economy: The Analysis of Rent-Seeking and DUP Activities*, 1–32. Cambridge, Mass.: Ballinger.

Brock, William A., and Stephen P. Magee. 1978. "The Economics of Special Interest Politics: The Case of the Tariff." *American Economic Review* 68 (May): 246–50.

Falvey, R. 1978. "A Note on Preferential and Illegal Trade under Quantitative Restrictions." *Quarterly Journal of Economics* 92, no. 1 (February): 175–78.

Feenstra, Robert, and Jagdish N. Bhagwati. 1982. "Tariff Seeking and the Efficient Tariff." In Jagdish N. Bhagwati, ed., *Import Competition and Response*. Chicago: University of Chicago Press.

Findlay, Ronald, and S. Wellisz. 1982. "Endogenous Tariffs, the Political Economy of Trade Restrictions, and Welfare." In Jagdish N. Bhagwati, ed., *Import Competition and Response*. Chicago: University of Chicago Press.

Grais, Wafik, Jaime de Melo, and Shujiro Urata. 1986. "A General Equilibrium Estimation of the Effects of Reductions in Tariffs and Quantitative Restrictions in Turkey in 1978." In T. N. Srinivasan and J. Whalley, eds., *General Equilibrium Trade Policy Modeling*. Cambridge, Mass.: MIT Press.

Hahn, Frank. 1985. "Recognising the Limits." *Times Literary Supplement*, December 6.

Hillman, Arye L. 1989. *The Political Economy of Protection*. Chur, Switzerland: Harwood Academic Publishers.

Hillman, Arye L., and John G. Riley. 1989. "Politically Contestable Rents and Transfers." *Economics and Politics* 1, no. 1 (Spring).

Hillman, Arye L., and Dov Samet. 1987. "Dissipation of Rents and Revenues in Small Numbers Contests." *Public Choice* 54: 63–82.

Hirschman, Albert O. 1970. *Exit, Voice, and Loyalty*. Cambridge, Mass.: Harvard University Press.

Irwin, Douglas A. 1989. "Political Economy and Peel's Repeal of the Corn Laws." *Economics and Politics* 1, no. 1 (Spring).

Jones, Ronald. 1971. "A Three-Factor Model in Theory, Trade and History." In Jagdish N. Bhagwati, ed., *Trade, Balance of Payments and Growth: Papers in International Economics in Honor of Charles P. Kindleberger*, 3–21. Amsterdam: North Holland.

Krasner, Stephen D. 1985. *Structural Conflict: The Third World against Global Liberalism*. Berkeley: University of California Press.

Krueger, Anne. 1974. "The Political Economy of the Rent-seeking Society." *American Economic Review* 64 (June): 291–303.

Lal, Deepak. 1987. "The Political Economy of Economic Liberalization." *World Bank Economic Review* 1, no. 2 (January).

Magee, Stephen P. 1984. "Endogenous Tariff Theory: A Survey." In David C. Colander, ed., *Neoclassical Political Economy: The Analysis of Rent-Seeking and DUP Activities*, 41–51. Cambridge, Mass.: Ballinger.

Magee, Stephen P., and William A. Brock. 1983. "A Model of Politics, Tariffs and Rent Seeking in General Equilibrium." In Burton Weisbrod and Helen Hughes, eds., *The Problems of Developed Countries and the International Economy: Human Resources, Employment and Development*, 497–523. Vol. 3. London: Macmillan.

Magee, Stephen P., William A. Brock, and L. Young. 1989. "Optimal Obfuscation and the Theory of the Second-Worst: The Politically Efficient Policy." In S. P. Magee, W. A. Brock, and L. Young, eds., *Black Hole Tariffs and Endogenous Policy Theory*. Cambridge: Cambridge University Press.

Mayer, Wolfgang, and Raymond G. Riezman. 1987. "Endogenous Choice of Trade Policy Instruments." *Journal of International Economics* 23, nos. 3 and 4 (November): 377– 81.

———. 1989. "Tariff Formation in Political-Economy Models." *Economics and Politics* 1, no. 1 (Spring).

Olson, Mancur. 1965. *The Logic of Collective Action: Public Goods and the Theory of Groups*. Cambridge, Mass.: Harvard University Press.

Srinivasan, T. N. 1989. "Recent Theories of Imperfect Competition and International Trade: Any Implications for Development Strategy?" *Indian Economic Review* 24, no. 1.

Tullock, Gordon. 1980. "Efficient Rent Seeking." In J. M. Buchanan, G. Tollison, and G. Tullock, eds., *Toward a Theory of the Rent Seeking Society*, 97–112. College Station: Texas A & M Press.

Wolf, Martin. 1987. "Differential and More Favorable Treatment of Developing Countries and the International Trading System." *World Bank Economic Review* 1, no. 4 (September): 647–68.

Chapter 6   Yujiro Hayami, "Land Reform"

Notes

1. Their efforts to promote land reforms are documented in detail in the three reports of the United Nations Department of Economic and Social Affairs (1954, 1956, 1962).

2. Such a view finds a classical expression in Wolf Ladejinsky's (1977: 355) work:

> The principal features that characterize the tenant's plight are stagnating agricultural economies; scarce land, yet concentrated in few hands; low yields but high rents; . . . absence of any change for advancement within agriculture; little margin for risk-taking; and subsistence farming with a lack of dynamic or regenerative capacity. Many of these conditions are due to institutional land arrangements over which the peasant has no control. An exploitative

system of tenancy prevails in most countries of the underdeveloped world. Rack renting and insecurity of tenure are its hallmarks. . . . The incentive to improve the land and produce more does not exist, nor is there a place for creative technology on a wide scale. To the extent that these conditions preclude a measure of equalization of opportunities, they stifle progressive impulses and tend to under-write stagnation in agriculture.

3. For the purpose of analysis, the land reform taxonomy used here is necessarily broad and abstract. For the large variety of actual cases, see Binswanger and Elgin (1988), together with UNDESA (1954, 1956, 1962).

4. For a concise summary of land reform and other agrarian reforms in Japan after World War II, see Hayami and associates (1975). For English readers interested in Japan's land reform in more detail, see Hewes (1950), Dore (1958), and Ogura (1963: 138–48).

5. Many case studies show that small family farms tend to have higher levels of labor input and yield per hectare than large farms. For a definitive empirical study, see Berry and Cline (1979). For a classic theoretical exposition, see Brewster (1950).

6. For the original text, see Marshall (1890: ch. 6). For the popular versions of "Marshallian inefficiency," see Schikele (1941) and Heady (1947).

7. This view, originally formulated by Cheung (1969), has stimulated heated discussions. For a comprehensive review of empirical evidence, see Otsuka and Hayami (1988).

References

Adams, Dale W., Douglas H. Graham, and J. D. von Pischke. 1984. *Undermining Development with Cheap Credit*. Boulder: Westview Press.

Anderson, Kym, and Yujiro Hayami with Associates. 1986. *The Political Economy of Agricultural Protection*. Sydney: Allen and Unwin.

Bale, Malcolm D., and Ernest Lutz. 1981. "Price Distortions in Agriculture and Their Effects: An International Comparison." *American Journal of Agricultural Economics* 63, no. 1: 8–22.

Bates, Robert H. 1981. *Markets and States in Tropical Africa*. Berkeley: University of California Press.

Berry, Albert R., and William R. Cline. 1979. *Agrarian Structure and Productivity in Developing Countries*. Baltimore: Johns Hopkins University Press.

Binswanger, Hans P., and M. Elgin. 1988. *What Are the Prospects for Land Reform?* Paper presented at the 20th International Conference of Agricultural Economists, Buenos Aires, August 24–31.

Breton, Albert. 1974. *The Economic Theory of Representative Government*. Chicago: Aldine.

Brewster, John M. 1950. "The Machine Process in Agriculture and Industry." *Journal of Farm Economics* 32, no.1: 69–81.

Buchanan, James M., and Gordon Tullock. 1962. *The Calculus of Consent*. Ann Arbor: University of Michigan Press.

Buchanan, James M., Richard D. Tollison, and Gordon Tullock, eds. 1980. *Toward a Theory of the Rent-Seeking Society*. College Station: Texas A & M University Press.

Cheung, Steven N. F. 1969. *The Theory of Share Tenancy*. Chicago: University of Chicago Press.

de Janvry, Alain. 1981. *The Agrarian Question and Reformism in Latin America*. Baltimore: Johns Hopkins University Press.

———. 1984. "The Role of Land Reform in Economic Development: Policies and Politics." In C. K. Eicher and J. M. Stanz, eds., *Agricultural Development in the Third World*. Baltimore: Johns Hopkins University Press.

Dore, Ronald P. 1958. *Land Reform in Japan*. Oxford: Oxford University Press.

Downs, Anthony. 1957. *An Economic Theory of Democracy*. New York: Harper and Row.

Hayami, Yujiro. 1988. *Japanese Agriculture under Siege*. London: Macmillan.

Hayami, Yujiro, Masakatsu Akino, Masahiko Shintani, and Saburo Yamada. 1975. *A Century of Agricultural Growth in Japan*. Tokyo: University of Tokyo Press; Minneapolis: University of Minnesota Press.

Hayami, Yujiro, and Toshihiko Kawagoe. 1989. "Farm Mechanization, Scale Economies and Polarization." *Journal of Development Economics* 31, no. 2: 221–39.

Hayami, Yujiro, and Vernon Ruttan. 1985. *Agricultural Development: An International Perspective*. Rev. ed. Baltimore: Johns Hopkins University Press.

Hayami, Yujiro, M. Agnes Quisumbing, and Lourdes S. Adriano. 1990. *Towards an Alternative Land Reform Paradigm: A Philippine Perspective*. Quezon City, Philippines: Ateneo de Manila University Press.

Heady, Earl O. 1947. "Economics of Farm Leasing Systems." *Journal of Farm Economics* 29, no. 3: 659–78.

Herring, Ronald J. 1983. *Land to the Tiller: The Political Economy of Agrarian Reform in South Asia*. New Haven: Yale University Press.

Hewes, Lawrence I. 1950. *Japanese Land Reform*. GHQ Natural Resources Section Report No. 127. Tokyo.

Johnson, D. Gale. 1973. *World Agriculture under Disarray*. London: Fontana.

Kawano, Shigeto. 1969. "Effects of the Land Reform on Consumption and Investment of Farmers." In K. Ohkawa, B. F. Johnston, and M. Kaneda, eds., *Agriculture and Economic Growth: Japan's Experience*. Tokyo: University of Tokyo Press.

Ladejinsky, Wolf. 1977. *Agrarian Reform as Unfinished Business: The Selected Papers of Wolf Ladejinsky*. Edited by L. J. Walinsky. Oxford: Oxford University Press.

Marshall, Alfred. 1890. *Principles of Economics*. London: Macmillan.

Mitrany, David. 1951. *Marx against Peasant*. Durham: University of North Carolina Press.

Myrdal, Gunnar. 1968. *Asian Drama*. New York: Random House.

North, Douglass C. 1981. *Structure and Change in Economic History*. New York: Norton.

Ogura, Takekazu, ed. 1963. *Agricultural Development in Modern Japan*. Tokyo: Fuji Publishing Co.

Olson, Mancur. 1965. *The Logic of Collective Action*. Cambridge, Mass.: Harvard University Press.

Otsuka, Keijiro, and Yujiro Hayami. 1988. "Theories of Share Tenancy: A Critical Survey." *Economic Development and Cultural Change* 37, no. 1: 31–68.

Schikele, Rainer. 1941. "Effects of Tenure Systems on Agricultural Efficiency." *Journal of Farm Economics* 23, no. 1: 185–207.

Schultz, Theodore W. 1964. *Transforming Traditional Agriculture.* New Haven: Yale University Press.

———, ed. 1978. *Distortions of Agricultural Incentives.* Bloomington: Indiana University Press.

Spillman, William J. 1919. "The Agricultural Ladder." *American Economic Review* 9, no. 1: 170–79.

Tollison, Robert D. 1982. "Rent-Seeking: A Survey." *Kyklos* 35, no. 4: 575–602.

United Nations Department of Economic and Social Affairs (UNDESA). 1954. *Progress in Land Reform.* New York: United Nations.

———. 1956. *Progress in Land Reform: Second Report.* New York: United Nations.

———. 1962. *Progress in Land Reform: Third Report.* New York: United Nations.

World Bank. 1982. *World Development Report 1982.* New York: Oxford University Press.

———. 1983. *World Development Report 1983.* New York: Oxford University Press.

———. 1986. *World Development Report 1986.* New York: Oxford University Press.

Thomas P. Tomich, "Comments"

Notes

1. An organizational theorist would stress the lack of institutional capacity to implement a reform as a key factor in its failure. In the article cited above, the *Asian Wall Street Journal* reports that "the bureaucracy has been overwhelmed by the task. . . . " Of course, policy failures resulting from nonrational organizational processes may increase opportunities for bureaucrats to manipulate the situation for their own ends. From this organizational process perspective, pursuit of self-interest by corrupt officials could be viewed as a symptom rather than a cause of policy failure.

2. One western diplomat, quoted by the *Asian Wall Street Journal*, reportedly said, "It's like the emperor without clothes. We have to pretend something's there because we believe in the concept."

References

"Corruption Is Bringing Manila's Land Reform Program to a Near Halt." 1989. *Asian Wall Street Journal Weekly* 11, no. 28 (July 10): 1.

Hayami, Yujiro, and Vernon W. Ruttan. 1985. *Agricultural Development: An International Perspective.* Rev. ed. Baltimore: Johns Hopkins University Press.

Johnston, Bruce F., and Thomas P. Tomich. 1985. "Agricultural Strategies and Agrarian Structure." *Asian Development Review* 3, no. 2: 1–37.

Meier, Gerald M. 1989. *Leading Issues in Economic Development*. 5th ed. New York: Oxford University Press.

Stiglitz, Joseph E. 1986. "The New Development Economics." *World Development* 14, no. 2: 257–65.

Chapter 7   Guy P. Pfeffermann, "Poverty Alleviation"

Notes

1. Efforts to alleviate poverty have not been particularly successful even in the industrialized countries. A 1988 study by Isabel Sawhill of the Washington Urban Institute was entitled "Poverty in the US: Why Is It So Persistent?" Her conclusions illustrate vividly how little we know about poverty and its remedies even in the United States:

> 1. For all their flaws, the existing "official" measures of poverty . . . have proved very useful, both to researchers and to policy makers.
>
> 2. The poor are a very diverse group, but thanks to the development of detailed . . . data, there is more appreciation of this fact now than in the past. . . .
>
> 3. Income poverty has declined only modestly since the mid-1960s and has actually increased in relative terms. However, some basic needs—health care in particular—are met more adequately now than in the past, and this does not show up in most measures of poverty.
>
> 4. This rather modest progress in the face of a large increase in real spending from income transfers and for human capital programs targeted on the poor is difficult to explain . . . it can be attributed, in part, to the failure of average real incomes to grow very much over the past 20 years. Even more important were the very high unemployment rates of the early 1980s compared to the very low rates of the late 1960s. Adverse demographic trends also played a role.
>
> 5. . . . anti-poverty programs . . . reduced poverty but it is hard to say by how much.
>
> 6. From a policy perspective, the greatest success story is the decline in poverty among the elderly induced by the growth of social insurance programs. . . .
>
> 7. . . . we can still understand very little about the basic causes of poverty—the extent to which it is a matter of genetic or cultural inheritance, a lack of human capital, a choice variable related to

work and family decisions, a result of macroeconomic failures or of
social stratification based on race, sex, or family background . . .
(Sawhill 1988: 1073–1119).

It may well be easier to alleviate poverty in societies such as Sri Lanka, where
traditional social relationships have endured, than in the United States, where
much of the poverty problem is one of social dislocation. In any case, poverty
alleviation is not a policy area where "best practice" can easily be spread from
North to South. Indeed, some of the most interesting ideas have been generated
in the South.

References

Chambers, Robert. 1980. "Rural Poverty Unperceived: Problems and Reme-
dies." World Bank Staff Working Paper no. 400. Washington, D.C.
Cornia, G. A., R. Jolly, and F. Stewart, eds. 1987. *Adjustment with a Human Face.*
Oxford: Oxford University Press.
Economic Commission for Latin America. 1988. "La Heterogeneidad de la
Pobreza: Una Aproximación Bidimensional." Montevideo, Uruguay.
Mimeo.
Fields, Gary S. 1989. "Poverty, Inequality, and Economic Growth." In G.
Psacharopoulos, ed., *Essays on Poverty, Equity, and Growth.* Oxford: Per-
gamon Press.
Knight, Peter T., and Ricardo Moran. 1981. "Brazil." Poverty and Basic Needs
Series. Washington, D.C.: World Bank. December.
Macedo, Roberto. 1988. "The (Mis)Targeting of Social Programs in Brazil: The
Federal Health and Nutrition Programs." Universidade de São Paulo, São
Paulo, Brazil. Mimeo.
Morawetz, David. 1977. *Twenty-five Years of Economic Development 1950 to 1975.*
Baltimore: Johns Hopkins University Press.
Pfeffermann, Guy P., and Charles C. Griffin. 1989. *Nutrition and Health Programs
in Latin America: Targeting Social Expenditures.* Washington, D.C.: World
Bank.
Pfeffermann, Guy P., and Richard C. Webb. 1983. "Poverty and Income Distribu-
tion in Brazil." *The Review of Income and Wealth,* series 29, no. 2: 101–24.
Sawhill, Isabel V. 1988. "Poverty in the US: Why Is It So Persistent?" *Journal of
Economic Literature* (September): 1072–1119.
Tendler, Judith. 1988. "Northeast Brazil Rural Development Evaluation: First
Impressions." Washington, D.C.: World Bank. Mimeo.
World Bank. 1986. *Poverty in Latin America: The Impact of Depression.* Washington,
D.C.
———. 1988a. *Rural Development: World Bank Experience, 1965–86.* Operations
Evaluation Department. Washington, D.C.
———. 1988b. *Targeted Programs for the Poor during Structural Adjustment.* Wash-
ington, D.C.

Roberto Macedo, "Comments"

References

Macedo, Roberto. 1988. "Growth Oriented Adjustment with Targeted Social Policies—A Proposal for Brazil." Paper presented at the "Symposium on Poverty and Adjustment," World Bank, 1988.

World Bank. 1988. *World Development Report 1988*. New York: Oxford University Press.

Chapter 8   Leroy P. Jones, Ingo Vogelsang, and Pankaj Tandon, "Public Enterprise Divestiture"

Notes

1. If "new" political economy assumes only perfectly rational, utility-maximizing actors, then "old" political economy presumably admits irrationality, and our approach is supra-adjectival. We do not propose a specific positive theory of divestiture, applicable to a particular mode of divestiture for a particular class of enterprise in a particular sociopolitical framework. Rather, we develop an accounting framework applicable across enterprises and countries. That is, we are less concerned with predicting the outcome of any particular game than with keeping score in all games.

2. For simplicity, we utilize single-period notation. Each term should be thought of as the discounted net present value of a stream. For the ugly way, see Jones, Tandon, and Vogelsang (1990).

3. The net present value of the future stream of profits.

4. And adding a multiplier on rents (λ_m) defined analogously to λ_p.

5. Specifically, one in the fiftieth percentile of the income distribution—that is, the median consumer.

6. Another possibility is to define a "base" consumer group whose welfare is just equal to a dollar of government revenue, as advocated in the extended method of the United Nations Industrial Development Organization (United Nations 1978: ch. 5). This has the advantage of making λ_g equal unity. So long as everything else is redefined accordingly, this makes no difference, but we prefer the reminder effect of keeping an explicit λ_g greater than one.

7. Note that the combination is not multiplicative, but additive. That is, if the efficiency multiplier on profits is 1.5 and the distributional multiplier is 0.2, the net multiplier is not 0.3 but 0.7. That is, the consumption component is only worth 0.2, but the external effects on investment, taxes, etc., are worth 0.5, for a total of 0.7.

8. This simply means replacing ΔS in equation (8.3) with $\lambda_s \Delta S$ and reinterpreting the other multipliers as including distributional components. Note that in equation (8.4) this has been disaggregated and appears as ΔS as the first term plus $(\lambda_s - 1)\Delta S$ as the last term. Similar decompositions have been applied to other terms.

9. Alternatively, the multiplier could be left with the ΔS term, implying that the consumers themselves get the extra benefits.

10. For documentation and elaboration on this and other assertions in this section, see Jones (1985).

11. An early statement is found in Tullock (1968). The notion received widespread professional attention only after the work of Krueger (1974). Downstream results may be found in Buchanan, Tollison, and Tullock (1980).

12. It is an approximation for at least two reasons: first, because of the cross-product term; and second, because of the neoclassical possibility that any ostensible cost reduction includes rent transfer, as explained below.

13. We admit the theoretical possibility that efficiency wage arguments could justify above-market wages, but we judge its explanatory power in the market for sweepers in Bolivia to be of footnote proportions.

14. The only savings that remain would be reductions in allocative efficiency. For the classic neoclassical exposition, see Stigler (1976).

15. Such a bald statement obviously must admit important exceptions (for example, the United Kingdom's divestiture of British Steel in 1953 and the divestiture of Korean Airlines in 1968) and fuzz things up with qualifications (for example, restricting the assertion to policy-generated change, recognizing that the sector can shrink absolutely as a result of recession and shrink relatively if large public-dominated sectors—read oil—are hit disproportionately).

16. For documentation through about 1980, see Short (1984).

17. This passage refers to the larger privatization trend and not merely its divestiture component.

18. The International Monetary Fund's approximation to "world" GDP grew at an average annual rate of 3.87 percent from 1959 to 1985 (IMF 1986), for a growth multiple of 2.68 over twenty-six years. Adding four years and cutting the growth rate a bit to reflect the assumption that the missing countries grew more slowly yields a rough tripling over thirty years.

19. This is because monopoly profits are then limited to the transportation margin.

20. For the well-documented case of increasing competitiveness in the United States, see Shepherd (1982). For the developing countries, statistics indicate the growing share of trade in GDP. Since 1980, exports have been growing faster than GDP for the low- and middle-income countries as a whole. See World Bank (1989).

21. The two-thirds rule says that the surface area of containers grows at roughly two-thirds the rate of growth of their volume. Therefore, the cost of building containers such as boilers grows less than proportionally to their capacity.

22. Recall that we are here referring to the degree of competition that characterizes the market before divestiture. If divestiture itself is accompanied by policies that increase competition, this is a clear plus.

23. For elaboration, see Jones and Vogelsang (1983).

24. For example, see Caves et al. (1982). For a survey, see Borcherding, Pommerehne, and Schneider (1982). For theoretical arguments, see De Alessi (1982), Borcherding (1983), and Vickers and Yarrow (1988). For empirical evidence, see Boardman and Vining (1989) and Millward and Parker (1983).

25. For an excellent survey of regulatory advances in the context of divestiture, see Vickers and Yarrow (1988), especially chapter 4, "Theories of Regula-

tion." Of those that have been implemented, one of the better known examples is the $RPI - X$ formula used to control prices in the divested British Telecom. Under this formula, price increases are limited to the rate of inflation in some consumer price index less a specified expected rate of productivity improvement, X percent. Although this scheme falls considerably short of the theoretical ideal, it has major advantages over traditional cost-plus-fair-return regulation: the long period before regulatory review provides increased incentives for cost cutting, and the preset rate puts some limits on exercise of market power.

26. Recall that we are talking about the rate of change here, not the level.

27. Since λ_g appears twice in equation (8.3), once with a positive sign and once with a negative sign, it might appear that the impact on ΔW could go either way. The second term, however, merely reduces the gains to government to the extent that they are passed to the purchaser through the process of bargaining over the price. Except in the unlikely event that the government actually accepts less than its minimum reservation price, the net effect of the two terms on ΔW will be positive. The effect of the second term is further reduced by the fact that what matters is $(\lambda_g - \lambda_p)$ and as λ_g rises, λ_p usually does too.

28. A partial exception is Bermeo, who compares privatization episodes in Greece, Portugal, and Spain and emphasizes the much greater influence on policy of the Spanish business community (1989: 14–18).

29. After divestiture, however, purchasers may become an important interest group blocking renationalization. The critical factor would be the price at which shares would be redeemed. Opposition could be expected if increased prospects for renationalization resulted in lower market prices or if the government considered redemption at a nonmarket price (for example, at the original undervalued issuance rate). This may have been one motive for underpricing shares in the United Kingdom. See Vickers and Yarrow (1988: 180–81).

30. Japan's experience in the 1880s is an exception. For details, see Smith (1955).

31. Note that in the United States, serious deregulation actually began in the Carter administration.

32. As we go to press, however, there is some indication that Egypt may get on the bandwagon.

33. In addition to Nellis, for the early record see Leeds (1988). For an update, see Waterbury (1989).

34. In 1980 the richest MDCs had a per capita GDP of about US$15,000 while the poorest LDCs had about US$100. The United Nations' International Comparison Project tells us that we need to multiply the lowest-income countries by a factor of about four to adjust for purchasing power differentials, yielding a ratio of 37.5 from top to bottom.

35. Calculation excludes Taiwan and South Korea, which are considered newly industrialized countries rather than LDCs. Were they included, the twenty-nine nation volume would still be only 70 percent of London volume.

References

Bermeo, Nancy. 1989. "The Politics of Public Enterprise in Portugal, Spain and Greece." In Ezra Suleiman and John Waterbury, eds., *The Political Economy of Public Sector Reform and Privatization.* Princeton University, May. Manuscript.

Boardman, A. E., and A. R. Vining. 1989. "Ownership and Performance in Competitive Environments: A Comparison of the Performance of Private, Mixed and State-Owned Enterprises." *Journal of Labor Economics* 32 (April): 1–36.

Boneo, Horacio. 1986. "Privatization: Ideology and Praxis." In William Glade, ed., *State Shrinking.* Austin: University of Texas Press.

Borcherding, T. E. 1983. "Toward a Positive Theory of Public Sector Supply Arrangements." In R. Prichard, ed., *Public Enteprises in Canada.* Toronto: Butterworth.

Borcherding, T., W. Pommerehne, and F. Schneider. 1982. "Comparing the Efficiency of Private and Public Production: The Evidence from Five Countries." *Journal of Economics,* Suppl. 2: 127–56.

Bos, Dieter. 1988a. "Privatization of Public Firms: A Government-Trade Union-Private Shareholder Cooperative Game." In M. Neumann, ed., *Public Finance and the Performance of Enterprises.* Detroit: Wayne State University Press.

———. 1988b. "Welfare Effects of Privatizing Public Enterprises." In D. Bos, M. Rose, and D. Seidel, eds., *Welfare and Efficiency in Public Economies,* 339–62. Berlin: Springer-Verlag.

Buchanan, J., R. Tollison, and G. Tullock. 1980. *Toward a Theory of the Rent-Seeking Society.* College Station: Texas A & M University Press.

Candoy-Sekse, Rebecca. 1988. *Techniques of Privatization of State-Owned Enterprises.* Vol. 3. World Bank Technical Paper no. 90. Washington, D.C.: World Bank.

Caves, D., L. Christensen, J. Swanson, and M. Tretheway. 1982. "Economic Performance of U.S. and Canadian Railroads: The Significance of Ownership and the Regulatory Environment." In W. T. Stanbury and Fred Thompson, eds., *Managing Public Enterprises,* 123–51. New York: Praeger.

Chandler, Alfred. 1977. *The Visible Hand: The Managerial Revolution in American Business.* Cambridge, Mass.: Harvard University Press.

Commander, Simon, and Tony Killick. 1988. "Privatization in Developing Countries: A Survey of the Issues." In Paul Cook and Colin Kirkpatrick, eds., *Privatization in Less Developed Countries,* 91–124. New York: St. Martin's Press.

De Alessi, L. 1982. "On the Nature and Consequences of Private and Public Enterprises." *Minnesota Law Review* 67: 191–209.

Hanke, Steve. 1987. "Toward a People's Capitalism." In Steve Hanke, ed., *Privatization and Development,* 213–22. San Francisco: ICS Press.

Ikenberry, John. 1989. "The International Spread of Privatization Policies: Inducements, Learning and 'Policy Bandwagoning.'" In Ezra Suleiman and John Waterbury, eds., *The Political Economy of Public Sector Reform and Privatization.* Princeton University, May. Manuscript.

International Finance Corporation. 1989. *Emerging Stock Markets Factbook: 1989.* Washington, D.C.

International Monetary Fund. 1986. *International Financial Statistics Yearbook 1986.* Washington, D.C.

Jones, Leroy. 1985. "Public Enterprise for Whom? Perverse Distributional Consequences of Public Operational Decisions." *Economic Development and Cultural Change* (January): 333–47.

Jones, Leroy, and Edward Mason. 1982. "Why Public Enterprise?" In L. Jones, ed., *Public Enterprise in Less-Developed Countries*. Cambridge: Cambridge University Press.

Jones, Leroy, Pankaj Tandon, and Ingo Vogelsang. 1990. *Selling Public Enterprises: A Cost-Benefit Methodology*. Cambridge, Mass.: MIT Press.

Jones, Leroy, and Ingo Vogelsang. 1983. *The Effects of Markets on Public Enterprise Conduct; and Vice Versa*. Ljubljana, Yugoslavia: International Center for Public Enterprises in Developing Countries.

Krueger, Anne. 1974. "The Political Economy of the Rent-Seeking Society." *American Economic Review* 64: 291–303.

Leeds, Roger. 1988. "Turkey: Rhetoric and Reality." In Raymond Vernon, ed., *The Promise of Privatization: A Challenge for American Foreign Policy*. New York: Council on Foreign Relations.

Marshall, J., and F. Montt. 1988. "Privatization in Chile." In Paul Cook and Colin Kirkpatrick, eds., *Privatization in Less Developed Countries*, 281–307. New York: St. Martin's Press.

Millward, R., and D. M. Parker. 1983. "Public and Private Enteprise: Comparative Behavior and Relative Efficiency." In R. Millward, D. M. Parker, L. Rosenthal, M. T. Sumner, and N. Topham, eds., *Public Sector Economics*. London: Longman.

Nellis, John. 1989a. "Contract Plans and Public Enterprise Performance." World Bank Discussion Paper no. 48. Washington, D.C.: World Bank.

———. 1989b. "Public Enterprise Reform in Adjustment Lending." World Bank Planning and Research Paper no. 233. Washington, D.C.: World Bank, August.

Ohasi, T. M., and T. P. Roth. 1980. *Privatization: Theory and Practice*. Vancouver: Fraser Institute.

Olson, Mancur. 1965. *The Logic of Collective Action: Public Goods and the Theory of Groups*. Cambridge, Mass.: Harvard University Press.

———. 1982. *The Rise and Decline of Nations*. New Haven: Yale University Press.

Park, Y. C. 1985. "Reform of Public Enterprise Sector in Korea." World Bank Public Sector Management Division. Washington, D.C.: World Bank, August.

Shapiro, Carl, and Robert D. Willig. 1989. "Economic Rationales for the Scope of Privatization." In Ezra Suleiman and John Waterbury, eds., *The Political Economy of Public Sector Reform and Privatization*. Princeton University, May. Manuscript.

Shepherd, William. 1982. "Increased Competition: Causes and Effects." Paper presented at the 9th European Association for Research in Industrial Economics (EARIE) conference, Louvain, Belgium, September.

Short, R. P. 1984. "The Role of Public Enterprises: An International Statistical Comparison." In Robert H. Floyd, Clive S. Gray, and R. P. Short, eds., *Public Enterprises in Mixed Economies: Some Macroeconomic Aspects*, 110–94. Washington, D.C.: International Monetary Fund.

Sigmund, Paul E. 1989. "Chile: Privatization, Reprivatization, Hyperprivatization." In Ezra Suleiman and John Waterbury, eds., *The Political Economy of Public Sector Reform and Privatization*. Princeton University, May. Manuscript.

Smith, T. C. 1955. *Political Change and Industrial Development in Japan: Government Enterprise, 1868–1880*. Stanford: Stanford University Press.

Squire, Lyn, and Herman B. van der Tak. 1975. *Economic Analysis of Projects*. Baltimore: Johns Hopkins University Press.

Stigler, George. 1976. "The Xistence of X-Efficiency." *American Economic Review* (March): 213–16.

Suleiman, Ezra, and John Waterbury, eds. 1989. *The Political Economy of Public Sector Reform and Privatization*. Princeton University, May. Manuscript.

Tanoira, Manuel. 1987. "Privatization as Politics." In Steve Hanke, ed., *Privatization and Development*, 53–64. San Francisco: ICS Press.

Trivedi, Prajapati. 1988. "Theory and Practice of the French System of Contracts for Improving Public Enterprise Performance: Some Lessons for LDCs." *Public Enterprise* 8, no. 1: 28–40.

Tullock, Gordon. 1968. "The Welfare Costs of Tariffs, Monopolies and Theft." *Western Economic Journal* 5: 224–32.

———. 1987. "Rent-Seeking." In John Eatwell, Murray Milgate, and Peter Newman, eds., *The New Palgrave: A Dictionary of Economics*. Vol. 4. London: Macmillan.

United Nations. 1978. *Guide to Practical Project Appraisal: Social Benefit Cost Analysis in Developing Countries*. New York.

Vernon, Raymond, ed. 1988. *The Promise of Privatization: A Challenge for American Foreign Policy*. New York: Council on Foreign Relations.

Vickers, J., and G. Yarrow. 1988. *Privatization: An Economic Analysis*. Cambridge, Mass.: MIT Press.

Waterbury, John. 1989. "The Political Context of Public Sector Reform and Privatization in Egypt, India, Mexico and Turkey." In Ezra Suleiman and John Waterbury, eds., *The Political Economy of Public Sector Reform and Privatization*. Princeton University, May. Manuscript.

World Bank. 1989. *World Development Report 1989*. New York: Oxford University Press.

Alice H. Amsden, "Comments"

References

Amsden, Alice H. 1989. *Asia's Next Giant: South Korea and Late Industrialization*. New York: Oxford University Press.

Kindleberger, Charles. 1978. *Manias, Panics, and Crashes*. Cambridge, Mass.: MIT Press.

Chapter 9   Stephan Haggard, "Inflation and Stabilization"

Notes

1. For example, it has been argued that corporatist arrangements are better able to generate stable and credible incomes policies than more decentralized systems of wage setting. See Cameron (1984) and Katzenstein (1985).

2. A crucial, and untested, assumption in the new political economy is that private interests—the effects of tax and expenditure policy on individual or group income—determine policy preferences. Preferences about public objectives, such as the financing of services, income distribution, promoting growth, or stabilization, are derived from the effect of policies on private income. This assumption reflects the general disregard in the new political economy for ideological and value conflicts separate from those rooted in material interests; in this, the new political economy bears an ironically close intellectual affinity to Marxist political economy.

3. For a concise statement, see Shepsle and Weingast (1984).

4. One study that has attempted a systematic cross-national study of the political business cycle in the developing world is Barry Ames' *Political Survival: Politicians and Public Policy in Latin America* (1987). Ames analyzes fiscal policy for a sample of seventeen Latin American countries between 1947 and 1982. He finds evidence of an increase in spending before electoral contests, and an even sharper increase in postelection spending by new, nonincumbent governments, presumably seeking to consolidate support.

5. This is true of the literature on rent seeking, the political business cycle, and partisan models of policy, but less true of the literature that treats the state as a self-interested *economic* actor seeking to maximize revenues or the gains from seigniorage.

6. There is also a growing literature on how institutional context can determine outcomes in democratic settings. An example is provided by U.S. trade policy. Before 1934, U.S. trade policy was made by Congress. As a result of the way that particular tariff schedules were farmed out to subcommittees dominated by interested members, logrolling occurred, producing the infamous Smoot-Hawley tariff in 1930. After 1934, authority over trade policy shifted to the executive. Congress retained powers of oversight, but industries seeking protection confronted a new institutional filter of liberal trade policy experts, a more technocratic decision-making process, and contending export interests. Previous channels of influence and even the mode of relevant argument were changed by the new legal structure.

7. This section and the following draw on Haggard and Kaufman (1989a, 1989b, 1990).

8. This description of the cycle draws on Dornbusch and Edwards (1989).

References

Aharoni, Yair. 1986. *The Evolution and Management of State-owned Enterprises.* Cambridge: Cambridge University Press.

Alesina, Alberto. 1987. "Macroeconomic Policy in a Two-Party System as a Repeated Game." *Quarterly Journal of Economics* 102 (August): 651–78.

Alesina, Alberto, and Guido Tabellini. 1987. "A Positive Theory of Fiscal Deficits and Government Debt in a Democracy." NBER Working Paper no. 2308. July. Cambridge, Mass.: National Bureau of Economic Research.

Alt, James, and K. Alec Chrystal. 1983. *Political Economics*. Berkeley: University of California Press.

Ames, Barry. 1987. *Political Survival: Politicians and Public Policy in Latin America*. Berkeley: University of California Press.

Barry, Brian. 1985. "Does Democracy Cause Inflation? Political Ideas of Some Economists." In Leon Lindberg and Charles S. Maier, eds., *The Politics of Inflation and Stabilization*. Washington, D.C.: Brookings Institution.

Bates, Robert. 1982. *Markets and States in Tropical Africa*. Berkeley: University of California Press.

Bienen, Henry S., and Mark Gersovitz. 1985. "Economic Stabilization, Conditionality, and Political Stability." *International Organization* 39, no. 4:729–54.

Cameron, David. 1984. "Social Democracy, Corporatism, Labor Quiescence, and the Representation of Economic Interests in Advanced Capitalist Society." In John H. Goldthorpe, ed., *Order and Conflict in Contemporary Capitalism*. Oxford: Clarendon Press.

Colander, David. 1984. *Neoclassical Political Economy: The Analysis of Rent-Seeking and DUP Activities*. College Station: Texas A & M University Press.

Cooper, Richard, and Jeffrey Sachs. 1985. "Borrowing Abroad: The Debtor's Perspective." In G. W. Smith and J. T. Cuddington, eds., *International Debt and Developing Countries*. Washington, D.C.: World Bank.

Dornbusch, Rudiger, and Sebastian Edwards. 1989. "The Macroeconomics of Populism in Latin America." Policy, Planning, and Research Working Paper. Washington, D.C.: World Bank. December.

Easterly, William R. 1989. "Fiscal Adjustment and Deficit Financing during the Debt Crisis." Policy, Planning and Research Working Paper no. 138. Washington, D.C.: World Bank. January.

Haggard, Stephan. 1990. *Pathways from the Periphery: The Politics of Growth in the Newly Industrializing Countries*. Ithaca: Cornell University Press.

Haggard, Stephan, and Robert Kaufman. 1989a. "Economic Adjustment in New Democracies." In Joan Nelson, ed., *Fragile Coalitions: The Politics of Stabilization and Structural Adjustment*. New Brunswick: Transaction Books.

———. 1989b. "The Politics of Stabilization and Structural Adjustment." In Jeffrey D. Sachs, ed., *Developing Country Debt and Economic Performance: The International Financial System*. Chicago: University of Chicago Press.

———. 1990. "The Political Economy of Inflation and Stabilization: East Asia and Latin America Compared." Policy, Planning, and Research Working Paper. Washington, D.C.: World Bank.

Hirschman, Albert. 1985. "Reflections on the Latin American Experience." In Leon Lindberg and Charles S. Maier, eds., *The Politics of Inflation and Economic Stagnation*. Washington, D.C.: Brookings Institution.

Katzenstein, Peter. 1985. *Small States in World Markets*. Ithaca: Cornell University Press.

Kaufman, Robert. 1989. "Economic Orthodoxy and Political Change in Mexico: The Stabilization and Adjustment Policies of the de la Madrid Administration." In Barbara Stallings and Robert Kaufman, eds., *Debt and Democracy in Latin America*. Boulder: Westview Press.

Krueger, Anne. 1974. "The Political Economy of the Rent-Seeking Society." *American Economic Review* 64, no. 3:291–303.

Nelson, Joan. 1984. "The Politics of Stabilization." In Richard Feinberg and Valeriana Kallab, eds., *Adjustment Crisis in the Third World*. New Brunswick: Transaction Books.

Sachs, Jeffrey. 1985. "External Debt and Macroeconomic Performance in Latin America and East Asia." *Brookings Papers on Economic Activity* 1985, no. 2:523–73.

———. 1989. "Social Conflict and Populist Policies in Latin America." NBER Working Paper no. 2897. March. Cambridge, Mass.: National Bureau of Economic Research.

Shafer, Michael. Forthcoming. "Sectors, States, and Social Forces: Korea and Zambia Confront Economic Restructuring." In *Comparative Politics*.

Shepsle, Kenneth A., and Barry R. Weingast. 1984. "Legislative Politics and Budget Outcomes." In G. Mills and J. Palmer, eds., *Federal Budget Policy in the 1980s*. Washington, D.C.: Urban Institute.

Vernon, Raymond. 1988. *The Promise of Privatization*. New York: Council on Foreign Relations.

World Bank. 1988. *World Development Report 1988*. New York: Oxford University Press.

William Easterly, "Comments"

References

Easterly, William. 1989. "Fiscal Adjustment and Deficit Financing during the Debt Crisis." In Ishrat Husain and Ishac Diwan, eds., *Dealing with the Debt Crisis*. Washington, D.C.: World Bank.

Chapter 10   Robert H. Bates, Stephan Haggard, and Joan M. Nelson, "A Critique by Political Scientists"

Robert H. Bates

Notes

1. For an all too short overview, see Keech, Lange, and Bates (1989). A more rigorous grounding is provided in Riker and Ordeshook (1973) and Ordeshook (1988). A superb overview is provided by Krebhiel (1988). See McCubbins and

Sullivan (1987) as well. I explore the utility of this kind of analysis for the study of the developing areas in Bates (1989).

2. The title of one of my own books is *Markets and States in Tropical Africa*; the work is cited in the chapters of both Findlay and Grindle. I note this to acknowledge that important parts of my own work are subject to the criticisms I make in this chapter.

3. Complicating the picture is that some of those most deeply involved with the "miracle of the market" theme in the new political economy have also made brilliant contributions to nonmarket, institutional analysis. See, for example, Lal (1984) and Lal and Collier (1980).

4. One of the clearest expositions of this argument is contained in Shepsle and Weingast (1984).

5. I hope that this discussion makes clear that abandoning the concept of the state is not the same thing as adopting a society-centric approach to the study of politics, as Grindle suggests. Rival interests are championed by competing politicians, rival ministries, and government agencies with contrasting visions of the public interest—and competing claims for the state's budget.

6. This rule is the closed rule employed in making financial legislation in the U.S. Congress. For more refined analysis, see the piece by Krebhiel cited above and the citation therein.

7. It should be noted that this is neither a "statist" analysis nor one that simply reduces political outcomes to societal preferences. This approach therefore offers a way out of the stark choices—statist or societal—posed by Grindle.

8. In performing this analysis, we attempted first to extract the effects of market shares and other sources of economic power in order to isolate the effects of votes on the assignment of quotas.

References

Arrow, Kenneth. 1951. *Social Choice and Individual Values*. New York: Wiley.
Bates, Robert H. 1981. *Markets and States in Tropical Africa*. Berkeley: University of California Press.
———. 1983. *Essays on the Political Economy of Rural Africa*. Berkeley: University of California Press.
———. 1989. *Beyond the Miracle of the Market: The Political Economy of Agrarian Development in Kenya*. Cambridge: Cambridge University Press.
Bates, Robert H., and Donald Lien. 1983. "On the Operations of the International Coffee Agreement." *International Organization* 39, no. 3 (September): 553–59.
Downs, Anthony. 1957. *An Economic Theory of Democracy*. New York: Harper and Row.
Fiorina, Morris. 1977. *Congress: Keystone of the Washington Establishment*. New Haven: Yale University Press.
Keech, William, Peter Lange, and Robert H. Bates. 1989. "Political Economy within Nations." Duke University Program in Political Economy, working paper no. 83 (July).
Krebhiel, Keith. 1988. "Spatial Models of Legislative Choice." *Legislative Studies Quarterly* 13, no. 3 (August): 259–319.

Lal, Deepak. 1984. "The Poverty of Development Economics." London: Institute of Economic Affairs.

Lal, Deepak, and Paul Collier. 1980. "Poverty and Growth in Kenya." World Bank Staff Working Paper no. 389. Washington, D.C.: World Bank.

McCubbins, Matthew C., and Terry Sullivan. 1987. *Congress: Structure and Policy.* Cambridge: Cambridge University Press.

Ordeshook, Peter C. 1988. *Game Theory and Politics.* Cambridge: Cambridge University Press.

Putterman, Louis. 1987. *The Economic Nature of the Firm.* Cambridge: Cambridge University Press.

Riker, William H., and Peter C. Ordeshook. 1973. *An Introduction to Positive Political Theory.* Englewood Cliffs, N.J.: Prentice-Hall.

Shepsle, Kenneth A., and Barry R. Weingast. 1984. "Political Solutions to Market Problems." *American Political Science Review* 77: 417–34.

———. 1987. "The Institutional Source of Committee Power." *American Political Science Review* 81: 935–45.

Williamson, Oliver. 1985. *The Economic Institutions of Capitalism.* New York: Free Press.

Stephan Haggard

References

Haggard, Stephan. 1988. "The Institutional Foundations of Hegemony: Explaining the Reciprocal Trade Agreements Act of 1934." In G. John Ikenberry, David A. Lake, and Michael Mastanduno, eds., *The State and American Foreign Economic Policy.* Ithaca: Cornell University Press.

Haggard, Stephan, and Robert Kaufman. 1989. "The Politics of Stabilization and Structural Adjustment." In Jeffrey Sachs, ed., *Developing Country Debt and Economic Performance: The International Financial System.* Chicago: University of Chicago Press.

Chapter 11   Nicolás Ardito-Barletta, "Experiences of Policy Makers"

Notes

1. The participants were Achi Atsain, from the Ivory Coast; Sergio de la Cuadra, Chile; Ernesto Fontaine, Chile; Roberto Junguito, Colombia; Guillermo Perry, Colombia; Francisco Swett, Ecuador; Leopoldo Solís, Mexico; José Luis Medina, Mexico; Augustine Tan, Singapore; Miguel Urrutia, Colombia; and Nicolás Ardito-Barletta, Panama. These participants have had extensive careers in public service in their countries and in international organizations, and their

positions have included cabinet minister, head of a central bank, senator, economic adviser, and president of a country.

2. I use "modern economics" here to mean the knowledge of economic theory and economic policy performance generated by the profession over the past forty years, and especially the past twenty.

3. Conference participants Roberto Junguito, Guillermo Perry, and Miguel Urrutia, for example, have held ministerial posts with governments of both parties and have worked in the same think tanks.

Chapter 12   Gerald M. Meier, "The Political Economy of Policy Reform"

Notes

1. Bhagwati (1989: 32) calls this the Determinacy Paradox: endogenizing policy generally removes the degree of freedom to vary policy interventions.

2. See, for example, Killick (1989). As Killick states, "In considering the desirable role of the state there are essentially two different issues, which are sometimes confused: (a) *how large* should the state be in relation to total economic activity; and (b) *what types of policy instrument* should the state employ? . . . Suggestions, for example, for a change in government import policies from quantitative restrictions to tariffs are not, *per se*, about the extent to which government action is necessary to limit imports but about the most efficient way of achieving that objective. . . . [S]hifting policies in more market-oriented directions is not synonymous with reducing the relative role of the state" (pp. 27–28). See also Lewis (1989: 80–82).

3. Simon calls rationality "bounded" when "complexity of the environment is immensely greater than the computational powers of the adaptive system."

4. Compare with Felix (1989: 1459).

5. An institution may be defined as a set of constraints that governs the behavioral relations among individuals or groups. Institutions may therefore be as diverse as markets, labor unions, employers' organizations, contracts, parliaments, administrative agencies, cultural rules, and codes of conduct (Nabli and Nugent 1989: 1335).

6. For an extended exposition of this statement, see March and Olsen (1989). Their book explores some ways in which the institutions of politics, particularly administrative institutions, provide order and influence change in politics.

7. For elaboration, see Matthews (1986: 903–18).

8. In Taiwan and South Korea (and other LDCs) there has been a transition from agricultural export and industrial import-substitution regimes to the present industrial export-promotion and agricultural import-substitution regimes. Anderson and Hayami conclude that this type of change occurs at an earlier stage of economic growth the weaker a country's comparative advantage in agriculture, and that the changes occur more rapidly the higher the rate of

economic growth and the faster the decline in agricultural comparative advantage (Anderson and Hayami 1986: 1). For South Korea and Taiwan, the structural adjustment costs would have been borne largely by a single generation of rural people.

Bates and Rogerson (1980) suggest that as the share of agricultural population declines, its desirability as a coalition partner rises. See also Ruttan (1989: 1380–82).

9. See also the chapter by Ranis in this volume. Moreover, although the governments of South Korea, Taiwan, and Singapore have been active, their policy choices have not been dominated by interest groups, and they have maintained the flexibility to modify or reverse policies in response to their economic consequences.

10. The major instruments of structural adjustment—public sector reform, devaluation, elimination of marketing boards—threaten to change not only the constituencies that political leaders look to for support, but also the way in which leaders relate to their supporters. For an expanded discussion, see Herbst (1990: 949–58).

References

Anderson, Kym, and Yujiro Hayami. 1986. *The Political Economy of Agricultural Protection: East Asia in International Perspective.* Sydney: Allen and Unwin.

Bates, Robert H. 1983. "Governments and Agricultural Markets in Africa." In D. Gale Johnson, ed., *The Role of Markets in the World Food Economy.* Part 4. Boulder, Colo.: Westview Press.

Bates, Robert H., and W. P. Rogerson. 1980. "Agriculture in Development: A Coalition Analysis." *Public Choice* 32, no. 5: 503–39.

Bhagwati, Jagdish. 1988. "Export-Promoting Trade Strategy: Issues and Evidence." *World Bank Research Observer* 3, no. 1 (January): 27–57.

———. 1989. "Is Free Trade Passé After All?" *Review of World Economics* 125, no. 1: 17–44.

Coase, Ronald H. 1984. "The New Institutional Economics." *Journal of Institutional and Theoretical Economics* 140, no. 1 (March): 229–31.

Dearlove, John. 1987. "Economists on the State." *IDS Bulletin* 18, no. 3: 5–10.

Ethier, W. 1974. "Some of the Theorems of International Trade with Many Goods and Factors" *Journal of International Economics* 4, no. 2: 199–206.

Evans, Peter. 1979. *Dependent Development: The Alliance of Multinational, State and Local Capital in Brazil.* Princeton: Princeton University Press.

Felix, David. 1989. "Import Substitution and Late Industrialization." *World Development* 17, no. 9 (September): 1455–69.

Findlay, Ronald. 1988. "Trade, Development and the State." In Gustav Ranis and Paul Shultz, eds., *The State of Development Economics.* Oxford: Basil Blackwell.

Findlay, Ronald, and Stanislaw Wellisz. 1982. "Endogenous Tariffs, the Political Economy of Trade Restrictions and Welfare." In J. Bhagwati, ed., *Import Competition and Response.* Chicago: University of Chicago Press.

———. 1986. "Tariffs, Quotas and Domestic-Content Protection." *Public Choice* 50, no. 1–3: 221–42.

Findlay, Ronald, and John D. Wilson. 1987. "The Political Economy of Leviathan." In Asswaf Raxin and Efraim Sadka, eds., *Economic Policy in Theory and Practice*. London: Macmillan.

Grindle, Merilee S. 1980. *Politics and Policy Implementation in the Third World*. Princeton: Princeton University Press.

———. 1986. *State and Countryside*. Baltimore: Johns Hopkins University Press.

Harberger, Arnold C. 1989. *The Economist and the Real World*. San Francisco: ICS Press.

Herbst, Jeffrey. 1990. "The Structural Adjustment of Politics in Africa." *World Development* 18, no.7 (July): 949–58.

Hirschman, Albert O. 1963. *Journeys toward Progress*. New York: Twentieth Century Fund.

———. 1975. "Policymaking and Policy Analysis in Latin America: A Return Journey." *Policy Sciences* 6, no. 4: 385.

Huntington, Samuel P. 1968. *Political Order in Changing Societies*. New Haven: Yale University Press.

Jones, Leroy, and Il SaKong. 1980. *Government, Business and Entrepreneurship in Economic Development*. Cambridge, Mass.: Council on East Asian Studies, Harvard University.

Keynes, J. M. 1923. *A Tract on Monetary Reform*. London: Macmillan.

Killick, Tony. 1989. *A Reaction Too Far*. London: Overseas Development Institute.

Krasner, Stephen D. 1988. "Sovereignty: An Institutional Perspective." *Comparative Political Studies* 21, no. 1 (April): 66–94.

Krueger, Anne O. 1990. "Asian Trade and Growth Lessons." *American Economic Review, Papers and Proceedings* 80 (May): 2.

Lal, Deepak. 1987. "The Political Economy of Economic Liberalization." *World Bank Economic Review* 1, no. 2 (January): 273–300.

———. 1989. "The Political Economy of Industrialisation in Primary Product Exporting Economies: Some Cautionary Tales." In Nurul Islam, ed., *The Balance between Industry and Agriculture in Economic Development*, 279–314. London: Macmillan Press.

Lewis, John P. 1989. "Government and National Economic Development." *Daedalus* (Winter).

Lipton, Michael. 1977. *Why Poor People Stay Poor: Urban Bias in World Development*. Cambridge, Mass.: Harvard University Press.

Magee, Stephen P. 1984. "Endogenous Tariff Theory: A Survey." In David C. Colander, ed., *Neoclassical Political Economy*, 41–54. Cambridge, Mass: Ballinger.

March, James G., and John P. Olsen. 1989. *Rediscovering Institutions*. New York: Free Press.

Matthews, R. C. O. 1986. "The Economics of Institutions and the Sources of Growth." *Economic Journal* 96 (December).

Michaely, Michael. 1989. "The Design of Trade Liberalization." *Finance and Development* (March).

Migdal, Joel S. 1988. *Strong Societies and Weak States*. Princeton: Princeton University Press.

Nabli, Mustapha K., and Jeffrey B. Nugent. 1989. "The New Institutional Economics and Its Applicability to Development." *World Development* 17, no. 9: 1333–47.

North, Douglass. 1990. "Economic Development in Historical Perspective: The Western World." Paper presented at a conference at the Hoover Institution, Stanford, Cal., March 7–8.

Ranis, Gustav. 1989. "The Role of Institutions in Transition Growth: The East Asian Newly Industrializing Countries." *World Development* 17, no. 9: 1443–53.

Ranis, Gustav, and John C. H. Fei. 1988. "Development Economics: What Next?" In Gustav Ranis and T. Paul Schultz, eds., *The State of Development Economics*. Oxford: Basil Blackwell.

Ruttan, Vernon W. 1989. "Institutional Innovation and Agricultural Development." *World Development* 17, no. 9: 1375–87.

Sachs, Jeffrey. 1985. "External Debt and Macroeconomic Performance in Latin America and East Asia." *Brookings Papers on Economic Activity* 2: 523–64.

Seers, Dudley. 1962. "Why Visiting Economists Fail." *Journal of Political Economy* 70, no. 4 (August).

———. 1967. "The Limitations of the Special Case." In Kurt Martin and John Knapp, eds., *The Teaching of Development Economics*. London: Frank Cass and Co.

Sen, Amartya. 1987. "Rational Behavior." *The New Palgrave*. London: Macmillan.

Simon, Herbert A. 1957. "A Behavioral Model of Rational Choice." In H. A. Simon, ed., *Models of Man: Social and Rational*. New York: John Wiley and Sons.

———. 1986. "Rationality in Psychology and Economics." *Journal of Business*, Supplement, 59: 5220–24.

Stigler, George. 1976. "Do Economists Matter?" *Southern Economic Journal* 42 (January).

Toye, John. 1988. *Dilemmas of Development*. Oxford: Basil Blackwell.

Van Arkadie, Brian. 1989. "The Role of Institutions in Development." *World Bank Review*, Supplement, Annual Conference on Development Economics 1989: 153–92.

Wellisz, Stanislaw, and Ronald Findlay. 1984. "Protection and Rent-Seeking in Developing Countries." In David C. Colander, ed., *Neoclassical Political Economy*, 141–53. Cambridge, Mass.: Ballinger.

World Bank. 1989. *Sub-Saharan Africa: From Crisis to Sustainable Growth*. Washington, D.C.

About the Contributors

GERALD M. MEIER is Konosuke Matsushita Professor of International Economics and Policy Analysis at Stanford University. Recipient of many professional awards and research grants, he is the author of a number of books in international economics and economic development. His most recent titles include *Leading Issues in Economic Development*; *Pioneers in Development*; *Pioneers in Development, Second Series*; *Financing of Asian Development*; and *Emerging from Poverty*.

ALICE H. AMSDEN is professor of economics at the New School for Social Research and is currently a visiting professor at the Massachusetts Institute of Technology. Amsden received her Ph.D. from the London School of Economics and has worked as an economist for the Organization for Economic Cooperation and Development. She is the author of *Asia's Next Giant: South Korea and Late Industrialization* and *Republic of Korea*, part of the series on Stabilization and Adjustment Policies and Programmes published by the World Institute for Development Economics Research.

NICOLÁS ARDITO-BARLETTA is general director of the International Center for Economic Growth. He has held a variety of government positions in his native Panama, including chairman of the National Banking Commission, minister of planning and economic policy, and president. Ardito-Barletta has also been vice-president of the Latin American and Caribbean Region of the World Bank, chairman of the board at the Banco Latinoamericano de Exportaciones, and director of the Department of Economic Affairs at the Organization of American States. He has written extensively on Latin American development, public finance, agricultural economics, and Panamanian national development plans.

PRANAB BARDHAN is a professor of economics at the University of California, Berkeley. His areas of research are international and development economics. He is currently the chief editor of the *Journal of Development Economics*. Bardhan's published books include *The Political Economy of Development in India*; *Land, Labor and Rural Poverty*; *Rural Poverty in South Asia* (with T. N. Srinivasan); and *Conversations between Economists and Anthropologists*.

ROBERT H. BATES is Henry R. Luce Professor of Political Economy at Duke University, where he also directs the Center on Political Economy. Bates has written extensively on agricultural policy reform in the developing countries of Africa. Among the many books he has written and edited are *States and Markets in Tropical Africa: The Political Basis of Agricultural Policy*, *Toward a Political Economy of Development: A Rationalist Perspective*, and *Beyond the Miracle of the Market: The Political Economy of Agrarian Development in Kenya*.

SERGIO DE LA CUADRA is senior partner of Sergio de la Cuadra y Asociados, Consultants. De la Caudra graduated from the Catholic University of Chile and received an M.A. from the University of Chicago. He has written numerous articles on the Chilean economy, and his most recent works are entitled "The Timing and Sequencing of Trade Liberalization Policies in Chile" and "Myths and Facts about Financial Liberalization in Chile: 1974–1982."

WILLIAM EASTERLY is an economist in the Macroeconomic Adjustment and Growth Division of the World Bank. He received a Ph.D. in economics from the Massachusetts Institute of Technology in 1985. Easterly worked previously with Data Resources, Inc., and El Colegio de México. He specializes in issues of exchange rate devaluation, management of fiscal deficits, and long-run growth in Latin America, Asia, and Africa.

RONALD FINDLAY is Ragnar Nurkse Professor of Economics at Columbia University. He received his Ph.D. from the Massachusetts Institute of Technology, and his areas of research are international economics, economic development, comparative systems, and political economy. Findlay is also the author of *Trade and Specialization* and *International Trade and Development Theory*.

MERILEE S. GRINDLE, who received her Ph.D. from the Massachusetts Institute of Technology, is a political scientist at the Harvard Institute for International Development (HIID) and a lecturer at the Kennedy School of Government at Harvard University. She has written extensively on the comparative analysis of policy making, implementation, and public management in developing countries. Her books include *Searching for Rural Development: Labor Migration and Employment in Mexico* and *State and Countryside: Development Policy and Agrarian Politics in Latin America*. She is currently a senior researcher on an HIID project that seeks to improve management capabilities in development assistance programs.

STEPHAN HAGGARD is an associate professor of government at Harvard University. In 1990, he was on leave from Harvard at the World Bank in the Macroeconomics and Growth Division. He is author of *Pathways from the Periphery: The Politics of Growth in the Newly Industrializing Countries*; coauthor with Tun-jen Cheng of *Newly Industrializing Asia in Transition*; and coeditor with Chung-in Moon of *Pacific Dynamics: The International Politics of Industrial Change*.

YUJIRO HAYAMI is a professor of economics at Aoyama Gakuin University, Tokyo, Japan. He has also been a professor of economics at Tokyo Metropolitan University and an agricultural economist at the International Rice Research Institute in the Philippines. His articles, books, and published research have won him many awards from the Agricultural Economics Society of Japan.

LEROY P. JONES is a professor of economics and director of the Program in the Economics and Management of Public Enterprise at Boston University. He has served as a consultant to many organizations and countries, including the World Bank, Venezuela, Indonesia, Peru, Pakistan, Chile, and Fiji. Jones has written *Public Enterprise and Economic Development: The Korean Case* and *Selling Public Enterprises: A Cost-Benefit Methodology* (with Pankaj Tandon and Ingo Vogelsang), and has edited *Public Enterprise in Less Developed Countries* (with Richard D. Mallon, Edward S. Mason, Paul Rosenstein-Rodan, and Raymond Vernon).

ROBERTO JUNGUITO has served the government of Colombia in several positions. He has been minister of agriculture and minister of finance and has served as his country's ambassador to the European Economic Community and to France. Currently he is the president of the board of the Banco Sudameris Colombia and the president of the Colombian Association of Coffee Exporters.

ROBERTO MACEDO is a professor of economics of the School of Economics and Management at the University of São Paulo, Brazil, and was dean of the school from 1986 to 1990. Macedo received a Ph.D. in economics from Harvard University. He is also president of the São Paulo Society of Economists and was awarded a Guggenheim Fellowship in 1986.

JOAN NELSON is a senior associate with the Overseas Development Council, where she has focused her work on links between market-oriented economic reforms and democratization in third and second world nations. She received her Ph.D. from Harvard University. Among the books Nelson has written and edited are *Access to Power: Politics and the Urban Poor, Fragile Coalitions: The Politics of Economic Adjustment*, and *Economic Crisis and Policy Choice*.

GUY P. PFEFFERMANN is director of the economics department and adviser to the executive vice-president of the International Finance Corporation of the World Bank. He has held a variety of other positions at the World Bank, including chief economist for the Latin American and Caribbean Region and chief of the Debt and Macroeconomic Adjustment Division. He has written many articles on Latin America and human development and is the author of *Industrial Labor in Senegal, Poverty in Latin America: The Impact of Depression*, and *Nutrition and Health Programs in Latin America* (with Charles Griffin).

GUSTAV RANIS is Frank Altschul Professor of International Economics at Yale University. He has written extensively on theoretical and policy-related issues of development. His books include *Japan and the Developing Countries, Comparative Technology Choice: The Indian and Japanese Cotton Textile Industries* (with K. Otsuka and G. Saxonhouse), and *Development of the Labor Surplus Economy: Theory and Policy* (with John Fei). He has served as assistant administrator for program and policy in the U.S. Agency for International Development and served as a consultant to the World Bank, the United Nations Development Program, the International Labor Organization, and many other organizations.

T. N. SRINIVASAN is Samuel C. Park, Jr., Professor of Economics and director of the Division of Social Sciences, Economic Growth Center at Yale University. He is a consultant to the Development Research Center of the World Bank and has written on food and rural issues and international economics. Srinivasan has written extensively on agricultural and

economic development in India, and has edited numerous books, in-
cluding *Population, Food, and Rural Development* (with R. Lee, W. Arthur,
A. Kelley, and G. Rodgers), *Handbook of Development Economics* (with H.
B. Chenery), *Rural Poverty in South Asia* (with Pranab Bardhan), and
General Equilibrium Trade Policy Modeling (with John Whalley).

FRANCISCO X. SWETT has had a distinguished career of public service in
his native Ecuador. Currently a congressman, he has also been economic adviser to the president, minister of finance and public credit,
economic adviser to the central bank, and president of the National
Board of Planning and Economic Coordination. His publications include *The Development of Capital Markets in Ecuador* and *Fiscal Policies in
Ecuador*.

AUGUSTINE H. H. TAN is an associate professor of economics and statistics at the National University of Singapore, and is a member of Parlia-
ment for Whampoa. From 1972 to 1976 he was the political secretary to
the prime minister, and he has been chairman of several parliamentary
committees. Tan, who received his Ph.D. from Stanford University, has
also served on the board of directors for the Economic Development
Board and the Housing and Development Board.

PANKAJ TANDON is an associate professor of economics and an associate
of the Public Enterprise Program at Boston University. He received his
Ph.D. in economics from Harvard University and also holds an M.A.
from the Dehli School of Economics. His primary research interests are
in the fields of public enterprise and the economics of technological
change. He has written numerous articles, and his first book is *Selling
Public Enterprises: A Cost-Benefit Methodology* (with Leroy P. Jones and
Ingo Vogelsang).

THOMAS P. TOMICH is an associate at the Harvard Institute for International Development and a lecturer on economics at Harvard University.
He has served as resident adviser at the Center for Policy and Implementation Studies for the Ministry of Finance, Indonesia. Tomich received his Ph.D. from Stanford University. He has written numerous
publications on agricultural policy, and is the author of *Agricultural
Development and Structural Transformation: Opportunities Seized, Opportunities Missed* (with Peter Kilby and Bruce F. Johnston).

JOHN TOYE is the director of the Institute of Development Studies at the
University of Sussex. He is the author of *Dilemmas of Development* and
Does Aid Work in India? (with Michael Lipton), and is currently research-
ing the impact of World Bank policy reform lending.

MIGUEL URRUTIA is director of Fedesarrollo, a private research institute dedicated to policy analysis in Bogota, Colombia. He was manager of the Economics and Social Development Department at the Inter-American Development Bank, vice-rector of the United Nations University, minister of mines and energy for Colombia, director of Colombia's national planning department, and deputy director for technical affairs of the Colombian central bank. He has written books on labor, income distribution, and economic planning, as well as articles on processes of decision making.

INGO VOGELSANG is a professor of economics and an associate of the Public Enterprise Program at Boston University. His fields of interest are public utility regulation, public enterprises, industrial organization in less-developed countries, and institutional problems in energy and tele-communications economics. Vogelsang's major publications include *Incentive Mechanisms to Regulate Electric Utilities: A Case Study in Institutional Economic Theory* (in German) and *Selling Public Enterprises: A Cost-Benefit Methodology* (with Leroy P. Jones and Pankaj Tandon).

Index